47052047

AF691978

WITHDRAWN
BEAVERTON CITY LIBRARY
Beaverton, OR 97005
Member of Washington County
COOPERATIVE LIBRARY SERVICES

Banking and Financial Institutions

Founded in 1807, John Wiley & Sons is the oldest independent publishing company in the United States. With offices in North America, Europe, Australia, and Asia, Wiley is globally committed to developing and marketing print and electronic products and services for our customers' professional and personal knowledge and understanding.

The Wiley Finance series contains books written specifically for finance and investment professionals as well as sophisticated individual investors and their financial advisors. Book topics range from portfolio management to e-commerce, risk management, financial engineering, valuation, and financial instrument analysis, as well as much more.

For a list of available titles, please visit our Web site at www.WileyFinance.com.

Banking and Financial Institutions

A Guide for Directors, Investors, and Counterparties

BENTON E. GUP

WILEY

John Wiley & Sons, Inc.

Copyright © 2011 by Benton E. Gup. All rights reserved.

Published by John Wiley & Sons, Inc., Hoboken, New Jersey.
Published simultaneously in Canada.

No part of this publication may be reproduced, stored in a retrieval system, or transmitted in any form or by any means, electronic, mechanical, photocopying, recording, scanning, or otherwise, except as permitted under Section 107 or 108 of the 1976 United States Copyright Act, without either the prior written permission of the Publisher, or authorization through payment of the appropriate per-copy fee to the Copyright Clearance Center, Inc., 222 Rosewood Drive, Danvers, MA 01923, (978) 750-8400, fax (978) 646-8600, or on the Web at www.copyright.com. Requests to the Publisher for permission should be addressed to the Permissions Department, John Wiley & Sons, Inc., 111 River Street, Hoboken, NJ 07030, (201) 748-6011, fax (201) 748-6008, or online at www.wiley.com/go/permissions.

Limit of Liability/Disclaimer of Warranty: While the publisher and author have used their best efforts in preparing this book, they make no representations or warranties with respect to the accuracy or completeness of the contents of this book and specifically disclaim any implied warranties of merchantability or fitness for a particular purpose. No warranty may be created or extended by sales representatives or written sales materials. The advice and strategies contained herein may not be suitable for your situation. You should consult with a professional where appropriate. Neither the publisher nor author shall be liable for any loss of profit or any other commercial damages, including but not limited to special, incidental, consequential, or other damages. For general information on our other products and services, or for technical support, please contact our Customer Care Department within the United States at (800) 762-2974, outside the United States at (317) 572-3993 or fax (317) 572-4002.

Wiley also publishes its books in a variety of electronic formats. Some content that appears in print may not be available in electronic books. For more information about Wiley products, visit our web site at www.wiley.com.

Library of Congress Cataloging-in-Publication Data

Gup, Benton E.
Banking and financial institutions : a guide for directors, investors, and counterparties / Benton E. Gup.
p. cm. – (Wiley finance series)
Includes bibliographical references and index.
ISBN 978-0-470-87947-4 (hardback); ISBN 978-1-118-08743-5 (ebk); ISBN 978-1-118-08744-2 (ebk); 978-1-118-08748-0 (ebk)
1. Banks and banking–United States. 2. Financial institutions–United States. I. Title.
HG2491.G865 2011
332.10973–dc22 2011005434

Printed in the United States of America

10 9 8 7 6 5 4 3 2 1

To
Jean, Andy, Jeremy, Lincoln, and Carol

Contents

Preface

The traditional role of commercial banks in the financial system, and how they operate, has changed dramatically in recent years. The reasons for the changes include:

1. Financial innovations such as credit default swaps, hedge funds, and securitization.
2. Globalization of banks and financial systems. Some of the biggest bank holding companies in the United States are owned by foreign banks.[1] Equally important, some of the biggest U.S. banks have global operations.
3. The global financial crisis that began in 2007. It continued to have negative repercussions around the world in 2011.
4. New laws, such as the Dodd-Frank Wall Street Reform and Consumer Protection Act of 2010, and new regulations that emerged from it.

Simply stated, the way that banks and financial institutions operate is changing. This book examines how they operate in the context of these and other changes.

The book consists of 13 chapters and a glossary of the terms used in it. Chapter 1, "Lessons Learned from Banking Crises," explains that banking crises are not new. They have been going on since biblical times, and they are not unique to the United States. Real estate booms and busts are a common cause of financial crises. The chapter explains why they may happen again.

Chapter 2 explains the economic role of financial intermediaries—the financial institutions that bring borrowers and savers together. It used to be that commercial banks were the primary financial intermediary, but their role has changed in recent years. A large part of what banks used to do is now being done by so-called shadow banks.

Chapter 3 delves into the evolving legal environment. Banks can do only what the laws allow them to do. This chapter examines the major laws affecting banks and bank regulation. There are a lot of laws that banks have to comply with unless they can figure out legal ways around those laws—regulatory arbitrage.

Chapter 4 is about asset and liability management (ALM). Banks earn most of their income from the difference between their borrowing and lending rates. In 2010, market rates of interest were at record low levels, and they can only increase over time. This chapter explains how banks can deal with this and related issues.

Chapter 5 explains how banks can hedge some of their interest rate and credit risks by using various types of derivatives contracts, options, and futures. It also covers the use of special purpose vehicles (SPVs) and enterprise risk management (ERM).

Chapter 6 covers the process of commercial and industrial (C&I) lending. These C&I loans are made to business concerns. The chapter covers how banks make loans, the types of C&I loans, the role of collateral, and other factors.

Chapter 7 is about real estate and consumer lending. Recall from Chapter 1 that real estate loans were a key factor in the financial crisis. For many banks, real estate loans account for most of their lending activities. This chapter explains some of the major features of real estate lending. It also covers consumer lending. One extremely important part of this chapter is how annual percentage rates (APRs) are computed on consumer loans. It also discusses real estate and consumer credit regulations.

Chapter 8 involves bank capital. Banks are very highly leveraged when compared with nonfinancial corporations. The high degree of leverage contributed to the large number of bank failures in recent years. However, because of new international and domestic standards, their capital ratios have increased. But is it adequate? This chapter deals with these issues.

Chapter 9 evaluates the financial performance of banks. Bank regulators require them to file periodic financial reports that are available to the public. This chapter explains how to evaluate their financial statements and their financial performance.

Chapter 10 explores the payments systems. Payments are the heart of the financial system, and they can take many different forms. Payments systems include cash, checks, credit cards, informal value transfer systems (e.g., Hawalas), wire transfers, and other means of payment. While most payments are legal, bankers and others have to report money laundering and suspicious activities to federal authorities—or suffer the consequences. Failure to comply with the bank secrecy act/anti-money laundering (BSA/AML) laws can result in large fines (e.g., $110 million) and going to jail.

Chapter 11 explains some of the other financial services offered by banks. These include cash management services for business concerns, trust services, private wealth management, and correspondent banking.

Chapter 12 is a guide to Islamic banking written by Professor Mohamed Ariff. Mohamed Ariff held a chair in finance and headed the finance faculty at Monash University in Melbourne, Australia, before moving to Bond University, where he is currently professor of finance. While Islamic banking is widely used in more than 80 countries around the world, it is new to the United States. Some U.S. banks are beginning to offer Islamic banking services, and this chapter explains some of the essential features.

In Chapter 13, John Harrison (Superintendent of Banks, Alabama State Department of Banking) gives some tips for bank directors, borrowers, and investors in banks. He also explains what lies ahead.

And finally, the language of banking and finance can be very confusing. The Glossary provides convenient brief definitions of the finance jargon used in this book.

Acknowledgments

I want to thank Professor Mohamed Ariff for writing Chapter 12 about Islamic banking and John Harrison, Alabama State Bank Commissioner, for providing his insights about the banking issues in Chapter 13.

About the Author

Professor Benton E. Gup holds the Robert Hunt Cochrane/Alabama Bankers Association Chair at the University of Alabama, Tuscaloosa. Dr. Gup is the author or editor of 29 books, and his articles on financial subjects have appeared in leading finance journals. His most recent books are *The Valuation Handbook* (with Rawley Thomas), 2010, and *The Financial and Economic Crises: An International Perspective,* 2010. In 2009, he was awarded the Midwest Finance Association's Lifetime Achievement Award.

Banking and Financial Institutions

CHAPTER 1

Lessons Learned from Banking Crises

This chapter examines the causes of the recent financial crisis that began in the United States and then spread around the world. It also explains seven lessons that can be learned from financial crises.

INTERNATIONAL FINANCIAL CRISES

Economic crises are not new. In A.D. 33, Emperor Tiberius had to inject 1 million gold pieces of public money into the Roman financial system to keep it from collapsing.[1] There have been at least 60 different crises since the early seventeenth century.[2] As shown in Table 1.1, there were 16 economic crises between 1987 and 2010. The impact of each crisis varied widely. For example, the removal of the British pound from the European Exchange Rate Mechanism in 1992 and the Russian ruble collapsing in 1997 did not have a major impact in the United States. However, the economic crisis that began in the United States in 2007 was the worst since the Great Depression in the 1930s. Equally important, it became a global crisis. In 2009, crises in Iceland and Dubai adversely affected global investors. In 2010, the financial crisis in Greece roiled the European Union. The European countries having financial problems were Portugal, Ireland, Italy, Greece, and Spain; they were referred to collectively as the PIIGS.

The crisis became global because the biggest banks in the world, most of which are foreign owned, have extensive operations in the United States. Equally important, the largest banks in the United States have extensive overseas operations. Citigroup, for example, has offices in 140 countries, JPMorgan Chase has offices in 60 countries, and Bank of America operates in more than 30 foreign countries.[3]

Table 1.2 lists the world's 10 largest banks in 2007. Royal Bank of Scotland (RBS, first on the list) owned Citizens Financial Group, Inc., the

TABLE 1.1 International Financial Crises, 1987–2010

1987	U.S. stock market crash
1990	Collapse of U.S. high-yield bond market
1991	Oil price surge
1992	Britain removes pound from the European Exchange Rate Mechanism
1994	U.S. bond market crashes
1995	Mexican crisis
1997	Asian crisis
1997	Russian default, ruble collapses; Long-Term Capital Management bailout
2000	Technology, media, and telecom sectors collapse
2001	September 11 payment system disruption
2002	Argentine crisis
2002	German banking crisis
2007	U.S. subprime mortgage turmoil
2009	Iceland's financial crisis
2009	Dubai's financial crisis
2010	Greece's financial crisis

Source for data through 2007. Leonard Matz. "Liquidity Analysis: Decades of Change," Federal Deposit Insurance Corporation (FDIC) *Supervisory Insights*, Winter 2007, Vol. 4, Issue 2 (Freely adapted from a presentation by Leonard Matz, International Director, BancWare Academy for SunGard BancWare, at Federal Financial Institutions Examination Council (FFEIC) Capital Markets Specialist Conference in June 2007).

TABLE 1.2 World's 10 Largest Banks in 2007

Rank	Name	Country	Assets
1	Royal Bank of Scotland (RBS)	United Kingdom	$3.81($ trillions)
2	Deutsche Bank	Germany	2.97
3	BNP Paribas	France	2.49
4	Barclays Bank	United Kingdom	2.46
5	HSBC Holdings	United Kingdom	2.35
6	Crédit Agricole Group	France	2.27
7	Citigroup	USA	2.19
8	UBS	Switzerland	2.01
9	Bank of America Group	USA	1.72
10	Société Générale	France	1.59

Source: "The World's Biggest Banks," *Global Finance,* October 2008, p. 111.

14th largest bank holding company in the United States.[4] A bank holding company (BHC) is a corporation that owns one or more banks or financial service organizations. Deutsche Bank, from Germany, owned Tannus Corporation, the 8th largest BHC, and BNP Paribas owned BancWest Corporation, the 22nd largest BHC. Crédit Agricole (6th on the list) is the only large bank without U.S. operations.

WHAT CAUSED THE CRISIS IN THE UNITED STATES?

Population Growth and Urbanization

Population growth was the most important driving force behind the real estate booms and busts. It created the demand for housing. The population of the United States increased from 205 million in 1970 to more than 302 million in 2007,[5] and about 100 million additional people had to live somewhere. They moved into urban areas such as Atlanta (Georgia), Dallas (Texas), Los Angeles (California), Las Vegas (Nevada), Miami (Florida), and other metropolitan areas located mostly in the south and southwestern parts of the United States.

The increased participation of women in the workforce is another demographic factor to be considered. Women accounted for 38 percent of the labor force in 1970, and 59 percent of the labor force in 2007. Two-income families tend to buy bigger and more expensive homes. In 1980, the average size of a single family home was 1,740 square feet, and it cost $64,600. In 2007, the average size was 2,521 square feet, and the cost soared to $247,900.[6]

Government Policies

Laws The U.S. Congress recognized that the increased population had increased the demand for housing, and they passed the laws that facilitated home ownership. The following is a partial list of those laws:

- Community Reinvestment Act (CRA, 1977) encouraged depository institutions to meet the credit needs of their communities, including low- and moderate-income neighborhoods. The CRA requires that each depository institution's record be evaluated periodically. The CRA examinations are conducted by the federal agencies that are responsible for supervising depository institutions. Depository institutions include Federal Deposit Insurance Corporation (FDIC) insured banks (commercial banks, savings banks, mutual savings banks), insured credit unions, and other institutions defined by law.[7]

- Depository Institutions Deregulation and Monetary Control Act (DIDMCA, 1980) preempted state interest rate caps on loans.
- Alternative Mortgage Transaction Parity Act (1982) permitted the use of variable interest rates and balloon payments.
- Tax Reform Act of 1986 eliminated the tax deduction for interest expense on credit cards. This induced borrowers to use home equity lines of credit (HELOC) or second mortgages on their homes. The interest on mortgage loans is a tax-deductible expense.
- Taxpayer Relief Act (1997) eliminated capital gains tax on the sale of homes priced up to $500,000 for married couples. People cashed out home equity profits to buy additional homes or condominiums. The snowbirds (people living in the colder northern part of the United States) bought second homes in the warmer southern and western parts of the country, in places such as Florida, Arizona, and Nevada.

Government-Sponsored Entities Government-sponsored entities (GSEs)—the Federal National Mortgage Association (FNMA, Fannie Mae), the Federal Home Loan Mortgage Corporation (FHLMC, Freddie Mac), and the Government National Mortgage Association (Ginnie Mae)—were chartered by Congress to provide liquidity, stability, and affordability to the U.S. housing and mortgage markets. Fannie Mae was established as a federal agency in 1938, and it became a private shareholder-owned company in 1968. Freddie Mac was chartered by Congress in 1970, and in 1989 it, too, became a publicly traded company. In 1968, Congress established Ginnie Mae as a government-owned corporation within the Department of Housing and Urban Development (HUD). It is still government owned.

Fannie Mae packages (i.e., securitizes) mortgage loans originated by lenders in the primary mortgage market into mortgage-backed securities (Fannie Mae MBSs) that can then be bought and sold in the secondary mortgage market. It also participates in the secondary mortgage market by purchasing mortgage loans (also called *whole loans*) and mortgage-related securities, including Fannie Mae MBSs, for its mortgage portfolio.[8] Freddie Mac's operations are similar to those of Fannie Mae.

Beginning in the1970s, Fannie Mae and Freddie Mac played a major role in changing the housing finance system from deposit-based funding to funding based on capital markets. By 1998, 64 percent of originated mortgage loans were sold by the mortgage originators to large financial institutions and the GSEs that securitized the mortgage loans and sold them to investors.[9] Fannie Mae and Freddie Mac also provided guarantees for their mortgage-backed securities. Subsequently, capital market investors funded the majority of housing finance. Non-GES securitizations also increased sharply in 2003–2006.

Because Fannie Mae and Freddie Mac are private shareholder-owned companies, management chose to grow the firms by acquiring low-quality, high-risk mortgages in order to maximize shareholder wealth.[10] It worked well until the real estate bubble burst, and the government placed them under conservatorship on September 6, 2008. The Federal Housing Finance Agency (FHFA) is the conservator.

Ginnie Mae deals exclusively in loans insured by the Federal Housing Administration (FHA) or guaranteed by the Department of Veterans' Affairs (VA). Other guarantors or issuers of loans eligible as collateral for Ginnie Mae MBSs include the Department of Agriculture's Rural Housing Service (RHS) and HUD's Office of Public and Indian Housing (PIH). Consequently, Ginnie Mae securities are the *only* MBS to carry the full faith and credit guaranty of the U.S. government.[11]

The Federal Home Loan Bank System was created in 1932 to provide funding for home mortgages.[12] Today, federal home loan banks (FHLBs) provide funding to banks for housing, development, and infrastructure projects. They are cooperatives owned by banks and other regulated financial institutions. Their advances to their member institutions provided an important source of funding and liquidity both before and during the banking crises.[13]

According to Sheila Bair, chairman of the FDIC,

> *Many of the products and practices that led to the financial crisis have their roots in the mortgage market innovations that began in the 1980s and matured in the 1990s. Following large interest-rate losses from residential mortgage investments that precipitated the thrift crisis in the 1980s, banks and thrifts began selling or securitizing a major share of their mortgage loans with the housing government sponsored enterprises (GSEs). By focusing on originating, rather than holding, mortgages, banks and thrifts were able to reduce their interest-rate and credit risk, increase liquidity, and lower their regulatory capital requirements under the rules that went into effect in the early 1990s. Between 1985 and the third quarter of 2009, the share of mortgages (whole loans) held by banks and thrifts fell from approximately 55 percent to 25 percent. By contrast, the share of mortgages held by the GSEs increased from approximately 28 percent to just over 51 percent, over the same time period (see Figure 1.1).*[14]

Figure 1.1 also shows the dramatic growth of home mortgages, the growth of GSEs, and banks' declining share of the home mortgage market.

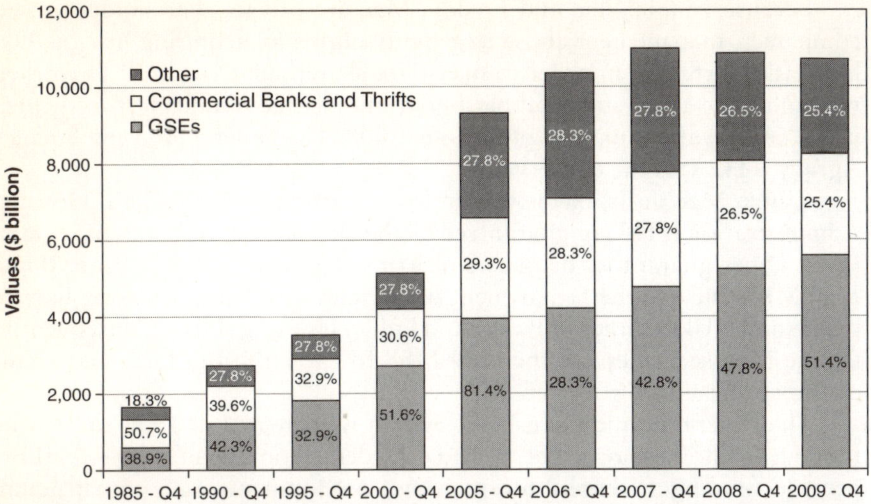

FIGURE 1.1 As Home Mortgage Volumes Grew, the Share Held by Banks and Thrifts Declined
Source: Sheila C. Bair, Chairman, FDIC, Statement on the Causes and Current State of the Financial Crises before the Financial Crisis Inquiry Commission, January 14, 2010.
Source: Haver Analytics, "Flow of Funds."

Declining Mortgage Rates and Increased Funding by Shadow Banks

The contract interest rate on a 30-year conventional fixed-rate mortgage peaked at 14.67 percent in July 1984.[15] Subsequently, mortgage rates declined gradually over the years, reaching 4.81 percent in May 2009, and remained below 5 percent until late December.

Both foreign investors and foreign governments invested heavily in the U.S. economy. These investors include, but are not limited to, Japan and China buying government bonds. Sovereign wealth funds (state-owned investment companies) invested billions of dollars in Citigroup, Morgan Stanley, Merrill Lynch, and other financial firms.[16] Unregulated financial institutions, such as hedge funds and private equity funds, also made billions of dollars available to borrowers and lenders. The so-called *shadow banking system*—"the whole alphabet soup of levered up non-bank investment conduits, vehicles, and structures"—helped to provide the liquidity that funded the real estate boom.[17] Shadow banks include investment banks, finance companies, money market funds, hedge funds, special purpose entities, and other vehicles that aggregate and hold financial assets. Shadow banks are unregulated or lightly regulated, and they do not have access to

central bank liquidity or public-sector credit guarantees.[18] "The shadow banking system was extremely vulnerable to financial stress in three ways: (1) some were highly leveraged; (2) they relied disproportionately on short-term funding markets; and (3) they did not benefit from explicit government support prior to the crisis. As a result, the shadow banking system was vulnerable to panics."[19]

The availability of funds and the decline in mortgage rates encouraged existing homeowners to refinance their mortgages at lower rates and others to take advantage of the falling rates to buy homes, condominiums, and investment properties. Between 2000 and 2005, housing prices in the United States rose 51 percent (34 percent when adjusted for inflation), double any period in the past 30 years![20]

Subprime Loans

The global financial crisis is associated with subprime real estate loans. A standard definition for *subprime* does not exist. Nevertheless, the term *subprime* typically refers to high-risk loans made to borrowers with low credit scores (e.g., Fair Isaac Corporation [FICO] credit scores below 620), and/or high loan-to-value ratios, and/or debt-to-income ratios above 50 percent, and other factors.[21] Some mortgage loans had little or no documentation (*low doc* and *no doc* loans). Subprime loans also include nonconforming loans. These are real estate loans that do not conform to the GSEs' loan standards. For example, Fannie Mae limited single-family homes to $359,650 in 2005 for one-unit properties.[22] The limit was raised to $417,000 in 2006 and remained at that level in 2010.

Many subprime real estate loans had *adjustable rate mortgages* (ARMs), which further increased the default risk. By way of illustration, consider a 2/28 ARM. Table 1.3 illustrates the difference between the payments of a fixed-rate mortgage and the 2/28 ARM when market rates of interest rise. The ARM has a low teaser interest rate for the first two years of a 30-year loan (2/28) to induce borrowers to use this method of financing.

TABLE 1.3 Sample ARM Comparison 2/28 ARM, $200,000 loan/30 years

Years and Interest Rates	Fixed Rate 7.5%	Reduced Initial Rate 2/28 ARM (7% for 2 years then adjusting to variable rate)
Years 1–2 7.5%	$1,598	$1,531
Year 3 10%	$1,598	$1,939
Year 4 11.5%	$1,598	$2,152
Years 5–30 13%	$1,598	$2,370

However, when market rates of interest rise, the monthly payments increase significantly. In some cases, the new payments exceed the borrower's ability to repay the loans, and the loans go into default.

The housing bubble burst in 2005. When housing prices began to decline sharply, the delinquency rate on subprime loans began to soar.[23] The delinquency rate on subprime ARMs was 10 percent in early 2005 and 28 percent in March 2009.[24] More will be said about that shortly. The decline in house prices and increase in delinquency rates contributed to increasing foreclosures.

The Role of Securitization, Mortgage-Backed Securities, Credit Default Swaps, and Models in the Crisis

Securitization *Securitization* is a financial innovation that gained widespread use in the 1970s.[25] It refers to packaging and selling mortgage loans, credit card loans, and other loans. Securitization is a great financial tool when used properly. However, the improper use of securitized mortgage loans was the time bomb that set off the financial crisis. The problem was that the originators of the securitized mortgage loans got paid when they sold the MBSs to other investors. They did not retain an equity interest in the MBSs. Stated otherwise, they had no skin in the game. This contributed to a moral hazard problem because the originators had no risk associated with selling high-risk, low-quality loans (i.e., subprime loans) to investors. The more loans they sold, the more money they earned. Thus, the basic business model of banking changed from originating and holding loans to originating and distributing loans.

The large foreign banks that were discussed previously acquired securitized mortgage loans, and they facilitated their distribution around the world. Thus, the impact of rising delinquency rates and defaults on mortgage loans that were originated in the United States was felt globally.

MBSs are a type of *collateralized debt obligations* (CDO). A CDO is an asset-backed security that pays cash flows based on the underlying collateral, which may be residential real estate, commercial real estate, corporate bonds, or other assets. The MBS CDOs are divided into classes, or *tranches*, that have different maturities and different priority for repayment.

The lack of transparency of complex MBSs was part of the problem. Investors did not know exactly what they were buying, and the credit rating agencies did not correctly estimate the risks of these securities. Two plausible reasons that the credit rating models did not work well are that they were based on historical data that didn't apply to subprime loans, and they

made certain assumptions about future economic conditions. When neither assumption is correct, the models did not accurately reflect credit risk.

Credit Default Swaps Because investors did not fully understand the risks associated with securitized loans, they bought *credit default swaps* (CDSs), a form of insurance or hedge for MBSs.[26] If the borrower defaults, the holder of the debt is paid by the insurer. The CDSs are also used by traders who make naked bets (i.e., they speculate and do not hold the debt) that the prices of certain debt securities will decline.

The CDS market increased from about $6.4 trillion in December 2004 to about $57.9 trillion in December 2007.[27]

American International Group (AIG) was the major issuer of CDSs. Its failure would have caused systemic risk in the financial markets. Consequently, when AIG got into trouble in September 2008, the Federal Reserve provided $85 billion in loans.[28] The loans had a 24-month term. Interest accrued on the outstanding balance at a rate of three-month London Interbank Offered Rate (LIBOR) plus 850 basis points.

Quantitative Models Mortgage lenders, insurance companies (AIG), credit rating agencies (Standard & Poor's, Moody's), credit scoring companies (Fair Isaac), and others make extensive use of quantitative models in their risk management and rating systems. According to Nobel Prize laureate in economics Robert Merton, models can be thought of as incomplete descriptions of complex reality: "The mathematics of financial models can be applied precisely, but the models are not at all precise in their application to the complex real world. Their accuracy as a useful approximation to that world varies significantly across time and place."[29]

Quantitative models, such as the Black-Scholes-Merton (BSM) option pricing model, are based on certain assumptions. For example, the BSM model assumes that markets are continuous in time and infinitely liquid. However, that is not a realistic assumption.[30] Similarly, the efficient market hypothesis (EMH)—that "competition among market participants causes the return from using information to be commensurate with its cost"—also has limitations.[31] According to Ball (2009), EMH is about the demand side of the market and is silent on the supply side of the information market (e.g., accounting reports, statements from managers, government reports). The information does not have the same meaning to investors with different investment objectives, markets are not costless to operate, taxes need to be considered, and other issues are also involved.

For the most part, the models used the credit ratings, and others were based on historical data that did not accurately foresee future events. Stated

otherwise, models have limits. When the markets exceed those limits, the models fail.

According to Richard Fisher, president of the Federal Reserve Bank of Dallas:

> *The excesses in subprime lending in the United States were fed by an excessive amount of faith in technically sophisticated approaches to risk management and a misguided belief that mathematical models could price securitized assets, including securities based on mortgages, accurately. These valuation methodologies were so technical and mathematically sophisticated that their utter complexity lulled many people into a false sense of security. In the end, complexity proved hopelessly inadequate as an all-encompassing measure of risk, despite its frequent advertisement as such. The risk models employed turned out to be merely formulaic descriptions of the past and created an illusion of precision.*[32]

Bank Business Models As a result of the growth of securitized assets and brokered deposits, the basic business model has changed for some banks. The term *deposit broker* is defined as any person engaged in the business of placing deposits, or facilitating the placement of deposits, of third parties with insured depository institutions. A *brokered deposit* is any deposit that is obtained, directly or indirectly, from a deposit broker.[33] The ability to buy and sell both loans and deposits has increased banks' liquidity. One consequence of the increased liquidity is that the basic business model of many banks is changing. It used to be to originate and hold loans. The new business model is to originate in order to distribute loans. Not all banks use the new model.

Dependence on short-term funds contributed to the increased liquidity crisis in 2008. A *liquidity crisis* is "defined as a sudden and prolonged evaporation of both market and funding liquidity with potentially serious consequences for the stability of the financial system and the real economy."[34] Market liquidity is the ability to trade a market instrument with little or no change in the price. Funding liquidity is the ability to raise cash or its equivalents by selling assets or borrowing funds. To avoid future liquidity crises, federal bank regulators sought comments on a proposed "Interagency Guidance on Funding and Liquidity Risk Management" in July 2009.[35] The proposed guidance is consistent with "Principles for Sound Liquidity Risk Management and Supervision" issued by the Basel Committee on Banking Supervision (BCBS) in September 2008.

Excessive Financial Leverage

Many subprime lenders and investment banks were very highly leveraged. An equity capital ratio of 3 percent means that for every $1 in equity capital, there are assets (i.e., loans, investments, other assets) of about $33. A $1 dollar loan loss translates into a 100 percent loss of the lender's capital. Bear Stearns had an equity capital ratio of 3 percent. It avoided failure in March 2008 by being acquired by JPMorgan Chase.[36]

Some hedge funds have lower equity capital ratios, such as 2 percent. In other words, they had $50 in assets for every $1 in equity capital. When highly leveraged borrowers default, the losses flow back to highly commercial banks. In 1999, the President's Working Group on Financial Markets said the following in its report on Long-Term Capital Management (LTCM), a hedge fund that almost failed.

> *When leveraged investors are overwhelmed by market or liquidity shocks, the risks they have assumed will be discharged back into the market. Thus, highly leveraged investors have the potential to exacerbate instability in the market as a whole. . . . These secondary effects, if not contained, could cause a contraction of credit and liquidity, and ultimately, heighten the risk of a contraction in real economic activity.*[37]

According to the Basel Committee on Banking Supervision:

> *One of the main reasons the economic and financial crisis became so severe was that the banking sectors of many countries had built up excessive on- and off-balance sheet leverage. This was accompanied by a gradual erosion of the level and quality of the capital base. At the same time, many banks were holding insufficient liquidity buffers. The banking system therefore was not able to absorb the resulting systemic trading and credit losses nor could it cope with the reintermediation of large off-balance sheet exposures that had built up in the shadow banking system. The crisis was further amplified by a procyclical deleveraging process and by the interconnectedness of systemic institutions through an array of complex transactions. During the most severe episode of the crisis, the market lost confidence in the solvency and liquidity of many banking institutions. The weaknesses in the banking sector were transmitted to the rest of the financial system and the real economy, resulting in a massive contraction of liquidity and credit availability. Ultimately the public sector had to step in with unprecedented injections of liquidity, capital support and guarantees, exposing the taxpayer to large losses.*[38]

The equity capital ratio for FDIC-insured commercial banks was 10.92 percent in the third quarter of 2009.[39] The *equity capital ratio* is the bank's equity capital, exclusive of the allowance for loan and lease losses, divided by the bank's total assets. Although the equity capital ratio for banks is substantially higher than that of hedge funds, banks are still highly leveraged compared with nonfinancial corporations, which have an equity capital ratio 58.6 percent.[40]

Bank Failures

The number of FDIC-insured bank and savings institution (hereafter called *banks*) failures increased from zero in 2005–2006 to 25 banks in 2008 and 140 banks in 2009 (as of December18). To put the number of failures in perspective, about 9,000 banks failed during the Great Depression of the early 1930s, and more than 1,600 banks failed during the 1980–1994 period (Table 1.4). The data also show that the number of banks has declined over the years, reflecting the consolidation and increased asset concentration of the banking system. In the first quarter of 2009, there were 8,246 FDIC-insured banks.[41] Out of that total, 115 banks with assets greater than $10 billion held 78 percent of the total assets.

Rather than letting the largest U.S. financial institutions fail, federal banking authorities arranged for Bank of America to buy Countrywide in January 2008 and Merrill Lynch in September. The government took over Fannie Mae and Freddie Mac in September, and the Federal Reserve invested in AIG. Nevertheless, the government let Lehman Brothers fail in September 2008.

TABLE 1.4 Bank Failures

Years	Number of Banks	Number of Bank Failures
Great Depression, 1930s	14,146 (12/1934)	9,000+
1980–1994	10,451 (12/1994)	1,600
1995–2004	8,976 (12/2004)	55
2005–2006	8,681 (12/2006)	0
2007	8,533 (12/2007)	3
2008	8,305 (12/08)	25
2009	8,200	140

Source: FDIC, *Statistics on Banking, Historical 1934–1994,* Vol. 1, 1995; FDIC, *History of the Eighties, Lessons for the Future,* Vol. 1, 1999; "FDIC Statistics at a Glance, Historical Trends as of March 31, 2009"; FDIC Failed Bank List.

Changes in the following banking laws contributed to bank consolidation and increasing banks' geographic footprint and the services and products that banks could offer their customers. These changes helped to reduce the number of bank failures by providing greater geographic and product diversification.

- Bank Holding Company Act of 1956 allowed bank holding companies to acquire banks in other states.
- Riegle-Neal Interstate Banking and Branching Efficiency Act of 1994 allowed interstate branch banking.
- Gramm-Leach-Bliley Act of 1999 (GLBA) permitted financial holding companies to engage in banking, selling insurance and securities, and other activities.

LESSONS LEARNED FROM FINANCIAL CRISES

Lesson 1: Financial Leverage—Caveat Emptor

Financial leverage is a double-edged sword. It can be beneficial to earnings per share when revenues are increasing, or it can result in bankruptcy when revenues decline. It should be used prudently. But it wasn't, and excessive financial leverage contributed significantly to the global financial crises.

Leveraged Borrowers Some corporate borrowers are highly leveraged. As previously noted, Bear Stearns, the former investment bank, had a leverage ratio of 33:1. Bear Stearns faced failure from its losses; it was acquired by JPMorgan Chase. Hedge funds may have even higher leverage ratios (e.g., 50:1), which makes them very risky borrowers. For every $1 in equity, there are $50 in assets. A $1 reduction in the value of the assets wipes out the equity.

Many individual borrowers increased their financial leverage through repeatedly cashing out and refinancing their homes. As home prices appreciated in value during the boom part of the real estate cycle, many home owners borrowed increasing amounts. The repeated refinancing of home mortgages resulted in an estimated $1.5 trillion in losses when real estate prices declined and the mortgage loans went into default.[42]

Leveraged Loans Consider the case of a 25-year, $1 million commercial real estate loan with a 7 percent fixed rate of interest. As shown in Table 1.5, Panel A, if 100 percent of the value of the real estate is borrowed, the expected annual income from the real estate project is $85,810. If the borrower

TABLE 1.5 Real Estate Values

Panel A 25-Year $1,000,000 Commercial Real Estate Loan at 7 Percent Fixed Rate

	Loan/Value 100%	Loan/Value 90%	Loan/Value 80%	Loan/Value 70%
25-Year real estate loan	$1,000,000	$1,000,000	$1,000,000	$1,000,000
Initial asset value	$1,000,000	$1,111,111	$1,250,000	$1,428,571
Expected annual income	$85,810	$95,346	$107,263	$122,586

Panel B Interest Rates Increase 200 Basis Points to 9 Percent

	Loan/Value 100%	Loan/Value 90%	Loan/Value 80%	Loan/Value 70%
25-Year real estate loan	$1,000,000	$1,000,000	$1,000,000	$1,000,000
Present value of asset at 9%	$842,877	$936,536	$1,053,602	$1,204,113
Asset value less loan amount	−$157,123	−$63,464	$53,602	$404,798
Probable outcome	Default likely	Default possible	Positive equity value	Positive equity value

borrows 90 percent of the value of the property, then the initial value of the property is about $1.1 million ($1,000,000/.90 = $1,111,111). Similarly, if the borrower borrows 70 percent, the initial value of the property is about $1.4 million. The table also shows the expected annual incomes.

Suppose that market rates of interest increase 200 basis points to 9 percent. As shown in Panel B, the value of the property declines. In the case of the 100 percent loan/value ratio, the property is worth $157,123 less than the amount of the loan, and default is likely. Similarly, when the loan/value ratio is 90 percent, default is likely. In both these cases, the property is worth less than the amount of the loan. Stated otherwise, the property is underwater.

When the loan/value ratios are lower, the owner has a positive equity value and will not default. The lesson to be learned here is that high loan/value ratios are risky, because the borrower is more likely to default if the property is underwater.

Leveraged Lenders Commercial banks are for-profit corporations whose objectives include maximizing shareholders' wealth. The faster a bank can

grow, the greater the potential profits. However, the success of their growth depends in part on how it is financed. An increasing number of banks are using *noncore funding sources* of funds. These include time deposits over $100,000, brokered deposits, and foreign office deposits. Banks also borrow funds from federal home loan banks. Noncore funding can increase a bank's financial leverage. It also increases its liquidity risk.[43]

Regulatory capital requirements limit the degree to which banks can be leveraged. In the third quarter of 2009, their risk-based core capital (leverage) ratio was 8.44 percent.[44] *Core capital* includes common equity capital plus noncumulative perpetual preferred stock plus minority interest in consolidated subsidiaries, less goodwill and other ineligible intangible assets. It does not take many loan losses to wipe out the bank's capital. In simple terms, commercial banks have about $12 in loans and other assets for every $1 of capital. In September 2010, bank regulators announced plans to increase bank capital requirements, thereby reducing financial leverage. The details are explained in Chapter 8.

On the other side of the coin, higher capital requirements for lenders may result in less lending. Thus, in the short run, there is a trade-off between lending and the growth rate of bank capital. How much capital banks should hold is debatable.

Collectively, when a large number of highly leveraged borrowers default on their loans, it has a cascading effect on the banks. Thus, if highly leveraged borrowers default on loans to highly leveraged hedge funds, which in turn default on bank loans, there will be a large number of bank failures.

Bank Failures in Iceland Iceland is a small country with a population of about 300,700. According to the Central Intelligence Agency's *World Fact Book*:

> *Much of Iceland's economic growth in recent years came as the result of a boom in domestic demand following the rapid expansion of the country's financial sector. Domestic banks expanded aggressively in foreign markets, and consumers and businesses borrowed heavily in foreign-currency loans, following the privatization of the sector in the early 2000s. Worsening global financial conditions throughout 2008 resulted in a sharp depreciation of the krona vis-à-vis other major currencies. The foreign exposure of Icelandic banks, whose loans and other assets totaled more than 10 times the country's GDP, became unsustainable. Iceland's three largest banks collapsed in late 2008.*[45]

The main source of the boom was financial leverage. "The country became a giant hedge fund. And once-restrained Icelandic households amassed debts exceeding 220% of disposable income—almost twice the proportion of American consumers."[46]

What is the right amount of leverage? Harry Markowitz (2009) said: "Excessive leverage is bad: too many illiquid assets are dangerous; and writing insurance against correlated risks without reinsuring, or without quite large reserves, is an accident waiting to happen." He goes on to say: "More generally, evaluating risks one at a time rather than considering them as a portfolio is an all-too-common error." That brings us to our next lesson: diversification.

Lesson 2: Diversification Is Good; High Loan Concentrations Are Bad for Banks

Colonial Bank Bobby Lowder created Colonial Bank in 1981 by acquiring a failed community bank, Southland Bancorp. His strategy was to build his deposit base by acquiring community banks and by investing primarily in real estate loans.[47] The strategy was successful for many years. Colonial took advantage of the booming real estate markets in Florida, Georgia, and Nevada. It operated 354 branches in Florida (57 percent of the branches), Alabama (26 percent), Georgia (5 percent), Nevada (6 percent), and Texas (6 percent).[48] The Colonial BancGroup, headquartered in Montgomery, Alabama, had more than $26 billion in assets when it failed in 2009.

In 2008, 85 percent of Colonial's loan portfolio was real estate loans: commercial real estate (34 percent), real estate construction (33 percent), and residential real estate (18 percent) loans.[49] In June 2009, commercial real estate loans were about 595 percent of Colonial's capital, and construction and development loans were 274 percent. When the real estate bubble burst, it did not take many loan losses to wipe out Colonial's capital.

Diversification means investing in assets whose returns are not perfectly positively correlated. Unfortunately for Colonial, the entire real estate market in the United States was adversely affected by the financial and economic crisis. The states that suffered the most were those that had the greatest population growth. They included Florida, Georgia, and Nevada, where Colonial's branches were located.

Colonial was the fifth largest bank failure in U.S. history. In August 2009, it was acquired by BB&T Corp., based in Winston Salem, North Carolina.

A significant number of the banks that failed during the 2007–2009 period had high concentrations of construction and land development loans that were secured by real estate. Such loans are made to finance the construction of new structures, additions, alterations, or demolitions to make way for new structures. They also depended heavily on brokered deposits.

Lesson 3: Loans Made to High-Risk Borrowers Are Risky

Subprime Borrowers and Mortgages The financial crisis that began 2007 is commonly associated with subprime loans, but it also involved *Alt-A mortgages* (i.e., alternative A-rated mortgages). Alt-A mortgages are riskier than prime-rated mortgages but less risky than subprime mortgages. Alt-A mortgages may lack full documentation, have higher loan-to-value ratios and debt-to-income ratios, or have other features that do not conform to GSEs' lending guidelines.

The delinquency on all residential real estate loans made by commercial banks soared from 1.6 percent in 2005 to 9.8 percent in the third quarter of 2009.[50] Similarly, the charge-off rates for commercial real estate loans increased from 1 percent to 8.7 percent.

The delinquency rate for prime ARMs on one- to four-unit residential properties in March 2005 was 2 percent.[51] By March 2009, it had increased to 12 percent. In contrast, delinquent subprime ARMs during that same period almost tripled, soaring from about 10 percent to 27.6 percent.[52]

Taking on too much risk is bad, but so is not taking on any risk. How much risk should lenders take?

Lesson 4: Be Aware of Interest Rate Risk

Rising Interest Rates Banks and other types of depository institutions generally finance their long-term assets with shorter-term liabilities. They profit from the difference between making long-term loans at high rates of interest and borrowing shorter-term funds at lower rates of interest. The difference between the two rates, called the net interest margin (NIM), is usually about 3 percent to 4 percent.

The Savings and Loan (S&L) crisis of the 1980s was due to the fact that long-term mortgage loans were made at low fixed rates, and they were financed with short-term deposits. Then market rates of interest soared to record levels. During the 1976–December 1981 period, 30-day CD rates increased from 5.08 percent to 15.94 percent, resulting in negative NIMs because of fixed-rate loans made at lower rates.[53]

Between 1980 and 1994, 1,600 banks and savings institutions failed. As previously noted, mortgage rates of interest peaked at 16.5 percent in 1981 and then declined to less than 5 percent in November 2009. Banks and other lenders that make fixed-rate mortgage loans when market rates of interest are low and then hold those loans instead of selling them will be subject to interest rate risk (i.e., negative NIMs) when market rates of interest rise.

Interest rate risk can be mitigated by hedging with interest rate swaps or other instruments. There were 8,099 FDIC-insured institutions in the United States in the third quarter of 2009.[54] However, only "1,110 insured U.S. commercial banks reported derivatives activities at the end of the second quarter.... Nonetheless, most derivatives activity in the U.S. banking system continues to be dominated by a small group of large financial institutions. Five large commercial banks represent 97% of the total banking industry notional amounts and 88% of industry net current credit exposure."[55]

Lenders can also mitigate their interest rate risk by selling the long-term fixed-rate loans to investors or government-backed entities, such as Fannie Mae and Freddie Mac, that are willing to hold them.

Another issue involving interest rates concerns fair value accounting, in which the assets and liabilities reflect market prices. Simply stated, an increase in market rates of interest will reduce the value of long-term bank assets more than short-term liabilities, resulting in lower bank equity capital. This issue is explained in more detail in Chapter 8.

Lesson 5: We Are Globally Interconnected

The financial crisis in Greece in 2010 had global impacts. One reason is that Greece is part of the European Union (EU) that includes 27 countries that share a common currency, the euro. Greece's economic problems had a negative impact on the value of the euro. That, in turn, affects all countries, including the United States, that have international trade relations with the EU. For example, a fall in the value of the euro has a negative effect on the value of the dollar because it is more expensive for EU countries to import goods and services from the United States. Thus, we are globally interconnected by trade, exchange rates, and financial markets. "A key lesson of the crisis is that keeping the economy in order does not necessarily insulate it from external shocks."[56]

Lesson 6: Real Estate Bubbles Will Probably Occur Again

Real estate bubbles are not limited to the United States. There were real estate bubbles in Japan, Spain, Sweden, and Thailand in the 1990s.[57] The most recent bubble in a foreign country was in Dubai.

Dubai Dubai is one of the seven United Arab Emirates (UAE), and it is located on the Persian Gulf coast. Dubai has a population of about

2.6 million. In 2000, if not before, Dubai began to engage in large-scale real estate projects with the intent of diversifying its economy and becoming a tourist destination and a global financial center. The large-scale real estate projects include one of the world's tallest skyscrapers (the Emirates Towers), the most expensive hotel (Burj Al Arab), and large residential projects (Palm Islands, built into the gulf).

The basic idea was to build the real estate projects and then people would come and buy or occupy them. However, the financial crisis that began in the United States in 2007, falling oil prices, and tighter credit had a chilling effect on Dubai's real estate projects. Some of the projects faltered, and the bubble burst.

The projects were run by Dubai's state-owned investment company, Dubai World. It wanted to restructure $26 billion in debt owed to global investors.[58] The global investors were surprised to learn that the Dubai government would not guarantee Dubai World's debts.[59] Investors with large exposures to Dubai World's debt included Abu Dhabi Commercial Bank,[60] Royal Bank of Scotland Group (UK), HSBC Holdings (UK), Barclays (UK), Lloyds Banking Group (UK), Standard Charter (UK), and ING Group (the Netherlands). Collectively, European banks had about $84 billion in exposure to UAE banks, including Dubai.[61]

Like previous real estate bubbles, the one in Dubai was financed with debt. But in this case, investors made the incorrect assumption about the quality of the debt. Thus, the risks associated with financial leverage are compounded by the quality of the debt.

The U.S. Population The population of the United States continues to grow. In January 2010, the population was 307 million.[62] The population is expected to increase to 439 million by 2050.[63] In other words, the demand for housing is going to continue to grow. Where are the additional 130 million people going to live? Is it going to fuel the next real estate bubble?

Lesson 7: Scotoma

Scotoma is a term used by psychologists that means a culturally induced blind spot. For example, in the 1400s, everyone believed that the world was flat and that if you went too far, you would fall off the edge. When Columbus went to the bank to borrow money for an expedition around the world, the banker refused. Who in their right mind would lend money to finance someone who was going to fall off the edge of the world? Today, most people know that the world is not flat. Nevertheless, each of us has scotomas. What they are and how they will affect future economic expansions and contractions are open for debate. Or are they? A 2003 study by experts at the Federal Reserve Bank of Chicago and a World Bank conference on asset price bubbles—long before the most recent crisis—concluded that:[64]

- Asset price bubbles are difficult to identify ex ante.
- Not all bubbles lead to economic crises.
- Bubbles occur with greater frequency in emerging economies than in developed economies.
- Countries that suffer longer and more destabilizing bubbles tend to have poor transparency, weak macroeconomic policies, and lack of diversification in their economies.

CHAPTER 2

The Economic Role of Financial Intermediaries

This chapter presents an overview of the financial system. In this context, the view from an airplane is entirely different from a view on the ground. At ground level, it is hard to visualize the shape and size of a town or a city or the winding course of a river. But they can be seen from an airplane. This chapter gives an airplane view of the financial system and how it relates to the economic system. The details of the financial landscape are explored in later chapters.

THE ECONOMIC AND FINANCIAL SYSTEM

How does that economic and financial system in the United States operate? To answer that question, think of the economic and financial system being divided into three types of economic units: business concerns, financial intermediaries, and individuals. To keep the explanation simple, we will not examine the role of government or taxes.

Figure 2.1 presents a simplified overview of how the three principal types of economic units relate to each other. Because the economic and financial systems are complex, this overview does not tell the whole story, but it does form a foundation for understanding how the system works. As shown in the figure, business concerns pay individuals wages, rent for the use of their labor, land, and other resources. By way of illustration, suppose that business concerns pay individuals $100. This is the *total income* (Y) in our economic system. Individuals use the $100 to buy goods and services from the business concerns. Economists call their purchases *consumption* (C). The top loop in the figure shows the flow of funds from business concerns to individuals, and then the funds flow back to the business concerns. This process is called the *circular flow of money*. In the top loop of the figure,

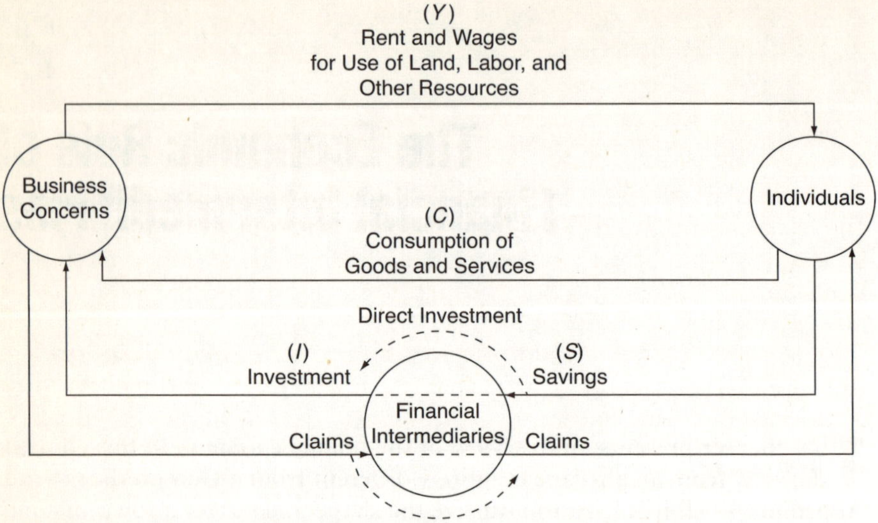

FIGURE 2.1 An Overview of the Economic and Financial System

total income Y is equal to total consumption C.

$$Y = C$$
$$\$100 = \$100$$

In the real world, money does not move in a perfect circle between business concerns and individuals because individuals do not spend all of the money they receive on goods and services. Savings (S) is the difference between income and consumption. If savings is \$20, then consumption will be \$80.

$$S = Y - C$$
$$\$20 = \$100 - \$80$$

Savings reduces the amount of funds that individuals return to business concerns. As shown in the lower loop of Figure 2.1, savings is channeled into financial intermediaries, which in turn invest that \$20 in business concerns. Thus, investment (I) is also equal to income less consumption.

$$I = Y - C$$
$$\$20 = \$100 - \$80$$

It follows that savings equal investment.

$$S = I$$
$$\$20 = \$20$$

Equally important, the savings and investment process takes place in financial intermediaries. They bring the savers and borrowers together by selling claims (securities) to the savers for money and investing or lending that money to borrowers. Some savers invest directly in business concerns and bypass the intermediaries.

Financial intermediaries are defined as economic entities whose principal function is to manage the financial assets of other economic entities, such as business concerns and individuals. Financial intermediaries bring savers, investors, and borrowers together by selling securities to savers and investors for money, and then they invest or lend the money to other entities.

The term *financial intermediaries* can be applied to a variety of institutions, including:

- Commercial banks.
- Credit unions.
- Finance companies.
- Hedge funds.
- Insurance companies.
- Investment companies.
- Mutual savings banks.
- Pension funds.
- Private equity funds.
- Savings and loan associations.
- Sovereign wealth funds.
- Stockbrokers and dealers.

INTERMEDIATION

Financial intermediaries could not exist without *intermediation*, the process that takes place when individuals and business concerns invest funds in banks or other financial intermediaries. The investors receive various types of claims. Some of the claims, such as bank demand deposits (checking accounts), have stable market values and a high degree of *liquidity* (they can be converted into cash quickly with little or no loss in value). Equally important, demand deposits are safe because they are insured by the Federal

Deposit Insurance Corporation (FDIC).[1] Other types of claims offered by financial intermediaries include savings accounts, time deposits, annuities, and insurance policies. In turn, the financial intermediaries invest the funds they receive in primary securities (stocks, bonds, mortgages, and the like) that may have unstable market values and low liquidity. In essence, the financial intermediaries change less risky secondary securities (their liabilities) into riskier primary securities (their assets). Primary and secondary securities are discussed later in this chapter.

Benefits of Intermediation

Pooling of Funds and Economies of Scale The intermediation process enables individuals to invest their funds and business firms to borrow funds, so that the borrowing-lending process in our economic system functions smoothly. Imagine what would happen if General Electric wanted to borrow $100 million and had to look for individuals who would lend them that amount. Or assume that you had $1,000 to lend. How would you find a borrower who wanted that exact amount and would provide the terms and liquidity you want? Fortunately, neither General Electric nor you face that problem because financial institutions serve as intermediaries by pooling the funds of individual savers and lending them to borrowers. The *pooling of funds provides administrative economies of scale* since it is less costly to administer one $10 million loan than it is to administer 10,000 loans of $1,000 each.

Reducing Risk Equally important, the pooling may *reduce the individual's risk* with respect to loan default if the funds are invested in a diversified portfolio of loans or other investments. Some financial intermediaries specialize in selected types of investments, which gives them a cost advantage in managing such assets. For example, a bank may specialize in credit cards, and a mutual fund may specialize in high-yielding bonds. Finally, intermediation reduces an individual's per dollar risk because some types of secondary securities are insured by the FDIC.

Nevertheless, financial intermediaries still face a variety of risks. For example, the Federal Reserve and Office of the Comptroller of the Currency (OCC) definitions of selected risks are:[2]

Compliance Risk: The current and prospective risk to earnings or capital arising from violations of, or nonconformance with, laws, rules, regulations, prescribed practices, internal policies and procedures, or ethical standards. Compliance risk also arises in situations where

the laws or rules governing certain bank products or activities of bank's clients may be ambiguous or untested.

Credit Risk: Arises from the potential that a borrower or counterparty will fail to perform on an obligation.

Foreign Exchange Transaction Risk: The risk to capital and earnings arising from the conversion of a bank's financial statements from one currency to another.

Legal Risk: Arises from the potential that unenforceable contracts, lawsuits, or adverse judgments can disrupt or otherwise negatively affect the operations or condition of a banking organization.

Liquidity Risk: Arises from the potential that an institution will be unable to meet its obligations as they come due because of an inability to liquidate assets or obtain adequate funding (referred to as *funding liquidity risk*) or to easily unwind or offset specific exposures without significantly lowering market prices because of inadequate market depth or market disruptions (*market liquidity risk*).

Market Risk: The risk to a financial institution's condition resulting from adverse movements in market rates or prices, such as interest rates, foreign exchange rates, or equity prices.

Operational Risk: Arises from the potential that inadequate information systems, operational problems, breaches in internal controls, fraud, or unforeseen catastrophes will result in unexpected losses.

Reputational Risk: Arises from the potential that negative publicity regarding an institution's business practices, whether true or not, will cause a decline in the customer base, costly litigation, or revenue reductions.

Strategic Risk: The current and prospective impact on earnings or capital arising from adverse business decisions, improper implementation of decisions, or lack of responsiveness to industry changes.

Liquidity Intermediaries also offer investors a wide range of denominations and securities, some of which can be converted into cash quickly with little or no loss in value. One can invest $1 or $1 million. Moreover, they offer various maturities on deposits. Deposits with longer-term maturities tend to have higher returns. The FDIC protects individual depositors of insured banks located in the United States against the loss of their deposits if an insured bank fails. The insurance covers all types of deposits received at FDIC-insured banks and thrift institutions for up to $250,000 (through December 31, 2013).[3] Similarly, investment company shares (mutual funds, exchange traded funds [ETFs]) can be liquidated easily.

Alternative Investments and Services Investors can also invest in other types of securities, including annuities, bonds, and mutual fund shares. It follows that investors have a choice of expected returns relative to the risk they are willing to take. The term *risk* refers to the probability of loss and the variability of returns. Low risk is usually associated with low returns, and high risk with high returns. For example, FDIC-insured deposits at commercial banks have very low risk, and they generally offer low returns. At the other end of the risk spectrum, many investors buy shares of mutual funds or common stocks that offer higher returns. However, stock prices are subject to large fluctuations, which means that they are much riskier than insured savings deposits.

Finally, a growing number of individuals, such as recent immigrants and low-income families who are underserved by banks, use alternative financial services (AFS),[4] including check-cashing outlets, money transmitters, car title lenders, payday loans, pawn shops, and rent-to-own stores.

To summarize, intermediation provides the following benefits:

- It facilitates the flow of funds from savers to borrowers.
- It provides economies of scale for savers and borrowers.
- It converts relatively safe secondary securities into relatively risky primary securities, thereby satisfying the needs of savers who want safety and borrowers who want investment capital.
- It provides specialization and expertise in particular types of financing, such as mortgages and consumer loans.
- It offers a wide variety of denominations, maturities, risks, returns, and liquidity.

Nonfinancial Business Concerns

Nonfinancial business concerns that produce goods and services for a profit are one of the principal customers of financial intermediaries. Most business concerns can be classified as sole proprietorships, partnerships, or corporations. For legal purposes, a sole proprietor is one who has the legal right or exclusive title to a business. A partnership is a voluntary contract between two or more individuals who agree to carry on a business together in specified terms of participation, profits, and losses. A corporation is an artificial person or legal entity with rights, privileges, and liabilities separate from those of the owners. The stockholders of a corporation have limited legal liability. In contrast, sole proprietors or partners may have unlimited liability or, in the case of limited partnerships where the general partner assumes personal liability, limited liability.

TABLE 2.1 Hypothetical Balance Sheet of a Nonfinancial Business Concern

Assets	Liabilities and Net Worth (Primary Securities [PS])
Financial assets (cash, demand deposits, securities, accounts receivable)	Trade debt (accounts payable)
Real assets (property, plant, equipment, inventories)	Loans (PS)
	Mortgages (PS)
	Leases (PS)
	Bonds
	Net Worth
	Stocks (PS)
	Retained earnings

To understand how a nonfinancial business concern is different than a financial intermediary, it is helpful to examine the simplified hypothetical corporate balance sheet shown in Table 2.1. The assets are what the companies own. The liabilities are what they owe. And the net worth, or equity, is the difference between the assets and liabilities that belongs to the owners of the corporation.

The financial assets of nonfinancial business concerns include cash, securities, deposits at financial intermediaries, and accounts receivable.

The real assets of nonfinancial business concerns vary according to the type of business. For example, the assets of Wal-Mart are largely inventories and their stores, and those of Delta Airlines consist mainly of airplanes and related equipment.

The liabilities on the other side of the balance sheet arise when firms borrow funds to finance their assets. Thus, Wal-Mart depends on short-term and intermediate-term borrowing to finance their inventories, while Delta Airlines finances their airplanes with longer-term debt. The basic idea is to match the life span of the assets with the maturity of the debt used to finance them.

The net worth represents the ownership of a business corporation. The stockholders are the owners, and they are entitled to receive dividends that are declared. They also have a right to vote on selected management issues.

Primary securities (PS) are all debt and equity securities issued by business concerns and individuals. Bonds, notes, loans, mortgages, and stocks are examples of primary securities issued by business concerns. Home mortgages and consumer installment debt are typical primary securities of individuals.

Some types of primary securities are considered risky by investors for two reasons. First, the market value or price on primary securities such as stocks, bonds, and mortgages change dramatically because of changing

TABLE 2.2 Selected Characteristics of Primary and Secondary Securities

Primary Securities	Degree of Liquidity	Price Changes
Stocks	High	Large
Bonds	Relatively high	Large
Mortgages	Relatively low	Large
Loans	Low (unless securitized)	Large
Leases	Low	Not applicable
Secondary Securities		
Short term		
Demand deposits	High	No change
Time and savings deposits	High	No change
Long term		
Mutual fund shares	High	Large
Pension fund policies	Low	No change
Life insurance policy reserves	High	No change

economic conditions and market rates of interest. The prices of these securities vary inversely with the level of market rates of interest. For example, when market rates of interest increase, the prices of outstanding stocks, bonds, and mortgages go down. Table 2.2 shows the price changes and degree of liquidity for selected primary and secondary securities. *Secondary securities* are claims against financial intermediaries and may take the form of demand deposits (checking accounts), savings deposits, life insurance policies, mutual fund shares, and other types of claims.

Second, some primary securities are not liquid. As previously mentioned, *liquidity* refers to assets that can be converted into cash quickly with little or no loss in value. Thus, an investor can call his or her stockbroker or go online and sell 100 shares of Google in minutes. However, an investor owning real estate or mortgage loans may not be able to sell them quickly with little or no loss of market value. In some cases, it takes months to sell real estate, which means that real estate is not a liquid asset. However, mortgage loans and some other types of loans can be securitized and sold.

Financial Intermediaries

As shown in Table 2.3, the assets of financial intermediaries consist of primary securities that are debt and equity claims against business concerns, individuals, and other obligors. In the case of business concerns, bonds, notes, bank loans, mortgages, and stocks are examples of their liabilities,

TABLE 2.3 Hypothetical Balance Sheet of Financial Intermediaries

Assets	Liabilities and Net Worth (Secondary Securities [SS])
Financial assets (cash and primary securities)	Demand deposits (SS)
Real assets (property, plant, equipment, inventories)	Time and savings deposits (SS)
	Insurance and pension fund reserves (SS)
	Mutual fund shares (SS)
	Stocks owned (SS)
	Bonds (SS)
	Net Worth
	Stocks (SS)
	Retained earnings

which are the primary securities of the financial intermediaries. Similarly, in the case of individuals, car loans, credit card debt, and mortgages are examples of their liabilities, which are the primary securities of the financial intermediaries.

Some financial intermediaries specialize in particular types of lending, such as credit cards or mortgage loans. Others, such as mutual funds, invest in stocks and bonds. Because the financial intermediaries are legal entities, they can do only what is permitted by law. Thus, a credit union cannot do the same things as a mutual fund or a sovereign wealth fund. Accordingly, some financial institutions engage in *regulatory arbitrage*, which refers to finding legal ways to get around restrictions imposed by laws. More will be said about it in the chapters that follow.

The remaining assets of financial intermediaries, including real estate owned and equipment, are a small part of their total assets. In December 2009, these other assets were only 9.5 percent of the total assets of commercial banks in the United States.[5]

The liabilities of financial intermediaries are secondary securities, such as demand deposits, time and savings deposits, and mutual funds shares. The secondary securities of financial intermediaries are assets held by business concerns and individuals.

Table 2.4 illustrates the types of primary and secondary securities held by several types of financial intermediaries. Secondary securities differ from primary securities in their degree of liquidity and their marketability. As previously noted, many types of primary securities have low liquidity and volatile market prices. In contrast, short-term secondary securities, such as savings accounts, have high liquidity and do not change in market value.

TABLE 2.4 Examples of Primary and Secondary Securities at Selected Financial Intermediaries

Financial Intermediary	Primary Securities	Secondary Securities
Commercial banks	Mortgage loans Commercial and industrial loans Consumer loans	Demand deposits Savings deposits, money market deposit accounts Certificates of deposit (CDs)
Credit unions	Consumer loans Mortgage loans	Credit union shares
Life insurance companies	Stocks Bonds Mortgages	Life insurance policies or certificates
Money market funds	Short-term securities	Shares
Pension funds	Stocks Bonds Mortgages	Pension fund policies

However, other types of secondary securities, such as mutual fund shares, can experience large changes in market value.

In summary, the assets and liabilities of financial intermediaries are mainly primary and secondary securities. To keep the role of these securities in perspective, recall that the liabilities of business concerns and individuals (i.e., secondary securities) are the assets of financial intermediaries (see Figure 2.2). Similarly, the liabilities of financial intermediaries are held as assets by business concerns and individuals. Thus, business concerns invest in deposits that are liabilities of financial intermediaries.

Long and Short Intermediation Chains

The description of the flow of funds from individual depositors to a financial intermediary, such as a bank, and then to a business borrower in Figure 2.2 is a simplified example of a short intermediation chain. A long intermediation chain presents a more complex view of the financial system. The following example and Figure 2.3 illustrate one possible long intermediation chain for household A that saves funds by investing in a money market fund. Then those funds are subsequently invested in a variety of institutions until they ultimately fund a mortgage for household B.[6]

- Step 1. In this example, household A buys shares of a money market fund (MMF)—an open-ended mutual fund that invests in short-term debt securities.

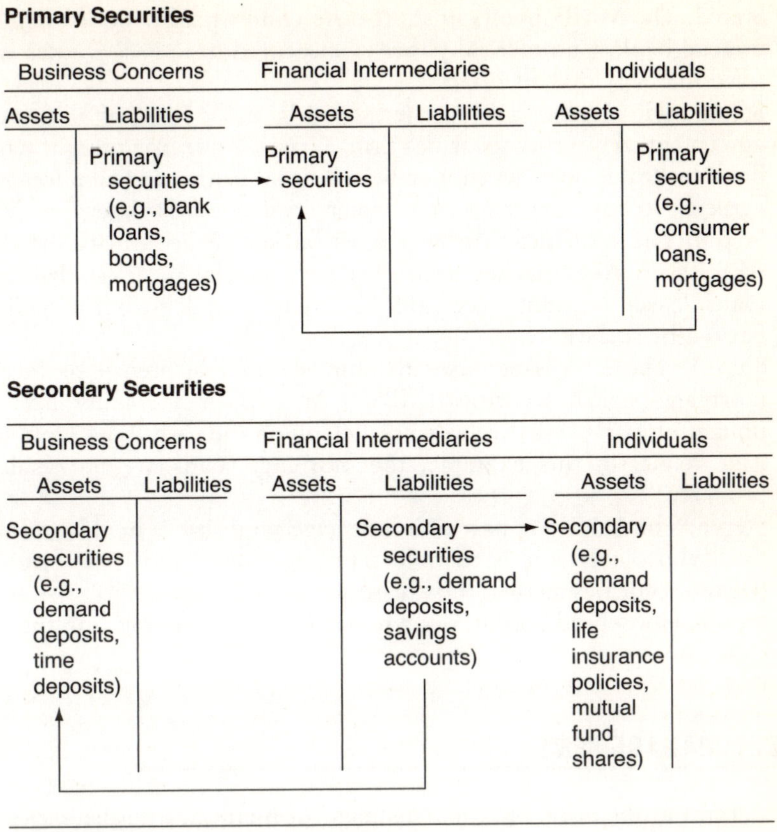

FIGURE 2.2 Primary and Secondary Securities

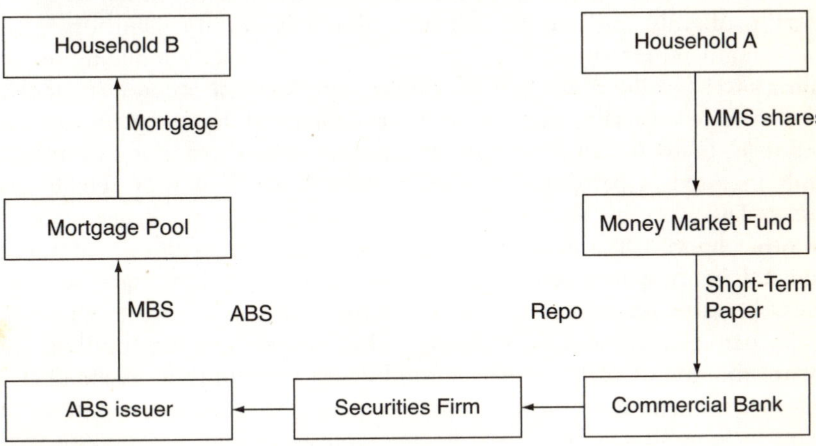

FIGURE 2.3 Long Intermediation Chain

- Step 2. The MMF invests in short-term commercial paper from a commercial bank. Commercial paper is unsecured promissory notes with a fixed maturity of 1 to 270 days.
- Step 3. The commercial bank lends funds, in the form of a repurchase agreement (repo) to a securities firm. A repo is a transaction in which a bank or dealer borrows money by selling securities and simultaneously agreeing to buy them back at a higher price at a later date.
- Step 4. The securities firm buys asset-backed securities (ABS) from an ABS issuer. Asset-backed securities are financial securities backed by loans, leases, accounts receivable, or credit card debt, but they are not backed by real estate.
- Step 5. The ABS issuer uses the funds raised in Step 4 to invest in mortgage-backed securities (MBSs). An MBS is a collateralized-debt obligation (CDO) that represents a claim on the cash flows from mortgage loans. In this example, the mortgage loans are on residential property.
- Step 6. The MBSs are part of a mortgage pool that is held by a passive firm whose sole role is to hold mortgage loans and issue mortgage-backed securities against those assets.
- Step 7. Household B takes out a mortgage loan that goes into the mortgage pool.

ASSET MANAGEMENT

The central problem of asset management of financial intermediaries is to maintain a sufficient amount of liquid assets to meet potential withdrawal of funds or make additional investments, while investing their remaining assets profitably and safely. When individuals want to withdraw their funds, financial intermediaries can satisfy their claims by reducing its cash, selling assets, or borrowing. If the dollar volume of the secondary securities is believed to be stable and long term, the financial intermediary can make long-term loans (i.e., buy long-term primary securities). For example, the funds invested in pension funds are not likely to be withdrawn on short notice. Therefore, pension funds tend to make long-term investments. On the other hand, if the dollar volume of secondary securities is volatile, the financial intermediary will focus on short-term liquid primary securities. Thus, because the dollar amount of large time deposits at commercial banks can change within a short period of time, banks holding large dollar amounts of such deposits should invest most of their assets in short- and intermediate-term liquid primary securities. Alternatively, they can invest in longer-term assets and hedge against the interest rate risk that is described later.

In trying to achieve the goals of asset management, financial intermediaries face various risks. The primary risks that banks face are credit risk and interest rate risk. Other risks include liquidity risk, legal risks, operational risk, price risk, and compliance risk.

- *Credit risk* is the risk to earnings and capital that a borrower or counterparty may not meet the terms of the loan contract (i.e., not paying principal or interest obligations), resulting in losses to the lender. Banks don't intentionally make bad loans. However, they do make loans that can go bad as a result of recessions, hurricanes, bad luck, or other factors. Banks can reduce their credit risk and interest rate risk by hedging—transferring the risk to others. Hedging and risk management are discussed in Chapter 5.
- *Interest rate risk* is the risk to earnings and capital that interest rates may change unfavorably. This risk arises from the timing of rate changes and the timing of cash flows, from changes in the shape of the yield curve, and from options embedded in bank products. For example, if market rates of interest decline, borrowers have a put option to repay the loan. Then they can make a new loan at a lower rate of interest. If the market rate of interest increases, the value of fixed-rate loans and securities declines.
- *Liquidity risk* is the risk to earnings and capital related to a financial intermediary's ability to meet its financial obligations to depositors or borrowers.
- *Legal risks* arise from unenforceable contracts, lawsuits, or adverse judgments that may negatively affect the operations or the financial condition of the bank.
- *Operational risk* is the risk to earnings and capital arising from problems associated with the delivery of a product or service. Fraud, financial misconduct, software problems, and power outages are a few examples.
- *Price risk* is the risk to earnings and capital related to taking positions in securities, derivatives, foreign exchange, or other financial instruments where the market price can change.
- *Compliance risk* is the risk to earnings and capital arising from the violation of laws, rules, regulations, and so on. For example, if a bank does not have adequate capital, bank regulators will take prompt corrective actions to require the bank to increase its capital to meet minimum standards, or be closed.

INDIVIDUALS

Individuals are the third part of the economic system. The term *individual* is used here in the broad sense of the word and refers to a person in contrast to a business.

One difference between the two is that individuals tend to be net savers and put their surplus funds into secondary securities. If the investment return on primary securities is significantly higher than the return on secondary securities, they may invest some of their funds in primary securities. However, they usually provide funds to financial intermediaries that invest in primary securities.

Another difference between persons and businesses is that individuals acquire real assets for the services they provide rather than for use as a capital good. Their real assets include their home, cars, TVs, and computers. The financial assets of individuals (their secondary securities) are mainly bank deposits, stocks, bonds, mutual funds, insurance, and pension funds. Their financial assets are held primarily for liquidity and investment purposes. The other side of an individual's balance sheet consists mainly of mortgage debt for their homes and consumer debt for cars and other purposes.

In the past, it was widely believed that individuals were more risk averse than business concerns. However, the financial crisis that began in 2007 cast some doubt on that notion. One of the primary drivers of the crisis was the growth of subprime mortgages to individual borrowers who could not afford them. As noted in the previous chapter, subprime mortgages refer to high-risk mortgage loans made to borrowers with low credit scores and/or high loan-to-value ratios, and/or high debt-to-income ratios. When the mortgage payments due began to exceed the borrowers' ability to pay them, the borrowers defaulted in mass on their loans, triggering the financial crisis.

INTEREST RATES

Interest rates are the price paid for the use of credit. They are a major factor governing the relationship between savers and borrowers. The disparity of interest rates among the different financial intermediaries and investment maturities are two of the principal factors that determine where savers and investors will allocate their funds. For example, a bank may offer a money market deposit account (MMDA) that pays a low rate of interest (e.g., 1 percent). There can be no more than six withdrawals per calendar month or statement cycle, of which no more than three can be by check, draft, or debit card. The bank also offers a regular savings account that pays 3 percent, where the funds can be withdrawn at any time. It also offers a one-year time deposit (or certificate of deposit [CD]) at 5 percent and a five-year time deposit at 7 percent. The funds invested in the time deposits can be withdrawn only at maturity. If they are withdrawn before maturity, there is a penalty. The penalty, for example, may be six months' interest on the amount withdrawn.

Financial intermediaries operate on a thin margin that is affected by the composition of their assets, liabilities, and interest rates. Suppose that the average cost of a bank's liabilities is 4 percent, and it earns an average of 7.5 percent on its assets. The 3.5 percent difference between the return on assets and its cost of funds is called the *net interest margin* (NIM)—interest income less interest expense divided by total assets.

At any given time, the level of interest rates is determined by the demand and supply of funds, which reflect the complex interactions within the economy. These include monetary policy, inflation, and other factors.

CURRENT TRENDS IN FINANCIAL INTERMEDIARIES

Consolidation

The number of banks in the United States peaked in 1921 at 31,076 and then declined to 6,839 at the end of 2009.[7] Bank failures during the Great Depression in 1933 reduced the number of banks to 14,771. Similarly, about 1,600 FDIC banks failed during the 1980–1994 period.[8]

Bank mergers and acquisitions also contributed to the reduction in the number of banks. By the end of 2009, there were 6,839 FDIC-insured commercial banks. As shown in Table 2.5, 93 percent of the banks in the United States are relatively small, with assets of less than $1 billion. That table also shows that the 85 largest banks, with more than $10 billion in assets

TABLE 2.5 FDIC-Insured Commercial Banks, Fourth Quarter, 2009

	All Institutions	Assets Less than $100 Million	Assets $100 Million to $1 Billion	Assets $1 Billion to $10 Billion	Assets Greater than $10 Billion
Number of banks	6,839	2,525	3,800	429	85
Percentage of banks	100%	37%	56%	6%	1%
Total assets $ billions	$11,846	$141	$1,113	$1,121	$9,472
Percentage of total assets	100%	1%	9%	10%	80%

Source: FDIC Quarterly Banking Profile, 4th Quarter 2009, Table IV-A. Data are rounded.

(i.e., 1 percent of the banks), controlled 80 percent of the total assets. Stated otherwise, a few big banks dominate the banking system in the United States.

Bank regulators call large banks with $250 billion or more in assets *core banks*. In the third quarter of 2009, there were six core banks in the United States: JPMorgan Chase National Association (NA), Bank of America NA, Wells Fargo Bank NA, PNC Bank NA, and U.S. Bank NA. Collectively, these six banks accounted for 56 percent of total bank assets.

Changes in Laws Contributed to Industry Consolidation

Banking laws permitting branch banking, bank holding companies, as well as financial holding companies, and interstate banking contributed to industry consolidation. For example, the Bank Holding Company Act of 1956 permitted bank holding companies to acquire multiple banks and businesses closely related to banking. The Gramm-Leach-Bliley Act of 1999 allowed bank holding companies to become financial holding companies that could acquire investment banking, insurance underwriting, and other types of businesses related to banking. The Riegle-Neal Interstate Banking and Branching Efficiency Act of 1994 allowed bank holding companies to acquire banks in other states. An extensive discussion of these and other banking laws is presented in Chapter 3.

Top Bank Holding Companies

In 2001, an article in the *Federal Reserve Bulletin* said: "Today a large proportion of assets held by U.S. banking organizations is concentrated in a small number of companies, and U.S. banking organizations have integrated into their product mix activities that extend well beyond traditional deposit taking and lending."[9] Table 2.6 lists the top 10 bank holding companies in the United States at the end of 2009. These bank holding companies are also financial holding companies, and they are called *large complex banking organizations* (LCBOs). The following criteria are considered for inclusion as an LCBO:[10]

- Total assets.
- Size of off-balance-sheet exposures.
- Activity in derivatives markets.
- Trading assets and trading revenue.
- Foreign assets and foreign deposits.
- Funding from market (nondeposit) sources.
- Securities borrowed and securities lent.
- Income from fiduciary activity.

- Mutual fund sales and mutual fund fee income.
- Revenue earned in mortgage markets.
- Assets under management.
- Activity in payment systems.
- Involvement in securities settlements.
- Geographic scope of operations.
- Merchant banking activities and proprietary investments.

TABLE 2.6 Top 10 Bank Holding Companies in the United States (as of December 31, 2009)

Rank	Institution Name	Location	Total Assets ($ Thousands)
1	Bank of America Corporation	Charlotte, NC	$2,224,539,279
2	JPMorgan Chase & Co	New York, NY	$2,031,989,000
3	Citigroup Inc.	New York, NY	$1,856,646,000
4	Wells Fargo & Company	San Francisco, CA	$1,243,646,000
5	Goldman Sachs Group, Inc.	New York, NY	$849,278,000
6	Morgan Stanley	New York, NY	$771,462,000
7	MetLife, Inc.	New York, NY	$539,314,240
8	HSBC North American Holdings Inc.	Mettawa, IL	$391,332,071
9	Taunus Corporation	New York, NY	$369,105,000
10	Barclays Group US Inc.	Wilmington, DE	$365,703,204

Source: National Information Center, www.ffiec.gov/nicpubweb/nicweb/Top50Form.aspx.

Defining an LCBO is not easy.

> *Large, complex banks are defined by both the Federal Reserve and OCC as those that generally have a functional management structure; a broad array of products, services, and activities; operations that span multiple supervisory jurisdictions; and consolidated assets of $1 billion or more. OCC has further designated the largest most complex banks, with assets of $25 billion or more, for supervision by one of three deputy comptrollers in Washington, D.C. The Federal Reserve has also identified certain large banks as being the largest and most complex and therefore subjects these institutions to heightened scrutiny, assigning a Federal Reserve Board analyst, in addition to staff from the Federal Reserve district bank.*[11]

Bank of America Corporation, for example, has $2.2 trillion in assets and 3,310 separate entities (corporations, partnerships, trusts, subsidiaries, structured investment vehicles [SIVs],[12] and so on) in its organization hierarchy.[13] It has more than 6,000 retail banking offices, more than 18,000

Automatic Teller Machines (ATMs), and nearly 30 million active users, and it serves clients in more than 150 countries.[14]

Similarly, JPMorgan Chase has $2 trillion in assets, 5,059 separate entities, and operations in more than 60 countries. It is "a leader in investment banking, financial services for consumers, small business and commercial banking, financial transaction processing, asset management and private equity."[15]

Table 2.6 also reveals that some of the bank holding companies are not traditional banks. For example, Goldman Sachs is known primarily for investment banking operations and Metlife for its insurance business.

There are also large foreign-owned banks: HSBC and Barclays Group are owned by banks in the United Kingdom. Taunus Corporation operates as a subsidiary of Deutsche Bank AG, in Germany.

Subchapter S Corporations At the other end of the bank size spectrum, a large number of smaller banks are organized as *subchapter S corporations.* Subchapter S corporations have 100 or fewer individual shareholders, and they are taxed as a partnership. Thus, the shareholders avoid the double taxation that is associated with cash dividends. Corporations are not allowed to own subchapter S stock. In June 2010, 2,444 FDIC-insured institutions were subchapter S corporations.[16]

THE CHANGING ROLE OF BANKS

Changing Technology

Changes in electronic and financial technology have tended to change the way that banks do business. As a result of the increased use of ATMs, direct deposits, and electronic banking (including the use of cell phones) for paying bills and buying goods and services, there is less need for physical contact between customers and banks. Today many banks package and sell loans (securitizing them), rather than holding the loans to maturity. Many banks buy brokered deposits—large dollar deposits ($100,000 or more) sold by deposit brokers—rather than depending on local customers for deposits. More will be said about this in later chapters.

Regulatory Disadvantage

Because banks are more heavily regulated than some other types of financial intermediaries, they are at a regulatory disadvantage.[17] Some other types of financial intermediaries, such as shadow banks, have greater flexibility in their operations.

Shadow Banking

Chairman Sheila Bair of the FDIC said: "By early 2007, the level of financial intermediation undertaken in the shadow banking sector exceeded the level of activity in the traditional banking sector."[18] She explained that activities such as commercial paper conduits, SIVs, hedge funds, private equity funds, money market repurchase agreements, and securities lending have become important parts of the intermediation process. Shadow banking also includes sale and repo, ABSs, CDOs, and asset-backed commercial paper (ABCP).[19] Shadow banking grew as a result of financial innovations, such as securitization, and regulatory changes that led to the decline of the traditional banking model. "Faced with competition from junk bonds and commercial paper on the asset side of bank balance sheets and from money-market mutual funds on the liability side, commercial banks became less profitable and sought new profit opportunities. Slowly traditional banks exited the regulated sector."[20] They began to increase their off-balance sheet activities, repos, securitization, off-balance sheet special purpose vehicles (SPVs), and similar activities.

Timothy Geithner, who was the president of the Federal Reserve Bank of New York in 2008, noted:

> *In early 2007, asset-backed commercial paper conduits, in structured investment vehicles, in auction-rate preferred securities, tender option bonds, and variable rate demand notes, had a combined asset size of roughly \$2.2 trillion. Assets financed overnight in triparty repo grew to \$2.5 trillion. Assets held in hedge funds grew to roughly \$1.8 trillion. The combined balance sheets of the then five major investment banks totaled \$4 trillion.*
>
> *In comparison, the total assets of the top five bank holding companies in the United States at that point were just over \$6 trillion, and total assets of the entire banking system were about \$10 trillion.*[21]

The comments by Bair and Geithner reflect the fact that an increasing amount of financial intermediation is taking place off the balance sheets. For example, banks create SIVs that issue ABSs that earn revenue from securitized loans.[22]

It follows that as a result of financial innovations, such as securitization, the basic business model of banking is changing from buy-and-hold strategies to what is called originate-and-distribute models.[23]

ALTERNATIVE FINANCIAL SERVICES

The 2009 FDIC Survey of Unbanked and Underbanked Households found that an estimated 7.7 percent of the U.S. households (9 million people) are *unbanked*—they do not have a checking or savings account.[24] About 17.9 percent (21 million people) are *underbanked*—they have a checking account or savings account, but they rely instead on alternative financial services. *Alternative financial services* are those offered outside the FDIC-insured institutions, including check-cashing outlets, money transmitters, car title lenders, payday lenders, pawnshops, and rent-to-own stores. It also includes the Internet, financial kiosks, and mobile phones.

Certain minorities are more likely to be underbanked than the population as a whole. These groups include Blacks, American Indians, Alaska Natives, and Hispanics. Asians and Whites are less likely to be underbanked.

The FDIC estimated that alternative financial services amount to more than $320 billion annually.

CHAPTER 3

The Evolving Legal Environment

Banks and other types of financial intermediaries have played a vital role in the history of the United States. Their role continues today, although their forms have changed over time. One reason for the changes is that they can do only what federal and state laws allow them to do. Another reason is that developments in financial technology, such as financial derivatives and securitization, electronic payments, and cell phones, are changing the way they do business.

Commercial banks have been the dominant financial intermediary, but their market share of loans has been declining as a result of the growth of government-sponsored entities (e.g., Fannie Mae and Freddie Mac), hedge funds, off-balance sheet activities (e.g., structured investment vehicles), shadow banks, and other types of financial institutions.

Against this background, this chapter focuses mainly on laws dealing with the evolution of banking and related institutions.[1]

WHAT IS A BANK?

Definitions

There is a saying that if something looks like a duck, walks like a duck, and quacks like a duck, it is a duck. However, a financial intermediary that looks like a commercial bank and acts like one is not necessarily a commercial bank. In general terms, a *commercial bank* is a financial institution that is owned by stockholders, operates for a profit, and engages in various lending activities.[2] Similarly, credit unions take deposits and make loans, but they are not commercial banks. *Credit unions* are financial cooperative institutions with a common federal, state, or corporate affiliation. As such, they are not-for-profit organizations designed to provide a variety of financial services for their members. Credit unions are exempt from paying income taxes. In contrast, commercial banks are for-profit organizations that serve the public at large, and they pay income taxes.

Simply stated, the term *bank* is widely applied to different types of financial institutions. But there are important differences among the various types of institutions. In the United States, a bank is defined by federal and state laws and by bank regulators. Therefore, we will examine the definitions of banking and the structure and organization of banks in a historical context by explaining selected banking laws. Table 3.1 defines different types of financial institutions. Notice that the term *bank* is used in the name of a number of different types of institutions. Also, the term *commercial bank* can have several definitions. For example, the definition of Federal Deposit Insurance Corporation- (FDIC) insured commercial banks and trust companies includes national banks and state-chartered banks and trust companies, but not savings banks. Commercial banks are either national or state chartered and insured by the FDIC Bank Insurance Fund (BIF) or the FDIC Savings Association Insurance Fund (SAIF).[3] Appendix 3B at the end of this chapter shows the evolution of the definition of commercial banks.

Shadow Banks

Shadow banks are a financial innovation of the 1980s. They can be defined as "financial intermediaries that conduct maturity, credit, and liquidity transformation without access to central bank liquidity or public sector guarantees."[4] Finance companies, asset-backed commercial paper (ABCP) conduits, money market funds, and hedge funds are examples of shadow banks. As explained in Chapter 1, they played a significant role in the financial crisis that began in 2007 by providing more credit than what was provided by traditional banks.[5]

WHY ARE BANKS REGULATED?

Why do we regulate banks, but we don't regulate McDonald's or Wal-Mart? The answer to that question is that banks are regulated for three reasons. The first two reasons involve *prudential regulation* of banks, meaning they deal with banks' safety and soundness to protect depositors' funds and the economic stability of the economy. The third reason concerns social goals.

Preventing Economic Disruption

Domestic Markets First, banks are regulated to reduce the risk of large-scale failures that would adversely affect the level of economic activity.

TABLE 3.1 All Institution Types Defined

Agreement Corporation Corporation chartered by a state to engage in international banking: so named because the corporation enters into an "agreement" with the Federal Reserve's Board of Governors that it will limit its activities to those permitted.

Bank Holding Company (BHC) A company that owns and/or controls one or more U.S. banks or one that owns, or has controlling interest in, one or more banks. A bank holding company may also own another bank holding company, which in turn owns or controls a bank; the company at the top of the ownership chain is called the top holder. The Board of Governors is responsible for regulating and supervising bank holding companies, even if the bank owned by the holding company is under the primary supervision of a different federal agency (Office of the Comptroller of the Currency (OCC) or FDIC).

Commercial Bank A financial institution that is owned by stockholders, operates for a profit, and engages in various lending activities.

Cooperative Bank State-chartered savings associations located in Massachusetts, New Hampshire, Rhode Island, and Vermont.

Credit Union Financial cooperative organization of individuals with a common affiliation. Credit unions can have federal, state, or corporate affiliations.

Data Processing Servicer Entities primarily engaged in providing infrastructure for hosting or data processing services. These establishments may provide specialized hosting activities, such as web hosting, streaming services or application hosting, provide application service provisioning, or may provide general time-share mainframe facilities to clients. Data processing establishments provide complete processing and specialized reports from data supplied by clients or provide automated data processing and data entry services.

Domestic Branch of a Domestic Bank A branch that resides in the United States, and whose parent is also located in the United States.

Domestic Entity Other Domestic institutions that engage in banking activities usually in connection with the business of banking in the United States.

Edge/Agreement Corporation An organization chartered by the Federal Reserve to engage in international banking and financial operations. Edge corporations can be broken into domestic branches, banking institutions, or investment institutions.

Finance Company Financial intermediary that makes loans to individuals or businesses.

Financial Holding Company A financial entity engaged in a broad range of banking-related activities, created by the Gramm-Leach-Bliley Act of 1999. These activities include: insurance underwriting, securities dealing and underwriting, financial and investment advisory services, merchant banking, issuing or selling securitized interests in bank-eligible assets, and generally engaging in any nonbanking activity authorized by the Bank Holding Company Act. The Federal Reserve Board is responsible for supervising the financial condition and activities of

(*continued*)

TABLE 3.1 (*Continued*)

financial holding companies. Similarly, any nonbank commercial company that is predominantly engaged in financial activities, earning 85% or more of its gross revenues from financial services, may choose to become a financial holding company. These companies are required to sell any nonfinancial (commercial) businesses within ten years.

Foreign Bank The term *foreign bank* generally refers to any U.S. operation of a banking organization headquartered outside the United States.

Foreign Banking Organization (FBO) Foreign banking organizations can acquire or establish freestanding banks or bank holding companies in the United States. These entities are regulated and supervised as domestic institutions.

Foreign Banking Organization of a BHC A foreign banking organization that is owned or controlled by a BHC.

Foreign Banking Organization as a BHC A foreign banking organization that also acts as a BHC and is thus supervised by the Board of Governors of the Federal Reserve.

Foreign Branch of a U.S. Bank A branch that resides outside of the United States but has a parent that is located in the United States.

Foreign Entity Other Foreign institutions that engage in banking activities usually in connection with the business of banking in the countries where such foreign institutions are organized or operating.

Industrial Bank A limited service financial institution that raises funds by selling certificates called *investment shares* and by accepting deposits. Often called Morris Plan banks or industrial loan companies. Industrial banks are distinguished from commercial loan companies because industrial banks accept deposits in addition to making consumer loans. Industrial banks differ from commercial banks because they do not offer demand deposit (checking) accounts. Industrial banks are not regulated by the Federal Reserve.

Insurance Company Provides compensation based on the happening of one or more contingencies.

Insured Branch of an FBO (Federal and State) An insured branch accepts retail deposits and must apply for federal deposit insurance.

Investment Bank/Company Acts as underwriter or agent that serves as intermediary between issuer of securities and the investing public.

Member Bank A bank that is a member of the Federal Reserve System, including all nationally chartered banks and any state-chartered or mutual savings banks that apply for membership and are accepted.

Mutual Savings Bank A financial institution that accepts deposits primarily from individuals and places a large portion of its funds into mortgage loans.

National Bank A commercial bank whose charter is approved by the OCC rather than by a state banking department.

TABLE 3.1 (*Continued*)

National banks are required to be members of the Federal Reserve System and belong to the FDIC.

Non-Member Banks This subset includes all commercial banks that are state-chartered and are NOT members of the Federal Reserve System. Commercial banks include all BIF-, SAIF-, and BIF/SAIF-insured commercial banks and industrial banks. (Please note: Effective March 31, 2006, the FDIC merged the BIF and the SAIF into a new fund, the Deposit Insurance Fund (DIF). All institutions carrying BIF, SAIF, and BIF/SAIF insurance were transitioned to DIF accordingly.)

Non-Depository Trust Company Accepts and executes trusts but does not issue currency. Non-depository trust companies can either be Federal Reserve members or Federal Reserve nonmembers.

Other Depository Institution Those financial institutions, not specifically listed, with authority to accept deposits of funds.

Other Non-Depository Institution Companies not specifically listed, but in which there is regulatory interest that are not authorized to accept deposits.

Savings and Loan Association A financial institution that accepts deposits primarily from individuals and channels its funds primarily into residential mortgage loans.

Savings Bank Banking institution organized to encourage thrift by paying interest dividends on savings. Savings banks can have state and federal affiliations, for example, state savings banks and federal savings banks.

Securities Broker/Dealer Entities primarily engaged in acting as agents (i.e., brokers) between buyers and sellers in buying or selling securities on a commission or transaction fee basis.

State Member Banks This subset includes all commercial banks that are state-chartered and members of the Federal Reserve System. Commercial banks include all BIF-, SAIF-, and BIF/SAIF-Insured commercial banks and industrial banks. (Please note: Effective March 31, 2006, the FDIC merged the Bank Insurance Fund (BIF) and the Savings Association Insurance Fund (SAIF) into a new fund, the Deposit Insurance Fund (DIF). All institutions carrying BIF, SAIF, and BIF/SAIF insurance were transitioned to DIF accordingly.)

Thrifts An organization that primarily accepts savings account deposits and invests most of the proceeds in mortgages. Savings banks and savings and loan associations and credit unions are examples of thrift institutions.

Uninsured Agency of an FBO (Federal and State) An uninsured agency does not accept retail deposits and need not apply for federal deposit insurance.

Uninsured Branch of an FBO (Federal and State) An uninsured branch does not accept retail deposits and need not apply for federal deposit insurance.

U.S. Branches and Agencies of FBOs U.S. branches and agencies of foreign banks are entities contained within and controlled by a foreign banking organization.

Source: National Information Center, "All Institution Types Defined," www.ffiec.gov/nicpubweb/Content/HELP/Institution%20Type%20Description.htm

This does not mean that an individual bank that is poorly run should not be allowed to fail. It does mean that the government and bank regulators are concerned that if one or more of the largest banks fails, or if a large number of banks fail, it could adversely affect the financial markets and the economy. That is what happened during the financial crisis that began in 2007. As noted in Chapter 1, there were large-scale failures of banks in the United States and various foreign countries that disrupted economic activity. The bank regulations that were in place then did not prevent the banks from failing.

Global Markets There is also concern about systemic risk. *Systemic risk* occurs when bank failures are potentially contagious, and only then if the losses in one bank cascade into other banks or to other economies throughout the world. All of the world's major economies are linked through the financial markets and other business relationships. A major shock in the U.S. economy has worldwide repercussions, and vice versa. Therefore, it is important to *harmonize,* or have uniform international bank regulations, to avoid divergent standards. Basel II bank capital standards provide one example of harmonization.

Guarding against Insurance Losses

Second, in any debtor-creditor relationship, the creditor limits the debtor's actions and monitors behavior to ensure repayment of the loan. In the case of banks, the largest number of creditors are small depositors, most of whom are not capable of evaluating the financial condition of banks or monitoring their actions. Therefore, it is in the public interest to protect small depositors by having their deposits insured by a government agency, the FDIC. Thus, the FDIC represents the depositors and the public's interests to ensure that banks operate in a safe and sound fashion. This helps to protect the deposit insurance fund. If bank failures are large enough to exhaust the deposit insurance fund, the remaining banks and taxpayers will be called on to repay depositors.

Achieving Social Goals

Third, banks are regulated to achieve desired social goals. This public choice approach to regulation serves to reallocate resources from one group to another. Thus, the goal of regulation in this regard is to promote an efficient and impartial allocation of credit to meet the needs of their customers and communities. Banks cannot discriminate against borrowers on the basis of race, sex, age, or other such factors. Borrowers must be judged on the basis of their creditworthiness. In addition, banks must supply borrowers with accurate information about the cost of borrowing.

SELECTED BANKING LAWS

This section examines some of the principal laws dealing with banking structure—the organization of banks. It includes the banking reforms of 2010.

Appendix 3A at the end of this chapter provides a more extensive list of banking legislation from 1864 through 2009. Some of these and other laws are discussed in other chapters of this book.

1781: The First Bank

The Bank of North America was founded in Philadelphia in 1781. It was chartered by the Continental Congress. Subsequently, it acquired a state charter. By 1862, there were 1,462 state-chartered banks in the United States.[6] At that time, bankers believed in the *real bills doctrine,* that banks borrowed short-term funds and made short-term self-liquidating loans. Because the banks concentrated on short-term loans and commercial paper (promissory notes, bills of exchange,[7] and the like), they were called *commercial banks.*

1863–1864: National Banks

Before and during the Civil War, there was a need for a national currency and national bank supervision. Accordingly, the National Currency Act of 1863 was passed and then replaced by the National Bank Act of 1864. It created the OCC and *national banks.* The OCC charters, regulates, and supervises national banks. National banks have the word *National* or National Association (NA) in their names.

1933: Separation of Banks and Investment Banking and Insurance

The Glass Steagall Act of 1933 (also known as the Banking Act of 1933) separated commercial banks from investment banking and insurance. Investment banking refers to underwriting stocks and bonds and selling insurance.

The National Bank Act of 1864 also *preempted* state laws that tried to direct or control the activities of the banks granted national status under federal law.

1956: Bank Holding Companies

The BHC Act of 1956 allowed BHCs to acquire other banks and businesses that were closely related and incident to banking. A BHC has control over one or more banks and other financial service organizations. Control means owning 25 percent or more of the voting shares. The term *insured bank* refers to FDIC-insured banks chartered in the United States that accept deposits (other than trust funds) and make loans.[8] The BHC Act also allowed the holding companies to acquire certain nonbank businesses that were closely related to banking. The company at the top of the ownership chain is called the *top holder*.

1994: Interstate Banking

The Riegle-Neal Interstate Banking and Branching Efficiency Act of 1994 opened the door for interstate banking by allowing BHCs to acquire banks in other states.

1999: Combining Banks, Investment Banks, and Insurance

The Gramm-Leach-Bliley Act (GLBA; also known as the Financial Services Modernization Act of 1999) repealed parts of the Glass Steagall Act of 1933. It allowed for the organization of financial holding companies. A financial holding company is a BHC that meets certain legal and regulatory requirements and can engage in merchant banking, developing real estate, and other complementary activities.

2010: Dodd-Frank Wall Street Reform and Consumer Protection Act

On July 17, 2010, the Dodd-Frank Wall Street Reform and Consumer Protection Act was signed into law.[9] It was passed in response to the financial crisis that began in 2007. The law contains 16 titles and 1,601 sections. Because of the length and complexity of the law, only selected parts of the act are discussed here. The Dodd-Frank Act gives government regulators the authority to rewrite some existing rules and generate new ones; therefore, the rules and regulations will evolve over time. There is a saying that the devil is in the details, which are yet to come.

- The law creates a Financial Stability Oversight Council (the Council) to identify risks to financial stability that could arise from financial distress or from the ongoing activities of large bank and nonbank financial companies and payment systems or that could arise outside the financial services marketplace. The 15-member council includes ten financial regulators, an independent member, and five nonvoting members. It will be chaired by the Treasury secretary and include the Federal Reserve Board, Securities and Exchange Commission (SEC), Commodities Futures Trading Commission, OCC, FDIC, Federal Housing Finance Authority, National Credit Union Administration, Consumer Financial Protection Bureau, and an independent employee with insurance expertise. The five nonvoting members include state banking, insurance, and securities regulators.
- The law provides for the "orderly liquidation of systemically important, failing financial companies" (Title II). In essence, it is designed to end "too big to fail" by establishing a resolution authority for banks with total assets of $50 billion or more and nonbank financial holding companies supervised by the Federal Reserve Board.[10]
- The law gives the Board of Governors of the Federal Reserve and Council the authority over BHCs with assets greater than $50 billion to limit their financial activities and/or to sell or transfer certain assets to unaffiliated entities.
- The powers and duties of the Office of Thrift Supervision, which regulated savings and loans, are transferred to the OCC, FDIC, and the Board of Governors of the Federal Reserve System.
- The Federal Insurance Office within the Department of Treasury will monitor insurance companies.
- The limit on federal deposit insurance is permanently increased to $250,000.
- The law requires advisers to hedge funds and private equity funds to register with the SEC and to provide the SEC with selected data.
- The law requires financial holding companies to be "well capitalized and well managed."
- The capital levels of BHCs, savings and loan holding companies, and insured depository institutions should be countercyclical, such that levels increase during times of economic expansion, decrease during

contractions in economic activity, and maintain levels consistent with the safety and soundness of the institution.

- There are prohibitions and/or limits on proprietary trading by banks.[11] This is the so-called *Volcker Rule*, which restricts banks from proprietary trading and sets limits on certain relationships and investments in hedge funds and private equity funds.
- The SEC and the Commodities Futures Trading Commission will regulate the over-the-counter swaps and security-based swap markets, including the regulation of dealers, major swap participants, and approval of new products. Standardized derivatives will be cleared through a clearinghouse and traded on an exchange.
- The proper functioning of the financial markets depends on efficient payment, clearing, and settlements. The Board of Governors of the Federal Reserve System and the National Credit Union Administration are charged with regulating financial market utilities, which are financial institutions and participants that are designated by the council as being systemically important.
- Concerning credit retention, institutions that securitize loans are required to retain no less than 5 percent of the credit risk for any asset.
- The SEC will establish an Investor Advisory Committee with the goal of increasing investor protection and improving the regulation of securities and markets. The SEC is also given increased regulatory enforcement powers, including increased authority over asset-backed securities, municipal securities, and credit rating agencies.
- A Bureau of Consumer Financial Protection, an independent bureau in the Federal Reserve System, is charged with regulating consumer financial products and services by administering, enforcing, or implementing federal consumer financial law and prohibiting unfair, deceptive, or abusive acts and practices.
- The law intends to improve access by low- and moderate-income people to mainstream financial institutions.
- Minimum standards for residential mortgage loans include that the borrower must be able to repay the loan.
- Incentive-based compensation should be prohibited when it encourages inappropriate risks by providing employees with compensation that is "excessive" or "could lead to material financial losses."[12]

SERVICES PROVIDED BY BANKS

The services provided by commercial banks can be divided into three broad areas: (1) payments, (2) intermediation, and (3) other financial services.[13]

Payments

Banks are the core of the *payments system.* The payment refers to the means by which financial transactions are settled. Banks also dispense coin and currency. Many financial transactions in the United States involve checking accounts, electronic deposits, and payments at commercial banks. Therefore, the means by which such payments are settled is an integral part of the payments system. The payments system also involves the settlement of credit card transactions, wire transfers, and other aspects in the movement of funds.

The role of banks in the payments system takes on an important social dimension because an efficient payments system is vital to economic stability and growth. At one time, commercial banks had a monopoly on transactions accounts, but that is no longer the case. Other depository institutions (i.e., savings and loans, savings banks, and credit unions), as well as money market mutual funds and brokerage firms, also offer transactions accounts.

Commercial banks, along with the Federal Reserve System, are the heart of the payments system. The payments system can be divided into two parts: the *retail payments system* that is used by individuals to pay their bills or receive funds and the *large-dollar payments system* that is used by business concerns and governments to handle large-dollar domestic and international payments and receipts.

The retail payments system in the United States makes extensive use of paper checks. However, electronic payments and credit and debit cards are becoming increasing important for retail payments. Thus, the use of paper checks has declined. Banks also provide coin and currency to businesses and individuals for cash transactions. Even the amount of cash in circulation has been affected by technology, as more people use credit and debit cards and electronic tools to pay for goods and services.

Large-dollar payments in the United States are electronic payments between commercial banks that are using the *Fedwire* (a wholesale wire transfer system operated by the Federal Reserve System). In addition, the Clearing House Interbank Payments System (*CHIPS*) is a private electronic transfer system operated by large banks in New York for transfers involving international movements of funds. The Society for Worldwide Interbank Financial Telecommunication (SWIFT) is operated by banks throughout the world to facilitate international payments.

Financial Intermediation

As noted in Chapter 2, the principal function of financial intermediaries is obtaining funds from depositors and others and then lending those funds to borrowers. They also provide other financial services. Banks are one type of financial intermediary. In financial terms, the deposits represent bank liabilities, and the loans are assets. Their profit from lending is the difference between the rates at which they borrow and lend, after taking into account all of their expenses. Banks also earn income from investments and from fees charged for various services.

Bank Balance Sheet

Assets	Liabilities and Eqity
Loans	Deposits
Other assets	Equity

Deposit Function Commercial banks act as intermediaries between those who have money (i.e., savers or depositors) and those who need money (i.e., borrowers). As financial intermediaries, they enhance economic efficiency and economic growth by allocating capital to its best possible uses. Banks obtain deposits from savers by offering:

1. A wide variety of denominations, interest rates, and maturities.
2. Risk-free (FDIC-insured) deposits.
3. A high degree of liquidity, depending on the maturity of the deposit. Short-term deposits tend to be the most liquid.

These are characteristics that meet the needs of most savers better than bonds and stocks, which may have high denominations, high risk, and less liquidity. Nonbank financial institutions may offer similar services, such as money market mutual funds, but mutual fund shares are not FDIC insured.

The FDIC is an independent agency of the U.S. government that insures selected deposits at FDIC-insured banks and savings associations. The basic FDIC insurance covers checking, Negotiable Order of Withdrawal (NOW), savings accounts, money market deposit accounts, certificates of deposit (CDs), and individual retirement accounts (IRAs) up to the insurance limit. The basic limits are $250,000 per owner in a single account (owned by one person), $250,000 per co-owner in joint accounts, $250,000 per owner in IRAs and certain other retirement accounts, and $250,000 for each beneficiary of revocable trust accounts. It is possible to have more than $250,000 in coverage at one insured bank or savings association if you own deposit accounts in different ownership categories. The principal ownership categories are single accounts, joint accounts, revocable trust accounts, and certain retirement accounts.[14]

The FDIC does not insure the money you invest in stocks, bonds, mutual funds, life insurance policies, annuities, or municipal securities, even if you purchased these products from an insured bank or savings association.

Loan Function Commercial banks use the deposits to make loans to borrowers. Historically, the loans were concentrated in short-term commercial lending. Today, however, banks make every type of loan that is legally permissible. By doing so, they gained expertise in evaluating and monitoring the risks associated with lending. They also make or acquire loans and then sell them to other intermediaries and investors.

Some banks specialize in particular types of lending and other activities. For example, Silicon Valley Bank in Santa Clara, California, is part of the "SVB Financial Group . . . that serves emerging growth and mature companies in the technology, life science, private equity, and premium wine industries."[15] While "Bank of America is one of the world's largest financial institutions, serving individual consumers, small- and middle-market businesses and large corporations with a full range of banking, investing, asset management, and other financial and risk management products and services,"[16] in contrast, Bank of New York Mellon Corporation (BNY Mellon) specializes in asset management and securities servicing. The point is that not all banks do the same things.

In terms of asset concentration, at the end of 2009, the three largest concentration groups of banks were commercial lenders (56 percent), agricultural lenders (20 percent), and mortgage lenders (10 percent).[17]

Other Financial Services

In addition to their traditional role of providing financial intermediation between depositors and borrowers, commercial banks provide a variety of other financial services.

- **Off-Balance Sheet Risk Taking.** Banks can generate fee income by dealing in financial derivatives: futures, options, interest rate swaps, financial futures, and other derivatives.[18] For example, a bank may guarantee the payment of another party. These guarantees are contingent claims (the bank must pay only if the party defaults) and do not appear on the bank's balance sheet. The *standby letter of credit* is perhaps the best known of those contingent claims and involves the agreement by a bank to pay an agreed-upon amount on presentation of evidence of default or nonperformance of the party whose obligation is guaranteed. Finally, banks make extensive use of interest rate swaps to hedge interest rate risk—the risk of adverse movements in market rates of interest.

- **Insurance-Related Activities.** Commercial banks currently are able to offer only a limited set of insurance products, such as annuities and credit life insurance.
- **Securities-Related Services.** Commercial banks provide a number of brokerage services in addition to selling mutual funds. They also offer limited investment banking services, such as underwriting municipal securities issued by state and local governments. They also trade foreign currencies and U.S. government securities.

  As domestic banks merge with or are acquired by international banks (such as Germany's Deutsche Bank's acquisition of Bankers Trust) that already have broad investment banking powers, it is only a matter of time before such broader investment powers are granted in the United States or they do it overseas.
- **Trust Services.** Commercial banks may operate trust departments in which they manage the funds of others for a fee, under the terms of a trust agreement. Because the bank does not own the assets held in trust, they do not show up on the bank's balance sheet. Thus, there is no regulatory capital requirement associated with trust assets. In its fiduciary role, trusts manage estates, employee pension, and profit-sharing programs, and a variety of securities-related activities for corporate businesses.

WHAT BANK REGULATORS DO

Commercial banks are private business corporations with a public role.[19] Their public role includes their role in the money supply, payments system, insured deposits, and more. It is because of this public side of banking that they are regulated. Bank regulators have four primary responsibilities: chartering, regulating, supervising, and examining banks. There are additional duties that are not covered here. For example, the Federal Reserve must approve bank mergers, it is specifically charged with the regulation of BHCs, it can lend money to banks at the discount window, and it acts as a lender of last resort.[20] Thus, not all bank regulators have exactly the same responsibilities.

Chartering

As previously noted, the OCC and state banking commissions have the authority to charter banks. In doing so, they have to determine if the proposed bank will have adequate capital and management for its respective market area. They also have to take into account the needs and convenience of the community, competition, and other factors.

Regulating

The terms *regulation* and *supervision* are sometimes used interchangeably. However, there is a technical difference: "Bank regulation entails issuing specific regulations and guidelines governing the operations, activities, and acquisitions of banking organizations."[21] Today, regulations involve the types of products that banks can offer, such as investment banking, insurance, and brokerage services; enforcement of laws such as the Truth in Lending Act; and rules involving safety and soundness.

Supervising

"Bank supervision involves the monitoring, inspecting, and examining of banking organizations to assess their condition and their compliance with relevant laws and regulations."[22] Bank examinations are one means of determining compliance with regulations.

Bank supervisors have a variety of techniques at their disposal to deal with problem banks—banks that are not in compliance with rules and regulations. The least intrusive technique is a *memorandum of understanding* (MOU) issued by the regulator to the bank, detailing the changes that must occur to put the bank back in good standing. Other techniques include *cease and desist orders* that prohibit the bank or a person from continuing a particular course of conduct. Finally, the regulators can close the bank.

Examining

As just noted, bank examinations are part of the supervisory process. Banks face two types of examinations. The first is to determine the safety and soundness of the bank. In this connection, bank examiners from the OCC, the Federal Reserve, the FDIC, and the Office of Thrift Supervision are required to use the Uniform Financial Institutions Rating System, commonly referred to as CAMELS. This acronym stands for:

- Capital adequacy—the amount of regulatory capital that banks are required to maintain.
- Asset quality—the risk associated with managing assets, including the quality of loans and investments. Assets are rated by federal bank examiners as passing or as problem assets because they represent potential

losses. Table 3.2 lists the problem asset categories and brief explanations of each. The worst thing that can happen to a loan is that it is classified as a loss, and it must be *charged off* (removed from the balance sheet). Lenders must charge off open-end loans (e.g., credit card loans) when they are 180 days past due and closed-end loans (e.g., mortgage loans) when they are 120 days past due.[23]

- Management—the capability of the board of directors and management to measure, monitor, and control risk.
- Earnings—the profitability of the bank and sources of those earnings, taking risk into account.
- Liquidity—the bank's ability to meet its financial obligations when they come due, and the needs of their customers (deposit withdrawals and loans).
- Sensitivity to market risk (interest rates, foreign exchange) and the ability of the bank to manage that risk.

Composite ratings of institutions range from 1 to 5. A composite score of 1 is the highest rating given. It means that the administration of the institution is sound in every respect, and there is no cause for supervisory concern. A composite score of 2 means that the institution is sound, but some strains need to be addressed. A composite score of 3 indicates that the bank has problems that must be addressed. Typically, an MOU is issued by the bank regulators explaining what actions need to be taken. This is considered an informal action. A composite score of 4 means that the bank has unsafe and unsound practices. The regulators take formal actions by issuing consent orders or cease and desist orders with the actions that the bank must take. A composite score of 5 means that the institution is in extremely bad condition and will most likely fail or be acquired by another institution unless immediate actions are taken to improve its financial condition. The composite ratings are not publicly available information, although many economists argue that such information would aid in the market discipline of banks.

Megabank mergers (e.g., Wells Fargo's acquisition of Wachovia Corp. in 2008), global banking, and the expanded used of derivative securities (e.g., interest rate swaps) have contributed to the increased size and complexity of the largest banking organizations. Bank regulators recognize that they can no longer rely on periodic examinations alone to ensure that the banks remain sound. Consequently, they are placing greater emphasis on banks' risk management practices and internal controls.

The second type of examination is to determine if the bank is in compliance with all of the relevant regulations and laws. Banks can do only those activities as permitted by laws, and how they do it is regulated, too. Table 3.3 lists the Federal Reserve regulations that banks must adhere to. Banks must comply with other regulations as well. Table 3.4 shows which regulators regulate which types of banking institutions.

Harmonization

Although the biggest banks are global in scope and operations, bank regulation is nationally based. Nevertheless, the Bank for International Settlements, located in Basel, Switzerland, "aims at promoting monetary and financial stability, [and] acts as a forum for discussion and cooperation among central banks and the financial community."[24] The Basel Committee on Banking Supervision and the Basel II Capital Accord are examples of international cooperation among bank regulators. The committee's members come from Argentina, Australia, Belgium, Brazil, Canada, China, France, Germany, Hong Kong SAR, India, Indonesia, Italy, Japan, Korea, Luxembourg, Mexico, the Netherlands, Russia, Saudi Arabia, Singapore, South Africa, Spain, Sweden, Switzerland, Turkey, the United Kingdom, and the United States.

IS PRUDENTIAL BANK REGULATION EFFECTIVE?

Is prudential bank regulation effective? One answer to that question depends on what one thinks prudential regulation is supposed to do. Prudential

TABLE 3.2 Problem Asset Categories

Category	Explanation
Other Assets Especially Mentioned (OAEM)	Has potential for weakness and needs close attention. If uncorrected, it may deteriorate further.
Substandard	Inadequately protected by current worth/paying capacity of obligor, or collateral. There is the distinct possibility of a loss.
Doubtful	Substandard and collection/liquidation in full is highly questionable or improbable.
Loss	Uncollectible, and of such little value that it should be removed from the balance sheet.

Source: William F. Treacy, "Credit Risk Ratings at Large U.S. Banks," *Federal Reserve Bulletin*, November 1998, 901.

TABLE 3.3 Federal Reserve Regulations

Regulation	Subject
A	**Extensions of Credit by Federal Reserve Banks** Governs borrowing by depository institutions and others at the Federal Reserve discount window.
B	**Equal Credit Opportunity** Prohibits lenders from discriminating against credit applicants, establishes guidelines for gathering and evaluating credit information, and requires written notification when credit is denied.
C	**Home Mortgage Disclosure** Requires certain mortgage lenders to disclose data regarding their lending patterns.
D	**Reserve Requirements of Depository Institutions** Sets uniform requirements for all depository institutions to maintain reserve balances either with their Federal Reserve Bank or as cash.
E	**Electronic Fund Transfers** Establishes the rights, liabilities, and responsibilities of parties in electronic funds transfers and protects consumers when they use such systems.
F	**Limitations on Interbank Liabilities** Prescribes standards to limit the risks that the failure of a depository institution would pose to an insured depository institution.
G	**Disclosure and Reporting of Community Reinvestment Act (CRA)-Related Agreements** Implements provisions of the Gramm-Leach-Bliley Act that require reporting and public disclosure of written agreements between (1) insured depository institutions or their affiliates and (2) nongovernmental entities or persons, made in connection with fulfillment of CRA requirements.
H	**Membership of State Banking Institutions in the Federal Reserve System** Defines the requirements for membership of state-chartered banks in the Federal Reserve System; sets limitations on certain investments and requirements for certain types of loans; describes rules pertaining to securities-related activities; establishes the minimum ratios of capital to assets that banks must maintain and procedures for prompt corrective action when banks are not adequately capitalized; prescribes real estate lending and appraisal standards; sets out requirements concerning bank security procedures, suspicious-activity reports, and compliance with the Bank Secrecy Act; and establishes rules governing banks' ownership or control of financial subsidiaries.

TABLE 3.3 (*Continued*)

Regulation	Subject
I	**Issue and Cancellation of Federal Reserve Bank Capital Stock** Sets out stock-subscription requirements for all banks joining the Federal Reserve System.
J	**Collection of Checks and Other Items by Federal Reserve Banks and Funds Transfers through Fedwire** Establishes procedures, duties, and responsibilities among (1) Federal Reserve Banks, (2) the senders and payors of checks and other items, and (3) the senders and recipients of Fedwire funds transfers.
K	**International Banking Operations** Governs the international banking operations of U.S. banking organizations and the operations of foreign banks in the United States.
L	**Management Official Interlocks** Generally prohibits a management official from serving two nonaffiliated depository institutions, depository institution holding companies, or any combination thereof, in situations where the management interlock would likely have an anticompetitive effect.
M	**Consumer Leasing** Implements the consumer leasing provisions of the Truth in Lending Act by requiring meaningful disclosure of leasing terms.
N	**Relations with Foreign Banks and Bankers** Governs relationships and transactions between Federal Reserve Banks and foreign banks, bankers, or governments.
O	**Loans to Executive Officers, Directors, and Principal Shareholders of Member Banks** Restricts credit that a member bank may extend to its executive officers, directors, and principal shareholders, and their related interests.
P	**Privacy of Consumer Financial Information** Governs how financial institutions use nonpublic personal information about consumers.
Q	**Prohibition against Payment of Interest on Demand Deposits** Prohibits member banks from paying interest on demand deposits.
R	**Exceptions for Banks from the Definition of Broker in the Securities Exchange Act of 1934** Defines the scope of securities activities that banks may conduct without registering with the SEC as a securities *broker* and implements the most important exceptions from the definition of the

(*continued*)

TABLE 3.3 (*Continued*)

Regulation	Subject
	term broker for banks under section 3(a)(4) of the Securities Exchange Act of 1934. Specifically, the regulation implements the statutory exceptions that allow a bank, subject to certain conditions, to continue to conduct securities transactions for its customers as part of its trust and fiduciary, custodial, and deposit "sweep" functions and to refer customers to a securities broker-dealer pursuant to a networking arrangement with the broker-dealer.
S	**Reimbursement to Financial Institutions for Providing Financial Records; Recordkeeping Requirements for Certain Financial Records** Establishes rates and conditions for reimbursement to financial institutions for providing customer records to a government authority and prescribes recordkeeping and reporting requirements for insured depository institutions making domestic wire transfers and for insured depository institutions and nonbank financial institutions making international wire transfers.
T	**Credit by Brokers and Dealers** Governs extension of credit by securities brokers and dealers, including all members of national securities exchanges. (See also Regulations U and X.)
U	**Credit by Banks and Persons Other Than Brokers or Dealers for the Purpose of Purchasing or Carrying Margin Stock** Governs extension of credit by banks or persons other than brokers or dealers to finance the purchase or the carrying of margin securities. (See also Regulations T and X.)
V	**Fair Credit Reporting** Proposed rules to implement the notice and opt-out provisions of the Fair Credit Reporting Act applicable to financial institutions that give their affiliates certain information about consumers.
W	**Transactions between Member Banks and Their Affiliates** Implements sections 23A and 23B of the Federal Reserve Act, which establish certain restrictions on and requirements for transactions between a member bank and its affiliates.
X	**Borrowers of Securities Credit** Applies the provisions of Regulations T and U to borrowers who are subject to U.S. laws and who obtain credit within or outside the United States for the purpose of purchasing securities.
Y	**BHCs and Change in Bank Control** Regulates the acquisition of control of banks and BHCs by companies and individuals, defines and regulates the nonbanking activities in

TABLE 3.3 (*Continued*)

Regulation	Subject
	which BHCs (including financial holding companies) and foreign banking organizations with United States operations may engage, and establishes the minimum ratios of capital to assets that BHCs must maintain.
Z	**Truth in Lending** Prescribes uniform methods for computing the cost of credit, for disclosing credit terms, and for resolving errors on certain types of credit accounts.
AA	**Unfair or Deceptive Acts or Practices** Establishes consumer complaint procedures and defines unfair or deceptive practices in extending credit to consumers.
BB	**Community Reinvestment** Implements the CRA and encourages banks to help meet the credit needs of their communities.
CC	**Availability of Funds and Collection of Checks** Governs the availability of funds deposited in checking accounts and the collection and return of checks.
DD	**Truth in Savings** Requires depository institutions to provide disclosures to enable consumers to make meaningful comparisons of deposit accounts.
EE	**Netting Eligibility for Financial Institutions** Defines financial institutions to be covered by statutory provisions that validate netting contracts, thereby permitting one institution to pay or receive the net, rather than the gross, amount due, even if the other institution is insolvent.
FF	**Obtaining and Using Medical Information in Connection with Credit** Creates exceptions to the statutory prohibition against obtaining or using medical information in connection with determining eligibility for credit.
GG	**Prohibition on Funding of Unlawful Internet Gambling** Requires U.S. financial firms that participate in designated payment systems to establish and implement policies and procedures reasonably designed to prevent payments connected to unlawful Internet gambling.

Source: Board of Governors of the Federal Reserve System, All Regulations (3/15/10); For additional information and the latest updates, see: www.federalreserve.gov/bankinforeg/reglisting.htm#R.

TABLE 3.4 Banking Institutions and Their Regulators

	Type of Institution	Chartering and Licensing	Supervision and Regulation
A	National banks	OCC	OCC
B	State member banks	State authority	Federal Reserve and state authority
C	FDIC-insured state nonmember banks	State authority	FDIC and state authority
D	Non-FDIC-insured state banks	State authority	State authority
E	Insured federal savings associations	Office of Thrift Supervision (OTS)	OTS
	Insured state savings associations	State authority	OTS and state authority
F	Non-FDIC-insured state savings associations	State authority	State authority
G	Federal credit unions	National Credit Union Administration (NCUA)	NCUA
	State credit unions	State authority	State authority
H	Bank/financial holding companies	Federal Reserve and state authority	Federal Reserve
I	Savings association holding companies	OTS and state authority	OTS
J	Foreign branches of U.S. national and state member banks	Federal Reserve and state authority	OCC or Federal Reserve
	Foreign branches of U.S. insured state nonmember banks	State authority	FDIC or state authority
K	Edge Act corporations	Federal Reserve	Federal Reserve
	Agreement corporations	State authority	Federal Reserve and state authority
L	Federal U.S. branches and agencies of foreign banks	OCC	OCC and Federal Reserve
	State U.S. branches and agencies of foreign banks	State authority	Federal Reserve and state authority

Source: Based on Federal Reserve Bank of New York (2003), "Banking Institutions and Their Regulators," www.newyorkfed.org/banking/regrept/BIATR.pdf.

regulation ranges from safety and soundness to consumer protection. In this context, it may be successful in accomplishing some goals of prudential regulation and less successful in other areas. However, one thing is clear: The safety and soundness of the banking system is the primary objective of prudential regulation. If banks fail in large numbers, the other objectives of prudential regulation cannot be met.

Another view is that the facts speak for themselves. During the 1980–1996 period, more than 130 International Monetary Fund member countries, including the United States, had significant banking sector problems or crises.[25] During the 1997–1999 period, there were banking crises in several Southeast Asian countries, Russia, and Brazil. The large numbers of bank failures and crises suggests that prudential regulation, at least in its present form, has limits and that it works better in some countries than in others. Systemic causes of bank failures are one of those limits. An FDIC study of banking crises in the 1980s and early 1990s concluded that "bank regulation can limit the scope and cost of bank failures, but it is unlikely to prevent bank failures that have systemic causes."[26]

Prudential regulation works best in a stable economic environment. The Basel Committee on Banking Supervision's Core Principles[27] state: "In the absence of sound macroeconomic policies, banking supervisors will be faced with a virtually impossible task." Most banking crises are associated with unstable economic conditions, such as asset price deflation, interest rate shocks, and foreign exchange rate shocks. The flip side of that coin is that prolonged stability and strong economic growth may lead to complacency with respect to risky lending. That, in part, is what happened in Asian countries when the stability and rapid economic growth encouraged banks to lend injudiciously, resulting in overspending in the government sector.

Beyond banking crises, heterogeneous financial conglomerates that cross regulatory and national boundaries, as well as changes in information technology, are testing the limits of prudential banking regulation.

Regulatory arbitrage is another factor that concerns bank regulators. *Regulatory arbitrage* refers to regulated financial institutions finding legal ways to get around bank regulations or laws. For example, JPMorgan Chase Chief Executive Jamie Dimon said that the Volcker Rule of the Dodd-Frank Act "won't limit J.P. Morgan's ability to do business with customers. But the bank will be moving its commodities and credit-default-swap businesses to a separate subsidiary."[28]

Similarly, some banks use conduits such as structured investment vehicles (SIVs) to remove loans from their balance sheets in order to avoid bank capital requirements. The SIVs are pools of investment assets that are funded by short-term debt that may be guaranteed by the bank.

Eliminating the capital requirement on the loans effectively increases the financial leverage of the loans.

APPENDIX 3A: FDIC DEFINITIONS OF COMMERCIAL BANKS[29]

1934—Two national banks in Alaska that are not members of the Federal Reserve System are included specifically.
1935—Morris Plan Banks that become insured are included.
1936—The definition of commercial banks is revised to read:

all operating national banks,

all incorporated state banks,

all trust companies and banks and trust companies regularly engaged in the business of receiving deposits
(except mutual savings banks, and in New Hampshire, guaranty savings banks),

all stock savings banks,

banks in conservatorship or operating under restrictions,
(provided they are authorized to and in fact do accept new deposits),

such industrial and Morris Plan banks as operate under general banking codes

or operate under the same codes of law as insured industrial banks,

branches of foreign banks which engage in a general deposit business,

cash depositories,

private banks under state supervision,

insured trust companies, even though not engaged in regular deposit banking (nondeposit trust companies),

the chief office in each of the US possessions of American banks engaged in a general deposit business in those possessions.

1937–1946—The last phrase of the 1936 definition of commercial banks is replaced by the following:

American branches engaged in a general banking business in US possessions
(where more than one branch is maintained by a given bank in any one possession, the chief or central office is classified (and counted) as a bank and the other offices are classified (and counted) as branches).

1947—The definition of commercial banks is revised to include:

national banks (except those not regularly engaged in deposit banking),

incorporated state banks,

trust companies,

banks and trust companies regularly engaged in the business of receiving deposits, whether demand or time (except mutual savings banks),

stock savings banks, including guaranty savings banks in New Hampshire,

industrial banks and Morris Plan banks that operate under general banking codes or are specifically authorized by law to accept deposits and in practice, do so, or the obligations of which are regarded as deposits for deposit insurance,

special types of banks of deposit,

cash depositories in South Carolina,

cooperative exchanges in Arkansas,

savings and loan companies operating under Superior Court charters in Georgia,

government-operated banks in American Samoa, Guam, and North Dakota,

a cooperative bank, usually classified as a credit union, operating under a special charter in New Hampshire,

two savings institutions, known as "trust companies," operating under a special charter in Texas,

Savings Bank Trust Company in New York,

branches of foreign banks that engage in a general deposit business in the continental United States or in the U.S. possessions,

in U.S. possessions, branches of American banks engaged in a general deposit business.

1948—The 1947 definition is revised to add a government bank in Puerto Rico.

1949—The 1947 definition is revised to include nondeposit trust companies with a national charter.

1950—The government-operated bank in Guam is dropped from the definition; it is no longer insured or no longer in operation.

1952—A revision indicates that there are four branches of foreign banks (counted as banks) that engage in a general deposit business in the continental United States or in Puerto Rico.

1961—The 1947 definition relating to the inclusion of cooperative exchanges in Arkansas is changed to the singular, indicating that there is only one insured cooperative exchange operating now.

There are now eight branches of foreign banks included.

1962—Nine branches of foreign banks are included.

1963—The number of foreign branches operating in the United States, Puerto Rico, and the Virgin Islands is 17.

1964—Foreign branches are now operating in New York, Oregon, Washington, Puerto Rico, and the Virgin Islands.

1966—The one cooperative exchange in Arkansas is dropped.

1970—The definition of commercial banks is revised to include:

national banks,

incorporated state-chartered banks,

trust companies,

bank and trust companies regularly engaged in the business of receiving deposits, whether demand or time (except mutual savings banks),

stock savings banks, including guaranty savings banks in New Hampshire,

industrial and Morris Plan banks that operate under general banking codes or are specifically authorized by law to accept deposits and, in practice, do so, or the obligations of which are regarded as deposits for deposit insurance,

special types of banks of deposit,

regulated certificated banks and a savings and loan company operating under a Superior Court charter in Georgia,

government-operated banks in North Dakota and Puerto Rico,

a cooperative bank, usually classified as a credit union, operating under a special charter in New Hampshire,

a savings institution, known as a "trust company," operating under a special charter in Texas,

the Savings Bank Trust Company in New York,

branches of foreign banks in Illinois, Massachusetts, New York, Oregon, Washington, Puerto Rico, and the Virgin Islands.

1975—Special types of banks of deposit and the savings and loan operating under a Superior Court charter in Georgia are no longer included, and the Savings Bank and Trust Company Northwest in Washington is added.

1976—The cooperative bank operating under a special charter in New Hampshire is no longer included.
1977—Guam is added to the list of states and U.S. territories and possessions with branches of foreign banks.
1978—Pennsylvania is added as having a branch of a foreign bank.
1982—The definition of commercial banks is revised to include:

national banks,

incorporated state-chartered banks and trust companies,

bank and trust companies regularly engaged in the business of receiving deposits, whether demand or time
(except mutual savings banks),

stock savings banks, including guaranty savings banks in New Hampshire,

industrial and Morris Plan banks that operate under general banking codes or are specifically authorized by law to accept deposits and, in practice, do so, or the obligations of which are regarded as deposits for deposit insurance.

1984—The definition of commercial banks is revised to include:

national banks,

FDIC-insured state-chartered banks and trust companies, except savings banks,

FDIC-insured industrial and Morris Plan banks that operate under general banking codes or are specifically authorized by law

to accept deposits and, in practice, do so, or the obligations of which are regarded as deposits for deposit insurance.

1989—The FIRREA enables SAIF-insured thrift institutions to change their charters to become commercial banks.
1990–1991—The definition of commercial banks is revised to include:

national banks,

state-chartered banks and trust companies, except savings banks,

industrial and Morris Plan banks that operate under general banking codes or are specifically authorized by law to accept deposits and, in practice, do so, or the obligations of which are regarded as deposits for deposit insurance.

commercial banks, either national or state chartered, insured by the FDIC Savings Association Insurance Fund (SAIF).

1992–Current—The definition of FDIC-insured commercial banks and trust companies is revised to include:

national banks,

state-chartered banks and trust companies, except savings banks,

commercial banks, either national or state chartered, insured by the FDIC Bank Insurance Fund (BIF) or the FDIC Savings Association Insurance Fund (SAIF),

other financial institutions that operate under general banking codes or are specifically authorized by law to accept deposits and, in practice, do so, or the obligations of which are regarded as deposits for deposit insurance.

APPENDIX 3B: SELECTED BANKING LEGISLATION

Many important laws that have affected the banking industry in the United States are listed here. The following list is based on FDIC data (www.fdic.gov/regulations/laws/important/index.html), and it covers some, but not all, of the laws affecting banks from 1864 through 2003. More recent legislation is also listed here.

- **National Bank Act of 1864** (Chapter 106, 13 STAT. 99). Established a national banking system and the chartering of national banks.
- **Federal Reserve Act of 1913** (P.L. 63-43, 38 STAT. 251, 12 USC 221). Established the Federal Reserve System as the central banking system of the United States.
- **To Amend the National Banking Laws and the Federal Reserve Act** (P.L. 69-639, 44 STAT. 1224). Also known as the McFadden Act of 1927. Prohibited interstate banking.
- **Banking Act of 1933** (P.L. 73-66, 48 STAT. 162). Also known as the Glass-Steagall Act. Established the FDIC as a temporary agency. Separated commercial banking from investment banking, establishing them as separate lines of commerce.
- **Banking Act of 1935** (P.L. 74-305, 49 STAT. 684). Established the FDIC as a permanent agency of the government.

- **Federal Deposit Insurance Act of 1950** (P.L. 81-797, 64 STAT. 873). Revised and consolidated earlier FDIC legislation into one act. Embodied the basic authority for the operation of the FDIC.
- **Bank Holding Company Act of 1956** (P.L. 84-511, 70 STAT. 133). Required Federal Reserve Board approval for the establishment of a bank holding company. Prohibited bank holding companies headquartered in one state from acquiring a bank in another state.
- **The Bank Secrecy Act of 1970** (See 31 USC 5311-5330 and 31 CFR 103). The BSA is also known as the Currency and Foreign Transactions Reporting Act. It requires U.S. financial institutions to assist U.S. government agencies in detecting and preventing money laundering.
- **International Banking Act of 1978** (P.L. 95-369, 92 STAT. 607). Brought foreign banks within the federal regulatory framework. Required deposit insurance for branches of foreign banks engaged in taking retail deposits in the United States.
- **Financial Institutions Regulatory and Interest Rate Control Act of 1978** (P.L. 95-630, 92 STAT. 3641). Also known as FIRIRCA. Created the Federal Financial Institutions Examination Council. Established limits and reporting requirements for bank insider transactions. Created major statutory provisions regarding electronic fund transfers.
- **Depository Institutions Deregulation and Monetary Control Act of 1980** (P.L. 96-221, 94 STAT. 132). Also known as DIDMCA. Established "NOW Accounts." Began the phaseout of interest rate ceilings on deposits. Established the Depository Institutions Deregulation Committee. Granted new powers to thrift institutions. Raised the deposit insurance ceiling to $100,000.
- **Depository Institutions Act of 1982** (P.L. 97-320, 96 STAT. 1469). Also known as Garn-St Germain. Expanded FDIC powers to assist troubled banks. Established the Net Worth Certificate program. Expanded the powers of thrift institutions.
- **Competitive Equality Banking Act of 1987** (P.L. 100-86, 101 STAT. 552). Also known as CEBA. Established new standards for expedited funds availability. Recapitalized the Federal Savings & Loan Insurance Company (FSLIC). Expanded FDIC authority for open bank assistance transactions, including bridge banks.
- **Financial Institutions Reform, Recovery, and Enforcement Act of 1989** (P.L. 101-73, 103 STAT. 183). Also known as FIRREA. FIRREA's purpose was to restore the public's confidence in the savings and loan industry. FIRREA abolished the Federal Savings & Loan Insurance Corporation (FSLIC), and the FDIC was given the responsibility of insuring the deposits of thrift institutions in its place.

The FDIC insurance fund created to cover thrifts was named the Savings Association Insurance Fund (SAIF), and the fund covering banks was called the Bank Insurance Fund (BIF).

FIRREA also abolished the Federal Home Loan Bank Board. Two new agencies, the Federal Housing Finance Board (FHFB) and the Office of Thrift Supervision (OTS), were created to replace it.

Finally, FIRREA created the Resolution Trust Corporation (RTC) as a temporary agency of the government. The RTC was given the responsibility of managing and disposing of the assets of failed institutions. An oversight board was created to provide supervisory authority over the policies of the RTC, and the Resolution Funding Corporation (RFC) was created to provide funding for RTC operations.

- **Crime Control Act of 1990** (P.L. 101-647, 104 STAT. 4789). Title XXV of the Crime Control Act, known as the Comprehensive Thrift and Bank Fraud Prosecution and Taxpayer Recovery Act of 1990, greatly expanded the authority of federal regulators to combat financial fraud.

  This act prohibited undercapitalized banks from making golden parachute and other indemnification payments to institution-affiliated parties. It also increased penalties and prison time for those convicted of bank crimes, increased the powers and authority of the FDIC to take enforcement actions against institutions operating in an unsafe or unsound manner, and gave regulators new procedural powers to recover assets improperly diverted from financial institutions.
- **Federal Deposit Insurance Corporation Improvement Act of 1991** (P.L. 102-242, 105 STAT. 2236). Also known as FDICIA, it greatly increased the powers and authority of the FDIC. Major provisions recapitalized the Bank Insurance Fund and allowed the FDIC to strengthen the fund by borrowing from the Treasury.

  The act mandated a least-cost resolution method and prompt resolution approach to problem and failing banks and ordered the creation of a risk-based deposit insurance assessment scheme. Brokered deposits and solicitation of deposits were restricted, as were the nonbank activities of insured state banks. FDICIA created new supervisory and regulatory examination standards and put forth new capital requirements for banks. It also expanded prohibitions against insider activities and created new Truth in Savings provisions.
- **Housing and Community Development Act of 1992** (P.L. 102-550, 106 STAT. 3672). Established a regulatory structure for government-sponsored enterprises (GSEs), combated money laundering, and provided regulatory relief to financial institutions.
- **RTC Completion Act** (P.L. 103-204, 107 STAT. 2369). Requires the RTC to adopt a series of management reforms and to implement

provisions designed to improve the agency's record in providing business opportunities to minorities and women when issuing RTC contracts or selling assets. Expands the existing affordable housing programs of the RTC and the FDIC by broadening the potential affordable housing stock of the two agencies.

Increases the statute of limitations on RTC civil lawsuits from three years to five or to the period provided in state law, whichever is longer. In cases in which the statute of limitations has expired, claims can be revived for fraud and intentional misconduct resulting in unjust enrichment or substantial loss to the thrift. Provides final funding for the RTC and establishes a transition plan for transfer of RTC resources to the FDIC. The RTC's sunset date is set at December 31, 1995, at which time the FDIC will assume its conservatorship and receivership functions.

- **Riegle Community Development and Regulatory Improvement Act of 1994** (P.L. 103-325, 108 STAT. 2160). Established a Community Development Financial Institutions Fund, a wholly owned government corporation that would provide financial and technical assistance to CDFIs.

  Contains several provisions aimed at curbing the practice of reverse redlining, in which nonbank lenders target low- and moderate-income homeowners, minorities, and the elderly for home equity loans on abusive terms. Relaxes capital requirements and other regulations to encourage the private-sector secondary market for small-business loans.

  Contains more than 50 provisions to reduce bank regulatory burden and paperwork requirements. Requires the Treasury Department to develop ways to substantially reduce the number of currency transactions filed by financial institutions. Contains provisions aimed at shoring up the National Flood Insurance Program.
- **Riegle-Neal Interstate Banking and Branching Efficiency Act of 1994** (P.L. 103-328, 108 STAT. 2338). Permits adequately capitalized and managed bank holding companies to acquire banks in any state one year after enactment. Concentration limits apply, and CRA evaluations by the Federal Reserve are required before acquisitions are approved. Beginning June 1, 1997, allows interstate mergers between adequately capitalized and managed banks, subject to concentration limits, state laws, and CRA evaluations. Extends the statute of limitations to permit the FDIC and RTC to revive lawsuits that had expired under state statutes of limitations.
- **Economic Growth and Regulatory Paperwork Reduction Act of 1996** (P.L. 104-208, 110 STAT. 3009). Modified financial institution regulations, including regulations impeding the flow of credit from lending

institutions to businesses and consumers. Amended the Truth in Lending Act and the Real Estate Settlement Procedures Act of 1974 to streamline the mortgage lending process.

Amended the FDIA to eliminate or revise various application, notice, and record-keeping requirements to reduce regulatory burden and the cost of credit. Amended the Fair Credit Reporting Act to strengthen consumer protections relating to credit reporting agency practices.

Established consumer protections for potential clients of consumer repair services. Clarified lender liability and federal agency liability issues under the CERCLA. Directed FDIC to impose a special assessment on depository institutions to recapitalize the SAIF and aligned SAIF assessment rates.

- **Gramm-Leach-Bliley Act of 1999** (P.L. 106-102, 113 STAT 1338). Repeals last vestiges of the Glass Steagall Act of 1933. Modifies portions of the Bank Holding Company Act to allow affiliations between banks and insurance underwriters. While preserving authority of states to regulate insurance, the act prohibits state actions that have the effect of preventing bank-affiliated firms from selling insurance on an equal basis with other insurance agents. Law creates a new financial holding company under section 4 of the BHCA, authorized to engage in underwriting and selling insurance and securities, conducting both commercial and merchant banking, investing in and developing real estate, and other complementary activities. There are limits on the kinds of nonfinancial activities these new entities may engage in.

  Allows national banks to underwrite municipal bonds. It restricts the disclosure of nonpublic customer information by financial institutions. All financial institutions must provide customers the opportunity to opt out of the sharing of the customers' nonpublic information with unaffiliated third parties. The act imposes criminal penalties on anyone who obtains customer information from a financial institution under false pretenses. Amends the Community Reinvestment Act to require that financial holding companies cannot be formed before their insured depository institutions receive and maintain a satisfactory CRA rating. Also requires public disclosure of bank-community CRA-related agreements. Grants some regulatory relief to small institutions in the shape of reducing the frequency of their CRA examinations if they have received outstanding or satisfactory ratings. Prohibits affiliations and acquisitions between commercial firms and unitary thrift institutions.

  Makes significant changes in the operation of the Federal Home Loan Bank System, easing membership requirements and loosening restrictions on the use of FHLB funds.

- **USA PATRIOT ACT of 2001** is the short title for the **International Money Laundering Abatement and Financial Anti-Terrorism Act of 2001** (P.L. 107-56) Legislation designed to prevent terrorists and others from using the U.S. financial system anonymously to move funds obtained from or destined for illegal activity. It authorizes and requires additional record keeping and reporting by financial institutions and greater scrutiny of accounts held for foreign banks and of private banking conducted for foreign persons.

  The law requires financial institutions to establish anti-money-laundering programs and imposes various standards on money-transmitting businesses. It amends criminal anti-money-laundering statutes and procedures for forfeitures in money-laundering cases and requires further cooperation between financial institutions and government agencies in fighting money laundering.
- **Sarbanes-Oxley Act of 2002** (P.L. 107-204). Sarbanes-Oxley establishes the Public Company Oversight Board to regulate public accounting firms that audit publicly traded companies. It prohibits such firms from providing other services to such companies along with the audit. It requires that CEOs and CFOs certify the annual and quarterly reports of publicly traded companies. The act authorizes, and in some cases requires, the SEC to issue rules governing audits.

  The law requires that insiders may no longer trade their company's securities during pension fund blackout periods. It mandates various studies, including a study of the involvement of investment banks and financial advisers in the scandals preceding the legislation. Also in the act are whistle-blower protections and new federal criminal laws, including a ban on alteration of documents.
- **Fair and Accurate Credit Transactions Act of 2003** (P.L. 108-159). The Fair and Accurate Credit Transactions (FACT) Act contains extensive amendments to the Fair Credit Reporting Act and is designed to improve the accuracy and transparency of the national credit reporting system, prevent identity theft, and assist victims. It contains provisions enhancing consumer rights in situations involving alleged identity theft, credit scoring, and claims of inaccurate information. It requires use of consumer reports to provide certain information to consumers who are offered credit on terms that are materially less favorable than the offers that the creditor makes to a substantial portion of its consumers. Companies that share consumer information among affiliated companies must provide consumers notice and an opt-out for sharing such information if the information will be used for marketing purposes.

RECENT LAWS

The Credit Card Accountability Responsibility and Disclosure Act of 2009, also called the Credit CARD Act of 2009 (P L 111-24), established fair and transparent practices relating to the extension of credit under an open-ended consumer credit plan and for other purposes. The act has eight major parts: (1) retroactive rate increases, (2) advance notice of rate hikes; (3) fee restrictions, (4) protects consumers younger than 21 years old, (5) ends the double-cycle billing, (6) fairer payment allocation, (7) more time to pay, and (8) safeguards for gift cards.

Dodd-Frank Wall Street Reform and Consumer Protection Act of 2010. As described earlier in this chapter, the law was passed in response to the financial crises that began in 2007.

CHAPTER 4

Asset/Liability Management

Asset/liability management (ALM) refers to the simultaneous management of both bank assets and liabilities for the purpose of maximizing profits, mitigating interest rate risk (IRR), providing liquidity, assuring its capital adequacy, and enhancing the market value of the bank.[1] It is an integral part of a bank's overall planning process. It is carried out by the bank's asset liability management committee (ALCO) and is usually considered short term in nature, focusing on near-term financial goals. Nevertheless, it is an integral part of the bank's overall planning and risk management processes.

The net interest margin (NIM) is a key part of ALM. It is the difference between interest and dividends earned on interest-bearing assets and interest paid to depositors and creditors, expressed as a percentage of average earning assets.[2] The average NIM was 3.5 percent in 2009.[3] To a large extent, NIM is affected by the level of interest rates.

AN OVERVIEW OF MARKET RATES OF INTEREST

The interest rate on 10-year U.S. Government Treasury bonds peaked in 1981 at 13.01 percent and declined to 10.62 percent in 1985, where the chart shown in Figure 4.1 begins.[4] The decline in market rates of interest continued through the end of 2009. Similarly, three-month Treasury bills peaked at 14.04 percent in 1981 and declined to 0.15 percent in 2009.

The major point to take away from Figure 4.1 is that the long-term decline in market rates of interest played a key role in the willingness and ability of borrowers to acquire funds and refinance existing loans at lower rates. Similarly, because banks typically borrow short-term funds and make longer-term loans, the fluctuating spread between the short-term Treasury bill rates and the long-term 10-year bond rates gives some idea of how

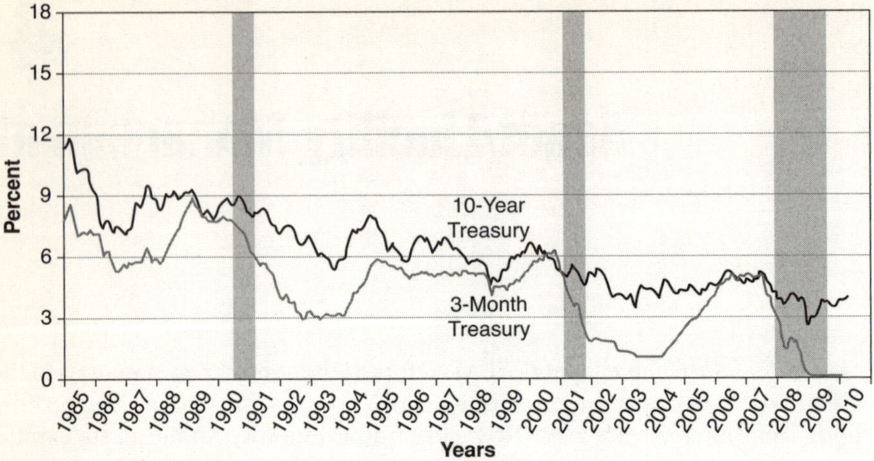

FIGURE 4.1 Interest Rates
Source: "National Economic Trends," Federal Reserve Bank of St. Louis, May 2010.

bank NIMs may have changed during the period shown. Both market rates of interest and NIMs change over time, and the changes are not always favorable to banks or borrowers.

Interest Rate and Price Risk

"Nowhere to Go but Up: Managing Interest Rate Risk in a Low-Rate Environment" was the title of the Federal Deposit Insurance Corporation (FDIC) *Supervisory Insights,* Winter 2009.[5] Because market rates of interest can only go up, the FDIC and other member agencies of the Federal Financial Institutions Examination Council (FFIEC) in January 2010 advised institutions of supervisory expectations for sound practices to manage IRR—the risk to earnings and capital that interest rates may change unfavorably.[6] The word *unfavorably* usually refers to unexpected changes in interest rates and prices.

In the current environment of historically low short-term interest rates, it is important for institutions to have robust processes for measuring and, where necessary, mitigating their exposure to potential increases in interest rates. Current financial market and economic conditions present significant risk management challenges to institutions of all sizes. For a number of institutions, increased loan losses and sharp declines in the values of some securities portfolios are placing downward pressure on capital and earnings. In this challenging environment, funding longer-term assets with shorter-term liabilities can generate earnings but poses risks to an institution's capital and earnings.... "The adequacy and effectiveness of an institution's IRR management process and the level of its IRR exposure are critical factors in the regulators' evaluation of an institution's sensitivity to changes in interest rates and capital adequacy."

Against this background, consider the effects of a change in market rates on debt securities. Consider the case of a manager of a bank's bond portfolio who is going to receive $1 million next week and must invest the funds for an indefinite period. The interest rates in early 2010 are about 6 percent, but the outlook is not clear. Some forecasters predict that interest rates will remain unchanged for the next three months; others predict that they will increase to 8 percent. If the bank invests all of the funds in 20-year bonds paying 6 percent and market interest rates do advance to 8 percent, it may have to sell the bonds for $802,000 (see Figure 4.2) and take a $198,000 loss. In other words, there is *price risk* associated with buying long-term debt securities because the price of the bonds declined.

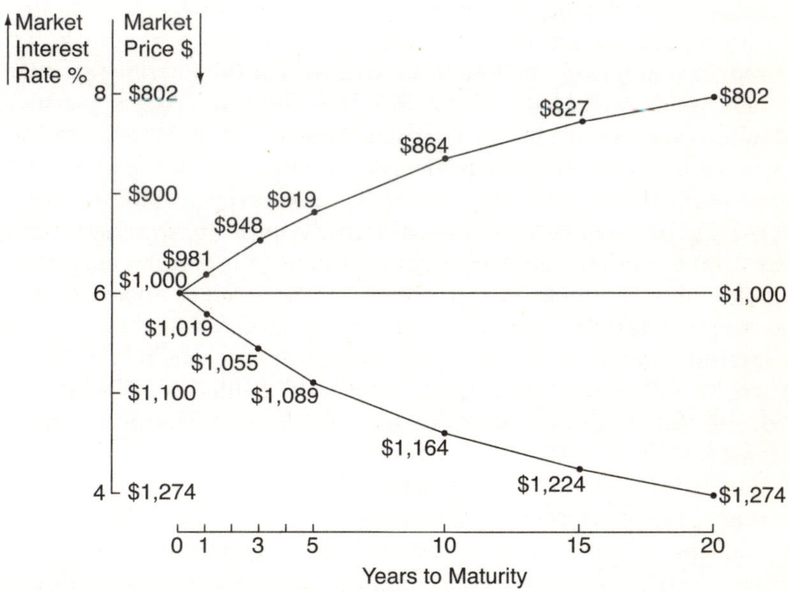

FIGURE 4.2 Relationship between the Market Price of a 6 Percent, 20-Year $1,000 Bond and Market Interest Rates of 8 Percent and 4 Percent.

On the other hand, if the bank invests in securities maturing in one year and has to sell them for $981,000, the loss will be $19,000. If interest rates are expected to decline, the bank can make the largest profit by buying long-term bonds. If it buys 20-year bonds and interest rates fall to 4 percent, it can sell the bonds and make a $274,000 profit. Had it invested in one-year securities, its maximum profit would have been $19,000.

Because of the difficulty of accurately forecasting interest rates, many investors prefer to invest in short-term securities to minimize their risk. Short-term debt securities, such as commercial paper, are commonly called *money market instruments*. Long-term securities such as stocks and bonds are called *capital market instruments*.

Income Risk

Income risk refers to the risk of losing income when movements in bank borrowing and lending rates are not perfectly synchronized. In banking jargon, it is a dollar gap problem. *Dollar gap* refers to the difference between the dollar amounts of rate-sensitive assets and rate-sensitive liabilities.

Assets and liabilities may be classified as rate sensitive or nonrate sensitive, depending on their maturity and how often they are repriced. *Interest rate repricing* refers to the frequency with which the interest rate on an instrument is adjusted (e.g., 30 days, 60 days, 90 days). Assets and liabilities with one year or less to maturity are considered rate sensitive. Some longer-term assets also may be rate sensitive, depending on the terms and conditions of that particular security. For example, some certificates of deposit (CDs) that offer variable rates feature multistep or bonus-rate structures where the interest rates can change over time according to a preset structure. Other variable-rate CDs track the performance of a specified index, such as the Dow Jones Industrial Average.[7] It should be noted that there are caps on the interest rates on various deposit products that can be paid by banks that are "less than well capitalized." The FDIC publishes "Weekly National Rates and Rate Caps" on their web site.[8] Bank capitalization is discussed in Chapter 8.

Equally important, *brokered deposits* are deposits issued by a financial institution and purchased by an investor through a third-party intermediary called a deposit broker. They tend to be more interest rate sensitive than core deposits. *Core deposits* are defined in the Uniform Bank Performance Report (UBPR) user's guide as the sum of demand deposits, all negotiable orders of withdrawal (NOW), and automatic transfer service (ATS) accounts, money market deposit accounts (MMDA) savings, other savings deposits, and time deposits under $100,000.[9]

> *Between 1978 and 2005, the percentage of U.S. banks that were able to fund at least two-thirds of their total assets with core deposits fell from nearly 91 percent to 59 percent. In addition to the declining share of core deposits, banks are facing increased interest costs since bank customers are reacting to higher interest rates and moving their money out of lower-yielding bank accounts and into certificates of deposit and other higher-paying accounts. As a result of these developments, bank liability management demands more attention today than it did just a few years ago.*[10]

Other sources of wholesale funding include *federal funds*,[11] *Federal Home Loan Bank advances*,[12] and the Federal Reserve's *primary credit* program.[13]

UBPRs are created by bank regulators for supervisory, examination, and bank management purposes.[14] Table 4.1 shows a few of the liquidity ratios that appear in the report for Ally Bank,[15] which is part of GMAC Inc., the 15th largest bank holding company in the United States.[16] The report covers the operations of the bank and that of a comparable group of peer banks (shown as Peer Group (PG) in the table). *PGs* are based on asset size, number of full-service branches, location, and other factors. Ally Bank had total assets of $55.2 billion.

It also shows the percentile (PCT) for each item listed compared with the peers. For example, Ally Bank is in the 83rd percentile for short-term investments as a percent of total assets. In other words, only 17 percent of the banks in the same peer group have a higher percentage of short-term investments as a percent of total assets. Similarly, it is in the 12th percentile for core deposits and the 91st percentile for noncore funding.

The table also shows several liquidity ratios. For example, it shows that Ally Bank is dependent on brokered deposits and it is in the 91st percentile of its peer banks. However, it should be noted that the previously cited article, "Nowhere to Go but Up: Managing Interest Rate Risk in a Low-Rate Environment," revealed that the average noncore funding for all banks was about 38 percent in June 2009—particularly at institutions where long-term assets are more than 40 percent of total assets.[17]

Liquidity Risk

Liquidity refers to the ability to liquidate an asset quickly with little or no loss in market value and the ability to raise funds through the sale of an asset or by borrowing. *Liquidity risk* is the risk to earnings and capital

TABLE 4.1 UBPR Liquidity Ratios for Ally Bank, March 31, 2010

	Bank	PG 1	PCT
Percent of Total Assets			
Short-term investments	17.52	8.60	83
Marketable equity sec (MES)	0.01	0.05	53
Core deposits	45.87	61.50	12
Short-term noncore funding	39.78	20.07	91
Liquidity Ratios			
Net S.T. noncore fund dependence	29.49	12.82	88
Net noncore fund dependence	50.93	27.26	85
Brokered deposits to deposits	31.93	7.00	91
Broker dep mat < 1 year to broker deps	81.84	70.75	51
Short-term inv to S.T. Ncore fund	44.04	51.73	57
Short-term asset to S.T. liabilities	82.45	107.29	47
Net S.T. liabilities to assets	8.30	1.89	64
Net loans & leases to deposits	113.22	82.70	92
Net LN&LS to core deposits	136.70	101.87	89
Net LN&LS & SBLC to assets	62.71	64.04	42

Abbreviations:
Mat = maturity.
MES = marketable equity securities.
Net LN&LS = net loans and leases.
S.T. = short term.
SBLC = standby letters of credit.
Source: Uniform Bank Performance Report, Ally Bank March 31, 2010, https://cdr.ffiec.gov/public/Reports/UbprReport.aspx?rptCycleIds=60%2c54%2c58%2c52%2c47&rptid=283&idrssd=3284070.

related to a financial intermediary's ability to meet its financial obligations to depositors or borrowers. Sound practices of liquidity risk management include the following corporate governance issues:[18]

- Effective corporate governance consisting of oversight by the board of directors and active involvement by management in controlling the institution's interest rate risk.
- Appropriate strategies, polices, procedures, and limits to manage and mitigate interest rate risk.
- Comprehensive measurement and monitoring systems that are commensurate with the complexity and business activities of the institution.
- Active management of intraday liquidity and collateral.
- An appropriate diverse mix of existing and potential funding sources.

- Adequate levels of highly liquid marketable securities free of legal, regulatory, or operational impediments that can be used to meet liquidity needs in stressful situations.
- Comprehensive contingency funding plans that sufficiently address potential adverse liquidity events and emergency cash flow requirements.
- Internal controls and internal audit processes to determine the adequacy of the liquidity risk management processes.

Examples of Liquidity Risk According to Federal Reserve Chairman Ben Bernanke:

> *A panic is possible in any situation in which longer-term, illiquid assets are financed by short-term, liquid liabilities, and in which suppliers of short-term funding either lose confidence in the borrower or become worried that other short-term lenders may lose confidence. Although, in a certain sense, a panic may be collectively irrational, it may be entirely rational at the individual level, as each market participant has a strong incentive to be among the first to the exit. . . . But liquidity risk management at the level of the firm, no matter how carefully done, can never fully protect against systemic events. In a sufficiently severe panic, funding problems will almost certainly arise and are likely to spread in unexpected ways.*[19]

Bernanke also said: "Lenders in the commercial paper market, and other short-term money markets, like depositors in a bank, place the highest value on safety and liquidity. Should the safety of their investments come into question, it is easier and safer to withdraw funds—'run on the bank'—than to invest time and resources to evaluate in detail their investment is, in fact, safe.[20]

IKB

> *On July 30, 2007, IKB, a medium-sized German bank, announced that in order to meet its obligations, it would be receiving extraordinary support from its government-owned parent and an association of German banks. IKB's problem was that its Rhineland off-balance-sheet vehicle was no longer able to roll over the asset-backed commercial paper (ABCP) it had been issuing in U.S. markets to fund its large portfolio of asset-backed securities. Although none of the securities in the Rhineland portfolio was in default and only some were subprime-related, commercial paper investors had become concerned about IKB's ability to meet its obligations in the event that the securities Rhineland held were downgraded.*[21] *. . . lenders in the commercial paper market and other short-term money markets, like depositors in a bank, place the highest value on safety and liquidity.*[22]

IndyMac Bank In July 2008, California-based IndyMac Bank, with $32 billion in assets, became the second largest bank failure after Continental Illinois Bank with $40 billion in assets in 1984. IndyMac Bank specialized in Alt-A mortgage lending that didn't require borrowers to disclose their incomes. It experienced large losses as home prices fell and foreclosures increased. IndyMac's failure was attributed to a liquidity crisis due to a run on bank deposits. Office of Thrift Supervision (OTS) Director John Reich "singled out Sen. Charles E. Schumer (D-N.Y.) as having helped to fuel massive withdrawals. On June 26, Schumer said in letters to the FDIC, the OTS and two other federal agencies that IndyMac might have 'serious problems' with its loan holdings."[23] Depositors withdrew $1.3 billion in the 11 days following Schumer's comments.

Wachovia Bank Wachovia Bank ($782 billion in assets) was one of the largest banks to require government assistance. Technically, it did not fail, but it was purchased by Wells Fargo corporation.[24] "During the week of September 15th (2008), following the Lehman bankruptcy, Wachovia experienced significant deposit outflows totaling approximately $8.3 billion, representing a mix of deposit types, but primarily large commercial accounts.... Liquidity pressures on Wachovia increased the evening of September 25th when two regular Wachovia counterparties declined to lend to the firm.... Wachovia's situation worsened as deposit outflows on Friday accelerated to approximately $5.7 billion, $1.1 billion in asset-back commercial paper and tri-party repurchase agreements could not be rolled over, and $3.2 billion in contingent funding was required on Variable Rate Demand Notes. By the end of the day, Wachovia management informed bank regulators that with the lack of market acceptance of Wachovia's liabilities, the institution faced a near-term liquidity crisis."[25]

Fixed- versus Variable-Rate Loans

The terms *fixed-rate loans* and *variable-rate loans* confuse the issue of rate sensitivity. The maturity and frequency of repricing assets determines rate sensitivity. For example, fixed-rate overnight loans are rate-sensitive assets because they are repriced every day. By contrast, a variable-rate 30-year mortgage that resets the interest rates once every three years is not a rate-sensitive asset. Selected examples of both rate-sensitive and non-rate-sensitive assets and liabilities are shown in Table 4.2.

Repurchase Agreements

Repurchase agreements, or *repos,* are short-term contracts to sell and repurchase financial assets, such as Treasury securities, at a future date. The

TABLE 4.2 Interest Rate Repricing

Non-Rate-Sensitive	
Assets	**Liabilities/Equity**
Long-term fixed-rate commercial and industrial loans	Long-term time deposits
Long-term bonds	Fixed-rate notes and debentures
Fixed-rate mortgages	Equity capital
Rate Sensitive	
Assets	**Liabilities/Equity**
Floating-rate loans	Short-term time deposits
Federal funds sold	Federal funds purchased
Short-term securities	Other short-term variable-rate sources of funds

maturity of repo contracts ranges from overnight to two years. When the contract expires, the seller repurchases the securities at the price at which they were sold and pays interest (the repo rate) for the use of the funds. From the point of view of the institution buying the security, it is a *reverse repo*.

Repos are widely used by banks, money market funds, and other institutions to help manage their liquidity positions. They are also used by the Federal Reserve to provide funds and liquidity to financial institutions.[26] Repo rate is the interest rate at which central banks, such as the Federal Reserve, repurchase government securities from banks.

Basel III Liquidity Standards

The Basel Committee on Banking Supervision's revised bank capital rules (called Basel III) include minimum liquidity standards called the liquidity coverage ratio (LCR) that will be implemented during the 2013–2019 period.[27] The LCR requires banks to have "high quality liquid assets" that should be equal to or greater than their net cash outflows over 30 days. Net cash outflows are the expected cash inflows less cash outflows adjusted for stress conditions.

$$\text{LCR} = \frac{\text{Stock of high qualty liquid assets}}{\text{Net cash outflow over 30 days}} \geq 100\% \tag{4.1}$$

The high-quality liquid assets are divided into two tiers. Tier 1, the most liquid assets, include cash, central bank reserves, marketable securities, and government or central bank debt. Tier 2 liquid assets include high-quality corporate debt, covered bonds (subject to some adjustments), and government and public sector assets. Tier 2 assets can contribute no more than 40 percent of the LCR.

Basel III also includes a net stable funding ratio (NSFR) that requires bank's "available stable funding" should at least equal its "required stable funding."

$$\text{NSFR} = \frac{\text{Avalable amount of stable funding}}{\text{Required amount of stable funding}} \geq 100\% \quad (4.2)$$

THE EFFECTS OF INTEREST RATE RISK ON INCOME AND MARKET VALUE

Dollar Gap and Net Interest Income

In banking jargon, the *dollar gap* is the difference between rate-sensitive assets (RSA) and rate-sensitive liabilities (RSL) expressed in dollars.

$$\text{GAP} = \text{RSA} - \text{RSL} \quad (4.3)$$

The dollar gap is widely used as a measure of interest rate sensitivity. When RSA is greater than RSL, a bank is said to be positively gapped. When RSA is less than RSL, a bank is negatively gapped. The dollar amount of the gap times the change in interest rates (Δr) gives the change in net interest income. *Net interest income* (NII) is interest income less interest expense.

$$\Delta\text{NII} = \text{GAP} \times \Delta\text{r} \quad (4.4)$$

For example, if a bank had a negative gap of \$100 million, and interest rates increase by 50 basis points (+0.005), NII will decline by \$500,000. Notice that the dollar amount of the negative gap is preceded by a minus (−) sign. The symbol Δ means change.

$$\Delta\text{NII} = \text{GAP} \times \Delta\text{r}$$

$$-\$500{,}000 = -\$100{,}000{,}000 \times 0.005$$

TABLE 4.3 GAP, Changes in Interest Rates, and NII

GAP	Change in Interest Rates	Change in NII
Positive RSA > RSL	Increase	Increase
Positive RSA > RSL	Decrease	Decrease
Negative RSA < RSL	Increase	Decrease
Negative RSA < RSL	Decrease	Increase
Zero RSA = RSL	Increase	No change
Zero RSA = RSL	Decrease	No change

If interest rates had declined by 20 basis points (–0.002), NII would have increased $200,000.

$$\Delta NII = GAP \times \Delta r$$

$$\$200,000 = \$100,000,000 \times -0.002$$

The effects of changing interest rates on NII are summarized in Table 4.3. For banks with a positive gap, NII will rise or fall as interest rates increase or decrease. For banks with a negative gap, NII will increase or decrease inversely with changes in interest rates. Stated otherwise, if interest rates increase, NII will decrease. In contrast, interest rate changes do not affect the NII of banks with a zero gap.

Effects on Market Value

If we assume that the value of a bank is positively related to its net interest income, we can illustrate graphically the effects of changes in interest rates on bank market values. The top panel of Figure 4.3 shows the effects on interest rate changes on a bank that is positively gapped (RSA > RSL; the symbol > means greater than, and < means less than). If interest rates increase, the returns on assets will increase more than the cost of the liabilities, thereby increasing the net interest income. Consequently, the value of the bank will increase.

If interest rates decline, the cost of the liabilities will exceed the returns on the rate-sensitive assets, and net interest income will shrink. The market value of the bank can decline, and it can become insolvent.

The lower panel of Figure 4.3 illustrates the effects of changes in interest rates on a bank that is negatively gapped (RSA < RSL). If interest rates increase, the market value of the negatively gapped bank will decline because

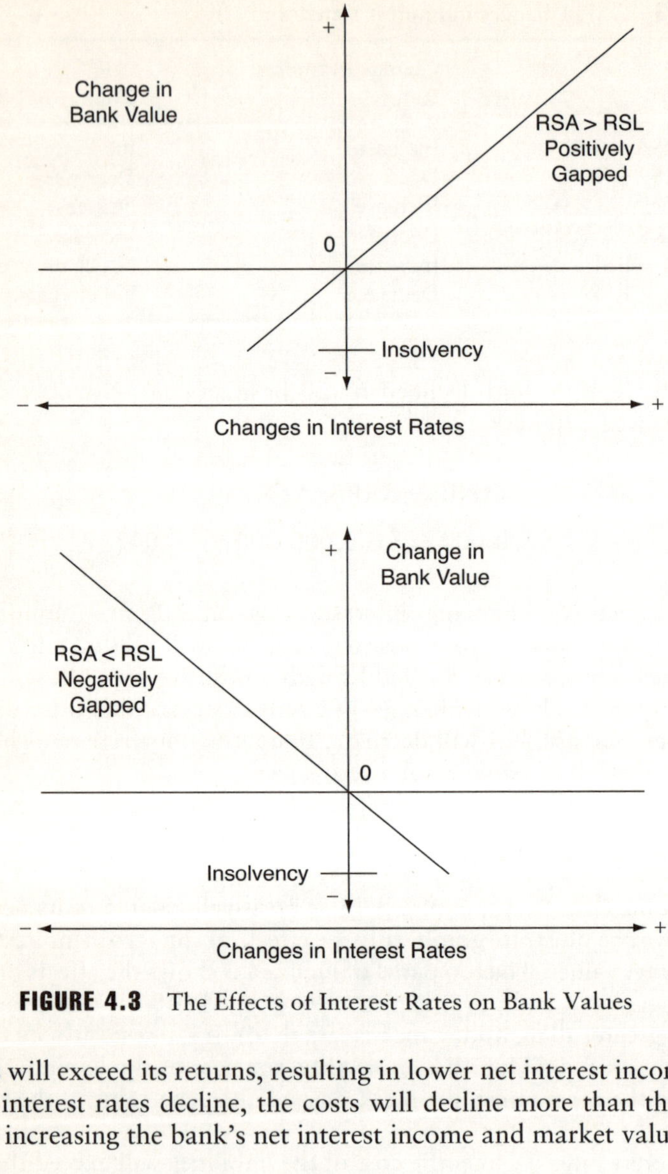

FIGURE 4.3 The Effects of Interest Rates on Bank Values

its costs will exceed its returns, resulting in lower net interest income. However, if interest rates decline, the costs will decline more than the returns, thereby increasing the bank's net interest income and market value.

MANAGING INTEREST RATE SPREADS

Interest rate risk affects net interest income and the value of banks. For banks that are positively gapped, an increase in interest rates results in

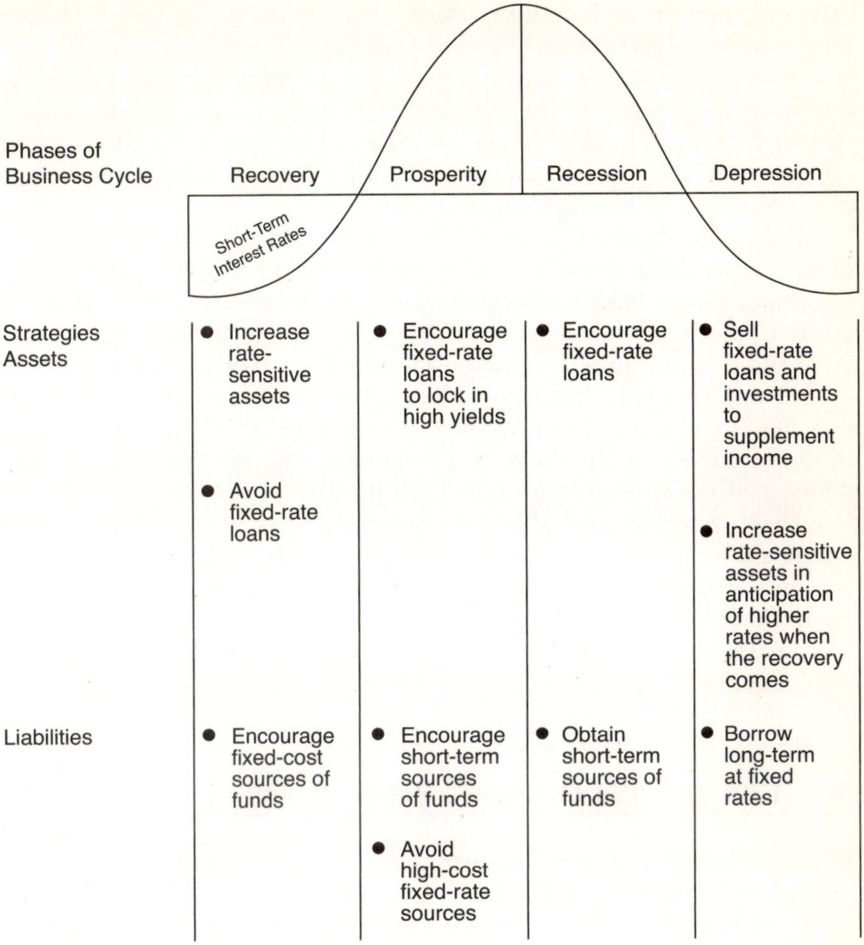

FIGURE 4.4 Spread Management Strategies

higher incomes and values. For banks that are negatively gapped, the reverse is true. This suggests that if banks gap correctly, they can increase incomes and values.

Recall from Figure 4.1 that short-term rates typically increased before the business cycles peaked, and then they declined (shown as the shaded area). Similarly, Figure 4.4 shows one possible path of short-term interest rates over the course of a business cycle.[28] During the recovery phase of the business cycle, short-term interest rates are expected to increase as business concerns borrow more for inventories and capital expansion. The rate of increase tapers off during the prosperity phase of the business cycle. Interest rates peak and then decline. During the recession, borrowers reduce their inventories, repay loans, and delay capital expenditures. Rates decline further during the final phase of the business cycle. Then the process starts again. Although this is a simplified version of what actually happens to interest rates over the course of a business cycle, it provides a useful framework for examining spread management strategies.

During the recovery phase of the business cycle, banks should increase their rate-sensitive assets and attempt to lock in longer-term fixed-rate sources of funds. Stated otherwise, they should be positively gapped. The positive gap should be the largest during the recovery phase of the business cycle and diminish in size as the business cycle matures. At the peak of the cycle, banks should lock in high-yield fixed-rate loans and obtain short-term variable-rate sources of funds. They should be negatively gapped. The size of the negative gap should be the greatest during the recession and then diminish as the cycle bottoms out. Then the process starts again.

These strategies work if interest rates behave as expected and the loans are repaid on schedule. The key word is *if*. As previously noted and shown in Figure 4.1, interest rates were at record lows in early 2010, and they will go up. The questions at that time were: (1) When will they go up? (2) How much will they go up? and (3) Will it be a parallel or nonparallel shift in the yield curve?

DURATION GAP AND ECONOMIC VALUE OF EQUITY

While the dollar gap analysis focuses on a bank's short-term net interest income, the duration gap takes a longer view and focuses on the economic value of equity. *Duration* is defined as the weighted average time to maturity to receive all cash flows from a financial instrument. Time is measured in terms of years and months.

Duration is a widely used measure of interest rate sensitivity. The concept of duration originated in 1938, when Frederick R. Macaulay wanted an alternative to the term to maturity for measuring a bond's life.[29] Duration is the weighted average time to maturity of the present value of all cash flows received from bonds, stocks, or the financial assets. For example, the duration of bonds that can be approximated by the following equation:

$$D = n - \frac{C[n - (1 + r)PVAIF_{r,n}}{P_0 \times r} \tag{4.5}$$

Where: D = duration in years
C = annual income ($) from bonds
n = number of years to maturity
r = rate of return, yield to maturity
P_0 = current market price of the bond
$PVAIF_{r,n}$ = present value of an annuity interest factor at a certain rate r for n years

Because it is cumbersome to calculate by hand, not much was done with it until calculators and computers could determine durations quickly. Today, it is widely used by academics, practitioners, and bank regulators as a means of reducing interest rate risk.

The maturity of a financial instrument does not account for the differences in cash flows. For example, the cash flow from a 20-year bond that pays 8 percent interest semiannually is different than the cash flow from a zero coupon bond that only pays the principal amount at maturity and has no periodic interest payments. As shown Table 4.4, the duration of the 20-year zero coupon bond is 20 years, while the duration of a 20-year bond that pays 8 percent interest semiannually is 10.29 years. The logic behind this is that all of the cash flows from the zero coupon bond ($1,000) are received at maturity, while interest payments ($1,600) over the life of the bond account for 62 percent of the total cash flows ($2,600) from the 8 percent bond are paid out.

Table 4.4 also shows the following:

Except for zero coupon bonds, duration is always less than the term to maturity.

For bonds with the same maturity, those with high coupon yields have shorter durations than those with lower coupon yields.

TABLE 4.4 Bond Durations for Selected Interest Rates and Maturities

Years to Maturity	0%	4%	6%	8%	10%	12%
1	1.00	0.99	0.99	0.98	0.98	0.97
5	5.00	4.99	4.39	4.22	4.05	3.90
10	10.00	8.34	7.56	7.07	6.54	6.08
20	20.00	13.95	11.90	10.29	9.01	7.97
40	40.00	20.27	15.55	12.44	10.29	8.75
50	50.00	21.98	16.27	12.74	10.42	8.81

Compounded semiannually. Assumes that the coupon and market yields are the same.

Longer terms to maturity generally mean longer durations.

Duration is inversely related to market yields.

The *duration gap* compares the effects of changes in interest rates on the duration of a bank's assets and liabilities to determine the economic value of stockholders' equity. The *economic value* is the theoretical value of the bank's equity, taking into account the duration of both the assets and liabilities. It is *not* the market value of the equity. The duration gap is equal to:

$$\text{DGAP} = \text{DA} - \text{WDL} \tag{4.6}$$

where: DGAP = Duration gap
DA = Average duration of assets
DL = Average duration of liabilities
W = Ratio of total liabilities to total assets

Suppose that the duration of a bank's assets is 4 years, the duration of its liabilities is 2 years, and the ratio of assets to liabilities is 90 percent. Using equation 4.5, the duration gap is 2.2 years.

$$\begin{aligned}\text{DGAP} &= 4.0 - (0.9)(2.0)\\ &= 2.2 \text{ years}\end{aligned}$$

Equation 4.7 gives an approximation for the expected change in the economic value of the equity relative to the total assets (A) for a given change in interest rates.

$$\$\Delta \text{ Net Worth} \cong -DGAP\frac{\Delta t}{1+i} \times \text{A} \tag{4.7}$$

where: DGAP = Duration gap
A = Total assets
i = Market rate of interest

Suppose that the current rate of interest is 7 percent and it is expected to increase by 100 basis points (1 percentage point) to 8 percent. Using

TABLE 4.5 Duration Gap, Change in Interest Rates, and Change in Equity

Duration Gap	Change in interest Rates	Change in Equity
Positive	Increase	Decrease
Positive	Decrease	Increase
Negative	Increase	Increase
Negative	Decrease	Decrease
Zero	Increase	No change
Zero	Decrease	No change

equation 4.4, we can determine the dollar amount of the change in net worth. The bank has total assets (A) of $100 million:

$$\$\Delta \text{ Net Worth} \cong (-2.2)\frac{1}{1.07} \times A \cong -2.06 \times \$100 \text{ million} = -\$2{,}060{,}000$$

The economic value of the bank's equity will decline by $2.06 million.

DURATION GAP MANAGEMENT STRATEGIES

Table 4.5 summarizes how the duration gap and changes in market rates of interest have an impact on a bank's equity. If the duration gap is positive and interest rates increase, the value of the equity will decline. Conversely, if the duration gap is positive and interest rates decrease, the value of the equity will increase. When the duration gap is negative, an increase in interest rates results in an increase in equity, while a decrease in rates results in a decrease in equity.

Immunization

Immunization occurs when the duration of a bank's assets and liabilities is equal to zero. Immunization protects the value of equity from changes in market rates of interest.

Duration Has Limitations

Duration is a useful tool for ALM, but it has limitations because of these issues:

- **Embedded Options:** The exercise of embedded options by bank customers can influence the duration of assets and liabilities. For example, the prepayment of loans can shorten the duration of loans. Similarly, deposits that are withdrawn before maturity will shorten the duration of deposits. Some bonds have call features that allow them to be called before maturity, which will shorten their duration if called.

- **Nonparallel Shifts in the Yield Curve:** Although not shown in the table, it is difficult to determine the interest-rate sensitivity of a bank's assets and liabilities when there is a nonparallel shift in the yield curve. It also follows that such shifts will change the bank's cost of funds and returns on invested assets.
- **Duration Drift:** Every day, bonds come closer to maturity. Similarly, the duration of debt instruments changes over time. Therefore, the durations of portfolios of assets and liabilities must be recalculated periodically to account for the duration drift.
- **Problem Loans:** It is difficult to estimate the duration of problem loans that do not earn income or pay interest.

Earnings Simulation Models and Stress Testing

Simulations are computer-generated scenarios about the future that permit banks to analyze interest rate risk and business strategies in a static or dynamic framework. The dynamic simulation techniques have the advantage that they can be used to simulate the effects of changes in interest rates and other variables such as lines of business, consumer behavior, and other inputs over different time horizons on balance sheets and income statements.[30] The data for the scenarios may include both historical data and what-if data. For example, what would be the effects of a prolonged 300- to 400-basis-point increase and a nonparallel shift in the yield curve on a bank's economic value? What if the interest rate shock was temporary? Analysis of such scenarios is part of good interest rate risk and capital management.

In 2009, The Basel Committee on Banking Supervision at the Bank for International Settlements (BIS) issued *Principles for Sound Stress Testing Practices and Supervision*.[31] Stress testing is a critical tool used by banks as part of their internal risk management and capital planning. The guidance sets out a comprehensive set of principles for the sound governance, design, and implementation of stress testing programs at banks. The report states that "stress testing . . . plays a particularly important role in:

- Providing forward-looking assessments of risk.
- Overcoming limitations of models and historical data.
- Supporting internal and external communication.
- Feeding into capital and liquidity planning procedures.
- Informing the setting of a bank's risk tolerance.

- Facilitating the development of risk mitigation or contingency plans across a range of stressed conditions."

The BIS report goes on to explain why stress testing is important in the context of the financial crises that began in 2007:

> *At the outset of the crisis, mortgage default shocks played a part in the deterioration of market prices of collateralised debt obligations (CDOs). Simultaneously, these shocks revealed deficiencies in the models used to manage and price these products. The complexity and resulting lack of transparency led to uncertainty about the value of the underlying investment. Market participants then drastically scaled down their activity in the origination and distribution markets and liquidity disappeared. The standstill in the securitization markets forced banks to warehouse loans that were intended to be sold in the secondary markets. Given a lack of transparency of the ultimate ownership of troubled investments, funding liquidity concerns were triggered within the banking sector as banks refused to provide sufficient funds to each other. This in turn led to the hoarding of liquidity, exacerbating further the funding pressures within the banking sector. The initial difficulties in subprime mortgages also fed through to a broader range of market instruments since the drying up of market and funding liquidity forced market participants to liquidate those positions which they could trade in order to scale back risk. An increase in risk aversion also led to a general flight to quality, an example of which was the high withdrawals by households from money market funds.*[32]

CHAPTER 5

Hedging and Risk Management

DERIVATIVES

Chapter 4 examined the interest rate and price risks associated with bank asset/liability management. This chapter examines how to hedge against those risks. The term *hedging* refers to trades used to reduce risk. Hedgers include financial institutions, commercial producers, processors, and users of agricultural commodities. The trades involve a variety of financial instruments, they take different forms of execution, and they have a lot of confusing terminology.

For example, hedges involve derivatives. A *derivative* is a financial contract whose value is derived from the performance of underlying market factors, such as interest rates, currency exchange rates, commodity, credit, and equity prices. Derivative transactions include a wide assortment of financial contracts, including structured debt obligations and deposits, swaps, futures, options, caps, floors, collars, forwards, and various combinations thereof.[1] Derivatives can be used to short risk to hedge, to reduce risk, or to speculate. These terms and others are explained as needed in the chapter. Because of the complexity of using derivatives and hedging, the intent of this chapter is to provide an introduction to the tools and concepts used in hedging. Additional educational resources are cited at the end of the chapter.

Speculators are traders who attempt to profit by anticipating the prices of financial instruments and commodities. By doing so, speculators and traders facilitate hedging by providing liquidity and price information to the markets.

At the end of 2009, there were 6,839 Federal Deposit Insurance Corporation (FDIC)-insured commercial banks in the United States.[2] Of that total, only 1,030 U.S. commercial banks reported derivatives activities.[3] As shown in Table 5.1, derivative activities were dominated by five large commercial banks that account for 96 percent of the total banking industry

TABLE 5.1 Notional Amounts of Derivative Contracts Held for Trading, Top 5 Commercial Banks and Trust Companies in Derivatives, June 30, 2010

Rank	Bank Name	Total Assets ($ millions)	Total Derivatives ($ millions)
1	JPMorgan Chase Bank NA	$ 1,568,093	$ 75,253,921
2	Bank of America NA	1,518,958	48,520,921
3	Citibank National Assn	1,157,877	45,990,989
4	Goldman Sachs Bank USA	95,515	42,087,305
5	HSBC Bank USA National Assn.	181,595	3,682,856
Total		$ 4,524,038	$215,535,430
	Other banks with derivatives	$ 5,945,572	$ 7,840,804
Total	All banks with derivatives	$10,469,610	$223,376,234

Source: Office of the Comptroller of the Currency, "OCC's Quarterly Report on Bank Trading and Derivatives Activities," Second Quarter 2010, Table 1.

notional amounts. The *notional amount* is the nominal or face amount that is used to calculate payments made on swaps and other risk management products. The term *notional* is used because the principal amounts rarely change hands.

RISKS ASSOCIATED WITH DERIVATIVES

Financial institutions and others use derivatives for (1) hedging, (2) reducing overall risk, (3) speculating, (4) price discovery, (5) obtaining better financial terms, and (6) changing the asset mix of their portfolios.[4]

Hedgers protect the value of their assets or liabilities by using derivative transactions whose values are expected to change in the opposite direction of their assets or liabilities. In other words, if the value of their asset declines, the decline will be offset by the increased value of the derivative product.

Speculators use derivatives to take advantage of anticipated price changes in interest rates, mortgages, commodities, and so on. As previously noted, they are essential in providing liquidity in the markets.

Derivatives can also be a lower-cost way to invest funds than buying for cash. For example, instead of buying $100,000 worth of U.S. Treasury bonds, an institution can buy a call option for a fraction of that price. It gives them the right to buy those bonds for a certain period of time if it is profitable to do so.

Although derivatives can be used to reduce risk, they are not risk-free. Those using derivatives should have knowledge and expertise in these instruments and be aware of the risks. The following comments on this issue are taken from the "OCC's Quarterly Report on Bank Trading and Derivatives Activities" (2009). They are intended to introduce the concepts, but they do not provide the details needed to measure and deal with credit risk, market risk, and other risks associated with derivatives. For example, one of the risks is that derivatives transactions are generally highly levered, which can result in large gains or in large losses.[5] Therefore, the FDIC states that institutions should have internal control systems covering all aspects of risk management, including validation of the models and financial instruments being used.[6] The risks include, but are not limited to, the following.

Credit Risk

> *Credit risk is a significant risk in bank derivatives trading activities. The notional amount of a derivative contract is a reference amount from which contractual payments will be derived, but it is generally not an amount at risk. The credit risk in a derivative contract is a function of a number of variables, such as whether counterparties exchange notional principal, the volatility of the underlying market factors (interest rate, currency, commodity, equity, or corporate reference entity), the maturity and liquidity of contract, and the creditworthiness of the counterparty.*
>
> *Credit risk in derivatives differs from credit risk in loans due to the more uncertain nature of the potential credit exposure. With a funded loan, the amount at risk is the amount advanced to the borrower. The credit risk is unilateral; the bank faces the credit exposure of the borrower. However, in most derivatives transactions, such as swaps (which make up the bulk of bank derivatives contracts), the credit exposure is bilateral. Each party to the contract may (and, if the contract has a long enough tenure, probably will) have a current credit exposure to the other party at various points in time over the contract's life. Moreover, because the credit exposure is a function of movements in market factors, banks do not know, and can only estimate, how much the value of the derivative contract might be at various points of time in the future.*[7]

Sometimes credit risk is referred to as *counterparty risk* that stems from the creditworthiness of banks, broker-dealers, and other financial institutions that fail to deliver on their over-the-counter (OTC) derivative obligations. There is a risk to the financial system if one or more banks or broker-dealers fail. Such failures could have a cascading effect in the market.[8] Stated otherwise, the failure of one large bank may contribute to the failure of additional banks. This was the case for Continental Illinois National Bank and Trust Company in Chicago in 1984. Comptroller of the Currency Todd Conover declared before a congressional committee that it was "too big to fail."[9] Bank regulators were concerned that Continental's problems might spread to more than 1,000 other banks that had deposits and/or federal funds there and that they, too, might fail if Continental failed. Similar concerns were expressed by the Federal Reserve in 2008 in connection with the failure of Bear Stearns. It was too interconnected to be allowed to fail. Contagion would have resulted, necessitating drastic action.[10]

Market Risk

> *Banks control market risk in trading operations primarily by establishing limits against potential losses.* Value at Risk (VaR) *is a statistical measure that banks use to quantify the maximum expected loss, over a specified horizon and at a certain confidence level, in normal markets. It is important to emphasize that VaR is not the maximum potential loss; it provides a loss estimate at a specified confidence level. A VaR of $50 million at 99 percent confidence measured over one trading day, for example, indicates that a trading loss of greater than $50 million in the next day on that portfolio should occur only once in every 100 trading days under normal market conditions. Since VaR does not measure the maximum potential loss, banks stress test trading portfolios to assess the potential for loss beyond the VaR measure. Banks and supervisors have been working to expand the use of stress analyses to complement the VaR risk measurement process that is typically used when assessing a bank's exposure to market risk.*[11]

Basis Risk

Basis is the difference between the spot or cash price of a commodity and the price of the nearest futures contract for the same or a related commodity (typically calculated as cash minus futures). Basis is usually computed in relation to the futures contract next to expire and may reflect different time periods, product forms, grades, or locations. *Basis risk* is the risk associated with an unexpected widening or narrowing of the basis between the time a hedge position is established and the time that it is lifted.[12]

DERIVATIVE CONTRACTS BY PRODUCT AND TYPE

Table 5.2 shows the derivative contracts by product and type. The data reveal that interest rate swaps are the most widely used contracts. In terms of products, the interest rates swaps are followed by options and futures, which are followed by options and futures contracts used mainly for foreign exchange and credit derivatives. These products are defined in the remainder of this section.[13]

Futures and Forwards

Futures are standardized contracts for the purchase and sale of financial instruments or physical commodities for future delivery on a regulated commodity futures exchange. Forwards are private, cash-market agreements between a buyer and seller for the future delivery of a commodity at an agreed price. In contrast with futures contracts, forward contracts are not standardized and not transferable.

Swaps

Swaps refer to the simultaneous purchase and sale of currencies or interest rate products in spot and forward market transactions.[14] The *spot market*

TABLE 5.2 Derivative Contracts by Product and Type, Second Quarter, 2010

Product	Notional Amounts ($ billions)
Futures and forwards	$ 36,790
Swaps	141,410
Options	31,301
Credit derivatives	13,876
Total	$223,376
Type	
Interest rate	$188,596
Foreign exchange	18,207
Equities	1,615
Commodities	1,093
Credit derivatives	13,876
Total	$223,376

Source: Office of the Comptroller of the Currency, "OCC's Quarterly Report on Bank Trading and Derivatives Activities Second Quarter 2010," Graphs 2 and 3. www.occ.treas.gov/topics/capital-markets/financial-markets/trading/derivatives/dq210.pdf.

is the market in which cash transactions for the physical commodity occur; currencies, stocks, and the like are bought and sold for cash and delivered immediately. The *forward market* refers to future delivery. Swaps contracts are traded over the counter. The most common plain vanilla interest rate swap is one party undertaking payments linked to a short-term floating interest rate index, such as the London Inter-Bank Offered Rate (LIBOR), and receiving a stream of fixed interest payments; the other counterparty undertakes the opposite set of transactions.

Options

Options are contracts that give the bearer the right, but not the obligation, to be long or short on a futures contract at a specified price within a specified time period. The specified price is called the *strike price*. The futures contract that the long may establish by exercising the option is referred to as the underlying futures contract.

Credit Derivatives

Credit derivatives are contractual agreements designed to shift credit risk between parties. They were originally used primarily by banks to hedge and diversify the credit risk of their customers in the event they could not pay back their loans. In most basic terms, a *credit default swap* is similar to an insurance contract, providing the buyer, usually a debt holder, with protection against the borrower not repaying the debt.

HEDGING WITH INTEREST RATE SWAPS

As shown in Table 5.2, interest rate swaps are the derivative product most widely used by banks and others.[15] To illustrate the use of interest rate spreads, consider ABC Bank that has a portfolio of fixed-rate loans that are funded primarily with short-term deposits. In other words, ABC Bank has a negative dollar gap. As explained in Chapter 4, a negative gap means that rate-sensitive liabilities exceed rate-sensitive assets (RSA < RSL). If market rates of interest increase, the bank's cost of borrowing will increase faster than the returns from the fixed-rate loans, resulting in reduced net interest margins (NIMs) and lower earnings.

To reduce its interest rate risk, ABC Bank can hedge by entering into a $10 million interest rate swap with XYZ Bank, which has a positive dollar gap (RSA > RSL). ABC Bank agrees to exchange a predetermined stream of fixed-rate interest payments at 8 percent to XYZ Bank for the next two years. Swap contracts have varying maturities, ranging from 1 to 30 years.

XYZ Bank agrees to pay ABC Bank a stream of interest payments based on a floating rate of interest such as LIBOR, the interest rate that highly rated banks (AA rating and above) charge each other for short-term loans. It is also the rate paid on *eurodollars* (ED)—U.S. dollar deposits placed with banks outside the United States. In this example, XYZ Bank will pay LIBOR plus 1 percent.

The bank that receives the fixed-rate stream of payments and pays the floating rate is the receiver. On the other side of the transaction, the bank that receives the floating rate in exchange for the fixed rate is the payer. Both the receiver and the payer are counterparties. Thus, ABC Bank is the receiver, and the counterparty XYZ Bank is the payer.

If market rates of interest increase, the interest rate swap agreement will provide ABC Bank with increased interest income, allowing it to reduce its interest rate risk. On the other side of the transaction, the interest rate swap will help to lock in XYZ bank's NIM.

In review:

ABC Bank pays an 8 percent fixed rate per annum to XYZ Bank based on a $10 million notional amount ($10,000,000 × 0.08 = $800,000/year for two years).

XYZ Bank pays a floating rate, LIBOR +1 percent, to ABC Bank, based on a $10 million notional amount. Assume that the current LIBOR rate is 6.5 percent ($10,000,000 × 0.065 = $650,000/year; LIBOR rates can change over time). Swap contracts are commonly netted against each other, so ABC Bank will pay XYZ Bank $150,000.

In this example, the counterparties were banks. They could have been speculators, corporations, or other types of financial institutions.

As previously noted, interest rate swaps are traded OTC. When swaps are initiated, the *swap rate* is the fixed interest rate that the receiver gets in exchange for the uncertainty of paying a floating rate (LIBOR) over time. The value of the swap's fixed-rate flows is called the *swap spread,* which is the difference between the swap rate and the government bond yields for the same maturity. As market conditions change over time, so will the value of swaps.

Swap spreads turned negative in March 2010 "amid rising demand for higher-yielding assets such as corporate and emerging market securities."[16] As shown in Table 5.3, selected spreads remained negative for several months. Explanations for the negative swap spread include the Lehman Brothers bankruptcy leading to the termination of contracts, expectations

TABLE 5.3 Swap Rates and Spreads

Years	Swap Rates	Treasury Rates, Constant Maturity	Swap Spread
1	0.72	0.36	0.0072
2	1.12	0.81	0.31
3	1.58	1.30	0.28
4	2.04	2.20	−0.16
5	2.42	2.90	−0.48
7	2.99	3.47	−0.48
10	3.47	4.17	−0.70
30	4.13	4.35	−0.22

Sources: Federal Reserve Statistical Release H.15, "Selected Interest Rates (Daily)," May 18, 2010, www.federalreserve.gov/releases/h15/update/.

that long-term rates might stay lower for a longer period of time than had been previously anticipated, turmoil in financial markets, and concerns about government creditworthiness in the face of large deficits.

HEDGING WITH CURRENCY SWAPS

A currency swap is a long-term agreement between counterparties to exchange principal and periodic interest payments in different currencies (e.g., foreign exchange) during the life of the contract. The principal amounts are usually exchanged at the beginning and end of the contract and are based on the current cash price (i.e., *spot rate*) of the currencies. The ratio of the currency amounts to be paid at the expiration of the currency swap is called the *forward price*. A currency swap is one type of foreign exchange derivative. Options and futures can also be used for foreign exchange trades.

The following is an example of a currency swap:[17] Company D borrows $25m (when $25m = £14m) at 6 percent fixed interest payable quarterly in arrears for two years. To hedge against any exchange loss should sterling depreciate against the dollar, it enters into a swap agreement with a bank. Under the agreement, there is either a notional or actual initial exchange of $25m for £14m. In addition, Company D agrees to pay quarterly to the bank a sum equal to 8 percent of £14m. The bank agrees to pay quarterly to Company D a sum equal to 6 percent of $25m.

The effect of the swap agreement is that Company D has converted its borrowing to a sterling loan of £14m at 8 percent.

If, for example, the first payments were made when £1 = \$1.6, then Company D will pay to the bank £14m × 8 percent × $\frac{1}{4}$ = £280,000 and will receive from the bank (\$25m × 6 percent × $\frac{1}{4}$ @ 1.6 = £234,375.

In practice, only a net sum of £45,625 (£280,000 less £234,375) may be paid by Company D to the bank.

As part of the swap agreement, the principal amounts are exchanged at the end of the two-year period. Company D pays the bank £14m in exchange for \$25m that it uses to pay off its borrowing. In effect, Company D has entered into a forward contract to acquire \$25m for £14m.

Credit Default Swaps

A *credit default swap* (CDS) is a bilateral financial contract in which a buyer seeking protection on loans or other assets makes periodic payments to a seller who is offering financial protection if a predefined *credit event* (e.g., default on a loan, bankruptcy, debt restructuring) occurs. A CDS covering multiple credit default events is called a *basket swap*. *Naked credit default swaps* are swaps in which the holder has no risk of financial loss if the underlying security fails. A naked CDS allows traders to speculate by buying insurance on corporate or government bonds that they do not own. Credit default swaps provide lenders with a form of insurance, and they provide sellers with a source of income.

A CDS does not eliminate the risks associated with lending for the buyer. But they are a form of hedging, and they transfer the risk to the seller. Nevertheless, there is the risk to the buyer that the seller of the CDS contract may default. This was a major concern in 2008 with the near-failure of American International Group, better known as AIG. As the largest insurance company in the United States, AIG was a major buyer of CDSs, which accounted for a large part of AIG's assets.[18]

> *AIG collapsed because collateral obligations embedded in the CDSs it wrote triggered a chain reaction that drained it of cash. Unable to raise funds in the private markets or quickly sell off some of its trillion dollars in assets, AIG was forced to accept a government bailout. In hindsight, it is easy to conclude that AIG should have never gotten into the CDS business, or at least not written the \$61.4 billion of CDSs on multi-sector Collateralized Debt Obligations (CDOs) with subprime mortgage loan exposure. Ultimately, however, AIG took a calculated business risk that turned out disastrous.*[19]

CDOs are a type of structured asset-backed security (ABS) whose value and payments are derived from a portfolio of fixed-income underlying assets.

The portfolio is divided into different risk classes and maturities called *tranches* or *slices*.

Securitization

The counterparty to the derivative contract could be either an investment bank or an insurance company, or it could be the capital markets through the process of securitization—the packaging and selling of loans, such as mortgages (mortgage-backed securities, (MBSs)) and credit card loans. In most cases, securitization of credit derivatives transfers the credit risk to the capital markets. Alan Greenspan, former chairman of the Board of Governors of the Federal Reserve System, testified before Congress: "It was the global proliferation of securitized U.S. subprime mortgages that was the immediate trigger of the current crisis" that began in 2007.[20]

Until the late 1990s, most securitizations of mortgage loans conformed to the underwriting standards of the government-sponsored agencies (GSEs) Fannie Mae and Freddie Mac.[21] These two GSEs were chartered by the federal government to support the secondary market for residential mortgages. In contrast, Ginnie Mae does not buy or sell loans or issue MBSs. However, it guarantees investors the timely payment of principal and interest on MBSs backed by federally insured or guaranteed loans—loans insured by the Federal Housing Administration (FHA) or guaranteed by the Department of Veterans Affairs (VA), the Department of Agriculture's Rural Housing Service (RHS), or the Department of Housing and Urban Development's Office of Public and Indian Housing (PIH). Ginnie Mae securities are the *only* MBSs that are guaranteed by the U.S. government.[22]

Subsequently, nonagency (private-label) MBSs issued by brokerage firms, banks, and others became widespread.[23] Fannie Mae and Freddie Mac were among the biggest buyers of subprime and Alt-A securitized mortgages. Alt-A *loans* have some characteristics of prime loans, but they lack full documentation of income and wealth. They are riskier than mortgages that are prime rated but less risky than subprime mortgages.

HEDGING WITH OPTIONS

Options are contracts that give the bearer the right, but not the obligation, to be *long* (own) or *short* (promise to sell) a futures contract on a security or commodity at a specified price within a specified time period. The option buyer pays a *premium* to the seller for the right to buy (a *call option*) or to sell (a *put option*) the underlying asset at an agreed price (strike or exercise price) until the contract expires (*expiry*). In *European-style* put and call options, the holder can exercise the option only on the last business day before the expiration date. Interest rate options are settled for cash, rather than the delivery of a security.

Interest rate options are options on the spot yields of U.S. Treasury securities.[24] They are based on the underlying values of short-, medium-, and long-term interest rates on U.S. Treasury securities. The following option contracts are traded on the Chicago Board Options Exchange (CBOE): short-term options based on the annualized discount rate on the most recently auctioned 13-week Treasury bill (ticker symbol IRX), intermediate-term options based on the yield to maturity of the most recently auctioned 5-year Treasury note (ticker symbol FVX), longer-term options based on the yield to maturity of the most recently auctioned 10-year Treasury note (ticker symbol TNX), and long-term options based on the yield to maturity of the most recently auctioned 30-year Treasury bond (ticker symbol TYX).

Keep in mind that bond prices move inversely with market rates of interest. If interest rates increase, bond prices decrease, and vice versa. Therefore, the holder of a yield-based call option holder will profit only if the underlying interest rate rises above the strike price plus the premium paid for the call. Similarly, the holder of a yield-based put option holder will profit only if the interest rate has declined below the strike price less the premium. These options can be exercised only at expiration. Finally, interest rate options are settled for cash rather than the delivery of a security.

Suppose that a bank has a positive dollar gap, which means that interest rate-sensitive assets are greater than rate-sensitive liabilities. If market interest rates increase, the bank's net interest margin (NIM) will increase. Conversely, if interest rates decline, the bank's NIM will decline. To hedge against falling interest rates, the bank can buy call options on Treasury securities if interest rates decline instead of increasing; the bank would lose in the cash or spot market, but the gain from its option position will completely or partially offset the loss. If interest rates increase, the higher net interest income will be reduced by the cost of the option premium.

HEDGING WITH FUTURES

The term *futures* refers to standardized contracts for the purchase and sale of financial instruments or physical commodities for future delivery on a regulated commodity futures exchange. Futures contracts are based on interest rates, equity indexes, foreign exchange, energy, agricultural commodities, metals, weather, and real estate. Although the primary focus here is on financial futures, it should be noted that banks also participate in other types of futures.[25] Futures can be used for hedging, speculation, and asset allocation. The principal commodities exchanges in the United States where futures are traded are operated by the CME Group.[26] They include the Chicago Mercantile Exchange (CME), Chicago Board of Trade (CBOT), New York Mercantile Exchange (NYMEX), and the Commodity Exchange (COMEX).

The commodity futures and options markets in the United States are regulated by the Commodity Futures Trading Commission (CFTC). The CFTC's mission is to protect market users and the public from fraud, manipulation, and abusive practices related to the sale of commodity and financial futures and options and to foster open, competitive, and financially sound futures and option markets.[27]

Each commodity traded in the futures market has unique contract specifications. Table 5.4 shows the contract specifications for the five-year U.S. Treasury note futures that are traded on the CBOT. Futures contracts based on U.S. Treasury securities are not obligations of the U.S. government. The basic trading unit has a face value (*par*) at maturity of \$100,000. Prices are quoted as a percentage of par; accordingly, 100 means 100 percent of par. A price of 98-16 means 98 and $^{16}/_{32}$ (98.5) percent of par. Each $^{1}/_{32}$ of a point is worth \$31.25 per contract (\$100,000 ÷ 100 ÷ 32 = \$31.25). The prices reflect current and expected levels of interest rates.

Similarly, Table 5.5 shows the contract specifications for three-month overnight index swap (OIS) futures. It can be used to hedge longer-term OIS exposures. A close examination of the contract specifications reveals significant differences between the underlying units, deliverable grades, price quotations, and other terms.[28] Stated otherwise, there are substantial differences between the futures contracts of the various commodities that are traded. It is essential to understand those details before trading them. There is a saying that the devil is in the details.

Futures contracts and contracts to buy and sell for cash differ in the following four respects:

1. Futures contracts specify standardized qualities and quantities while cash transactions can be for any quantity or quality of a commodity. Hedgers who use Treasury futures chiefly to minimize interest rate risk are seldom interested in using futures as a means of buying Treasury securities. They typically liquidate their outstanding futures positions before the contracts require delivery and buy new contracts to maintain their positions. The practice of rolling over contracts is so widespread that only about 4 percent of Treasury futures are delivered.[29] The deliverable grade Treasury notes and bonds are debt instruments backed by

TABLE 5.4 Contract Specifications for Five-Year U.S. Treasury Note Futures

Underlying Unit	One U.S. Treasury note having a face value at maturity of $100,000.	
Deliverable Grades	U.S. Treasury notes with an original term to maturity of not more than five years and three months and a remaining term to maturity of not less than four years and two months as of the first day of the delivery month. The invoice price equals the futures settlement price times a conversion factor, plus accrued interest. The conversion factor is the price of the delivered note ($1 par value) to yield 6 percent.	
Price Quote	Points ($1,000) and quarters of $^1/_{32}$ of a point. For example, 119-16 represents $119^{16}/_{32}$, 119-162 represents $119^{16.25}/_{32}$, 119-165 represents $119^{16.5}/_{32}$, and 119-167 represents $119^{16.75}/_{32}$. Par is on the basis of 100 points.	
Tick Size (minimum fluctuation)	One-quarter of one thirty-second ($^1/_{32}$) of one point ($7.8125, rounded up to the nearest cent per contract), including intermonth spreads.	
Contract Months	The first five consecutive contracts in the March, June, September, and December quarterly cycle.	
Last Trading Day	Last business day of the calendar month. Trading in expiring contracts closes at 12:01 P.M. on the last trading day.	
Last Delivery Day	Third business day following the last trading day.	
Delivery Method	Federal Reserve book-entry wire-transfer system.	
Settlement	U.S. Treasury Futures Settlement Procedures	
Position Limits	Current Position Limits	
Block Minimum	Block Trade Minimums	
All or None Minimum	All or None Minimums	
Rulebook Chapter	CBOT Chapter 20	
Trading Hours (All times listed are Central Time)	OPEN OUTCRY	MON–FRI: 7:20 A.M.–2:00 P.M.
	CME GLOBEX	SUN–FRI: 5:30 P.M.–4:00 P.M.
Ticker Symbol	OPEN OUTCRY	FV
	CME GLOBEX	ZF
Exchange Rule	These contracts are listed with, and subject to, the rules and regulations of CBOT.	

Source: CMEGroup, "Interest Rate Products," www.cmegroup.com/trading/interest-rates/us-treasury/5-year-us-treasury-note_contract_specifications.html.

TABLE 5.5 Contract Specifications for Three-Month OIS Future

Underlying Instrument	U.S. domestic interbank deposit having a principal value of $1,000,000 that pays interest at a rate equal to the compounded daily effective federal funds rate during the contract's reference quarter.
Reference Quarter	*First Day:* Third Wednesday of the month that is three whole months before the contract's named expiry month. *Last Day:* The day immediately preceding the day that follows the first day by three calendar months. The reference quarter is inclusive of the first day and the last day.
Price Quote	100 minus R where R is the realized interest rate during the reference quarter, with daily compounding of the effective overnight federal funds rate: R = [Î i = 1 . . . n{1 + (di/360) * (ri/100)} – 1] × (360/D) × 100
Tick Size (minimum fluctuation)	Contracts with four months or less to expiry: one-quarter of one basis point (0.0025 = USD 6.25). All other contract months: one-half of one basis point (0.005 = USD 12.50)
Contract Months	First eight months in the March quarterly cycle (i.e., White and Red expiry years)
Last Trading Day	Last day of reference quarter. Trading in expiring contracts ceases at 4:00 P.M. Chicago time (CT) on the last trading day.
Final Settlement	Final settlement price = 100 – R. Cash settled on the first business day following the last day of the reference quarter. Final settlement price is rounded to the nearest one-tenth (1/10) of one basis point.
Position Limits	Current position limits
Block Minimum	Block trading minimums
All or None Minimum	All or none minimums
Rulebook Chapter	CME Chapter 460
Trading Hours (All times listed are Central Time)	OPEN OUTCRY MON–FRI: 7:20 A.M.–2:00 P.M. CME GLOBEX SUN–FRI: 5:00 P.M.–4:00 P.M. CT
Ticker Symbol	OPEN OUTCRY OSP CME GLOBEX OSS
Exchange Rule	These contracts are listed with, and subject to, the rules and regulations of CME.

Source: CMEGroup, "Interest Rate Products," www.cmegroup.com/trading/interest-rates/stir/3-month-ois_contract_specifications.html.

the full faith and credit of the U.S. government. Any Treasury security may be tendered for delivery, as long as it meets the futures contract's criteria for delivery. For example, the deliverable grade for 10-year 100,000 Treasury notes must have a remaining term to maturity of at least 6 years 6 months and not more than 10 years. Similarly, the deliverable grade for 5-year 100,000 Treasury notes is a security with an original term to maturity of not more than 5 years 3 months, and the remaining term to maturity must be at least 4 years 2 months.

2. Futures contracts specify future months for delivery, while delivery can be in any month for cash contracts.
3. Futures contracts are traded on organized commodity exchanges, while the cash market is analogous to an OTC market.
4. Futures contracts can be offset—a long position can be liquidated through the sale of an equal number of contracts for the same delivery month. Similarly, a short position can be covered with an equal number of contracts for the delivery month. As previously noted, only about 4 percent of the contracts are delivered.

Table 5.6 shows how financial institutions can use futures contracts to manage their interest rate risk. A net short futures position decreases the rate sensitivity of assets and increases the rate sensitivity of liabilities. The reverse is true for net long futures position.

For example, suppose that a bank expected intermediate-term interest rates (e.g., three–five years) to increase, and it had a large position in fixed-rate intermediate-term loans. To increase the rate sensitivity of its assets, the bank could take a net long position in five-year U.S. Treasury note futures. A long net futures position or a short net position occurs when all open long futures positions and open short positions in an account are offset against each other, and the difference is either a surplus of long or of short positions. In other words, the bank wants to protect its net interest margin—the difference between interest earned and interest expense—by

TABLE 5.6 Hedging with Futures for Asset/Liability Management

	Short Net Futures Position	Long Net Futures Position
Assets	Decreases the rate sensitivity of assets	Increases the rate sensitivity of assets
Liabilities	Increases the rate sensitivity of liabilities	Decreases the rate sensitivity of liabilities

buying futures contracts that will provide increased income if interest rates move as expected.

COVERED BONDS

Covered bonds are debt obligations issued by financial institutions. They are backed by the institution's promise to pay and by a dynamic pool of assets (i.e., cover pool) that are pledged as collateral. The underlying assets are typically high-quality assets (e.g., mortgages, government debt) that are subject to the eligibility requirements.[30] If any loans and other assets in the cover pool become delinquent, they must be replaced with performing assets. Thus, covered bonds are overcollateralized, which provides additional security to the bondholders. If the issuing bank fails to pay on the covered bond, then the investors have recourse to the cover pool as secured creditors. This means that investors have dual recourse over the cover pool and the financial institution.

On the other side of the coin,

> *The obligation to replace delinquent loans means that there is a continuing demand for new originations, which can act as a liquidity drain if delinquencies increase. This also means that, as poorer loans are taken out of the cover pool, the remaining balance sheet will consist of more and more delinquent loans.... The potential stress on issuing banks is illustrated by Washington Mutual Bank, which had to increase the cover pool to almost 150 percent overcollateralization in a failed effort to maintain high ratings for the transaction. This further exacerbated Washington Mutual's asset and liquidity problems.*[31]

Washington Mutual Bank and its subsidiary, Washington Mutual FSB, Park City, Utah, had combined assets of $307 billion. On September 25, 2008, the Office of Thrift Supervision (OTS) seized Washington Mutual Bank from Washington Mutual, Inc., and placed it into the receivership of the FDIC. Washington Mutual Bank's operations were acquired by JPMorgan Chase.[32]

Covered bonds are a primary source of funding in European banks. They were introduced in Prussia in the eighteenth century.[33]

Covered bonds are one alternative to securitization. While securitization provides off-balance-sheet financing, covered bonds remain on the bank's balance sheet. Because they are typically used to finance mortgages or other long-term assets, the covered bonds lengthen the maturity profile of the issuing bank's liabilities. However, they require the bank to hold more capital than if the loans (e.g., mortgages) were securitized. Finally, covered bonds may be a less costly source of funding long-term assets than senior unsecured debt.

Federal Reserve Chairman Ben Bernanke said:

> *Covered bonds do help to resolve some of the difficulties associated with the originate-to-distribute model. The on-balance-sheet nature of covered bonds means that the issuing banks are exposed to the credit quality of the underlying assets, a feature that better aligns the incentives of investors and mortgage lenders than does the originate-to-distribute model of mortgage securitization.*[34]

SPECIAL PURPOSE VEHICLES

Special Purpose Vehicles (SPVs), also called *special purpose entities* (SPEs), are legal entities created by a sponsoring firm (also called the sponsor, originator, seller, or administrator). The sponsor can be a bank, finance company, investment bank, or insurance company. The SPV can be a corporation, trust, partnership, or a limited liability company organized in the United States or elsewhere. Its operations are generally limited to the acquisition and financing of specific types of assets and liabilities. For example, asset securitizations by banks and finance companies usually involve bonds backed by the cash flows from income-generating assets such as residential mortgage loans and credit card receivables. Liability securitizations are usually by insurance companies that issue bonds that assume the risk of a potential insurance liability, such as a catastrophic natural event or unexpected claims on a product.[35]

The sponsors use the SPVs for risk management. They can transfer credit risk, interest rate risk, market risk, event risk, and insurance risks to other parties. They are considered *bankruptcy remote,* meaning that the bankruptcy of the sponsor will not affect the assets of the SPV. They can also be used as an additional source of funds, liquidity, and regulatory arbitrage. For example, the capital requirements for certain types of loans held on the balance sheet are higher than those in SPVs. Finally, there are accounting differences between the on- and off-balance-sheet treatment of loans involving Financial Accounting Standards (FAS) 166 and 167.[36] Banks affected by the new accounting standards generally will be subject to higher minimum regulatory capital requirements in asset-backed commercial paper (ABCP) programs.

Although SPVs are a useful and widely used tool, they were misused by Enron in 2001 to hide large losses and boost earnings.

ENTERPRISE RISK MANAGEMENT

Federal Reserve Governor Susan Schmidt Bies said: "All financial institutions need sound risk-management practices. An enterprise-wide approach is appropriate for setting objectives across the organization, instilling a culture attuned to risk, and ensuring that key activities and risks are being monitored regularly."[37]

As noted in Chapters 1 and 2, financial institutions face a wide range of risks.[38]

- *Compliance Risk*. The current and prospective risk to earnings or capital arising from violations of, or nonconformance with, laws, rules, regulations, prescribed practices, internal policies and procedures, or ethical standards. Compliance risk also arises in situations where the laws or rules governing certain bank products or activities of bank's clients may be ambiguous or untested.
- *Credit Risk*. Arises from the potential that a borrower or counterparty will fail to perform on an obligation.
- *Foreign Exchange Transaction Risk*. The risk to capital and earnings arising from the conversion of a bank's financial statements from one currency to another.
- *Legal Risk*. Arises from the potential that unenforceable contracts, lawsuits, or adverse judgments can disrupt or otherwise negatively affect the operations or condition of a banking organization. For example, a bank might knowingly or unknowingly break the law, such as facilitating money laundering in violation of the Bank Secrecy Act.
- *Liquidity Risk*. Arises from the potential that an institution will be unable to meet its obligations as they come due because of an inability to liquidate assets or obtain adequate funding (referred to as *funding liquidity risk*) or that it cannot easily unwind or offset specific exposures without significantly lowering market prices because of inadequate market depth or market disruptions (*market liquidity risk*).
- *Market Risk*. The risk to a financial institution's condition resulting from adverse movements in market rates or prices, such as interest rates, foreign exchange rates, or equity prices.
- *Operational Risk*. Arises from the potential that inadequate information systems, operational problems, breaches in internal controls, fraud, or unforeseen catastrophes will result in unexpected losses. Examples are

the 9/11 terrorist attack on the World Trade Center, Hurricane Katrina, floods, snowstorms, and electric power outages.

- *Reputational Risk.* Arises from the potential that negative publicity regarding an institution's business practices, whether true or not, will cause a decline in the customer base, costly litigation, or revenue reductions.
- *Security Risk.* Arises from cyber attacks, bank robberies, fraud, or other such problems.
- *Strategic Risk.* The current and prospective impact on earnings or capital arising from adverse business decisions, improper implementation of decisions, or lack of responsiveness to industry changes.

Collectively, these and other risks must be dealt with as part of enterprise risk management (ERM). Dealing with ERM begins with the board of directors, as part of their fiduciary duties, and senior management, which sets the tone at the top of the organization that becomes part of the corporate culture. *Corporate culture* can be defined as the way we do things in this organization. In the context of this discussion, it includes the degree of risk that an organization is willing to take in managing its assets, liabilities, and operations. Thus, risk management policies must be established, applied, and carefully monitored to ensure that they are being carried out across the entire firm. This is not easy to do in large, global firms and when the risks are evolving over time.

The Committee of Sponsoring Organizations of the Treadway Commission (COSO)[39] framework can be used by managements to evaluate and improve their organizations' ERM: "*Enterprise risk management* is defined as a process, effected by an entity's board of directors, management, and other personnel, applied in strategy setting and across the enterprise, designed to identify potential events that may affect the entity, and manage risk to be within its risk appetite, to provide reasonable assurance regarding the achievement of entity objectives."[40] The intent of ERM is to expand on internal controls by providing a more robust and extensive effort to strike a balance between growth and return goals and related risks. The COSO report goes on to say that although ERM provides important benefits, it does have limitations "that result from the realities that human judgment in decision making can be faulty, decisions on responding to risk and establishing controls need to consider the relative costs and benefits, breakdowns can occur because of human failures such as simple errors or mistakes, controls can be circumvented by collusion of two or more people, and management has the ability to override ERM decisions. These limitations preclude a board and management from having absolute assurance as to achievement of the entity's objectives."[41]

The Senior Supervisors Group (representing France, Germany, Switzerland, the United Kingdom, and the United States) made the following "Observations on Risk Management Practices" in their report to the Financial Stability Forum, Bank of International Settlement, in connection with the financial crisis in 2007:[42] The firms that dealt most successfully with the financial market crisis had (1) effective firm-wide risk identification and analysis; (2) consistent application of independent and rigorous valuation practices across the firm; (3) effective management of funding liquidity, capital, and the balance sheet; and (4) informative and responsive risk management and management reporting and practices.

For additional discussion of ERM and the economic capital requirements associated with it, see Chapter 8, "Bank Capital." Also see the discussion of the economic value of equity and stress testing in Chapter 4, "Asset Liability Management."

ADDITIONAL EDUCATIONAL RESOURCES

The following organizations and their web sites provide additional educational resources concerning derivatives and swaps:

Chicago Board Options Exchange (CBOE), The Options Institute
cboe.com/LearnCenter.

CME Group
cmegroup.com. Click on the Education tab.

Eurex
www.eurexchange.com/index_en.html. Click on the Education tab.

International Securities Exchange (ISE)
ise.com. Click on the Education tab.

International Swaps and Derivatives Association Inc. (ISDA)
www.isda.org. Click on the Education tab.

Options Industry Council (OIC)
Optionseducation.org.

CHAPTER 6

Commercial and Industrial Loans

This is the first of two chapters about lending and managing loan portfolios. This chapter deals primarily with commercial and industrial loans (C&I loans) and the process of lending.[1] These loans are those made to businesses to finance their day-to-day activities (e.g., inventories and receivables), longer-term needs (e.g., plant and equipment), and for other business purposes. The next chapter deals with real estate and consumer loans.

The average size of C&I loans at all commercial banks in February 2010 was $473,000, and they had an average maturity of 372 days.[2] The size of the loans and length of maturities were related to bank size. The average loan size for large domestic banks with assets of $3.7 billion or more was $400,000, and the average maturity of the loans was 400 days. In contrast, the average loan size for small banks was $95,000 and the average maturity was 698 days.

THE ROLE OF ASYMMETRIC INFORMATION IN LENDING

Three theoretical concepts are examined in this section concerning the relationships between banks and the customers who borrow from them. These concepts underlie much of the material that is presented in this chapter and the next one.

Asymmetric Information and Adverse Selection

Before banks make loans, they must evaluate imperfect information about prospective borrowers to determine if they are creditworthy. Information is difficult and costly to obtain. Information about large firms that are publicly traded, such as Microsoft, is easier to obtain than information about small, privately held firms. The information that prospective borrowers provide to the banks may be sufficient to make a credit decision. However, it is usually incomplete in the sense that borrowers know more about the risk of their proposed investment projects than they reveal to the bank. We are using the term *investment project,* but the concept applies to the use of any funds borrowed from the bank, including consumer loans. The inequality of information between the bank and the borrower is called *asymmetric information.* Simply stated, asymmetric information means that the borrowers have more information about themselves than is available to the bank.

Because of asymmetric information, banks tend to charge an interest rate that reflects the average rate of risk of all borrowers. The average interest rate is too high for borrowers with low-risk investment projects and too low for borrowers with high-risk investment projects.

Adverse Selection

Adverse selection means that high-risk borrowers try to get loans from banks because they are willing to pay the average rate of interest, which is less than they would have to pay if their true condition were known to the bank. It also follows that low-risk creditworthy borrowers may be able to borrow directly from the money and capital markets at lower rates than those offered by banks. Market rates of interest confirm this. In May 2010, the prime rate was 3.25 percent. The *prime rate* is the base rate on corporate loans made by banks. However, the rate on Aaa (top quality) corporate bonds (long-term debts) was 4.99 percent, and the rate on 30-day *commercial paper* (short-term paper issued by major corporations) was 0.22 percent.[3] The banks tend to attract the higher-risk borrowers that do not have direct access to the money and capital markets. Note that adverse selection occurs before the loan is made.

Moral Hazard The asymmetric information also gives rise to a moral hazard problem after the loan is made. *Moral hazard* is the risk that the borrower, who now has the loan, might use the funds to engage in higher-risk activities in expectation of earning higher returns. The higher-risk activities increase the probability of default on the loan. The moral hazard problem is most likely to occur when the lender is unable to monitor the borrower's activities.

THE COMPETITIVE ENVIRONMENT

The Business of Lending

Lending money can be profitable, but it is risky. The profits come from collecting the interest income and fees earned on the loans. To the extent possible, banks and other lenders try to charge high-risk borrowers higher interest rates than low-risk borrowers. Therefore, lenders have an incentive to take greater risks in expectation of earning higher returns. The major risk they face is credit risk. *Credit risk* is the risk to earnings and capital that a borrower or counterparty may not meet the terms of the loan contract, resulting in losses to the lender. Credit risk applies to loans, derivatives, foreign exchange transactions, the investment portfolio, and other financial activities.

Banks do not intentionally make bad loans. They do, however, make loans that can go bad over time. For example, two years after a bank grants a loan, a severe recession may adversely affect a borrower's ability to repay the loan, and the borrower defaults. The fact that economic conditions changed for the borrower helps to explain why banks must monitor their loans.

The decision to default on a loan is the borrower's. In theory, borrowers have a put option to put the loan back to the lender when it is to their advantage to do so. This usually occurs when borrowers are unable to make the required loan payments or meet other terms of the loan agreement. If a large number of borrowers exercise their put options to default, and the losses are sufficiently large, the lender may fail. Fearing losses and failure, lenders try to control their credit risk.

Increasing Competition

Economic theory tells us that the expectation of high returns attracts competition, and the loan business is no exception. In the past, banks dominated commercial and consumer lending. It was thought that banks were special because they had particular expertise in making, monitoring, and collecting loans. However, banks did not have a sustainable competitive advantage, and today they are facing increasing competition from nonbank lenders such as credit unions, hedge funds, sovereign wealth funds, and shadow banks. In 2010, it was estimated that shadow banks financed about $8 trillion in assets, making that sector almost as large as the real banking system.[4] In an effort to retain their share of the debt markets, banks securitize and sell loans.

The growth of nonbank lenders has resulted in highly competitive terms of lending on loans and the standards used to make those loans. Stated otherwise, some lenders who are trying to maximize revenue or market share may not give credit risk the weight it deserves in their lending decisions. Nevertheless, there is some differential in pricing risk at banks. The average interest rate on all C&I loans at commercial banks in a February 2010 Federal Reserve survey was 2.77 percent.[5] Recall that market rates of interest were near record low levels. The average rates ranged from 1.57 percent for daily rates to 4.35 percent for loans of more than 365 days. The rate on high-risk loans of more than 365 days was 5.58 percent.

Competition also affects the nonprice terms of loans, such as the degree of tightness in loan covenants and the release of guarantees to make it easier to obtain loans. *Loan covenants* are conditions in the loan contract that the borrower must meet. For example, the borrower must provide audited financial statements annually.

Both nonbank and bank lenders have shifted their portfolios to higher-yielding, higher-risk loans in recent years. The result was the economic crisis that began in 2007 that was attributable, in part, to subprime real estate loans, weak standards for securitization, and other factors that were discussed in Chapter 1.

Changes in Technology

Developments in financial technology changed how banks operate their lending activities. These developments are securitization of loans, credit scoring, and electronic banking. Other changes in technology, such as the use of credit derivatives to manage portfolio risks, have also been important.

Securitization Securitization is packaging and selling otherwise unmarketable loans to other financial institutions and investors. For example, residential mortgage loans are packaged in large volumes and sold as mortgage pools, some of which are guaranteed by government agencies. Other securitized loans include automobile loans, credit card loans, and small business loans. The small business loans may be guaranteed by the Small Business Administration. Alternatively, the issuer may overcollateralize the loans—putting up more collateral loans than is required—to enhance the package.

The growth of securitization means that loans that were formerly funded in local markets are now being funded in global capital markets. Removing geographic financial constraints for borrowers and lenders allows demand for such loans and the supply of funds to grow and provides increasing liquidity for the secondary loan market. It also provides lenders and investors who buy those loans a means of diversifying their portfolios.

Unbundling of Loans The growth of securitization has contributed to the unbundling of loans. Traditionally, banks made and held loans in their portfolios. Today, the lending process can be divided into the following four activities:

1. Originating loans.
2. Packaging loans for sale to others.
3. Servicing loan portfolios.
4. Investing in loan-backed credit instruments.

A bank, or some other organization, can do any one or all of these activities. Accordingly, one firm may originate the loans, another package them for resale, and so on.

Syndicated Loans/Shared National Credits Both domestic and foreign loans can be syndicated. Syndication is presented here because it permits banks of different sizes to participate in international lending. The syndication of international loans is explained later in this chapter.

The *syndication* of large loans has advantages for both the borrower and the lender. Syndication of any loan or loan commitment of at least $20 million that is shared by three or more unaffiliated federally supervised institutions, or a portion of which is sold to two or more unaffiliated federally supervised institutions, is called a *shared national credit* (SNC).[6]

From the borrower's point of view, syndication provides more funds than may be available from any single lender. In addition, the credit terms may be better than for a large number of smaller loans. From the lender's point of view, syndication provides a means of diversifying some of the risks of foreign lending. Another advantage of syndication is that it provides the lead bank with off-balance-sheet income for that portion of the loan that is sold to other participants. The lead bank and other banks that co-manage the loan receive fee income for their management services. Typically, the management fee is paid by the borrower at the time the loan is made. Such fees range from 0.5 percent to more than 2 percent of the total amount of the loan. Finally, syndication can enhance relations with foreign governments because it is a means of financing their domestic economic activity.

Credit Scoring Credit scoring is the use of statistical models to determine the likelihood that a prospective borrower will default on a loan. Credit scoring models are provided by Fair Isaac Corporation (FICO)[7] to credit bureaus including Experian, Equifax, and TransUnion. Credit scoring models, such as FICO scores, are widely used to evaluate small business, real estate, and consumer loans.[8] In the case of small business loans, for example, the models may be based on data from credit applications, personal financial statements, business financial statements, and credit bureau reports. The cutoff scores (e.g., a FICO score of 680) used by lenders depend on the degree of risk they are willing to take. Therefore, different lenders use different scores, and they have so-called override policies. A customer who receives a low score may still receive a loan if the lender decides to override the model because of other considerations.

The major advantages of credit scoring models are the reduced time and lower cost of processing loans. Another advantage is that the same measures are applied to all customers, thereby demonstrating a consistent credit policy.

Banks and other lenders use credit scoring models. However, because of economies of scale and the standardized treatment of loans, the use of credit scoring encourages automated lending decisions on a large scale from a single location, such as monoline banks, and no closing cost or fees.[9] An advertisement said:

Nationwide Financing Services

- New Business Loans.
- Acquisition Financing.
- Business Lines of Credit.
- Working Capital Loans.
- Loan Restructuring.

The point here is that there is increasing competition to make small business loans.

THE BOARD OF DIRECTORS' WRITTEN LOAN POLICY

The Role of Directors

The board of directors has the ultimate responsibility for all of the loans made by their bank. Because the board delegates the task of making loans to others, it must have a written loan policy that establishes the guidelines and principles for the bank's lending activities.

Loan policies vary widely from bank to bank. The loan policies for a small bank that lends primarily to local consumers are going to differ from the policies of a large bank that specializes in lending to business concerns. In either case, the policy would state that the bank is in the business of making sound and profitable loans. Therefore, the loan policy must make it clear that an important part of the lending process is that all loans should have a repayment plan at the time the loan is made.

Other parts of the loan policy deal with:

- Loan authority—who has the authority to make loans. The lending limits relative to capital, deposits, or assets. The loan approval process.
- Loan portfolio—the types of loans the bank wants to make, such as consumer loans, loans to start up businesses, loans to large businesses, farm loans, or international loans. The policy should also put limits on the concentration of particular types of loans.

- Geographic limits of the bank's trade area where it may grant loans.
- Policies for determining interest rates, fees, and contractual terms of the loans.
- Limits and guidelines for off-balance-sheet exposures from loan commitments, letters of credit, securitized loans, and derivative products (swaps, options, futures, and so on).
- A loan review process to evaluate lending procedures and the quality of the loan portfolio.

Although this list is incomplete, it is sufficient to give you an overview of some of the key topics that are covered in a loan policy. The policy also may specify the types of loans that the board considers undesirable. For example, the bank should not make loans to persons whose integrity or honesty is questionable. It should not make capital loans to a business where the loan cannot be repaid within a reasonable period except by liquidation of the business. And finally, it should not make loans secured by stock in a closed corporation where there is no market for that stock.

Reducing Credit Risk

Banks use a wide variety of techniques to reduce their credit risk. Some of the techniques are listed here in alphabetical order.

Avoid making high-risk loans. For example, a small bank located in Cincinnati, Ohio, should reject a loan proposal to buy deep-sea fishing boats in New England. While this might be a good loan for a bank in New England that is familiar with that industry, it would be a high-risk loan for a Midwest bank that has no expertise in lending on deep-sea fishing boats.

Collateral reduces the risk to the lender, and the threat of loss of the collateral provides an incentive for the borrower to repay the loan. Collateral is considered a secondary source of repayment in the event of loan default.

Diversify the loan portfolio. Diversification means making investments or loans to a variety of borrowers whose cash flows are not perfectly positively correlated and avoiding undue concentration to a borrower or in a particular type of loan whose returns are related. For example, Colonial Bank in Alabama made real estate loans in Florida, Georgia, Nevada, and Alabama. The financial real estate crisis that began in 2007 had devastating effects on real estate prices in Florida, Georgia, and Nevada.

Documentation refers to all of the documents needed to legally enforce a loan contract and protect a bank's interest. Documents typically include promissory notes, guarantees, financial statements, UCC (Uniform Commercial Code) filings for collateral, and notes about meetings with the customers. An unsigned promissory note is not enforceable. Moreover, failure to renew a UCC filing on collateral can turn a secured loan into an unsecured loan. The successful collection of loans may depend on documentation.

Guarantees do not eliminate default risk or the riskiness of a loan portfolio. In fact, they may contribute to increased risk as banks substitute financial guarantees for high credit standards or higher rates charged on risky loans. Nevertheless, the federal government loan guarantees pay important roles in agriculture, commerce, and housing. The Small Business Administration (SBA), for example, assists small businesses by guaranteeing all or parts of qualifying loans made by banks and other lenders. Private guarantees (those not backed by government) are also widely used by borrowers. A parent company guaranteeing the loan of a subsidiary is one example.

Limit the amount of credit extended to any single borrower or group of borrowers with related cash flow patterns in order to avoid undue loan concentration. For example, national banks are limited in the amount of their capital that they can lend to a single borrower. The maximum amount is 15 percent of the unimpaired capital and unimpaired surplus of the bank.[10]

Monitor the behavior of the borrower after the loan is made to ensure compliance with the loan agreement. Recall that the decision to default on a loan is a put option held by the borrower. Some borrowers have a moral hazard problem and take excessive risks. Other borrowers may be adversely affected by external factors such as oil price shocks, recessions, floods, or droughts. Therefore, monitoring should take into account those external factors that might impede the borrower's ability to repay the loan.

The outside monitor may know that the borrower has used the loan funds to buy assets, such as inventory or equipment. However, the monitor may not be able to verify the value of those assets. The difference between what the monitor knows and what can be verified contributes to the agency problems between the lender and borrower. Agency problems, as used here, refers to the ability of the lender (the principal) to influence the behavior of the borrower (the agent).

Transfer risk to other parties by selling securitized loans and loan participations and syndications of loans (SNCs) and by hedging with interest rate and credit derivatives.[11]

SEVEN WAYS TO MAKE LOANS

The seven ways that banks make loans are presented in alphabetical order.

Banks Solicit Loans

Banks actively solicit loans in person, by mail, and on the Internet by offering loans and other services they provide. These sales efforts are typical of banks seeking new customers and those trying to cross-sell their services. For example, a branch manager or loan officer may explain to a prospective borrower how the bank's cash management services, including lock boxes and cash concentration accounts, can improve the firm's cash flow. *Lock boxes* are mail boxes where retail customers send their payments for goods and services purchased. The lock boxes are serviced by the bank, and funds can be concentrated and forwarded to the firm's treasury for investment.

Buying Loans

Participations Banks buy parts of loans, called *participations,* from other banks. The acquiring banks have pro rata shares of the credit risk. Participations by three or more unaffiliated banks in loans or formal loan commitments in excess of $20 million are called SNCs.[12] Suppose that a large bank is making a $100 million loan to an airline, but the originating bank does not want to keep such a large loan in its loan portfolio. It may sell parts (participations) of that loan to other banks. The sale of participations downstream to smaller banks allows smaller banks to participate in loans that they could not originate. In addition, it is one way for a bank with slack demand for loans to increase its loan portfolio. It also allows all of the banks involved to diversify their loan portfolios. Participations can originate from small banks, too. Suppose that a small bank wants to make a loan that exceeds its lending limits. It can make the loan and sell participations upstream to larger banks. Banks also buy and sell securitized loans.

Secondary Market for Small Business Loans A study by the SBA found that a "relatively small existing secondary market for conventional small business loans results from an overarching sense of uncertainty. This uncertainty is exacerbated by the lack of standard lending and servicing practices followed by loan originators"[13] However, because of the 2009 Recovery Act, the Treasury Department committed up to $15 billion to help unlock the secondary markets for small business loans.[14] For most purposes, the SBA's maximum guarantee for any borrower is $1.5 million, or 75 percent of a $2 million loan.[15]

Commitments

About 81 percent of all commercial and industrial loans are made under loan commitments.[16] A *loan commitment* is an agreement between a bank and a firm to lend funds under terms that are agreed on in writing. Loan commitments specify the amount of the commitment fee and the amount of funds to be borrowed, but the cost of borrowing depends on the prevailing rates at the time the loan is made. The pricing on the loan is usually specified when the commitment is made. For example, the bank may charge the *prime rate* (the base rate on corporate loans) plus two percentage points when the funds are borrowed.[17]

Firms pay a commitment fee to banks for the call option of borrowing at some future date. Commitment fees range from 0.25 percent to 0.50 percent per annum of the total amount to be borrowed. Commitment fees contribute to bank's income, and they do not require immediate funding. For example, assume a 45-day commitment for $5 million and a commitment fee of 0.50 percent per annum computed on a 360-day basis. The bank earns $3,125 without investing any assets, but it does have a contingent claim.

$$\text{Commitment} \times 0.50\%$$

$$\$5{,}000{,}000 \times 0.005 = \$25{,}000$$

$$\text{Daily fee} = \text{total fee}/360$$

$$\$25{,}000/360 = \$69.444$$

$$\text{Fee for 45 days} = \text{daily fee} \times 45 \text{ days}$$

$$\$69.444 \times 45 = \$3125.00$$

Banks may compute the fee on a 365-day basis. Using 365 days, the daily fee is $68.493 and the bank earns $3,082.19. The bank is better off using 360 days.

Customers Request Loans

A customer asks for a commercial loan. Unfortunately, many potential borrowers are denied loans or do not get what they need because they do not know what information the bank needs in order to grant a loan request. Some borrowers, for example, do not know what type of loan (e.g., line of credit, term loan) will meet their financial needs or what type of collateral (e.g., accounts receivable, bill of lading, second mortgage) is suitable for their loans. Good loan officers work with prospective borrowers who do not know the procedures by explaining to them what information they must provide to the bank.

Loan Brokers

Loan brokers sell loans to banks and other lenders. *Loan brokers* are individuals or firms who act as agents or brokers between the borrower and the lender. For example, a loan broker may contract with a real estate developer to find financing for a particular project. The broker will seek out lenders and arrange for the loan. Once the loan is made and the fees are paid, the broker is out of the picture.

Overdrafts

An *overdraft* occurs when a customer writes a check on uncollected funds or when there are insufficient funds in the account to cover the withdrawal. If a bank pays on a check written against insufficient balances, it is extending an unsecured loan.

Some overdrafts are written with prior permission of the bank, but most are not. In the latter case, the overdraft represents a loan that the bank may not want to make. The borrower did not ask the bank for the funds in advance.

Overdrafts can be for less than one day (*daylight overdraft*) when a check is written or funds transferred out by wire in the morning and the deposit to cover that check or wire transfer is not made until that afternoon. Suppose that a firm located in New York City deposits a check drawn on a bank located in El Paso, Texas. It will take about two days for the check to be collected by the New York bank from the bank in Texas. Although the New York firm's balance has increased, it cannot use those funds to write checks without the bank's permission. Many banks analyze their customers' out-of-town checks and permit them to write checks only on their average collected balances. Under the Competitive Banking Equality Act of 1987, no more than one business day may intervene between the deposit of a local check and the availability for withdrawal of those funds; four business days are allowed for nonlocal checks.

As more funds are being transferred electronically, the number of checks being written has declined dramatically. More will be said about the role of electronic banking in Chapter 10, "Payment Systems."

Refinancing

Borrowers refinance loans. Suppose that interest rates on loans have declined from 10 percent to 6 percent and that borrowers with high fixed-rate loans want to take advantage of the lower rates. They can make a new loan at the lower rate and pay off the high-rate loan. The refinancing is at the borrower's option and occurs only when it is to their advantage.

COLLECTING LOANS

Making loans is the easy part of the lending process. Collecting the loans is the hard part. There are two primary sources of repayment that lenders consider when they make loans: from the borrowers' cash flow (e.g., earnings) and from the sale of the assets being financed (e.g., inventory). Collateral serves as a secondary source of repayment.

In the event that neither the primary nor the secondary sources of loan repayment satisfy the debt, the bank will have to take appropriate action to protect its interests. If the loan is guaranteed (such as a guarantee from the SBA), the bank will turn to the guarantor for repayment.

The SBA provides a variety of loan guarantee programs for start-ups and existing small businesses; private, nonprofit corporations are set up to contribute to the economic development of their communities. Their lending programs include microloans (small loans up to $35,000), export loan programs, rural loan programs, venture capital loans, and disaster assistance loans.[18]

Finally, if no other options for repayment are available, the bank may force the borrower into bankruptcy. This is the costliest and least effective method of repayment.

PRINCIPAL LENDING ACTIVITIES

The principal lending activities are loans and leases. The types of loans presented here are lines of credit, revolving loans, term loans, and bridge loans. Banks make other types of loans that are not described here. Each type of loan has its own purpose. The concept of different types of loans for different purposes is illustrated in Figure 6.1. As shown in the figure, the total assets of a firm can be divided into two categories, permanent assets and temporary assets. Permanent assets include plant and equipment as well as that portion of working capital (cash, accounts receivable, and inventory) that will be sustained over time. Temporary assets include that portion of working capital that fluctuates with periodic changes in sales and revenues. For example, the inventory of The Toy Store is expected to increase before Christmas. When the toys are sold, the inventory will be reduced, but the accounts receivable will increase. As the receivables are collected and the cash is used to repay debts or acquire new long-term assets, working capital will be reduced.

The figure also shows that temporary assets should be financed with temporary loans and permanent assets with permanent loans. Stated otherwise, a safe lending strategy is to match the maturity of the asset being financed with the maturity of funds used to finance it. For example, it makes sense to finance The Toy Store's seasonal inventory loan for up to one year, although one would expect it to be repaid in less time. It does not make sense to provide funds for five years to finance an inventory of toys for one

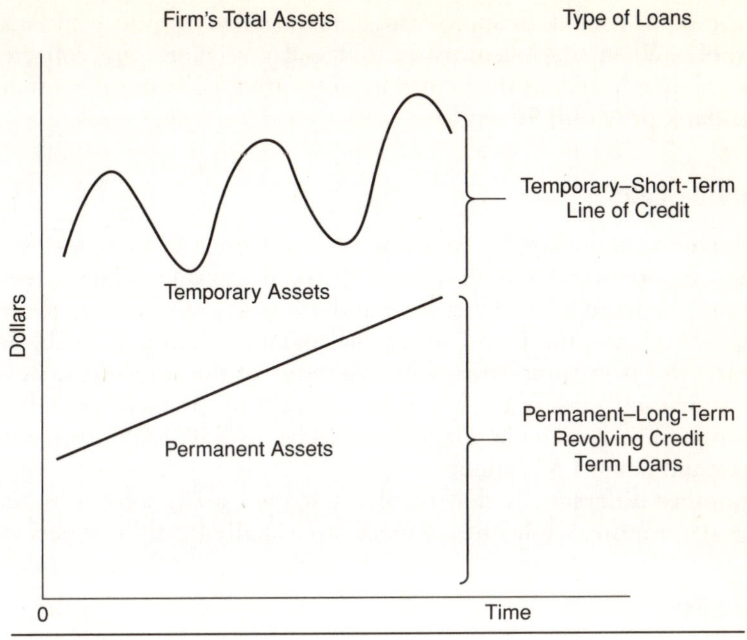

FIGURE 6.1 The Financing Mix

Christmas season. Sometimes this kind of mismatch occurs when funds are lent to finance both temporary and permanent assets in one loan rather than as separate loans.

Next, we examine specific types of loans and *credit facilities* (agreements which may or may not result in loans).

Line of Credit

A *line of credit* is an agreement between a customer and the bank that the bank will entertain requests from that customer for a loan up to a predetermined amount. The line of credit is established when the bank gives a letter to the customer stating the dollar amount of the line, the time it is in effect (e.g., 1 year), and other conditions or provisions, such as the relationship the customer must maintain with the bank and the customer's financial condition. If the borrower does not meet all of the terms and conditions of the letter, the bank is not obligated to make the loan or continue the line of credit.

The line of credit is the maximum amount that can be borrowed under the terms of the loan. The loans are made for periods of one year or less, and they should be used to finance seasonal increases in inventory and accounts receivable. When the inventory is sold and receivables are collected, the funds are used to reduce the loan. The loans are usually payable on demand by the bank or within 90 days.

Revolving Loan

Revolving loans are similar to a line of credit because they, too, are used to finance borrowers' temporary and seasonal working capital needs. One difference between a revolving loan and a line of credit is that the bank is obligated to make the loans, up to the maximum amount of the loan, if the borrower is in compliance with the terms of the agreement. Revolving loans commonly specify the minimum amount of the increments that may be borrowed. For example, the loan could be for $30,000 increments up to a maximum limit of $3 million.

Another difference is that revolving loans usually have a maturity of two years or more, while lines of credit are usually for shorter periods.

Term Loan

A *term loan* is usually a single loan for a stated period of time or a series of loans on specified dates. A term loan is used for a specific purpose, such as acquiring machinery, renovating a building, or refinancing debt. It should not be used to finance day-to-day operations.

Term loans may have an original maturity of five years or more. From the lender's point of view, the maturity of the loan should not exceed the economic life of the asset being financed if that asset is collateral for the loan. Equally important, the value of the asset being financed always should exceed the amount of the loan. The difference between the value of the asset and the amount being financed is the borrower's equity, which represents the borrower's investment in the asset being financed. It also provides the bank with a cushion in the event of default. The borrower will lose funds before the bank experiences a loss. Borrowers not wanting to lose their equity investment have an incentive to operate their business so that the loan will be repaid.

Term loans may be repaid on an amortized basis or at one time. Recall that the planned repayment of loans should come from the borrower's operating revenues or from the sale of assets. These concepts are illustrated in the top panel of Figure 6.2. The point of these concepts is to protect the bank's security interest in the loan.

The lower panel illustrates improper lending procedures: a loan that exceeds the value of the asset that it is financing. In addition, the maturity

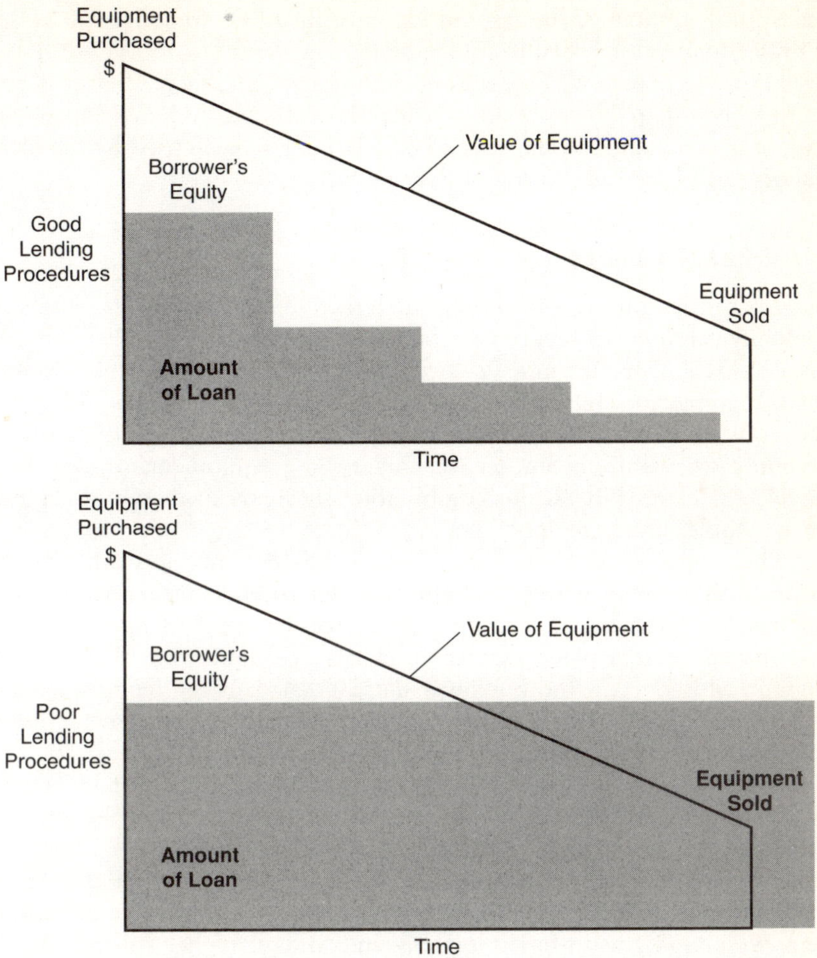

FIGURE 6.2 Term Loans for Machinery

of the loan exceeds the life of the asset. If the borrower defaults when the value of the equipment is less than the amount of the loan, the bank will incur a substantial loss.

Bridge Loan

Bridge loans bridge a gap in a borrower's financing until some specific event occurs. For example, a firm wants to acquire a new warehouse facility but needs funds to finance the transaction until the old warehouse can be sold. A bridge loan can be used to fill the gap.

Similarly, a firm needs working capital now, and next week it is going to issue commercial paper to provide those funds. A bank can provide temporary financing. In this case, the bank loan is being used by the firm as a short-term substitute for other debt financing.

Asset-Based Lending

Asset-based lending is a form of commercial lending where the assets of a company are used to secure the company's obligation to the lender. Most asset-based lenders are finance companies, although some banks do asset-based lending, too. In the broadest sense, all secured loans could be classified as asset-based lending. Asset-based loans have as their collateral base accounts receivable, inventory, machinery and equipment, or real estate, singly or packaged in various combinations (e.g., receivables and inventory or receivables and machinery).

The major distinctions between asset-based loans and other secured loans is that much greater weight is given to the market value of the collateral in asset-based lending than in regular C&I loans. In addition, asset-based lenders place greater emphasis on monitoring than do bank lenders. Moreover, if the borrower defaults, asset-based lenders are more willing to liquidate the borrower's collateral than is the case for regular C&I loans.

Asset-based loans require a higher level of monitoring than other secured commercial loans. The degree of monitoring to ensure the existence, value, and integrity of the collateral further differentiates asset-based loans from other secured commercial loans. The combination of a higher level of monitoring and a greater willingness to liquidate in the event of default may help explain why asset-based lenders tend to have higher spreads and fees and lower write-offs than other secured lenders.

Leasing

Leases are used to finance tangible assets such as cars, airliners, and ships. A *lease* is a contract that enables a user (the lessee) to secure the use of a tangible asset over a specified period of time by making payments to the owner (the lessor). The contract also specifies the details of the payments, the disposition of income tax benefits, provisions for maintenance, renewal options, and other clauses that permit the contract to qualify as a *true lease* under the Internal Revenue Code.[19]

We will consider two types of leases, operating leases and financial leases.

1. *Operating leases* are short-term leases used to finance equipment such as computers, where the term of the lease is a fraction of the economic life of the asset. The asset is not fully amortized over the term of a lease. Operating leases may be canceled.
2. *Financial leases* are used in connection with financing long-term assets and have a term that is equal to the economic life of the asset. For example, a communications satellite may be leased for 12 years. Such leases are usually not canceled.

COLLATERAL

Sound banking practices require that certain types of loans be backed by collateral. *Collateral* refers to an asset pledged against the performance of an obligation. If a borrower defaults on a loan, the bank takes the collateral and sells it. Therefore, it is frequently referred to as a secondary source of repayment.

Collateral reduces the bank's risk when it makes a loan. However, collateral does not reduce the risk of the loan per se. The risk of the loan is determined by the borrower's ability to repay it and other factors.

While collateral reduces the bank's risk, it increases the costs of lending and monitoring. The higher costs are due to the need for documentation and the expense of monitoring the collateral. In an effort to cut costs, some banks are not requiring collateral on lines of credit issued to small businesses. However, without collateral, some borrowers could not obtain loans.

Collateral benefits both borrowers and lenders in certain type of loans. In other types of loans collateral is not used. For example, a large credit-worthy corporation borrowed $20 million for one day until it sold its own commercial paper. The minimal risk and the large volume of paperwork to obtain liens against specific assets mitigated the need for collateral in this case.

Characteristics of Good Collateral

Almost anything that is lawful may be used as collateral, but some things are better than others. The five factors listed here determine the suitability of items for use as collateral.

Durability This refers to the ability of the asset to withstand wear or to its useful life. Durable goods make better collateral than nondurables. Stated otherwise, crushed rocks make better collateral than fresh flowers.

Identification Certain types of assets are readily identifiable because they have definite characteristics or serial numbers that cannot be removed. Two examples are a large office building and an automobile that can be identified by make, model, and serial number.

Marketability For collateral to be of value to the bank, the collateral must be marketable. That is, you must be able to sell it. Specialized equipment that has limited use is not as marketable as trucks that have multiple uses.

Stability of Value Bankers prefer collateral whose market values are not likely to decline dramatically during the period of the loan. Common stocks, for example, are not as desirable as real estate for collateral because the stock prices are more variable than real estate prices.

Standardization Certain types of grains have been graded by the U.S. Department of Agriculture. For example, soybeans are graded as No. 1 yellow, No. 2 yellow, or No. 3 yellow. These grades indicate the quality of the beans. Likewise, other types of commodities and merchandise have been graded to facilitate their use in trade and as collateral. The standardization leaves no ambiguity between the borrower and the lender as to nature of the asset that is being used as collateral.

Types of Collateral

The most common types of collateral used in commercial lending are examined here.

Accounts Receivable There are three ways that accounts receivable can be used as collateral: pledging, factoring, and bankers' acceptances.

Pledging A borrower can pledge accounts receivable with his or her bank. In this case, the borrower retains ownership of the receivables, and there is usually no notification made to the buyer of the goods for which the receivables have been pledged.

The percentage of face value of the accounts receivable that the banker is willing to advance depends on the size, number, and quality of the receivables. Most bankers prefer to advance funds for receivables from a few well-established firms with good credit ratings.

Factoring Factoring is the sale of accounts receivable to a factor, which is usually a bank or finance company. When the receivables are sold, the buyer of the goods is usually notified to make payments to the factor.

Like pledging, factors prefer receivables from well-established firms. One important difference between the two methods is that factors usually buy receivables on a nonrecourse basis. *Nonrecourse* means that it cannot be returned to the firm that is selling the receivables. Thus, the factor accepts the credit risks for the receivables it purchases. To reduce risk, the factor may advance only 80 percent or 90 percent of the face value; the remainder is held in reserve until the receivables are collected or until some predetermined date. In addition, the factor charges a commission that ranges from 1 percent to 3 percent of the total face value and monthly interest charges on the advances.

For example, suppose that Southern Mill Outlet wants to factor $100,000 in receivables. The factor holds a reserve of 10 percent (advances 90 percent) and charges a 3 percent commission and 2 percent monthly interest. The Southern Mill Outlet receives $85,260, and the factor earns $4,740 plus what it can earn on investing the reserve.

Face value of the accounts receivable	$100,000
Reserve held by factor (10%)	10,000
Commission (3%)	−3,000
Funds that may be advanced	$87,000
Less monthly interest charge (2%)	−1,740
Funds available to Southern Mill Outlet	$85,260

Bankers' Acceptance A bankers' acceptance usually arises from foreign trade. Suppose an American exporter sells computer parts to a French concern. The French importer agrees to pay for the parts 30 days after they have been delivered. The means of payment is a *time draft,* which is similar to a predated check. The American manufacturer can send the time draft, which from the American's point of view is the same as an account receivable, to the French importer's bank and have it accepted. This means that the French bank becomes responsible for the payment of the draft and will collect the funds from the importer when the draft becomes due. In other words, the French bank is guaranteeing payments of the French importer's obligation. The accepted draft is called a bankers' acceptance. It is a negotiable instrument that can be traded in the securities markets. The American manufacturer can sell the bankers' acceptance at a discount (i.e., below face value) to compensate investors who bought it and cannot collect the full value until it matures.

Inventory Inventory is widely used as collateral against commercial loans. The inventory may consist of raw materials or finished goods, such as automobiles. Other types of inventory may include natural resources, livestock, and crops.

Marketable Securities Marketable securities including corporate stocks and bonds, certificates of deposit, and U.S. Treasury securities may be used as collateral for business loans. The amount of credit extended on such securities varies widely. One problem with securities as collateral is that the market value of publicly held stocks and bonds can vary widely from day to day. The value of publicly traded securities is readily available in the press. In contrast, the market value of privately held companies may not be determinable without going to considerable expense.

Real Property and Equipment Real property refers to real estate that includes houses, office buildings, shopping centers, and factories. Such property is widely used as collateral. In addition, equipment of various sorts may be used. Equipment includes trucks, forklifts, drill presses, and robotics. Appraisals by qualified real estate appraisers and equipment appraisers are essential before the loan is made.

Guarantees Bankers can improve their security by having a third party guarantee the payments. The third party may be an individual, insurance company, or U.S. government agency such as the Small Business Administration. For example, a parent company may guarantee a loan made by a subsidiary. Without the guarantee, the loan would not have been made. With the exception of the government agencies, the quality of guarantee depends on the financial strength of the guarantor.

■ ■ ■

In summary, many banks require collateral and/or a guarantee when they make business loans. Small businesses frequently use the personal assets of the principals as collateral. Personal assets can be real estate, cars, the surrender value of life insurance policies, or anything else of value.

THE LENDING PROCESS

The process of lending begins before a loan is made. The board of directors establishes a loan policy and considers the risk-reduction techniques previously described. The process ends when the loan is repaid or when it is determined to be uncollectible. At that point, if it no longer has value, it is removed as an asset from the bank's balance sheet. Even then, the bank still may be able to collect some of the proceeds. Both the lender and the borrower perform certain tasks over the term of the lending process.

Evaluating a Loan Request

A key part of the lending process involves the six C's of credit. Banks that use credit scoring models incorporate data from credit reporting agencies and other sources that cover some of them. While the use of credit scoring models is growing in importance, many loans must be evaluated using the traditional methods described here.

- Character (personal characteristics of the borrower, honesty, and attitudes about willingness and commitment to pay debts).
- Capacity (the borrower's success in running a business—cash flows).
- Capital (the financial condition of the borrower—net worth).
- Collateral (pledged assets).
- Conditions (economic conditions).
- Compliance (compliance with laws and regulations).

Character Banks must know their customer before they make loans, and character is the place to start. Character refers to a combination of qualities that distinguishes one person or a group from another. To some extent, the words *character* and *reputation* overlap in meaning. We use the term *character* here to refer to a borrower's honesty, responsibility, integrity, and consistency, on which we can determine willingness to repay loans. Evidence of character traits can be found in reports from credit bureaus (e.g., Equifax, Experian, TransUnion) and credit reporting agencies, such as Dun and Bradstreet (D&B).

Capacity This refers to success of the borrower's business as reflected in its financial condition and ability to meet financial obligations via cash flow and earnings. Banks generally require prospective borrowers to submit their financial statements and/or federal and state income tax statements to determine their creditworthiness.

Credit scoring is widely used to aid in decision making. In addition, credit analysts may use analytical software programs that provide a wide range of financial ratios and comparative data to evaluate the data and to do pro forma projections and stress testing. However, most loans are for relatively small amounts and do not warrant the cost of doing pro forma statements or stress tests. Credit scoring for consumer loans is discussed in Chapter 7.

Capital Capital represents the amount of equity capital a firm has that can be liquidated for payment if all other means of collection of the debt fail. Equity capital is equal to total assets less total liabilities. However, there can be a substantial difference between the *book value* and the *market value* of assets and liabilities. For example, land purchased 20 years ago can be carried on the books at its historical cost. However, the market value of the land could be substantially higher or lower than the book value.

Collateral Collateral refers to assets that are pledged for security in a credit transaction. The fact that borrowers may lose their collateral if they default on their loans serves as an incentive for them to perform in accordance with the loan contract.

Conditions Conditions refer to external factors that are beyond the control of a firm but may affect their ability to repay debts. Excess capacity in commercial real estate is one example. If there is excess capacity in that market, the lender should take it into account before granting a loan to add to the capacity. Changes in conditions, such as recessions, interest rate shocks, and asset price deflation, adversely affect borrowers and contribute to their defaulting on loans.

Compliance While the previous categories concerned the borrower, compliance applies to the lender. Compliance with court decisions, laws, and regulations is an increasingly important part of the lending process. Banks must comply with the Community Reinvestment Act (CRA), the Environmental Superfund Act, and dozens of other laws to operate in accordance with the law and bank regulations and to avoid lender liability. *Lender liability* means that the lender may be sued by borrowers or others for losses and damages. For example, in the case *of U.S. v. Maryland Bank and Trust Company,* the Environmental Protection Agency (EPA) sued the bank for reimbursement of cleanup costs of a hazardous waste dump after the bank foreclosed on the property. However, in *U.S. v. Fleet Factors,* the Eleventh Circuit Court of Appeals ruled that a secured lender can be liable under federal environmental laws, even absent foreclosure, if the lender participates in management to a degree that it influences the firm's treatment of hazardous waste.

Structuring Commercial Loan Agreements

When the bank decides to grant a loan, all of the terms of the loan are put into a contract called a *loan agreement*. The contract is structured to control the borrower to the extent necessary to assure timely repayment of the loan. All commercial loans have the following six elements:

1. The type of credit facility (e.g., term loan) and amount to be borrowed.
2. The term of the loan (e.g., 2 years).
3. The method and timing of repayment (e.g., the loan is to be repaid monthly from the sale of inventory).
4. Interest rates and fees to be paid by the borrower to the banker. The interest rates can be fixed rate or floating rate, based on the prime rate or London Inter-bank Offered Rate (LIBOR), and so forth.
5. Collateral if required.
6. Covenants—promises by the borrower to take or not take certain actions during the term of the loan. For example, the borrower will provide the bank with quarterly financial statements. The borrower will not incur additional long-term debt without the bank's prior permission.

Pricing Commercial Loans

One key element in the process of commercial lending is loan pricing—determining what interest rate to charge the borrower and how to calculate that rate. The interest rate may be determined by using a *loan pricing model*. The purpose of loan pricing models is to determine the minimum price that a bank should charge on a commercial loan. Before we examine loan pricing, let's consider the effective yield.

How to Calculate Effective Yield There is a difference between the *nominal interest rate*—the interest rate that is stated in the loan agreement—and the *effective yield*, which takes the payment accrual basis and the payment frequency into account. The method for calculating effective yields is explained after some terms have been defined.

The *payment accrual basis* refers to the number of days used in the interest rate calculation. One part of the calculation involves the number of days in a year. Interest may be calculated on the basis of a 365-day year or a 360-day year. To illustrate the difference, consider a $1 million loan at a 10 percent nominal rate of interest. The daily interest payment (interest income to the bank and interest expense to the borrower) of the loan is determined by multiplying the amount of the loan by the nominal interest rate and then dividing by the appropriate number of days (365 or 360) and multiplying that figure by the amount of the loan. Accordingly, the cost of a $1 million loan at 10 percent interest is $273.97 on a 365-day basis and $277.78 on a 360-day basis. These calculations will be presented again.

Another part of the calculation involves the number of days that the loan is outstanding. One can use the actual number of days the loan is outstanding, or one can use a 30-day month base.

The final variable is the frequency of interest payments. Typically, term loans are structured with monthly, quarterly, or annual payments. Because of the time value of money (money is worth more today than if the same amount is received in the future), frequent payments are favored by bankers but harder to sell to borrowers. The effect of payment frequency on interest earned and yields will be explained shortly.

To illustrate the effective yield, let's consider a 345-day term loan beginning on January 1 and ending on December 11. The principal amount is $1 million and the interest rate is 10 percent. The calculations for a 360-day year and 30-day month are as follows:

1. $1,000,000 Principal amount
2. ×0.10 Annual interest rate
3. $100,000 Annual interest amount
4. 360 Divide by number of days in year (360 or 365)
5. $277.78 Daily interest payment
6. × (30 days × 11 months + 11 days) Times 11 30-day months plus 11 days (341 days) or the actual number of days
7. $94,722.22 Total interest paid

$$\text{Effective} = \frac{\text{Total interest paid}}{\text{Principal amount}} \times \frac{365}{\text{Term of loan in days}}$$

$$= \frac{\$94{,}722.22}{\$1{,}000{,}000.00} \times \frac{365}{345} = 10.02\% \tag{6.1}$$

The same process (with the appropriate number of days in lines 4 and 6) may be used to calculate the effective yields for 360-day years with actual number of days and 365-day year with actual number of days. The effective yields for the three methods are as follows:

Effective Yield	
360-day year/30-day month	10.02%
360-day year/actual number of days	10.14%
365-day year/actual number of days	10.00%

Effect of Payment Frequency on Interest Earned and Yields The frequency of loan payments has a major impact on interest earned and the yield received on loans. Suppose a bank is considering making a one-year, \$100,000 loan at 12 percent interest. The \$100,000 loan will be repaid at the end of the year. The bank earns \$12,000.00 if interest is paid annually and \$12,747.46 if it is paid daily. The bank earns more when interest is collected frequently.

Payment Periods	Interest Earned on \$100,000 Loan	Yield
Continuous	\$12,748.28	12.748%
Daily	\$12,747.46	12.747%
Monthly	\$12,682.50	12.683%
Quarterly	\$12,550.88	12.551%
Annually	\$12,000.00	12.000%

The amount that the bank receives at the end of the period may be determined by the equation for the future value of \$1:

$$FV_n = PV_o(1 + i/m)^{nm} \tag{6.2}$$

where: FV_n = future value at end of n periods
PV_o = present value (\$100,000 in this example)
i = interest rate
n = number of periods
m = number of interyear periods (days, months, quarters)

Thus, the amount earned if interest is collected monthly is

$$\begin{aligned} FV_{12} &= \$100{,}000(1 + 0.12/12)^{1\times 12} \\ &= \$112{,}682.50 \end{aligned}$$

Interest earned is the difference between FV_{12} and PV_o, which is:

$$\$112{,}682.50 - \$100{,}000 = \$12{,}682.50$$

It follows that the annual yield is[20]

$$\begin{aligned} FV_n &= PV_o(1 + 0.12/12)^{n\times 12} \\ &= 12.683\% \end{aligned}$$

Many loans are amortized, which means that the principal is reduced with periodic payments. Methods for computing the annual interest rates Annual Percentage Rate (APR) on such loans are explained in connection with consumer loans in Chapter 7.

Loan Pricing

When profit margins on commercial loans are razor thin, precise estimates of cost are necessary to price the loans correctly. Overpricing loans results in some borrowers going elsewhere to obtain loans. Underpricing loans results in banks earning less than they should for a given level of risk. Consistent underpricing could adversely affect both the profits and the value of banks making that error.

Many banks price commercial loans by using an index rate (e.g., prime rate) plus a markup of one or more percentage points. Other banks use the cost of borrowed funds (e.g., 90-day certificate of deposit (CD) rate) plus a markup. The advantage of using markups above prime of the cost of CDs is that they are simple and easy to understand. Markups are supposed to compensate the bank for the risk it takes in making a loan, as well as providing a return on its investment. The disadvantage of using markups is that they may not properly account for risk, the cost of funds, and operating expenses. The result may be that some loans are mispriced. The alternative is to use loan pricing models that properly account for risk, costs, and returns.

Return on Net Funds Employed There are many types of loan pricing models. The one presented here is to illustrate some of the factors going into loan pricing. This loan pricing model establishes the required rate of return that the bank wants to earn on the loan, and then it must determine the net income that the loan must generate to provide that return. If the loan cannot generate sufficient net income to earn the required rate of return, the bank should consider rejecting it. We will examine each of the components of the model below, and then solve for loan income.

$$\text{Marginal cost of funds} + \text{Profit goal} = \frac{(\text{Loan income} - \text{Loan expense})}{\text{Net bank funds employed}} \tag{6.3}$$

Required Rate of Return In this model, the required rate of return is equal to the marginal cost of funds plus a profit goal. The marginal cost of capital (funds) is the rate of return required by debt and equity investors on newly issued funds they provide to the bank.[21] That rate may differ from the rate of return required by the bank's management. We make the simplifying assumption that the marginal cost of capital is the *weighted average cost of capital* (WACC).[22] In this example, we further assume that WACC is 6 percent.

$$k_w = k_d(1 - T)L + k_e(1 - L) \tag{6.4}$$

where: kw = weighted average cost of capital of new funds
kd = cost of interest-bearing liabilities
ke = cost of equity
T = corporate tax rate
L = ratio of liabilities to assets.

Profit Goal While the cost of capital takes into account the average risk of the bank, the profit goal must consider the specific risk of each loan, including the risk of bankruptcy as measured by a loan's Z (zeta) score.[23]

The percentages we discuss here reflect the profit goal and are added to the WACC. The size of the markup is directly related to the risk of the loan under consideration. High-risk loans require larger markups than low-risk loans. The criteria for classifying the riskiness of the loan may include the strength of the financial statement, relative position the firm holds in the industry, collateral, and other factors. When all of these factors are considered, the firms may be classified as having, say, very low, low, average, or high risk.

Liquidity, measured in terms of years, must be considered when evaluating the profit goal. Short-term loans are more liquid than long-term loans.

The combination of risk and liquidity can be used to determine a profit goal. For example, the profit goal shown here for a very low-risk loan made for one year or less is 1.0 percent. If the loan had a maturity of three to five years, a 1.2 percent return would be required. The profit goal increases with the risk and the maturity of the loan. The determination of the profit goals based on risk and liquidity are based on management's judgment. Thus, they vary from bank to bank.

Profit Goal for Term of Loans		
Class of Risk	Under 1 year	3–5 years
Very low	1.0	1.2
Low	1.5	1.8
Average	2.0	2.4
High	2.6	3.1

Loan Expense

Loan expense includes all direct and indirect costs associated with making, servicing, and collecting the loan. However, it does not include the bank's cost of funds. Making effective cost estimates to be used in the model is difficult to do. To illustrate the difficulty, suppose that a loan officer spent 35 hours of working time trying to attract a new loan customer. Let's consider only the officer's time, which is worth $100 per hour. The cost is $3,500. If the customer borrows $10,000 for 90 days, the equation suggests that the bank would have to charge more than $3,500 (35 percent) to cover that cost alone. Obviously, the bank would not attempt to charge that amount. Nevertheless, someone has to pay for the loan officer's time. This is done by using cost accounting data and trying to make reasonable estimates about the cost of making, servicing, and collecting loans.

Net Bank Funds Employed The net bank funds employed is the average amount of the loan over its life, less funds provided by the borrower, net of Federal Reserve System reserve requirements. Borrowers provide funds in the form of compensating balances or other balances held at the bank. The bank cannot use the entire amount on deposit because it is required by the Federal Reserve System to maintain a specified amount of reserves against those balances.

To illustrate the use of Eq. (6.4), let's make the following four assumptions:

1. Marginal cost of funds is 6 percent.
2. Profit goal is 2 percent.
3. Loan expense is $2,000.
4. Net bank funds employed is $100,000.

Given these assumptions, we use Eq. (6.4) to solve for loan income, which comes out to $10,000.

$$(6\% + 2\%) = \frac{(\text{Loan income } - \$2{,}000)}{\$100{,}000}$$

$$\text{Loan income} = \$10{,}000$$

The $10,000 is the amount of income this loan must generate for the bank to earn its required rate of return. This figure understates the correct amount because it does not take the time value of money into account. Nevertheless, it is a good ballpark estimate of the income that is needed.

This loan pricing model is best suited for banks that have effective cost accounting data and can estimate the order data that are required. If this model is used to price variable-rate loans, the rate of return to the bank will change whenever the loan rate changes. This problem is resolved in the next model.

Relationship Pricing The loan pricing model that was examined did not take into account other business relationships that the borrower may have with the bank. For example, the borrower may be using cash management services, have a pension fund managed by the bank, and use other bank facilities. Each of these activities generates positive income. When and under what circumstances should a borrower's relationships be considered?

To answer that question, we must think about making a loan as a new investment opportunity. All of the relevant cash flows must be evaluated. If the loan is the only business that the borrower has with the bank, then only the cash flows associated with the loan are relevant. However, if the loan is one of many services provided by the bank, then all of the cash flows associated with that borrower's relationship with the bank must be evaluated. The projected cash flow from each service, including the loan, should be adjusted to take risks into account. In *relationship pricing,* the rate charged on a loan may differ from the rate indicated by the loan pricing model presented previously.

Minimum Spread Some banks price loans by determining the minimum spread they will accept between their lending rate and their costs plus a profit margin. For example, assume that a bank's costs are 8 percent and the profit margin is 2 percent. If the bank wants to encourage lending, it will accept a smaller profit margin and charge borrowers 9 percent. If the bank wants to retard lending, it will increase the spread and charge borrowers 11 percent or more. Encouraging and discouraging lending is a common practice and reflects banks' changing financial needs. The banks know that many large commercial loans are repriced every day or every 30, 60, or 90 days. Large borrowers regularly shop for the lowest rates. A bank that increases its lending rate in one period to discourage borrowers may decide to make the loan the next time it is repriced. Loans to corporations waiting to sell commercial paper are an example of loans that are repriced frequently.

Average Cost versus Marginal Cost The costs used in this model include the cost of funds and operating costs. Here, too, there are problems determining the relevant costs. Since operating costs have been discussed previously, let's focus on the cost of funds. Should the bank use the *average cost of funds* or the marginal cost of funds? In the explanation of the cost of capital, the marginal and average costs were the same. But that is not always the case. To illustrate this problem, suppose that a firm wants to borrow $1 million for 90 days. The bank's lending rate is the cost of funds plus 1 percentage point per annum. The hypothetical bank raised $0.5 million by selling a 90-day CD at 10 percent. In addition, the bank has $0.5 million in other interest-rate-sensitive liabilities that cost 8 percent. For simplicity, we ignore equity. The average cost of borrowed funds, which is determined by dividing total interest cost by total funds employed, is 9.0 percent. The marginal cost of funds, or the 90-day CD rate, is 10 percent.

Should the bank use the average cost of funds or the marginal cost of funds to price the loan? When market rates of interest are rising, the bank is better off using the marginal cost of funds because it is higher than the average cost of funds. However, when market rates of interest are falling, it is better off using the average cost of funds, which is higher than the marginal cost.

Another consideration is how the loan is funded. If the $1 million, 90-day loan was *match funded* by selling a $1 million 90-day CD, the CD rate could be used to represent the borrowed funds. Although not mentioned previously, the bank would have to raise more than $1 million to cover reserve requirements. Suppose that reserve requirements are 5 percent. The bank would have to raise $1,052,632 ($1,000,000/0.95 = $1,052,632) in order to lend $1 million.

If the bank views all of its deposits as a pool of funds used to finance loans, the answer is still the marginal rate. In theory, the marginal loan (the next loan to be made) should be charged the marginal cost of funds, including the cost of equity.

All of the examples used here suggest that in order to make a profit, a bank's lending rate should be greater than its cost of funds, including equity.

Performance Pricing The price of a loan reflects the riskiness of the borrower. When the borrower's riskiness changes, the price of the loan should be changed accordingly. One way to do this is with *performance pricing*, which allows banks and borrowers to change the price of a loan without renegotiating it. The price can be tied to specific financial ratios, the amount of the loan outstanding, the borrower's debt ratings, or other criteria that are mutually agreeable.

Monitoring and Loan Review

After the loan has been granted, the bank must monitor the loan to determine if the borrower is complying with the terms of the loan agreement. Part of the monitoring process is a loan review. This is an internal audit system for the lending functions of the bank. Loan reviews help to identify potential problems with particular loans, as well as weaknesses in loan procedures. In addition, it is used to help quantify the risk in the loan portfolio.

Payoffs or Losses?

One of four things can happen to an outstanding loan: (1) It can be repaid on schedule. (2) It can be renewed or extended. (3) The bank can sell the loan to another investor. (4) The loan can go into default, and the bank may sustain losses. Items 1 to 3 are desirable outcomes. Item 4 is the worst-case scenario for the bank.

INTERNATIONAL LENDING

Some features of international lending are different from domestic lending. There are some similar practices, also. This section examines only those lending practices that are typically associated with international lending.

Syndicated Loans

As previously noted, both domestic and foreign loans can be syndicated. Syndication is presented here because it permits banks of different sizes to participate in international lending.

The *syndication* of large loans has advantages for both the borrower and the lender. From the borrower's point of view, syndication provides more funds than may be available from any single lender. In addition, the credit terms may be better than for a large number of smaller loans. From the lender's point of view, syndication provides a means of diversifying some of the risks of foreign lending that were discussed previously. Another advantage of syndication is that it provides the lead bank with off-balance-sheet income for that portion of the loan that is sold to other participants. The lead bank and other banks that co-manage the loan receive fee income for their management services. Typically, the management fee is paid by the borrower at the time the loan is made. Such fees range from 0.5 percent to more than 2 percent of the total amount of the loan. Finally, syndication can enhance relations with foreign governments because it is a means of financing their domestic economic activity.

The Syndication Process

There are two types of syndicated bank loans. The first occurs when there is an agreement between the borrower and each lender. The second, which is the one we are concerned with, is a *participation loan,* which is a cross between traditional bank lending and underwriting. In this form of participation, there are three levels of banks in the syndicate: lead banks, managing banks, and participating banks. The lead banks negotiate with the borrower on the terms of the loan and assemble the management group that will underwrite it. They are also responsible for all documentation of the loan (notes, security agreements, legal opinions, and so on). Moreover, they are expected to underwrite a share of the loans themselves, at least as large as that of the other lenders. After the underwriting group has been established, information will be sent to other banks that may be interested in participating. For example, the initial telex cables advise the name of the borrower, maturity of the loan, and interest rates. If a bank is interested in participating, it advises a member of the underwriting group and receives additional information that permits it to analyze the credit. Although the loan may be attractive, some banks may reject it because they have already reached their lending limits in that country or region. Finally, syndication does not relieve each participating bank from doing its own credit analysis and assessment of risks.

Loan Pricing

Eurocurrency syndicated loans, as well as many domestic commercial and industrial loans, are priced at LIBOR plus a certain number of points. *LIBOR* is the rate at which banks lend funds to other banks in the Euromarket. It is usually about $\frac{1}{8}$ to $\frac{1}{4}$ percent above *LIBB,* the London interbank bid—the rate at which they buy funds. Accordingly, a syndicated loan may be priced at, say, LIBOR plus 0.5 percent for the next five years. In the Pacific basin, there is *SIBOR,* which is the Singapore interbank offered rate. Singapore is the center of the Asia dollar market, and SIBOR is widely used in Asian trade.

Although LIBOR changes on a day-to-day basis, the interest rates on the loans are usually adjusted every three or six months. Additional loan costs include commitment fees, underwriting fees, and other charges. Like domestic loans, commitment fees are based on the unused portion of the credit that is available to the firm under the terms of the agreement. For example, the fee may be 0.5 percent annually of that amount.

Unlike domestic loans, there may be an underwriting fee, which is a one-time front-end cost. Such fees are divided among the lead banks and the other banks in proportion to their participation.

Finally, the loans may also have clauses dealing with foreign taxes and reserve requirements, so that the lenders receive all the payments that are necessary to pay for the principal and interest on the loans.

SUMMARY

Banks make most of their money by lending, and lending accounts for most of their risk—credit risk. Recall from Chapter 1 that credit risk is the primary cause of bank failure. Simply stated, credit risk is the risk to earnings and capital that an obligor will fail to meet the terms of a contract with the bank. Asymmetric information and adverse selection play important roles in credit risk. Asymmetric information refers to the fact that borrowers know more about their business prospects than banks, and banks tend to attract higher-risk borrowers. This, coupled with increased competition for lending from nonbank lenders, has resulted in banks shifting their portfolios to higher-risk loans in hopes of increasing their profitability. Changes in technology, such as securitization and credit scoring, also have affected the ways loans are made and serviced.

The process of lending begins with the board of directors' written loan policy that sets out the guidelines within which the bank must operate. Given those limits, which vary from bank to bank, various techniques for reducing credit risk (avoiding high-risk loans, diversification, and so on) were presented. Against this background, the ways (soliciting loans, buying loans, commitments, and so on) that banks make C&I loans were explained. Loans should be made with the expectation that they will be repaid from earnings or the sale of assets. Collateral is a secondary source of repayment.

Banks make different types of C&I loans for different purposes. Lines of credit, for example, are used to finance temporary or seasonal working capital needs; term loans are used to finance the acquisition of real assets and for other purposes. The use of collateral is a common practice in C&I lending. Collateral reduces the risk to a bank and serves as an incentive to the borrower to repay the loan. Almost anything that is legal can be used as collateral. However, the most common forms of collateral include accounts receivable, inventory, equipment, and real estate.

Before loans are granted, the lender must evaluate the creditworthiness of the prospective borrower. The borrower's character, financial condition, and ability to repay the loan from future income or the sale of assets are of primary importance. The bank must also comply with numerous federal regulations before and after credit is extended. In addition, the bank must price the loan so that it is fair to the customer and profitable for the bank. Different pricing models result in different interest earnings. Once all of this is done, the loan agreement is developed that provides details about how the funds will be used, how they will be repaid, and other terms. After the loan is granted, the bank must monitor the loan to assure repayment. The best outcome is that the loan is repaid in full. The worst outcome is that it is charged off as a loss.

CHAPTER 7

Real Estate and Consumer Lending

Federal Deposit Insurance Corporation (FDIC) Chairman Sheila C. Bair said:[1]

> *For many decades U.S. government policies have promoted housing in general and homeownership in particular. These policies have been very successful in raising the quality of our housing stock while extending the benefits of homeownership to more than two-thirds of American households.... But now that our housing bubble has burst... we must recognize that the financial crisis was triggered by a reckless departure from tried and true, common-sense loan underwriting practices.... Traditional mortgage lending worked so well in the past because lenders required sizeable down payments, solid borrower credit histories, proper income documentation, and sufficient income to make regular payments at the fully-indexed rate of the loan. Not only were these bedrock principles relaxed in the run-up to the crisis, but they were frequently relaxed all at once in the same loans in a practice regulators refer to as "risk layering." ... As all of you know, the long-term credit performance of a portfolio of mortgage loans can only be as sound as the underwriting practices used to originate those loans.*[2]

REAL ESTATE LENDING

Mortgage Debt Outstanding

The term *mortgage* is used in connection with real estate lending. In general terms, a mortgage is a written conveyance of title to real property. It provides the lender with a security interest in the property, if the mortgage is

TABLE 7.1 Mortgage Debt Outstanding by Type of Property, Fourth Quarter 2009 ($ millions)

1- to 4-family residences	$ 10,772,272	75%
Multifamily residences	898,852	6
Nonfarm, nonresidential (commercial)	2,477,614	17
Farm	138,602	1
Total	$ 14,287,340	100%

Source: Board of Governors of the Federal Reserve System, "Mortgage Debt Outstanding, March 2010," Totals do not add to 100 percent due to rounding. www.federalreserve.gov/econresdata/releases/mortoutstand/current.htm.

properly recorded in the county courthouse. It also provides that the property being used as collateral for the loan will be sold if the debt is not repaid as agreed. The proceeds from the sale of the property are used to reimburse the lender. As shown in Table 7.1, 1- to 4-family residential mortgage debt accounts for 75 percent of the total mortgage debt outstanding. Nonresidential and nonfarm commercial buildings and other business real estate loans are called *commercial mortgage loans,* which are the second largest category of mortgage loans. Multifamily residences and farm mortgages account for the remainder.[3]

Mortgage loans are *originated* by commercial banks and other financial institutions. The originating institutions may hold the mortgages in their loan portfolios or sell them in the secondary market. The *secondary mortgage market,* in which securities representing pools of mortgage loans are purchased and sold, increases the liquidity of residential mortgages and lessens the cyclical disruptions in the housing market. The pools of mortgage loans are one type of *asset-backed securities.*

The process of transforming individual loans into marketable asset-backed securities is called *securitization.* The process involves the issuance of securities that represent claims against a pool of assets (e.g., mortgages, car loans, credit card receivables, and small business loans) that are held in trust. The originator of a loan sells the assets to a trust. It must be a *true sale,* which means that the assets cannot be returned to the originator's balance sheet. The trustee then issues securities through an investment banker (underwriter) to investors. Some banks act as packagers of asset-based loans, and they take on the risk of an underwriter. Some act as originators and packagers, and they service (collect loan payments, deal with delinquencies, and so on) the loans, too. As the principal and interest payments are made on the loans, they are paid out to investors by the trustee or *servicer,* who retains a small transaction fee. In many cases, the cash flows to investors are guaranteed (*credit enhanced*) by bank guarantees (standby letters of credit), by government agency guarantees (e.g., Government National Mortgage Association), or by having more loans than is necessary to secure the value of the pools (*overcollateralize*). Credit rating agencies, such as Standard and Poor's, assign ratings to asset-backed securities just as they do for stocks and bonds. The quality of the credit enhancement is an important part of the rating. The credit enhancements, credit ratings, and the reputations of the investment banker or packager help to standardize the quality of asset-backed loans. However, the financial crisis that began in 2007 revealed that many of the credit ratings and enhancements were flawed.

The Dodd-Frank Act of 2010 requires that firms that originate mortgage-backed securities must retain at least 5 percent of the credit risk. In other words, they must have some skin in the game to ensure that these securities meet new credit standards that are aimed at reducing risk.

One benefit of the secondary mortgage market is that it permits lenders to increase the liquidity of their mortgage portfolio. Stated otherwise, they can package otherwise unmarketable individual mortgage loans and sell them to investors. Another benefit is that the secondary market has attracted investors from outside the traditional mortgage investment community who want to buy mortgage-backed securities. Thus, the secondary mortgage market has increased the breadth, depth, and liquidity of the capital market that is available for mortgage financing.

The three major participants in the secondary market are the Federal National Mortgage Corporation (Fannie Mae), the Federal Home Loan Mortgage Association (Freddie Mac), and the Government National Mortgage Association (Ginnie Mae).[4] These organizations were created by Congress, and they developed a secondary mortgage market. They issue mortgage pools or trusts of one- to four-family real estate, multifamily real estate, and certain other properties. Congress also created the Farmers Home Administration, but it is a very small factor in the secondary mortgage market. Some private organizations also operate in the secondary mortgage market. As shown in Table 7.2, mortgage pools and trusts hold more than half of the total mortgage debt outstanding. The table also reveals that commercial banks hold more mortgage debt than savings institutions, life insurance companies, and federal and related agencies.

The *Federal Home Loan (FHL) Banks* also play an important role in providing liquidity to the mortgage market. More than 8,000 banks, thrifts, credit unions, community development financial institutions, insurance companies, and state housing finance agencies are members of the Federal Home Loan Bank system. They have branches throughout the 50 states and the

TABLE 7.2 Mortgage Debt Outstanding by Type of Holder, Fourth Quarter 2009 ($ millions)

Commercial banks	$3,818,960
Savings institutions	633,339
Life insurance companies	328,867
Federal and related agencies	785,152
Mortgage pools and trusts	7,592,919
Individuals and others	1,128,105
Total	$14,287,340

Source: Board of Governors of the Federal Reserve System, "Mortgage Debt Outstanding, March 2010," www.federalreserve.gov/econresdata/releases/mortoutstand/current.htm.

U.S. territories. Member institutions are eligible to borrow funds (called *advances*) from the FHLBanks. To qualify for advances, members must pledge high-quality collateral in the form of mortgages, government securities, or loans on small business, agriculture, or community development.[5] At year-end 2009, the FHLBanks had more than $631 billion in outstanding advances. They also hold mortgage-backed securities.

CHARACTERISTICS OF MORTGAGE LOANS

Table 7.3 lists selected characteristics of new home mortgages in May 2003. The average purchase price of a new home was $350,600, and the average amount lent was $267,152. The difference between those two amounts, $83,448, represents the *down payment*, or borrower's equity. *Equity* is the difference between the market value of the property and the borrower's mortgage debt. From the lender's perspective, the percentage loaned to

TABLE 7.3 Selected Characteristics of New Home Mortgages, 2008

Purchase price	$350,600
Amount of loan	$267,152
Loan-to-price	76.2%
Contract interest rate	5.9%
Fees and charges	$2,945 (0.84% of loan amount)
Maturity	29.1 years

Source: U.S. Federal Housing Finance Board, "Rates & Terms on Conventional Home Mortgages, Annual Summary," www.census.gov/compendia/statab/2010/tables/10s1156.xls.

the borrowers, or the loan-to-price ratio, was 76.2 percent. Bank regulators have established loan-to-value (LTV) limits for different categories of loans. For example, the LTV limit for raw land is 65 percent, and for 1- to 4-family residential construction, it is 85 percent, but there is no limit on owner-occupied homes.[6] Bank regulators also placed limits on the aggregate of real estate loans. For example, the aggregate of high LTV one- to four-family residential loans should not exceed 100 percent of the institution's total capital.

In option pricing theory, bank loans are considered compound options containing the rights to prepay (call options) and to default (put options) on each of the scheduled payment dates. When the put options are in the money (the value of the asset is less than the loan amount), borrowers have an incentive to exercise their put options and default on the loans. The lower the loan-to-price ratio (i.e., the higher the borrower's equity), the less likely it is that borrowers will default.

When market interest rates decline, borrowers with fixed-rate loans may exercise their call options and prepay the loans. That is, they refinance their loans at lower rates. For example, Table 7.3 shows that the average contract interest rate on mortgage loans was 5.9 percent, and borrowers paid fees, commissions, discounts, and points to make the loan amounting to $2,945. The fees and the interest earned on the loan are income for the lenders. If interest rates and fees decline sufficiently, say, 200 basis points, many borrowers with fixed-rate mortgages will refinance at the lower rates.

The average maturity of new home mortgage loans is about 29 years. However, because borrowers may sell their home or refinance when rates decline, the average life of a mortgage portfolio is substantially less. For example, the weighted average life may be about 12 years.

The Real Estate Portfolio

Banks make an investment decision as to the percentage of their loan portfolio that they want to invest in various types of real estate loans. The decision takes into account risks and returns of the various types of real estate loans they make (residential, commercial, and so forth). In the first quarter of 2010, residential real estate loans accounted for 25 percent of bank loans, nonfarm nonresidential real estate loans were 15 percent, and construction loans were 6 percent.[7] These figures include mortgage-backed securities.

The risks include defaults, declining real estate values, prepayments, and lack of liquidity. Bankers also must decide what proportions of their loans should be made at fixed rates or at adjustable rates. These decisions reflect the characteristics of the lender, the market, and the borrowers. Lenders mitigate some of these risks by raising their credit standards and excluding less creditworthy borrowers, by requiring borrowers to make larger down payments (lower loan-to-price ratios), by selling real estate loans in the secondary market, and by changing origination fees to influence borrowers' behavior. The returns banks receive on real estate lending come from interest earned on the loans; fees for transaction, settlement, and closing costs; and fees for servicing loans that are sold. In addition, they charge points that are fees paid to the lender, and they are often linked to the interest rate. One point equals 1 percent of the loan. Finally, some lenders require *private mortgage insurance* (PMI) when the down payment is less than 20 percent. The PMI protects the lender in the event of default.[8]

Collateral Residential real estate is good collateral because it is durable and easy to identify, and most structures cannot be moved elsewhere. Despite these fine qualities, the value of real estate can go up or down. During periods of inflation, residential real estate in many parts of the country appreciated in value, thereby enhancing its value as collateral. During deflation and recessions, however, the value of residential real estate in some areas declined. When real estate values decline during periods of economic distress, delinquencies and default rates on real estate loans increase.

The fact that real estate has a fixed geographic location is both good and bad. It is good in the sense that the collateral cannot be removed. It is bad in the sense that its value is affected by adjacent property. If a toxic waste dump site were to locate in what was previously a golf course, the value of the adjacent residential property would decline. Finally, real estate is illiquid. That is, it is difficult to sell on short notice at its fair market value. These comments on residential real estate also apply to commercial real estate.

Residential Mortgage Loans

Residential mortgage loans differ from other types of loans in several respects. First, the loans are for relatively large dollar amounts. As shown in Table 7.3, the average loan for a new home was $350,600. Second, the loans tend to be long-term, with original maturities as long as 30 years. Third, the loans are usually secured by the real estate as collateral. However, real estate is illiquid, and its price can vary widely.

The two basic types of 1- to 4-family residential mortgage loans are fixed-rate mortgages and adjustable-rate mortgages (ARMs). The interest rate charged on fixed-rate mortgages does not change over the life of the loan. In contrast, ARMs permit lenders to vary the interest rate charged on the mortgage loan when market rates of interest change. The basic idea behind ARMs is to help mortgage lenders keep the returns on their assets (mortgage loans) higher than the costs of their funds. However, it is the borrowers who decide what type of mortgage loans they want, and that choice is influenced by the level of interest rates. When interest rates are high, borrowers prefer ARMs that will provide lower rates when interest rates decline. Alternatively, they can refinance their fixed-rate mortgages, but that costs more to do. Lenders, on the other hand, prefer ARMs when interest rates are expected to increase, so that they can benefit from the higher rates.

Conventional mortgage loans are those that are not insured by the Federal Housing Administration (FHA) or guaranteed by the Veterans Administration (VA). Mortgage loans that are insured by the FHA or guaranteed by VA are called *government-backed or insured mortgages*. However, some conventional mortgages are insured against default by PMI companies.

Fixed-Rate Mortgages Fixed-rate, fully amortized, level-payment mortgages are a widely used form of financing residential mortgage loans. *Fixed-rate, fully amortized, level-payment mortgage* means that the interest rate does not change and the debt is gradually extinguished through equal periodic payments on the principal balance. In other words, the borrower pays the same dollar amount each month until the mortgage loan is paid off. Partially amortized, fixed-rate mortgages also are used for financing home loans. In this case, only a portion of the debt is extinguished by level periodic payments over a relatively short period, say, five years, and the unamortized amount is paid in one large lump sum payment—a *balloon payment*. Alternatively, the loan can be refinanced when it matures.

Monthly Mortgage Payments The dollar amount of monthly payments depends on the size of the loan, the interest rate, and the maturity. Table 7.4 shows the monthly mortgage payments for a $1,000 mortgage loan with

TABLE 7.4 Monthly Payments for a $1,000 Mortgage Loan

Annual Interest Rate	Years to Maturity				
	10 Years	15 Years	20 Years	25 Years	30 Years
6%	$11.10	$8.44	$7.16	$6.44	$6.00
8	12.13	9.56	8.36	7.72	7.34
10	13.22	10.75	9.65	9.09	8.78
12	14.35	12.00	11.01	10.53	10.29
14	15.35	13.32	12.44	12.04	11.85
16	16.76	14.69	13.92	13.59	13.45

selected annual interest rates and maturities. A close examination of the body of the table reveals two important facts. First, the dollar amount of the monthly mortgage payment increases as the interest rate increases. For example, the monthly mortgage payment for a loan with 10 years to maturity ranges from $11.10 when the interest rate is 6 percent to $16.76 when the interest rate is 16 percent. Second, the dollar amount of the monthly mortgage payment declines as the maturity of the loan is extended. When the interest rate is 6 percent, the monthly mortgage payment declines from $11.10 when the maturity is 10 years to $6.00 when the maturity is 30 years.

The monthly mortgage payments shown in Table 7.4 can be determined by using equation 7.1 to solve for the present value of an annuity. By way of illustration, we will compute the monthly mortgage payment for a $1,000 mortgage loan at 6 percent interest for 10 years. Because we are solving for a monthly payment, the number of payments over the 10 years is 120 (10 years × 12 months per year). Moreover, only one-twelfth of the 6 percent annual interest rate (0.06/12 = 0.005) is charged each month. The present value of the annuity is the $1,000 mortgage loan in this example. The monthly payment is $11.10.

$$\text{PV of annuity} = \text{PMT}\left[\frac{1-(1+i)^{-n}}{i}\right]$$

$$\$1{,}000 = \text{PMT}\left[\frac{1-(1+0.005)^{120}}{0.005}\right]$$

$$\text{PMT} = \$11.10 \tag{7.1}$$

where: PV = Present value of the annuity.
PMT = Payment per period
i = Interest rate per period
n = Number of periods

Maturity Don't be fooled by low monthly payments. For a given interest rate and maturity, the total cost of the loan is higher with longer maturities (smaller monthly payments) than shorter maturities (higher monthly payments). The total cost is determined by multiplying the mortgage payment per $1,000 of loan for each interest rate by the dollar amount of the loan (in thousands) and the number of months. By way of illustration, consider a $100,000 mortgage loan at 12 percent with a maturity of 10 years. The monthly payment is $1,435 ($14.35× 100 = $1,435), and the total cost

TABLE 7.5 Mortgage Amortization, $100,000 at 12 Percent for 25 Years, Months 1–12, Monthly Payment = $1,053.00

Month	Principal	Interest	Balance
1	$53.00	$1,000.00	$99,000.00
2	63.00	990.00	98,010.00
3	72.90	980.10	97,029.90
4	82.70	970.30	96,059.60
5	92.40	960.60	95,099.00
6	102.01	950.99	94,148.00
7	111.52	941.48	93,206.53
8	120.93	932.07	92,274.46
9	130.26	922.74	91,351.72
10	139.48	913.52	90,438.20
11	148.62	904.38	89,533.82
12	157.66	895.34	88,638.48
Totals	$1,274.48	$11,361.52	

over the life of the loan is $172,200 ($1,435 × 120 months = $172,000). If the maturity were 25 years, the monthly payment would be reduced to $1,053, but the total cost would be $315,900, which is $143,900 more than the cost of the shorter-term loan.

Principal and Interest Let's examine the monthly mortgage payment in greater detail and consider the amount that is allocated to principal and to interest. Table 7.5 shows the breakdown between principal and interest for the first year's payments of a $100,000 loan at 12 percent for 25 years. The striking feature of this table is the disproportionate amount of the monthly payment that is applied to interest payments. Total mortgage payments amounted to $12,636 ($1,053 × 12 = $12,636) during the first 12 months of the loan. Of that amount, $11,361.52 was applied to interest and only $1,274.48 was used to reduce the principal amount of the loan.

The implication of the data presented in Table 7.5 is that lenders earn most of their interest income during the early years of a mortgage loan. Therefore, all other things being equal, a high turnover of the mortgage loans contributes more interest income to earnings than having mortgage loans remain in their portfolio until they mature.[9]

Adjustable-Rate Mortgages An ARM is one in which the interest rate changes over the life of the loan. The change can result in changes in monthly payments, the term of the loan, and/or the principal amount.

Index The idea behind ARMs is to permit lenders to maintain a positive spread between the returns on their mortgage loans (assets) and their cost of borrowed funds (liabilities) when benchmark interest rates change. This is accomplished by linking the mortgage rate to a standard benchmark rate, such as the rate on one-year Constant Maturity Treasury yield or the Federal Reserve's District Cost of Funds Index (COFI).[10]

When an index changes, the lender can (1) make periodic changes in the borrowers' monthly payments, (2) keep the monthly payment the same and change the principal amount of the loan, (3) change the maturity of the loan, or (4) any combination of these. Some mortgage loans have fixed rates for 3 years, 5 years, 7 years, or 10 years but may adjust one time or annually after that.

The best adjustment, from the lender's point of view, depends on whether interest rates are expected to rise or fall over the life of the mortgage. If they are expected to rise, increased monthly payments will increase the lender's cash flow. If they are expected to fall, the second option will permit the lender to more or less maintain the spread between earning assets and costs of funds. The adjustment period may be monthly, annually, or any other time period, according to the terms of the contract.

Caps ARMs have *caps* that limit how much the interest rate or monthly payments can change annually or over the term of the loan. For example, the interest rate may change no more than 2 percentage points annually nor more than 6 percentage points over the life of the loan. Alternatively, a $50 payment cap means that the monthly payment cannot increase more than $50 per year.

Margin *Margin* is the number of percentage points that the lender adds to the index rate to determine the rate charged on the ARM each adjustment period. The equation for the ARM rate that is charged is:

$$\text{ARM interest rate} = \text{index rate} + \text{margin} \tag{7.2}$$

Suppose the index rate is 6 percent and the margin is 2 percent. The interest rate that will be charged on the ARM is 8 percent (6% + 2% = 8%). The margin usually remains constant over the life of the loan. However, the size of the margin can vary from lender to lender.

Rates Lenders may offer prospective home buyers a lower interest rate or lower payments for the first year of the mortgage loan to induce the buyer to use an ARM. After the discount period, the ARM rate will be adjusted to reflect the current index rate. The lower rate is commonly called a *teaser rate,* because lenders expect it to increase in future years.

Even without teaser rates, the initial interest rates charged on ARMs are lower than the rates charged on fixed-rate mortgages. The extent to which they are lower depends on the maturity of the loans and varies widely, but differences of 100 or more basis points are not uncommon. For example, in June 2010, the average 5/1-year ARM available in the United States was 3.78 percent, the average 15-year fixed-rate mortgage was 4.18 percent, and the 30-year rate was 4.80 percent.[11] The 5/1 ARM means that the interest rate is fixed for five years and then adjusted on an annual basis thereafter. The interest rate for a 30-year jumbo mortgage was 5.76 percent. A *jumbo mortgage* is one that is larger than the limits set by Fannie Mae and Freddie Mac. In 2010, the single-family loan limit was $417,000 in the 48 adjacent states and $625,500 in Alaska, Hawaii, and the Virgin Islands.[12] In high-cost-of-living cities, the amounts were $729,750 in the 48 states and $938,250 in Alaska, Hawaii, and the Virgin Islands. The amount is adjusted annually. Mortgage loans exceeding these loan limits are called *nonconforming loans.*

Subprime Mortgages As explained in Chapter 1, the term *subprime* typically refers to high-risk loans made to borrowers with low credit scores (e.g., Fair Isaac Corporation (FICO) credit scores below 660), and/or high LTV ratios, and/or debt-to-income ratios above 50 percent, and other factors.[13] Some mortgage loans had little or no documentation (low doc and no doc loans). Subprime loans also include nonconforming loans.

Alt-A mortgages may lack full documentation, have higher LTV ratios and debt-to-income ratios, or have other features that do not conform to the Government Sponsored entities' (GSEs') lending guidelines. They are riskier than mortgages that are prime rated but less risky than subprime mortgages.

Shifting the Risk Lenders shift some of their interest rate risk of holding mortgage loans from themselves to borrowers by using ARMs. However, the lenders may have traded reduced interest rate risk for increased default risk and lower income. First, ARMs are riskier than fixed-rate mortgages because they generate less interest income during periods of declining interest. Second, ARMs have higher delinquency and default risks than fixed-rate mortgages. One reason for this may be that LTV ratios are higher for ARMs than for fixed-rate mortgages. Another may be that ARMs are used more frequently by younger, first-time buyers. The delinquency rates reported here occurred during a period of falling interest rates. The delinquency rates may get worse if interest rates increase because borrowers' ability to repay loans may be diminished. Borrowers' disposable income may not increase sufficiently to cover the higher interest payments. These risks are reflected in the relatively narrow spread between the effective rates charged on fixed-rate mortgages and ARMs that were mentioned previously.

Lenders can reduce their risk by requiring borrowers to have PMI on their loans. PMI is usually required when the down payment, or borrower's equity, is less than 20 percent. PMI companies consider ARMs riskier than their fixed-rate counterparts, and the insurance premiums on ARMs are higher than those on fixed-rate mortgages.

Finally, some lenders use *credit default swaps* (CDSs) as a form of insurance to protect against potential losses in the event that borrowers default on their loans. However, CDSs are not insurance in the legal sense of the word. The seller of the CDS may not be a regulated insurance company or have reserves to pay off the buyers. In addition, the buyer of the CDS does not need to own the underlying asset that is covered by the CDS.

Additional Terms

Assumable Mortgage Some mortgage loans, such as VA-backed home loans, are assumable, which means that they can be passed on to a new owner if the property is sold. Most mortgage loans are not assumable.

Buydown A high mortgage interest rate is offset by paying points at the time of closing.

Due-on-Sale Clause Some mortgage loans contain a *due-on-sale clause,* which means that the mortgage loan is not transferable to the new buyer, and the balance of the loan must be paid to the lender when the house is sold. The clause is exercised at the option of the lender. Other loans, however, are *assumable,* which means that the mortgage loan can be transferred to the buyer, if the buyer meets the lender's credit requirements and pays a fee for the assumption.

Late Charges Borrowers are required to make their monthly payments by a certain date or pay a late charge. Late charges cover the costs of handling delinquent accounts and add to the lender's fee income.

Mortgage Insurance PMI for conventional mortgage loans is required by some lenders to reduce the default risk by insuring against loss on a specified percentage of the loan, usually the top 20 to 25 percent.

Points In addition to interest on the borrowed funds, lenders charge both fixed-rate and adjustable-rate mortgage borrowers additional fees or points to increase their income and to cover the costs of originating and closing mortgage loans. A *point* is 1 percent of the principal amount of a mortgage loan, and points are prepaid interest. One point on a $100,000 mortgage is $1,000. The points usually are paid by the borrower at the time of the closing. They may be deducted from the face amount of the loan or paid as a cash cost. If they are deducted from the face amount of the loan, a one point closing cost on a $100,000 mortgage loan would result in a disbursement to the borrower of $99,000. Points are charged on government-backed (FHA, VA, FmHA) mortgages when the market rate of interest on conventional mortgage loans exceeds the rate permitted on such mortgages. The points make up the difference in rates between the two types of mortgages.

Points increase the *effective interest rate* of a mortgage loan. The effective interest rate is the contract interest rate plus points and other costs amortized over the payback period of the loan. As a rule of thumb, each point (1 percent of the loan amount) increases the interest charge by one-eighth (0.125) of 1 percent. The $\frac{1}{8}$ factor corresponds to a *payback period* (number of years until the loan is paid off) of about 15 years. For example, suppose that the contract interest rate on a mortgage loan is 13 percent, and 4 points are charged at the closing. The effective interest rate for a 15-year payback is 13.5 percent ($13\% + 0.125 \times 0.04 = 0.135$). If the loan is repaid before or after 15 years, the rule of thumb does not apply.

Settlement Charges *Settlement* is the formal process by which ownership of real property, evidenced by the title, is transferred from the seller to the buyer. The settlement process for most residential mortgage loans is governed by the Real Estate Settlement Procedures Act (RESPA). Part of the settlement costs may include fees that enhance the lender's income. Examples of such fees are:

- Loan discounts or points.
- Loan origination fees, covering the lender's administrative costs.
- Lender's inspection fees to inspect the property.
- Assumption processing fees may be charged when the buyer takes on the prior loan from the seller.
- Escrow, which means funds held to ensure future payment of real estate taxes and insurance. No interest is paid on the funds.
- Settlement or closing fee, a fee paid to the settlement agent.
- Title search and guarantee.
- Survey of the property.

These settlement fees and others not mentioned here may amount to 3 percent or more of the total amount borrowed.

Alternative Mortgage Instruments

Alternative mortgage instruments is a generic term that covers a smorgasbord of mortgage instruments where the terms of the contract can change or where they differ from the traditional mortgage loan. Following are the principal types of alternative mortgage instruments.

Balloon Mortgage Balloon mortgage loans are relatively short-term loans, such as five years. At the end of that period, the entire amount of the loan comes due, and a new loan is negotiated. The initial payments are usually based on a 20- to 30-year amortization. This is similar to the *Canadian rollover mortgage* or *renegotiable mortgage,* where the maturity is fixed, but the interest payments are renegotiated every three to five years.

Graduated Payment Mortgage Because of the high cost of housing, many young buyers cannot afford large monthly mortgage payments. Graduated payment mortgages (GPMs) address this problem by making a fixed-rate loan where monthly payments are low at first and then rise over a period of years.

Because the monthly payments on GPMs are so low in the early years, there is *negative amortization:* The monthly payments are insufficient to pay the interest on the loan. The unpaid interest accrues, and borrowers pay interest on the interest. If the borrowers decided to sell their residence in the early years, and it did not appreciate in value, the principal balance on the loan would have increased due to negative amortization. In other words, they would owe more than they originally borrowed on the house, and the sale of the mortgaged property might not provide sufficient funds to pay off the loan.

Growing Equity Mortgage Growing equity mortgages (GEMs) are 15-year fully amortized home mortgage loans that provide for successively higher debt service payments over the life of the loan. They are made with a fixed rate, and the initial payments are calculated on a 30-year schedule. However, they are paid off more rapidly because there is an annual increase in the monthly payments, all of which goes to reduce the principal balance of the loan. In addition, the interest rate is made below the prevailing rate for 30-year loans. Borrowers who can afford the increased payments can save thousands of dollars in interest payments over the term of the loan.

Interest-Only Mortgages The interest-only mortgage lets the borrower pay only the interest portion of the loan for some predetermined period, and then the loan payments are adjusted to fully amortize over the remaining life of the loan. For example, a 30-year mortgage loan may be interest only for the first 10 years, and then the loan payments are changed to amortize the loan over the remaining 20 years. One of the major advantages from the borrower's point of view is that monthly payments during the interest-only period are lower than they would be for a fully amortized mortgage. On the other side of the coin, the borrower may have little or no equity stake in the real estate.

Reverse Mortgages The reverse mortgage is designed for senior citizens, 62 and older, who own their houses free and clear and want to increase their incomes by borrowing against the equity in their houses. In this case, the lender pays the property owner a fixed tax-free annuity based on a percentage value of the property. The owner would not be required to repay the loan until his or her demise, at which time the loan would be paid from the proceeds of the estate, or until the house is sold. The interest rate on the loan may be adjustable, and the loan may have a refinancing option.[14]

Second Mortgage/Home Equity Loan (HELOC) Many homeowners use a second mortgage when they need funds for business or as a substitute for consumer loans. Other than selling their homes, a home equity loan is the only way homeowners can convert their equity into funds they can spend. As previously noted, *equity* is the difference between the market value of the property and the mortgage debt. A traditional second mortgage is made in addition to the first mortgage and uses the same property as collateral. Second mortgages usually provide for a fixed dollar amount to be repaid over a specified period of time, requiring monthly payment of principal and interest. Second mortgages have a subordinated claim to property in the event of foreclosure.

Home Equity Loan It can be a traditional second mortgage or a revolving line of credit, in which case the line of credit has a second mortgage status but would be the first lien if the borrower has no mortgage debt outstanding when the credit line was established. The line of credit has more a flexible repayment schedule than the traditional second mortgage. Under the home equity line of credit, the borrower with a fixed credit line can write checks up to that amount. In the case of a home equity loan, the loan is a lump sum that is paid off in installments over time. Interest charges on home equity loans may be tax deductible, unlike the interest on consumer loans.

Moreover, since home equity loans have the borrower's home as collateral, the interest rate charged on such loans may be less than the interest rate on credit cards. The home equity loan can be for a fixed amount, or it can be a line of credit.

The relative dollar amount of home equity loans that is allowed varies from state to state. In Texas, for example, 20 percent equity is required on mortgage loans.[15] The maximum amount of a loan on real estate that has a fair market value of $100,000 is $80,000. The equity is $20,000. If the mortgage debt outstanding is $30,000, then the consumer can borrow up to $50,000 ($80,000 – $30,000 = $50,000).

Shared Appreciation Mortgage A shared appreciation mortgage (SAM) is a mortgage loan arrangement whereby the borrower agrees to share in the increased value of the property (usually 30 percent to 50 percent) with the lender in return for a reduction in the fixed-interest rate at the time the loan is made. The increased value of the property is determined at some specified date in the future when the loan can be refinanced or when the property is sold. Sharing a decline in value is not part of the loan agreement.

The Internal Revenue Service considers the bank's portion of the appreciation as contingent or residual interest, which means that it is ordinary income. Thus, the bank has no equity position in the property. Similar arrangements can be applied to other types of mortgage loans, such as large commercial mortgage loans and reverse annuity mortgages. While such arrangements between banks and real estate borrowers are not common, they are used by insurance companies and other long-term lenders making commercial real estate loans.

Commercial Real Estate Loans

Commercial mortgages include loans for land, construction, and real estate development and loans on commercial properties such as shopping centers, office buildings, and warehouses. Commercial real estate loans often are linked to commercial loans. For example, suppose a delivery firm wants to expand, buy new trucks, and build a warehouse. The bank would make a term loan to finance the trucks and a construction loan to build the warehouse; the bank would then refinance the construction loan for the warehouse with a mortgage loan when it is completed. The mortgage loan on the warehouse cannot be pooled and sold like home mortgage loans. Nevertheless, it is a profitable loan. It is financed on a floating rate basis for seven years, and it is cross-collateralized with the trucks.

After land is acquired and financed, *construction and land development loans* call for the bank to make irregular disbursements to the borrower-builder. One method of making the disbursements is based on completion of certain phases of construction. For example, 30 percent may be paid when the foundation is completed, 30 percent when the project is under roof and the plumbing and wiring have been completed, and the remainder when the structure is complete and ready for occupancy. Another method is to pay the builder upon presentment of bills from suppliers and subcontractors as the building progresses. Construction loans have to be flexible to meet the needs of the borrower and the lender.

Construction and development loans are considered interim financing. That is, the loans are only in effect during the development and construction phase of the real estate project. When the project is complete, the builder is expected to get permanent (i.e., long-term) financing. The permanent financing is usually determined before interim financing is provided.

In the case of home loans, the permanent financing will be provided when the homes are sold and the buyers obtain mortgage loans. In the case of commercial property, long-term financing can be obtained from life insurance companies, Fannie Mae, Freddie Mac, or pension and retirement plans, as well as banks. It is common practice for life insurance companies to share in the equity or profits from large commercial real estate ventures they finance.

During the construction phase of development, the land and partially completed structures serve as collateral for the loan. If the developer-builder is unable to complete the project for one reason or another and defaults on the loan, the lender may take possession of the partially completed structure. Then the lender has to consider finishing the structure or liquidating it. Because there may be considerable risk involved with interim financing, the interest rates charged are relatively high for some borrowers.

Interest rates on construction loans are frequently priced at the prime rate plus one or more percentage points, depending on the risk involved. In addition, an origination fee of 1 percent to 3 percent of the amount of the loan may be charged. This fee is charged to cover the cost of the paperwork involved and to increase the effective yield on the loan to the bank.

CONSUMER LENDING

Consumer credit outstanding was $2.4 trillion in April 2010. Commercial banks held 48 percent of total, and the remainder was held by finance companies, credit unions, and others.[16] *Consumer credit* is loans to individuals for personal, household, or family consumption. Consumer lending is the heart of *retail banking*—banking services provided to individuals and to small business concerns. Services provided to medium-size and large business concerns and governments are called *wholesale banking*. Most banks do both retail and wholesale banking, although some specialize more than others. Small banks tend to specialize in retail banking because they do not have sufficient assets to do large-scale wholesale lending.

Types of Consumer Loans

Consumer loans differ from commercial and real estate loans (including home equity loans) in several respects. First, except for automobile and mobile home loans, most consumer loans are for relatively small dollar amounts compared with a home or car loan. The average size of new car loans in April 2010 was $27,797.[17] Second, most consumer loans are not secured by collateral because they are used to buy nondurable goods and services where collateral is not practical. Airline tickets, food, gasoline, and doctor bills are examples of such goods and services. Third, with the same exceptions, many consumer loans are *open-end* (no maturity) lines of credit, whereby consumers may increase their loans and pay off their loans over an indefinite period of time. Credit card loans are one example of *open-end* or *revolving loans*. Loans with definite maturities are called *closed-end loans* or nonrevolving loans. Automobile loans that must be repaid within 48 months are an example of closed-end loans. As shown in Table 7.6, nonrevolving loans account for 66 percent of consumer credit.

The greatest risk associated with consumer installment credit is *default risk*—the risk that the borrower will not repay the loan or may violate other terms of the loan agreement. Defaults tend to increase with the size of the loan and with longer-term maturities, and they are inversely related to the

TABLE 7.6 Consumer Credit, June 2010

Type	Amount ($ billions)	Percentage
Nonrevolving	$1,602	66%
Revolving	$838	34%
Totals	$2,440	100%

Source: Federal Reserve Statistical Release, "Consumer Credit," G19, June 7, 2010, www.federalreserve.gov/releases/g19/20100607/.

value of the collateral relative to the size of the loan. Defaults also tend to increase during recessions when unemployment is high.

Because the market for consumer loans is highly competitive, there is competition on interest rates, amounts lent, fees, and noncredit services provided by credit issuers. The services offered include liability insurance on automobile rentals, frequent flyer mileage on airlines, travel accident insurance, discounts on long-distance phone calls, and extended warranties on items purchased. Some credit cards have a cash-back bonus that pays cardholders a small percentage of the items charged on their credit card. In addition, *affinity card plans* offer bank credit cards to members of a particular organization (e.g., universities, clubs, and unions). Affinity cards carry the organization's logo, and the organization may benefit financially when the cards are used.

Consumer installment loans can be profitable. One obvious reason is that the rates charged on such loans are relatively high when compared with rates charged on commercial and real estate loans. A credit card loan, for example, may have an interest rate of 15 percent, the commercial loan a 10 percent rate, and the real estate loan an 8 percent rate. Of course, the size, risk, and maturity of each of the loans differ substantially. Another reason for the high profitability is that much of the processing and monitoring work concerning consumer loans (e.g., credit cards) can be automated. The automation provides economies of scale in managing large portfolios of such loans. A large consumer loan portfolio consists of many small loans over a wide geographic area. This allows the lender to diversify the risk of lending. It also means that the few loans that default will not have a major impact on the bank's capital. In contrast, banks that have small loan portfolios of large commercial real estate loans may not have sufficient capital to withstand the failure of a few large commercial real estate loans. As noted in Chapter 1, failures of real estate loans were one of the primary causes of bank failures in the United States and other major countries.[18] More will be said about income from the credit card business shortly.

Automobile Loans Automobile loans account for about a third of the nonrevolving credit that is shown in Table 7.6. Nonrevolving credit includes motor vehicle loans, mobile home loans, and other loans that are not included in revolving credit, such as loans for education, boats, and trailers. New car loans may have an original maturity of 62 months or longer, and some lenders will finance 90 percent or more of the cost.[19] The average new car loan in March 2010 was about $28,000. Long-term car loans result in the consumer owing more than the car is worth. In industry parlance, this is called *upside down*.[20] In the case of a 60-month car loan at 5 percent, the loan will be upside down for the first three years. Consumers wanting to sell their cars during this period will have to write a check to the bank.

The average LTV ratio was 88 percent for new cars and 95 percent for used ones. Although most automobile loans are paid off in installments, some are balloon loans with a repurchase agreement that makes them look like a closed-end lease from the customer's point of view. Closed-end leases will be discussed shortly. Under a *repurchase agreement,* the bank (or some other third party) will repurchase the automobile at the end of the term of the loan, at the customer's option, for a price that is equal to the balloon obligation. In other words, the bank takes the automobile instead of the final payment. Suppose that the amount borrowed for the loan is $18,000 and the automobile is expected to have a value of $10,000 at the end of the loan period—which is the same dollar amount as the balloon payment. At the end of the loan period, the customer can:

- Sell or trade in the car and pay off the balance of the loan.
- Keep the car and pay off or refinance the balance.
- Exercise the repurchase agreement instead of paying off the loan.

The repurchase agreement stipulates that the vehicle must be within certain standards for mileage and wear and tear. The mileage limit may be 15,000 miles per year, and the buyer is required to provide normal maintenance. The trade-in value of the automobile is usually supported by an insurance policy, thereby reducing the risk to the bank.

The monthly payments on balloon loans are often 300 to 500 basis points higher than the monthly payments on a lease because the lender does not get the tax advantage of the depreciation from the vehicle.

Like mortgage loans, automobile loans can be pooled and sold to investors. Thus, securitization provides lenders with increased liquidity and flexibility in managing their loan portfolios.

Revolving Consumer Loans Revolving loans account for 34 percent of consumer credit (Table 7.6). In *revolving loans,* or *open-end credit,* the borrower has a line of credit up to a certain amount and may pay off the loans and credit charges over an indefinite period of time. Revolving loans have no definite maturity. The terms of repayment are flexible and largely at the discretion of the borrower. Most revolving loans charge interest on the amount borrowed only if the borrower pays less than the full amount of the loan at the end of a grace period of 25 to 30 days or less. This does not apply to cash advances, which may incur finance charges beginning on the transaction date. Bank credit cards, such as VISA and MasterCard, account for most revolving loans.

Credit Cards A *credit card* is any card, plate, or device that may be used from time to time and over and over again to borrow money or buy goods and services *on credit*.[21] A credit card should not be confused with a debit card or a prepayment card. A *debit card* looks like a plastic credit card and may be used to make purchases, but no credit is extended. The funds are withdrawn or transferred from the cardholder's account to pay for the purchases. Debit and credit cards are the preferred method of payment for in-store sales. More will be said about payment methods in Chapter 10.

In the case of *prepayment (stored-value) cards,* a certain dollar amount is prepaid into an account, and deductions are made for each transaction. They are widely used to make telephone calls and in New York, San Francisco, and Washington in lieu of coins for subway fares. *Smart cards* containing silicon chips that are capable of storing data and making simple computations are being introduced into the payments system in China, Europe, and the United States.

In 2009, there were about 576 million credit cards and 509 million debit cards in the United States.[22] Credit cards are successful because they are convenient to use and are widely accepted as a form of payment. The user does not have to carry cash or a check that may not be an acceptable form of payment. They are also a convenient source of unsecured credit.

The growth of credit card–related consumer debt is attributable to automation and the fact that credit cards are mass-marketed like a commodity. That is, credit cards are sold as a cluster of services at one price, and there is no personal contact with the issuer. Mass mailings of credit card applications are sent to selected segments of the population based on demographic criteria, such as income and housing. The applications are evaluated by computer programs using credit scoring. Qualified applicants receive cards, and their accounts are monitored by computer programs. The use of automation keeps labor costs at a minimum for the large number of transactions processed. This process allows credit card issuers located in Delaware, North Dakota, or elsewhere to sell their cards anywhere in the United States. Obviously, they must be sold in sufficient quantity to justify the cost of credit card operations.

In addition to the mass marketing of credit cards, individual banks issue them to their customers. There are three types of credit card plans for banks. The first type of plan utilizes a single principal bank to issue the credit card, maintain accounts, bill and collect, and assume most of the other functions associated with credit cards.

In the second type of plan, one bank acts as a limited agent for the principal bank. The principal bank issues the card, carries the bulk of the credit, and performs the functions described in the first plan. The functions of the agent bank are to establish merchant accounts and accept merchant sales drafts; it receives a commission on the business it generates without incurring the costs of a credit card operation. The limited agent bank may have its own name and logo on the card. Cardholders assume that the card is issued and managed by that bank, which is not the case.

In the third plan, a bank affiliates with one of the major *travel and entertainment card* (T & E) plans such as American Express. A travel and entertainment card is a credit card; but cardholders must pay the amount owed when billed. They do not have the option of making small payments over time. However, American Express also issues other credit cards that are credit cards in the true sense of the word.

All bank credit cards have the following common features:

- The credit card holder has a prearranged line of credit with a bank that issues credit cards. Credit is extended when the credit card holder buys something and signs (or approves) a sales draft at a participating retail outlet. The retail merchant presents the sales draft to its bank for payment in full, less a *merchant discount* that is based on:
  a. The retail outlet's volume of credit card trade.
  b. The average size of each credit card sale.
  c. The amount of compensating balances kept at the bank.
  d. Some combination of these factors.

The merchant discounts range from nothing to 6 percent or more. Some merchants do not accept certain credit cards that have high merchant discounts. Thus, not all credit cards are equal in the eyes of the merchants.

The merchant's bank will get part of the merchant discount for handling the transaction and routing it to the major credit card company (i.e., VISA, MasterCard, American Express, and Discover) that issued the card.[23] The credit card company determines the amount that the card-issuing bank owes. The card-issuing bank pays the credit card company, and the credit card company pays the merchant bank. Finally, the card-issuing bank presents the sales draft to the credit card holder for payment.

> *The majority of the merchant discount fee is generally paid from the acquiring institution to the issuing institution in the form of an* interchange fee. *A merchant does not pay the interchange fee directly.*

Rather, the Visa or MasterCard network transfers the interchange fee portion of the merchant discount fee from the acquiring institution to the issuing institution. The acquiring institution retains the balance of the merchant discount fee to cover its costs for processing the transaction.... [For] example, when a cardholder makes a $100 purchase, the merchant pays $2.20 in merchant discount fees for the transaction. This amount is divided between the issuing institution, which received $1.70 in interchange fees, and the acquiring institution, which receives 50 cents for processing the transaction.[24]

- Under the Credit CARD Act of 2009, all creditors offering any type of open-end credit that has a *grace period* (the period within which any credit extended can be repaid without incurring a finance change due to a periodic interest rate) must mail or deliver periodic financial statements at least 21 days before the expiration of the grace period when the payment is due.[25]

Banks depend on interest income earned on these credit balances as the major source of income from their credit card operations.

Banks also earn *fee income* from credit cards. For example, a bank may charge an annual fee (say, $50) for the privilege of having a credit card. However, for competitive reasons, some banks charge no annual fees.

Fees are also charged for other account activities such as:

Cash advances: 3 percent of the cash advance or a minimum of $5 and no maximum amount.

Late payments: The issuer will add $35 to the purchase balance for each billing period the borrower fails to make the minimum payment due.

Exceeding the credit line: The issuer will add $20 to the purchase balance for each billing period the balance exceeds the line of credit.

Returned check fees: When payments are not honored, $20.

Fees are also charged for foreign transactions, balance transfers, returned payments, and returned checks.

Finally, banks earn fees for the sale of products, vacation packages, magazine subscriptions, and insurance in connection with their credit cards. Under the Credit CARD Act, the total amount of fees that can be charged in the first year after an account is opened cannot exceed 25 percent of the credit limit.[26]

- The final feature is the plastic credit card itself, which serves special purposes. First, it identifies the customer to the merchant. Some Citibank

TABLE 7.7 Ten Largest Credit Card Issuers as of Year-End 2008

Card Issuer	Percentage of Total U.S. Credit Card Market by Credit Card Balance Outstanding
JPMorgan Chase	21
Bank of America	19
Citi	12
American Express	10
Capital One	7
Discover	6
Wells Fargo	4
HSBC	3
U.S. Bank	2
USAA Savings	2
Total	88

Source: U.S. Government General Accountability Office, "Credit Cards: Rising Interchange Fees Have Increased Costs for Merchants, but Options for Reducing Fees Pose Challenges," GAO 10-45, November 2009, p. 6.

credit cards have the customer's picture on the card to enhance its security. This does not apply to credit transactions by Internet, mail, or telephone. Second, it is used to transfer account information to the sales draft by use of a machine. Finally, the card may be encoded with a magnetic strip or computer chip that provides additional information about the card holder's financial condition.

About 56 percent of credit card debt outstanding is *convenience* use, in which the cardholder uses the credit card instead of cash or checks and pays the amount owed in full when billed, thereby avoiding interest charges.[27] Therefore, the amount of consumer credit shown in Table 7.6 is overstated.

More than 6,000 depository institutions issue credit and debit cards.[28] But at year-end 2008, the 10 largest issuers accounted for 88 percent of the total credit card balances outstanding (see Table 7.7).

Manufactured Home Loans Because of their origins as trailers pulled behind cars, manufactured home (formerly known as mobile homes) loans are included in consumer credit. A manufactured home is a structure that is transportable in one or more sections. In traveling mode, the home is 8 feet or more in width and 40 feet or more in length. A *manufactured home* is designed and constructed to meet the Federal Manufactured Construction and Safety Standards (U.S. Dept. of Housing and Urban Development [HUD] Code) and is labeled as such.[29] They are not considered the same as travel trailers, motor homes, or modular housing.

Manufactured home loans are direct and indirect loans made to individuals to purchase manufactured homes. In the case of indirect loans, banks may require the dealers from whom they purchased loans to stand behind them in the event of default. Additional protection for the lender can be obtained in the form of insurance. Mobile home loans may be guaranteed by the FHA, VA, and Rural Housing Services (RHS) under the Department of Agriculture.

Noninstallment Loans Commercial banks also make noninstallment consumer loans. These are loans that are scheduled to be repaid in a lump sum. The largest component of the noninstallment loans is the single payment loan that is used to finance the purchase of one home while another home is being sold. Loans used for this purpose are called *bridge loans.* Other noninstallment loans are used to finance investments and for other purposes.

Leases

Leasing is an alternative method of financing consumer durables such as automobiles, trucks, airplanes, and boats. In the case of cars, low monthly costs and getting a new car every few years are two reasons for their popularity.

Under a lease, the bank owns the automobile and rents it to the customer.[30] The lease may be open-end, in which case the bank is responsible for selling the automobile at the end of the lease period. If the amount received is less than a previously agreed-on residual value, the customer pays the difference—a balloon payment. Suppose that an automobile is leased under a three-year open-end lease. The lessor estimates that the car will be worth \$25,000 after three years of normal wear. If the auto is returned in a condition that reduces its value to \$20,000, the lessee may owe the lender \$5,000. On the other hand, if the appraised value is more than the residual value, the customer receives the difference.

Under a closed-end lease, the bank assumes the risk of the market value being less than the residual value of the automobile. National banks must have insurance on the residual on closed-end leases. The monthly payments for closed-end leases are higher than those for open-end leases because the bank has a greater risk. However, since the bank owns the automobile and gets the tax benefit (depreciation), the monthly payments may be less than that of a loan of an equivalent amount to buy the automobile outright.

Under the Consumer Leasing Act of 1976 (and Federal Reserve Regulation M), consumer leases must meet the following criteria:

- A lease of personal (not real estate) property.
- The term of the lease must exceed four months.
- It must be made to a natural person (not a corporation).
- The total lease obligation must not exceed $25,000.
- The lease must be for personal, family, or household purposes. It covers leases for cars, furniture, and appliances but does not cover daily car rentals or apartment leases.

FINANCE CHARGES

Federal Reserve *Regulation Z* (Truth in Lending), requires lenders of consumer loans to provide borrowers with written information about finance charges and annual percentage rates (APRs) before they sign a loan agreement, so that they may compare credit costs. APR is the percentage cost of credit on an annual basis. For example, the same credit card can have different APRs for different types of transactions. There may be (1) a low introductory rate for six months, (2) a different rate for cash advances, (3) a purchase rate for the purchase of goods and services that is charged on the balance owed, and (4) a penalty rate for late or returned payments. Also, the rates can vary over time if they are based on the prime rate, the Treasury bill rate, or some other rate that can change.

The *finance charge* is the total dollar amount paid for the use of credit. The finance charge includes interest, service charges, and other fees that are charged the borrower as a condition of or incident to the extension of credit. For example, a customer borrows $1,000 for one year and pays $80 in interest, a $10 service charge, and a $10 origination fee; the finance charge is $100.

Computation Methods

Adjusted Balance Method Using this method,[31] the finance charge is applied against the amount that has been billed, less any payments made prior to the due date. Purchases are not counted. The amount billed in this example is $100 and the payment was $20, resulting in $80. The monthly finance charge is 1.5 percent per month (18 percent annually) times $80, which amounts to $1.20.

Amount billed	$100
Payment	−20
	$ 80
× % rate/month	×1.5%
Finance charge	$1.20

Previous Balance Method According to this method, the finance charge is applied against the original amount billed, and no consideration is given to the $20 payment. The monthly finance charge is 1.5 percent times $100, which amounts to $1.50.

Amount billed	$100
× % rate/month	×1.5%
Finance charge	$1.50

Daily Balance Method (Excluding Current Transactions) According to this method, the finance charge is based on the daily balance outstanding over the current 30-day period but does not include current transactions. The daily balance is $90 ($100 for 15 days and $80 for 15 days) and the finance charge is $1.35 ($90 × 1.5 percent = $1.35).

Average daily balance first 15 days	
$100	= $100
Average daily balance second 15 days	
$100 – $20	= $80
Average daily balance for 30 days = $90	
× % rate/month	×1.5%
Finance charge	$1.35

Average Daily Balance Method (Including Current Transactions) According to this method, the finance charge is based on the average daily balance outstanding during the current 30-day period, including new purchases made during that time. The average daily balance is $200 for the first 15 days ($100 from April and $100 purchased on June 1) and $180 for the last 15 days ($200 less $20 = $180), so the average balance for the entire period is $190.

The finance charge is 1.5 percent times $190, which amounts to $2.85.

Average balance for the first 15 days	
$100 + $100	= $200
Average balance for the second 15 days	
$200 – $20	= $180
Average balance for the 30 days	= $190
× % finance charge/month	×1.5%
Finance charge	$2.85

A borrower who skips a payment on a month's purchases or makes a partial payment may lose the grace period. The grace period is the time in which the bill can be paid in full to avoid interest on the most recent month's charges. The reason is that many card issuers calculate interest on the account's average daily balance retroactive to the first purchase. The average daily balance including the current transactions method illustrates the impact this has on finance charges. Some banks that promote their low interest rates use the most expensive methods of computing their finance charges.

Methods	Finance Charge
Adjusted balance	$1.20
Previous balance	1.50
Average daily balance excluding current transactions	1.35
Average daily balance including current transactions	2.85

In review, by using different methods for determining the unpaid balance, finance charges on the same transaction based on an 18 percent annual interest rate (1.5 percent monthly) ranged from a low of $1.20 to a high of $2.85! All of these methods for determining unpaid balances are widely used.

The Truth in Lending Act does not tell creditors how to calculate the finance charges; it only requires that they inform borrowers of the methods that are used and provide them with information about the annual percentage rate.

ANNUAL PERCENTAGE RATE

Single Payment, End of Period

The APR is the percentage cost of credit on an annual basis. The APR may be used to compare credit costs of loans of various sizes and maturities.[32] The APR is the annualized *internal rate of return* (IRR) on the loan. Readers who are familiar with financial management will recognize that the IRR is that rate of interest that equates the present value of the periodic payments with the principal amount of the loan.

The APR for a given series of payments can be calculated easily by calculators programmed to calculate the IRR. For textbook exercises, we recommend such calculators. Most banks use computer programs or tables to compute the APR. Finally, the IRR may be determined by using the following equation when the payments are the same in each period:

$$\mathrm{P} = \sum_{t=1}^{n} \mathrm{PMT} \frac{1}{(1+\mathrm{i})^t} \tag{7.3}$$

where: P = original principal amount ($), or the amount received by the borrower in the case of discount loan rate
PMT = periodic payments ($)
i = periodic interest rate (%)
n = number of periodic payments (number)

Other equations (methods) also may be used to calculate APRs.[33] The Federal Reserve allows some flexibility in how to compute APRs. The APRs are considered acceptable as long as they are within 1/8 of 1 percent of one of the two so-called actual APRs computed by the Federal Reserve. The Federal Reserve uses the IRR (actuarial method) and/or the U.S. Rule method (not described here) to compute the actual APR. The methods give slightly different results.

By way of illustration of the use of the IRR to compute APRs, assume that a customer wants to borrow $1,000 for one year at 10 percent. The bank can offer the customer monthly amortization, an add-on rate, or a discount rate. The APRs for each method are substantially different.

Monthly Amortization

Amortization refers to the gradual repayment of debt over time. In this example, the loan is amortized by 12 monthly payments of $87.92 each. Using equation 7.3, we determine that the IRR/periodic rate is

$$\mathrm{P} = \sum_{t=1}^{n} \mathrm{PMT} \frac{1}{(1+i)^t}$$

$$\$1{,}000 = \sum_{t=1}^{12} \$87.92 \frac{1}{(1+i)^t}$$

$$i = 0.83407$$

$$\mathrm{APR} = 0.83407 \times 12 = 10.01\%$$

Because the periodic rate is monthly, the nominal annual rate is determined by multiplying the periodic rate by 12 to get the percentage. Accordingly, the APR in this example is 10.01 percent ($12 \times 0.83407 = 10.01$).

Add-on Loan Rate

The term *add-on* means that the finance charge is added to the amount borrowed. Consider a $1,000 loan for one year at 10 percent add-on interest. For purposes of illustration, the finance charge, FC, is determined by multiplying the amount borrowed P by the add-on interest rate expressed as a decimal R, times the life of the loan in years T. The FC may include fees and charges not considered in these examples. In this example, one year is used, so T = 1. If the loan had been for 15 months, T would be equal to 1.25; if it were for 18 months, T would be equal to 1.5, and so on.

$$
\begin{aligned}
\mathrm{FC} &= \mathrm{P} \times \mathrm{R} \times \mathrm{T} \\
&= \$1{,}000 \times 0.10 \times 1 \\
&= \$100
\end{aligned} \tag{7.4}
$$

The $100 finance charge is added to the amount borrowed so that the total amount owed is $1,100. The monthly payments PMT are determined by dividing the total amount owed, which is principal amount plus the finance charge, by the number of payments n.

$$
\begin{aligned}
\mathrm{PMT} &= \frac{\mathrm{P} + \mathrm{FC}}{n} \\
&= \frac{\$1{,}000 + \$100}{12} = \$91.67
\end{aligned} \tag{7.5}
$$

Using equation 7.3, the APR is 17.98 percent.

$$
\begin{aligned}
\mathrm{P} &= \sum_{t=1}^{n} \mathrm{PMT}\frac{1}{(1+i)^t} \\
\$1{,}000 &= \sum_{t=1}^{12} \$91.67\frac{1}{(1+i)^t} \\
i &= 1.498 \\
\mathrm{APR} &= 1.498 \times 12 = 17.98\%
\end{aligned}
$$

Discount Loan Rate

In a discount loan, the creditor deducts the finance charge from the principal amount of the loan, and the borrower receives the difference. Consider a \$1,000 loan discounted at 10 percent. The creditor deducts the \$100 finance charge from the \$1,000 principal amount and the borrower receives \$900. Nevertheless, the borrower must repay \$1,000 in 12 monthly payments of \$83.33 (\$1,000/12 = \$83.33). When calculating the APR on discount loans, the amount P received by the borrower (\$900) is set equal to the discounted monthly payments. The APR for the discount loan is 19.9 percent.

$$P = \sum_{t=1}^{n} \mathrm{PMT} \frac{1}{(1+i)^t}$$

$$\$900 = \sum_{t=1}^{12} \$83.33 \frac{1}{(1+i)^t}$$

$$i = 1.6587$$

$$\mathrm{APR} = 1.6587 \times 12 = 19.90\%$$

In summary, the APRs are:

Monthly amortization	10.01 percent
Add-on rate	17.97 percent
Discount rate	19.90 percent

From the bank's point of view, the discount method produces the highest returns, followed by the add-on method.

As mentioned previously, the APR may be used to compare the cost of credit. The concept of *cost of credit* is multidimensional, and it includes the amount of the monthly payments, the amount of the down payment, the method of payment (e.g., cash, payroll deduction), and other factors. By way of illustration, consider loans A and B, each for \$6,000, and each having an APR of 14 percent. Loan A has a maturity of three years, and loan B has a maturity of four years. Because loan B has a longer maturity, the monthly payments are lower than those of loan A. However, the total finance charge and total payments of loan B are higher than those of loan A. Although the finance charges are lower with loan A, consumers who prefer lower monthly payments may choose loan B.

	APR (%)	Maturity (Years)	Monthly Payments	Finance Charge	Total Payments
Loan A	14	3	$205.07	$1,382.52	$7,382.52
Loan B	14	4	$163.96	$1,870.08	$7,870.08

REAL ESTATE AND CONSUMER CREDIT REGULATION

Federal laws prescribe certain terms and conditions under which lenders can make residential real estate and consumer loans. Highlights of selected laws are presented here. The legislation and regulations impose substantial costs on lenders, who must maintain detailed records of their actions and submit to examinations to determine if they are complying with the legislation and relevant regulations. A 1998 study of the costs of complying with all bank regulations by U.S. banks estimated them to be 12 percent to 13 percent of banks' noninterest expense.[34] A 2003 study of banks in the United Kingdom estimated that the compliance cost was equivalent to 1.6 percent of the firms' nonregulatory operating costs.[35] The two estimates are not strictly comparable, but in either case, the cost of compliance is significant.

Community Reinvestment Act

The Community Reinvestment Act (CRA) is directed at federally regulated lenders that take deposits and extend credit. Such institutions are required to serve the needs and convenience of their respective communities. The intent of the legislation is to facilitate the availability of mortgage loans and other types of loans to all qualified applicants, without regard to their race, nationality, or sex.

Equal Credit Opportunity Act and the Fair Housing Act

The Equal Credit Opportunity Act (ECOA) (Federal Reserve Regulation B) and Fair Housing Act collectively prohibit lenders from discriminating against borrowers on the basis of age (provided that the applicant has the capacity to contract), color, family status (having children under age 18), handicap, marital status, national origin, race, receipt of public assistance funds, religion, sex, or the exercise of any right under the Consumer Protection Act. The use of credit scoring models, such as FICO scores, can help to ensure consistency and uniformity in making credit decisions.[36]

Fair Credit Billing Act

A customer who believes there is an error on a bill must contact the lender, *in writing,* within 60 days after the first bill in which the error appears is sent. A telephone call to the lender does not preserve the customer's rights. The amount in dispute, including finance charges, accrues until the issue is resolved. The lender has 90 days to correct the error or explain why the bill is correct.

Home Mortgage Disclosure Act

The Home Mortgage Disclosure Act (HMDA, Federal Reserve Regulation C) of 1975 and its amendments were intended to make available to the public, information concerning the extent to which financial institutions are serving the housing credit needs of their communities. The HMDA data are also used by government officials to assess public-sector investments in housing and to identify possible discriminatory lending patterns.

Real Estate Settlement Procedures Act

Settlement is the process by which the ownership of real estate, which is represented by the title, passes from the seller to the buyer. The intent of the Real Estate Settlement Procedures Act (RESPA) is to provide buyers and sellers with information about the settlement process. The law covers most residential real estate loans, including lots for houses or mobile homes. When a buyer applies in writing for a loan covered by RESPA, the lender must send the borrower good faith estimates of the settlements costs within three business days of the application and a booklet called *Settlement Costs–a HUD Guide,* describing the settlement and charges. One day before settlement, the borrower has the right to see the completed Uniform Settlement Statement that will be used.

Truth in Lending Act

The purpose of the Truth in Lending Act (Federal Reserve Regulation Z) is for creditors to disclose to individual consumers who are borrowers (not business borrowers) the amount of the finance charge and the APR they are paying, to facilitate their comparison of finance charges from different sources of credit. In addition, credit card issuers are required to disclose, in written applications or their telephone solicitations, fees, grace periods, and the method of calculating balances. Finance charges and APR were discussed earlier in this chapter. The law requires that the disclosures be clear and conspicuous, grouped together, and segregated from other contractual matters to make it easier for consumers to understand.

In 2008, Regulation Z was revised to prohibit creditors from making higher-priced mortgage loans that were based on the value of the consumer's collateral without regard to the consumer's ability to repay the loan from their current or expected income and assets, other than their collateral and mortgage related obligations.[37]

IF CREDIT IS DENIED

Credit denial must be based on the creditworthiness of the applicant. If credit is denied, the creditor must notify the applicant within 30 days. The notification must be in writing and explain the reasons for the denial, or tell you that you have the right to ask for an explanation if one is not provided. Frequently, the denial is based on information received from a *credit bureau*—a firm that provides credit information for a fee to creditors. Credit bureaus obtain their information from creditors, and sometimes errors are made or information is out of date. For example, bankruptcies must be removed from credit histories after 10 years, and suits, judgments, tax liens, and arrest records must be removed after 7 years.

Under the *Fair Credit Reporting Act*, applicants who have had credit denied based on information from a credit bureau have the right to examine the credit file and correct errors or mistakes in it. If the request is made within 30 days of the refusal, the credit bureau may not charge a fee for providing the information. The credit bureau is required to remove any errors that the creditor who supplied the information admits are there. If a disagreement still remains, applicants can include a short statement in the file with their side of the story. However, removal of incorrect information from one credit bureau does not change the files of the other credit bureaus.

Under the *Fair and Accurate Credit Transactions Act* of 2003 (the Fact Act), everyone can obtain a free credit report once a year from the three major credit bureaus, Exquifax Inc., Experian, and Transunion. It also provides another free credit report for victims of identity theft.

PRIVACY ISSUES

Banks collect information about their customers from the customers themselves, from third parties such as credit reporting agencies, and from the customers' transactions with the bank and its affiliates.

Under the *USA PATRIOT Act* (Section 326), financial institutions are required to implement reasonable procedures to verify the identity of their customers, maintain information about that person, and determine if that person is on any list of known or suspected terrorists or terrorist organizations. This is part of an effort to prevent money laundering, terrorist financing, identity theft, and other forms of fraud.

The *Gramm-Leach-Bliley Act* of 1999 gives consumers of financial institutions the right to opt out of sharing some of their personal financial information with unrelated third parties. Examples of personal private information include Social Security number, assets, income, transactions history, and account balances.

CREDIT CARD ACCOUNTABILITY, RESPONSIBILITY, AND DISCLOSURE ACT OF 2009 (CREDIT CARD ACT)

What consumers need to know about that act has been explained by the Federal Reserve.[38]

What Your Credit Card Company Has To Tell You

When they plan to increase your rate or other fees. Your credit card company must send you a notice 45 days before they can increase your interest rate; change certain fees (such as annual fees, cash advance fees, and late fees) that apply to your account; or make other significant changes to the terms of your card.

If your credit card company is going to make changes to the terms of your card, it must give you the option to cancel the card before certain fee increases take effect. If you take that option, however, your credit card company may close your account and increase your monthly payment, subject to certain limitations.

For example, they can require you to pay the balance off in five years, or they can double the percentage of your balance used to calculate your minimum payment (which will result in faster repayment than under the terms of your account).

The company does *not* have to send you a 45-day advance notice:

- You have a variable interest rate tied to an index; if the index goes up, the company does not have to provide notice before your rate goes up.

- Your introductory rate expires and reverts to the previously disclosed go-to rate; your rate increases because you are in a workout agreement and you haven't made your payments as agreed.

How long it will take to pay off your balance. Your monthly credit card bill will include information on how long it will take you to pay off your balance if you make only minimum payments. It will also tell you how much you would need to pay each month to pay off your balance in three years. For example, suppose you owe $3,000 and your interest rate is 14.4 percent. Your bill might look like this:

New balance	$3,000.00
Minimum payment due	$90.00
Payment due date	4/20/12

Late Payment Warning: If we do not receive your minimum payment by the date listed, you may have to pay a $35 late fee and your APRs may be increased up to the penalty APR of 28.99 percent.

Minimum Payment Warning: If you make only the minimum payment each period, you will pay more in interest, and it will take you longer to pay off your balance. For example:

If you make no additional charges using this card and each month you pay...	You will pay off the balance shown on this statement in about...	And you will end up paying an estimated total of...
Only the minimum payment	11 years	$4,745
$103	3 years	$3,712 (savings = $1,033)

New Rules Regarding Rates, Fees, and Limits

No interest rate increases for the first year. Your credit card company cannot increase your rate for the first 12 months after you open an account. There are some exceptions:

- If your card has a variable interest rate tied to an index; your rate can go up whenever the index goes up.
- If there is an introductory rate, it must be in place for at least six months; after that your rate can revert to the go-to rate the company disclosed when you got the card.

- If you are more than 60 days late in paying your bill, your rate can go up.
- If you are in a workout agreement and you don't make your payments as agreed, your rate can go up.

Increased rates apply only to new charges. If your credit card company does raise your interest rate after the first year, the new rate will apply only to new charges you make. If you have a balance, your old interest rate will apply to that balance.

Restrictions on over-the-limit transactions. You must tell your credit card company that you want it to allow transactions that will take you over your credit limit. Otherwise, if a transaction would take you over your limit, it may be turned down. If you do not opt in to over-the-limit transactions and your credit card company allows one to go through, it cannot charge you an over-the-limit fee.

- If you opt in to allowing transactions that take you over your credit limit, your credit card company can impose only one fee per billing cycle. You can revoke your opt in at any time.

Caps on high-fee cards. If your credit card company requires you to pay fees (such as an annual fee or application fee), those fees cannot total more than 25 percent of the initial credit limit. For example, if your initial credit limit is $500, the fees for the first year cannot be more than $125. This limit does not apply to penalty fees, such as penalties for late payments.

Protections for underage consumers. If you are under 21, you will need to show that you are able to make payments or you will need a cosigner to open a credit card account.

- If you are under age 21, have a card with a cosigner, and want an increase in the credit limit, your cosigner must agree in writing to the increase.

Changes to Billing and Payments

Standard payment dates and times. Your credit card company must mail or deliver your credit card bill at least 21 days before your payment is due. In addition:

- Your due date should be the same date each month (for example, your payment is always due on the 15th or always due on the last day of the month).

- The payment cutoff time cannot be earlier than 5 P.M. on the due date.
- If your payment due date is on a weekend or holiday (when the company does not process payments), you will have until the following business day to pay. (For example, if the due date is Sunday the 15th, your payment will be on time if it is received by Monday the 16th before 5 P.M.).

Payments directed to highest interest balances first. If you make more than the minimum payment on your credit card bill, your credit card company must apply the excess amount to the balance with the highest interest rate. There is an exception:

- If you made a purchase under a deferred interest plan (for example, "no interest if paid in full by March 2012"), the credit card company may let you choose to apply extra amounts to the deferred interest balance before other balances. Otherwise, for two billing cycles prior to the end of the deferred interest period, the credit card company must apply your entire payment to the deferred interest-rate balance first.

No two-cycle (double-cycle) billing. Credit card companies can impose interest charges only on balances in the current billing cycle.

CONCLUSION

Real estate and consumer lending are the heart of retail banking. Mortgage lending for 1- to 4-family homes accounts for about 75 percent of the mortgage debt outstanding, and nonrevolving credit accounts for 66 percent of consumer credit. Changes in technology are having a major influence in the conduct of retail banking. Credit scoring to make lending decisions and securitization to manage portfolios are changing the way lenders operate. The economies of scale in both credit scoring and securitization favor both increased concentration (size) of lenders and increased specialization. In addition, an increasing number of lenders are using the Internet and other technologies to sell their products, thereby expanding the geographic markets in which they operate from local market to global markets.

This chapter examined some of the details of real estate and consumer lending. One significant difference between commercial and industrial loans, which were examined in the previous chapter, and real estate and consumer loans is that the latter are becoming standardized commodity products that can be securitized. Nevertheless, there are still a very large number of real estate and consumer loans that are not securitized and remain on the lender's books.

Finally, retail banking is more heavily regulated than wholesale banking in order to help consumers make informed credit decisions, protect their financial interests, and meet social goals mandated in the CRA and other acts.

CHAPTER 8

Bank Capital

Capital Adequacy

The traditional role of bank capital is to protect depositors against loss, but realistically, the role is much broader than that. Among other things, bank capital provides the working capital required when a new bank is chartered. It also acts as a buffer to absorb temporary losses so that a bank can continue to operate and improve earnings. It is a source of funds necessary to fund growth. However, the real significance of bank capital concerns what is commonly referred to as *capital adequacy.*

Unlike most business concerns, commercial banks are required by federal and state laws to maintain a minimum amount of capital to open a new bank. Similarly, federal and state laws place limits on the amount of loans to one party, limits on the size of a loan relative to a bank's capital and surplus, and other constraints. Finally, bank regulators have minimum capital standards that they apply to individual banks to determine if the bank is well capitalized. Although there are bank capital standards, "one of the reasons the economic and financial crisis (of 2007–2009) became so severe was that the banking sectors of many countries had built up excessive on- and off-balance sheet leverage. This was accompanied by a gradual erosion of the level and quality of the capital base. At the same time, many banks were holding insufficient liquidity buffers. The banking system was not able to absorb the resulting systemic trading and credit losses."[1]

In the United States, the Dodd-Frank Wall Street Reform and Consumer Protection Act, enacted in 2010, requires financial holding companies to be "well capitalized and well managed." It also requires that the capital be countercyclical in the sense that it should increase during economic expansions and decrease during periods of contraction.[2]

Because banks are for-profit businesses, management prefers the lowest amount of capital that will permit the bank to grow. If equity capital is kept relatively low, shareholders can earn a higher return on equity (ROE).

TABLE 8.1 U.S. Bank Equity/Asset Ratios

Date	U.S. Banks	Nonfinancial Corporations
1896	23.5%	—
1900	17.9%	—
1980	5.8%	69.1%
1988	6.2% (Basel I)	—
2000	8.5%	51.7%
2010 First Quarter	10.92%	54.6% (2008)

Sources: All-bank Statistics, United States, 1896–1955, *Statistical Abstract of the United States* 1989, 1993, 2010. Note that the latest data for nonfinancial corporations equity is the market value (Table 735 Nonfinancial Corporate Business) for 2008. FDIC Quarterly Banking Profile, First Quarter 2010, Table III-A. FDIC-Insured Commercial Banks.

Some international banks could hold as low as 2 percent common equity to risk-based assets.[3] Therefore, there is a continual struggle between bank managers, who want the minimum amount of capital, and bank regulators, who want more capital for safety and soundness.

Table 8.1 shows the equity capital to asset ratios of U.S. banks from 1896 to the first quarter of 2010. It provides a historical perspective by showing how equity capital declined from the 1800s to the 1980s and then increased after the Basel I Capital Accord was implemented in 1988. More will be said about Basel 1 later in the chapter. *Equity capital* is defined as the book value of assets less the book value of liabilities. It is different than *regulatory capital,* which can include subordinated debt and adjustments for off-balance-sheet items. For example, regulatory *core capital* is defined as "common equity capital plus noncumulative perpetual preferred stock plus minority interest in consolidated subsidiaries, less goodwill and other ineligible intangible assets. The amount of eligible intangibles (including servicing rights) included in core capital is limited in accordance with supervisory capital regulations."[4] Although not shown in Table 8.1, the core capital leverage ratio varied by bank size. The smallest banks with assets of less than $100 million had a core capital leverage ratio of 11.19 percent, and banks with more than $10 billion in assets had a ratio of 8.19 percent.

Finally, equity capital (the book value of assets less the book value of liabilities) also differs from economic capital, which is a statistical estimate of risk and capital that will be discussed shortly.

As shown in Table 8.1, banks in the United States had equity/asset ratios of 23.5 percent in 1896. The ratios in 1896 and 1900 reflect a time when many banks were operating under the real-bills doctrine: borrowing short-term and lending short-term.

The equity/asset ratio gradually declined to less than 5.8 percent in 1980. Over the years, bankers expanded their lending horizons and made longer-term loans, including real estate loans. They were still borrowing short-term, but the longer-term loans increased their risk. During the 1985–1992 period, 1,373 banks that were insured by the Federal Deposit Insurance Corporation (FDIC) failed.[5] In addition, 1,073 savings and loan associations and 1,707 credit unions failed. All were federally insured. Thus, there was pressure in the United States for increased regulation of bank capital. The end result was the passage of the *Federal Deposit Insurance Corporation Improvement Act of 1991* (FDICIA) that increased bank capital requirements. It included *prompt correct action* (PCA) rules of how to deal with undercapitalized banks that have total risk-based capital ratios of 6 percent or less, or tier 1 capital of 3 percent or less. Well-capitalized banks have total risk-based capital ratios of 10 percent or more.

The definitions of bank capital are complex and very confusing. Without going into a detailed explanation of each term, tier 1, tier 2, and total capital are defined as follows.

Total Capital includes:

Tier 1 Capital plus tier 2 minus investments in unconsolidated subsidiaries.

Tier 1 Capital includes:

1. *Common stock, undivided profits, paid-in-surplus;*
2. *Noncumulative perpetual preferred stock;*
3. *Minority interests in consolidated subsidiaries;*

Minus

1. *All intangible assets (with limited exceptions);*
2. *Identified losses;*
3. *Deferred tax assets in excess of the limit set forth in section 325.5(g).*

Tier 2 Capital includes:

1. *Allowance for loan and lease losses, up to 1.25% of risk-weighted assets;*
2. *Cumulative perpetual preferred stock, long-termed preferred stock (original maturity of at least 20 years), and any related surplus;*
3. *Perpetual preferred stock (where the dividend is reset periodically);*

4. *Hybrid capital instruments, including mandatory convertible debt; and*
5. *Term subordinated debt and intermediate-term preferred stock.*[6]

Federal Reserve Chairman Ben Bernanke said that a "long-standing Federal Reserve policy holds that common equity should be the dominant component of Tier 1 capital because it provides permanent loss absorption capacity and increased flexibility around the timing and amount of dividends and other distributions."[7]

As shown in Table 8.2, PCA is based primarily on three capital ratios: (1) tier 1 risk-based capital ratio, (2) total risk-based capital ratio, and (3) tier 1 leverage ratio. The minimum total risk-based capital ratio to be adequately capitalized is 8 percent. *Total risk-based capital ratio* is the sum of tier 1 risk-based capital and tier 2 risk-based capital.

Tier 1 risk-based capital ratio is tier 1 capital divided by risk-weighted assets. Tier 1 capital is the core capital that was defined previously. The *risk-weighted assets* are assigned four risk weights: 0 percent, 20 percent, 50 percent, and 100 percent, depending on their relative risk: U.S. Treasury securities are assigned a 0 percent risk, and real estate loans are assigned a 100 percent risk. The minimum tier 1 risk-based capital ratio to be adequately capitalized is 4 percent.

Tier 1 leverage ratio is tier 1 capital divided by average quarterly consolidated assets (from the most recent Call Report), less goodwill and other intangibles. Here, too, the minimum for being adequately capitalized is 4 percent.

Tier 2 risk-based capital ratio is tier 2 capital divided by risk-weighted assets. Tier 2 capital is the sum of allowance for loan and lease losses (limited to 1.25 percent of risk-weighted assets), perpetual preferred stock that is not part of tier 1 capital, intermediate-term preferred stock, and subordinated debt.

TABLE 8.2 Risk-Based Capital Groups

Percent	Total Risk-Based Capital	Tier 1 Risk-Based Capital	Tier 1 Leverage Ratio
Well capitalized	≥ 10%* and	≥ 6%* and	≥ 5%*
Adequately capitalized	≥ 8% and	≥ 4% and	≥ 4%
Undercapitalized	≥ 6% and	≥ 3% and	≥ 3%
Significantly undercapitalized	< 6% or	< 3% or	< 3%

*% of risk weighted assets.

Source: FDIC Quarterly, 2010, Volume 4, No. 2, p. 25.

Two additional factors contributed to increased growth opportunities and risks for banks. The first one is the laws that allowed commercial banks to form multibank holding companies and then expand into underwriting securities, insurance, merchant banking, insurance, and other complementary activities.[8] This opened the door for banks to become large complex banking organizations (LCBOs). They are determined by their asset size, the extent of international operations, participation in large-value payment and settlement systems, and other factors. Second was the growth of securitization in mortgage lending. As noted in previous chapters, securitization is packaging and selling mortgage loans to investors.[9] Securitization can involve complex structures such as mortgage-backed securities (MBSs), collateralized debt obligations (CDOs), and structured investment vehicles (SIVs) backed by pools of MBS and CDO bonds.

Table 8.1 also shows that nonfinancial corporations had equity/asset ratios that ranged from 69 percent to about 55 percent. This is substantially greater than the banks' equity/asset ratios for several reasons. First, the equity/asset ratios for nonfinancial corporations reflect market values rather than the book values shown for banks. Therefore, the numbers are not strictly comparable. The second reason is that banks are regulated by federal and state agencies and subject to various laws such as the previously mentioned FDICIA.

BASEL CAPITAL ACCORDS

International bank capital standards are established by the Basel Committee on Banking Supervision at the Bank for International Settlements (BIS), located in Basel, Switzerland. The BIS is an international organization that fosters international monetary and financial cooperation and serves as a bank for 56 central banks around the world.[10] In the 1970s and 1980s, the Basel Committee became increasingly concerned about the failure of large banks and cross-border contagion. In particular, they were concerned that large banks did not have adequate capital in relation to the risks they were assuming. In the 1980s, their concerns were directed at Japanese banks that were expanding globally. They also were concerned about competitive equality in terms of capital requirements for banks. The end result was a uniform, one-size-fits-all, 8 percent capital requirement for banks that became known as the 1988 Capital Accord, or Basel I.

Basel I

Under Basel I, bank capital consisted of two tiers. Tier 1 includes shareholder equity and retained earnings, and it is 4 percent. Tier 2 includes additional internal and external funds available to the bank and also is 4 percent.[11] Thus, Basel I required 8 percent risk-adjusted capital.

Basel I focused primarily on credit risk, and risk-weighted assets ranged from 0 percent weight for claims on Organization for Economic Cooperation and Development (OECD) central banks and governments to 100 percent weights for commercial and consumer loans and loans to non-OECD governments.

Along this line, banks were required to hold more capital against ordinary mortgages than against pools of mortgages that were securitized. Therefore, banks began to change the way they did business from holding the mortgage loans to securitizing them and selling them to other investors. While banks continued to make mortgages and other loans, the securitization process allowed them to shift the risk to the investors who bought the loans.[12]

The 8 percent risk-based capital ratio is an arbitrary ratio that is used to monitor risk. The 8 percent "minimum capital is a guidepost. . . . It was not and is not intended as a level toward which the firms should aim nor as a standard for internal risk management."[13] It does not measure risk. Equally important, a large number of failed banks had capital ratios in excess of 8 percent shortly before failure. According to an FDIC study *History of the Eighties: Lessons for the Future,* 26 percent of the 1,600 U.S. banks that failed between 1980 and 1994 had CAMEL ratings of 1 or 2, one year before failure.[14] (*CAMEL* stands for capital, asset quality, management, earnings, and liquidity.) The CAMEL ratings are used by bank regulators to evaluate banks. The ratings range from a high of 1 to a low of 5.[15] *History of the Eighties: Lessons for the Future* went on to say that "bank capital positions are poor predictors of failure several years before the fact."[16]

A number of changes in financial technology and banking operations undermined the effectiveness of Basel I.[17] These changes include developments in derivatives, globalization, and the consolidation of LCBOs. Equally important, the basic business model of commercial banks has shifted from the real bills doctrine (borrowing short-term and lending short-term) to borrowing short-term and lending long-term (i.e., buy and hold) and, more recently, to borrowing short-term and selling assets (i.e., originate and distribute to other investors through syndications, securitization, and credit derivatives).[18]

Basel II

Basel II is an attempt to align regulatory capital with the risks that banks face. There are two distinctly different but related aspects of Basel II. One involves the three pillars, and the other involves enterprise risk management (ERM), which was explained in Chapter 5.

Pillar 1: Minimum Capital Requirements—The regulatory capital requirements are based on credit risk (defaults by counterparty), market risk (price changes on and off balance sheet), and operational risk (failed processes, people, systems, events). The definition of total capital in Basel II is the same as in Basel I. Total capital divided by credit risk, market risk, and operational risk must be equal to or more than 8 percent.

$$\frac{\text{Total Capital (definition unchanged)}}{\text{Credit risk} + \text{Market risk} + \text{Operational risk}} \geq 8\% \text{ minimum capital ratio} \qquad (8.1)$$

Pillar 2: Supervisory review process—Foster supervisor-bank dialogue on risk management.

Pillar 3: Market discipline—Based on disclosure of information.

Without going into the all of the details, banks quickly discovered that it is relatively easy to get around the Basel II capital requirements—a process called *regulatory arbitrage*. Simply stated, it means that if regulators have principles rather than strict rules, banks will find a way to get around them. For example, a bank can avoid minimum capital charges on mortgage loans through sale or securitization of those assets that would have higher capital charges if they were kept on the bank's balance sheet. In essence, regulatory arbitrage allows banks to achieve so-called effective capital requirements well below the minimum 8 percent.[19]

Basel II provides three options for calculating risk-weighted assets for credit risk.

1. The standardized approach is similar to the 1988 Accord. However, some adjustments to the risk weights are made for sovereign exposures, nongovernmental public sector entities, and multilateral development banks. A 100 percent risk weight means a full capital charge equal to 8 percent of that value. A 50 percent risk weight means a capital charge of 4 percent (0.5 × 8 percent) of that value. For corporate lending, Basel II provides risk weights of 20 percent, 50 percent, 100 percent, and 150 percent. The standardized approach is appropriate for smaller banks, and Internal Ratings-Based (IRB) approaches are for the larger banks.[20]
2. The foundation IRB approach. Supervisors provide the estimates of the values used to establish the losses—for example, loss given default

(LGD), exposure at default (EAD), and maturity (M)—that are used in the models.

3. The advanced IRB approach. The advanced IRB approach is similar to the foundation IRB approach. However, under the foundation IRB, the bank supervisors provide the estimates of the values used in establishing losses (e.g., LGD, EAD, and M) that are used in the models. Under the advanced IRB, the bank provides the probability of default (PD), LGD, EAD, and M. The range of risk weights under the foundation and advanced IRB approaches is greater than under the standard approach. Credit risk mitigation and securitization are considered under both approaches.

The advanced IRB approach is very complex and very costly to apply. It is also the easiest one to use to take advantage of statistical models that provide the lowest capital requirements.

The data in Table 8.3 show that the minimum capital for a $100 commercial loan can vary from $1.81 to $41.65, depending on the credit risk and the approach used to calculate the required capital.

Table 8.4 provides another illustration of regulatory arbitrage for two $1 million loans where the expected loss (EL) is equal to the PD times the loss given default (LD). Although the PD and LD of the two loans vary widely, they both have the same capital charge.

Banks can avoid charge-offs by restructuring loans that may become nonperforming loans. Alternatively, they can make a second loan to the obligor that would cover the payments of the first loan and keep it from defaulting. Finally, they can securitize loans—get them off the balance sheet.

The bottom line is that market discipline did not forestall the global financial crisis that began in 2007.[21]

TABLE 8.3 Basel II: Minimum Capital for a $100 Commercial Loan

	AAA Credit Risk	BBB– Credit Risk	B Credit Risk
Standardized approach	$1.81	$8.21	$12.21
Foundation IRB	$1.41	$5.01	$18.53
Advanced IRB	$0.37 to $4.45	$1.01 to $14.13	$ 3.97 to $41.65

Source: Susan Burhouse, John Field, George French, and Keith Ligon, "Basel and the Evolution of Capital Regulation: Moving Forward and Looking Back," an update on emerging issues in banking, FDIC, January 14, 2003.

TABLE 8.4 Regulatory Arbitrage: Two Loans for $1 Million Each

EL =	PD x	LD
Loan 1 EL = 1%	5%	20%
Loan 2 EL= 1%	2%	50%
Capital charges $1 million × 1%	= $10,000	= $10,000

Basel II Revisions

The Basel II market risk framework was revised to make adjustments to capital requirements concerning net long and net short securitization positions held in a bank's trading book.[22] Banks will be subject to the Basel II securitization charges, similar to those held in the banking book. "So-called correlation trading books are exempted from the full treatment for securitization positions, qualifying either for a revised standardized charge or a capital charge based on a comprehensive risk measure."[23] Equally important, changes are being made to the definition of tier 1 capital: "significant investments in the common shares of unconsolidated financial institutions (banks, insurance, and other financial entities); mortgage servicing rights, and deferred tax assets from timing differences.... Instead of a full deduction, [the previous items] may each receive limited recognition when calculating the common equity component of Tier 1, with recognition capped at 10% of the bank's common equity component."[24] There are also changes in accounting standards concerning International Financial Reporting Standards (IFRS), and liquidity ratios.

If this sounds confusing, that's because it is confusing. Therefore, the Basel Committee proposed a "Tier 1 Leverage Ratio" of 3 percent to provide "a simple, transparent, non-risk based measure that is calibrated to act as a credible supplementary measure to the risk based requirements."[25] They proposed a transition to the leverage ratio that will begin in January 2013 and run until January 2017. Other changes under consideration were a minimum global standard for funding liquidity and a liquidity ratio, a countercyclical capital buffer, recommendations to reduce the systemic risk-associated resolution of cross-border banks, and a capital surcharge to mitigate the risk of systemic banks.[26] It took time for all of the bank regulators to agree on changes that resulted in Basel III.

Basel III

On September 12, 2010, the G-10 Governors and Heads of Supervision (GHOS), the oversight body of the Basel Committee on Banking Supervision, announced higher global minimum capital standards.[27] The U.S. bank regulators supported the new capital requirements for risk-weighted assets.[28] The new capital standards are commonly referred to Basel III, although that is not their official name. The reforms will be phased in by 2019. The major changes include the following, which are summarized in Table 8.5:

- The minimum requirement for common equity will be increased from 2 percent (before some regulatory adjustments) to 4.5 percent.
- The tier 1 capital requirement, which includes common equity and other qualifying financial instruments, will have to meet stricter criteria. The tier 1 capital requirement will be increased from 4 percent to 6 percent.
- The minimum total capital is 8 percent.
- A capital conservation buffer of 2.5 percent common equity above the minimum capital requirement is required to ensure that financial institutions can absorb losses during periods of financial distress.
- A countercyclical buffer of 0 percent to 2.5 percent common equity, or other fully loss-absorbing capital, will be implemented based on national circumstances.
- A liquidity coverage ratio (LCR) will be introduced on January 1, 2015.
- A revised net stable funding ratio (NSFR) will move to a minimum standard by January 1, 2018.

TABLE 8.5 Minimum Risk-Based Capital Ratios

	Common Equity after Deductions	Tier 1 Capital	Total Capital
Minimum	4.5%	6.0%	8.0%
Conservation buffer		2.5%	2.5%
Minimum plus conservation buffer	7.0%	8.5%	10.5%
Countercyclical buffer		0.0%–2.5%	
Leverage ratio	—	3.0%	—

Source: BIS, "Group of Governors and Heads of Supervision announces higher global minimum capital standards," Press Release, September 12, 2010.

Banks are also required to have a non-risk-based tier 1 leverage ratio of 3 percent during the parallel run period. The leverage ratio incorporates potential leverage from off-balance-sheet exposures and makes adjustments for derivative transactions and some international accounting differences for derivatives.[29]

ENTERPRISE RISK MANAGEMENT AND ECONOMIC CAPITAL

Bank regulators and others recognized that Basel II had significant limitations and that additional measures were needed. Basel II creates an uneven playing field for the large but not for the largest banks in the United States that can use the costly and complex advanced IRB approach to achieve minimum capital requirements. As shown in Table 8.3, the advanced IRB approach permits each bank to have vastly different capital charges for the same type of loan, depending on the model that they use. Thus, bank regulators began to consider ERM. The Committee on Sponsoring Organizations of the Treadway Commission (COSO) defines ERM as a process affected by an enterprise's board of directors, management, and other personnel that is applied across an enterprise to identify, assess, and manage risks within its risk appetite to provide reasonable assurance of achieving its objectives.[30]

Federal Reserve Governor Susan Schmidt Bies (2006) commented on the COSO definition of ERM that it can mean different things to different people, but "all banking organizations need good risk management. An enterprise-wide approach is appropriate for setting objectives across the organization, instilling an enterprise-wide culture, and ensuring that key activities and risks are being monitored regularly." Governor Bies went on to say that ERM includes:[31]

- Aligning the entity's risk appetite and strategies.
- Enhancing the rigor of the entity's risk-response decisions.
- Reducing the frequency and severity of operational surprises and losses.
- Identifying and managing multiple and cross-enterprise risks.
- Proactively seizing on the opportunities presented to the entity.
- Improving the effectiveness of the entity's capital deployment.

The key point here is that ERM is forward looking. It takes into account economic conditions and a wide range of risks and other factors affecting banks in the future. Regulatory capital is history—not the future. But as noted in Chapter 5, although ERM provides important benefits, it is does have limitations,

> *that result from the realities that human judgment in decision making can be faulty, decisions on responding to risk and establishing controls need to consider the relative costs and benefits, breakdowns can occur because of human failures such as simple errors or mistakes, controls can be circumvented by collusion of two or more people, and management has the ability to override enterprise risk management decisions. These limitations preclude a board and management from having absolute assurance as to achievement of the entity's objectives.*[32]

ERM employs the concept of *economic capital*—a statistical concept measuring risk—and the bank's estimate of the amount of capital needed to support its risk-taking activities. It is not the amount of *regulatory capital* held.[33]

> *Economic capital measures may be one of several key factors used to inform decision-making in areas such as profitability, pricing, and portfolio optimization—particularly at the business-line level. Economic capital measures may also feed into senior management decisions relating to issues such as acquisitions and divestitures. Such measures are also used, primarily at the consolidated entity level, to assess overall capital adequacy.*[34]

A study of risk-based capital by the Government Accountability Office (GAO) found that "economic capital models may explicitly measure a broader range of risks, while regulatory capital as proposed in Basel II will explicitly measure only credit, operational, and where relevant, market risks."[35] In the context of ERM, risks for global banks go far beyond credit risk, market risk, and operational risk. They include, but are not limited to, breakdown of critical infrastructure, changing laws and regulations, changes in technology, defaults of sovereign debts, foreign exchange, hurricanes, oil prices, terrorism, and political instability in the Middle East. Thus, economic capital reflects the bank's estimate of the amount of capital (not book value capital or regulatory capital) needed to support its risk-taking activities. In statistical terms, it is a conditional random variable.

Risk is measured in terms of probability, expected values, and standard errors. Thus, *economic capital* is the difference between a given percentile of a loss distribution and the expected loss. It is sometimes referred to as unexpected loss at the 99.97 percent confidence level. That means a

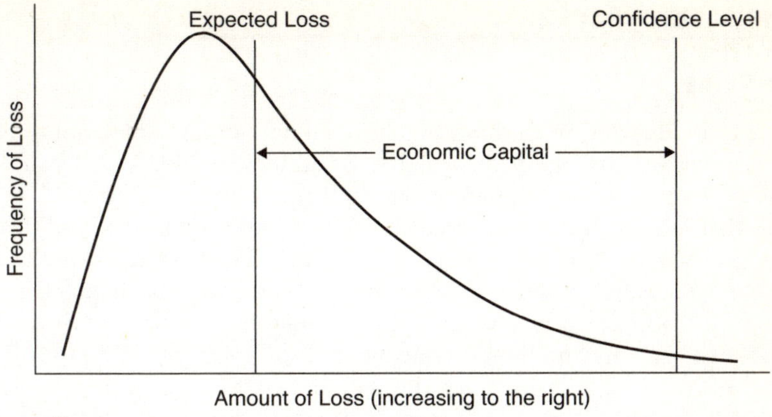

FIGURE 8.1 Economic Capital

3 in 10,000 probability of the bank becoming insolvent during the next 12 months. It is important to recognize that measures of economic capital will vary from bank to bank and over time as conditions change. Figure 8.1 illustrates the concept of economic capital.

In theory, economic capital sounds good. In practice,

> *The Federal Reserve conducted a review across a number of large banking organizations to assess these firms' use of so-called "economic capital" practices, which are a means for firms to calculate, for internal purposes, their capital needs given their risk profile. Consistent with other findings, we found that some banks relied too extensively on the output of internal models, not viewing model output with appropriate skepticism. Models are dependent on the data used to construct them. When data histories are short or are drawn mostly from periods of benign economic conditions, model results may not be fully applicable to an institution's risk profile. We concluded that banks would generally benefit from better evaluation of inputs used in their internal capital models, stronger validation of their models, and broader use of stress testing and scenario analysis to supplement the inherent limitations of their models.*[36]

In practice, "There remain significant methodological, implementation, and business challenges associated with the application of economic capital in banks, particularly if economic capital measures are to be used for internal assessments of capital adequacy."[37] The bottom line is that economic capital is a work in process.

ACCOUNTING ISSUES

Fair Value

Changes in accounting methods can have an impact on bank capital. Financial Accounting Standards Board (FASB) Statement No. 157, "Fair Value Measurements," issued in September 2006, and FASB Statement No. 159, "The Fair Value Option for Financial Assets and Financial Liabilities," issued in February 2007 were effective in 2008.[38] The FDIC defines *fair value* as "the valuation of various assets and liabilities on the balance sheet—including trading assets and liabilities, available-for-sale securities, loans held for sale, assets and liabilities accounted for under the fair value option, and foreclosed assets—involves the use of fair values. During periods of market stress, the fair values of some financial instruments and nonfinancial assets may decline."[39]

Both FASB 157 and 159 will have an impact on bank regulatory capital when market rates of interest change.[40] "They require banks to value their assets and liabilities in such a way that assets and liabilities reflect market prices." Kevin Bailey, deputy comptroller of the Office of the Comptroller of the Currency, testified before Congress that as of December 31, 2008, approximately 25 percent of national banks' assets were subject to Fair Value accounting treatment.[41]

Bailey noted that an increasing number of banks have chosen an "originate and distribute approach to asset designations in order to permit Fair Valuations and ultimately transfer risk to investors rather than holding the assets to maturity. Eventually most assets and liabilities will be subject to Fair Valuation."[42]

Loans held for sale are marked to market. When market rates of interest increase, the market price of long-term debt instruments such as bonds and fixed-rate mortgages declines. If the value of the loans declines sufficiently, they may wipe out a bank's regulatory capital. As shown in Table 8.6, Panel A, "Fair Value Hypothetical Bank" is funding its long-term loan with a long-term deposit, and it is well capitalized. However, this bank does not hedge its interest rate risk.

Let's see what happens if market rates of interest increase 100 basis points, and the loan was funded with shorter-term sources of funds. As shown in Table 8.6, Panel B, capital adequacy is inversely related to the maturity of the bank's liabilities. In other words, the bank that funded the 20-year loan with 5-year deposits will be significantly undercapitalized, and the bank will fail.

Although five-year deposits are not short term in the strict sense of the phrase, the effect of accounting rules must be considered in banks' asset/liability management strategies. Along this line, changes in FASB 166 and

TABLE 8.6 The Effects of Funding Maturities on the Equity/Asset Capital Ratio of "Fair Value Hypothetical Bank"

Panel A: Bank's Initial Position ($ thousands)

Assets	**Liabilities and Equity**	**Equity/Assets**
$10,000 Loan (20 years, 8% fixed rate, semiannually)	$9,000 Certificate of deposit (CD) (20 years, 5% fixed rate, semiannually)	
	$1,000 Equity	
Total assets	Total liabilities and equity	
$10,000	$10,000	10% (well capitalized)

Panel B: Bank's Position with Alternative Funding Options ($ thousands)

Market Rates of Interest Increase 100 Basis Points for Both Assets and Liabilities	**Alternative Funding Maturities**	**Equity/Asset Ratios when the Bank Is Funded by CDs with Different Maturities**
Assets (market value) (20 years maturity)	**Liabilities (market value) (maturity of CD)**	**Equity/asset**
$9,080 (20 years)	$7,959.6 (20 years)	12.34% (well capitalized)
$9,080 (20 years)	$8,330.4 (10 years)	8.26% (adequately capitalized)
$9,080 (20 years)	$8,615.7 (5 years)	5.11% (significantly undercapitalized)
$9,080 (20 years)	$8,913.6 (1 year)	1.83% (critically undercapitalized)

FASB 167 pertaining to securitization and special purpose entities changed in 2009.[43] They will have an impact on the bank capitalization and stress tests.

WHAT'S NEXT?

Everyone agrees that bank capital is important, but there is less agreement on how much capital banks should hold. In the past, former Federal Reserve Chairman Alan Greenspan said:

> *[Central banks] have chosen implicitly, if not in a more overt fashion, to set capital and other reserve standards for banks to guard*

> *against outcomes that exclude those once or twice in a century crises that threaten the stability of our domestic and international financial systems. . . . I do not believe any central bank explicitly makes this calculation. But we have chosen adverse loss outcomes. There is implicit in this exercise the admission that, in certain episodes, problems at commercial banks and other financial institutions, when their risk-management systems prove inadequate, will be handled by central banks. At the same time, society on the whole should require that we set this bar very high. Hundred-year floods come only once every hundred years. Financial institutions should expect to look to the central bank only in extremely rare situations.*[44]

Recently, Secretary General Stefan Walter of the Basel Committee on Banking Supervision said: "The pre-crisis financial system was characterized by—too much leverage in the banking and financial system and not enough high quality capital to absorb losses—and other factors."[45]

Similarly, Nout Wellink, chairman of the Basel Committee on Banking Supervision and president of De Nederlandsche Bank, said: "Now, in the face of this experience, minimum standards for capital and liquidity need to be raised substantially so that the banking sector can withstand future periods of stress, thus enhancing financial stability and promoting more sustainable growth. The banking sector must serve as a stabilizing force and not as an amplifier of shocks."[46] Along this line, the Basel Committee on Banking Supervision is proposing a countercyclical capital buffer.[47] The aim of the countercyclical buffer is to ensure that the banking sector has sufficient capital to "help maintain the flow of credit in the economy without its solvency being questioned, when the broader financial system experiences stress after a period of excess credit growth. This should help to reduce the risk of the supply of credit being constrained by regulatory capital requirements that could undermine the performance of the real economy and result in additional credit losses in the banking system."[48] The amount of the buffers may vary by country and by banks. In other words, it is not a one-size-fits-all capital requirement.

The Basel Committee on Banking Supervision recommended supplementing the risk-based capital requirements with a simple *leverage ratio* that would take into account both on- and off-balance-sheet leverage.[49] It should be noted that there are several leverage ratios. The following three for example:

1. Tier 1 Leverage Capital ratio (Tier 1 Capital/Average Assets).
2. Tier 1 Risk-Based Capital ratio (Tier 1 Capital/Risk-Weighted Assets).
3. Total Risk-Based Capital ratio (Total Capital/Risk-Weighted Assets).

According to FDIC Chairman Sheila Bair:

> *There are differences in regulatory capital between banks and holding companies. Capital requirements for bank holding companies are less stringent, qualitatively and quantitatively, than those applicable to insured banks. Specifically, leverage ratio requirements are lower for bank holding companies and, unlike insured banks, bank holding companies are permitted to include, within limits, certain types of hybrid capital instruments and subordinated debt as regulatory tier 1 capital.... The capital differences have created a situation where certain large bank holding companies became significantly more leveraged on a consolidated basis. The policy rationale for lower capital requirements at the holding company was presumably that these entities did not enjoy an explicit federal safety net.*[50]

That assumption was wrong.

So will central banks increase regulatory capital sufficiently to avoid future large-scale bank failures? In June 2010, the Basel Committee on Banking Supervision revised some aspects of the Basel II market risk framework that will take several years to implement.[51] An FDIC publication in 2003 asked: "How much capital is enough?"[52] Only time will tell because bank capital is a work in progress.

CHAPTER 9

Evaluating Bank Performance

It is said that beauty is in the eye of the beholder. Similarly, the value of a bank and its financial condition depend on what you are looking for. For example, a stockholder's perspective is different from that of a bank regulator. Stockholders are interested in maximizing their wealth. In contrast, bank regulators are interested in the bank's safety, soundness, and compliance with laws and regulations. Other points of view include large depositors who are interested in high returns but also want to ensure that their funds are safe. Borrowers are interested in the availability and the cost of funds. Finally, communities are also interested in the availability of funds to support their growth.

Because there are different perspectives on evaluating bank performance, this chapter is organized as follows: The first part of the chapter examines banks whose stock is publicly traded. In reality, they are bank/financial holding companies or financial service companies rather than individual commercial banks. The second part of the chapter focuses on analyzing commercial banks.

EVALUATING PUBLICLY TRADED BANKS

Bank Stocks

A Google search of "bank stocks" produced 19.5 million results in 0.15 seconds. One of the first items listed was the NASDAQ Bank Index (symbol IXBK). NASDAQ is the largest U.S. electronic stock market. The NASDAQ Bank Index includes 474 NASDAQ-listed companies classified according to the Financial Times and Stock Exchange (FTSE) Global Classification System as banks.[1] The banks included in the index provide a broad range of financial services, including retail banking and money transmission. Figure 9.1 shows the performance of the NASDAQ Bank Index (XBK) from 2004 to July 2010. The index was developed in 1971 with a base level of 100. In 2004,

FIGURE 9.1 NASDQA Bank Index (XBK)
© Copyright 2010, The NASDAQ OMX Group, Inc. Reprinted with permission.

the index was about 2,450. Bank stock prices increased to about 3,450 in October 2007, when the global financial crises started to affect the economy. Then bank stock prices plunged below 1,200 in early 2009. Subsequently, they began a long and painful recovery. In July 2010, they were still far below the high levels reached in 2007. In simple terms, the chart shows that bank stock performance is closely tied to the level of economic activity.

A second bank index is the American Bankers Association (ABA) NASDAQ Community Bank Index (ABAQ) that includes banks, thrifts, or their holding companies listed on the NASDAQ Stock Market that have been selected by the ABA.[2] This index measures price returns. The third bank index is the NASDAQ XABQ that measures total returns of reinvested cash dividends of the stocks in the ABAQ index. There is some overlap between the XBK and the two NASDAQ Community Bank Indices.

Other banks, such as Bank of America, Citigroup Inc., JPMorgan Chase & Co., and Wells Fargo Co., are traded on the New York Stock Exchange (NYSE). Keep in mind that these are large complex banking organizations (LCBOs). Typically, LCBOs are global financial service companies that engage in a wide variety of permissible activities. For example, Citigroup Inc. has approximately 200 million customer accounts, and it operates in approximately 140 countries.[3] In addition, Citigroup had 2,343 separate entities listed under its "Organization Hierarchy" report that is provided by the National Information Center (NIC), a source of financial information and institution characteristics collected by the Federal Reserve System.[4] Citigroup's hierarchy included 71 institutions classified as commercial banks located around the world.

Securities and Exchange Commission Filings Securities sold to the public must be registered with the Securities and Exchange Commission (SEC). There are some exceptions. The exceptions include private offerings to a limited number of persons or institutions, offerings of limited size, intrastate offerings, and securities of municipal, state, and federal governments.[5]

Companies that are registered with the SEC are required to file periodic financial and other reports. Accordingly, the SEC provides investors with the following information:

SEC Filings

10-K (audited annual financial statements).

10-Q (unaudited quarterly financial statements).

8-K (current information including preliminary earnings announcements).

Registration statements including Form S-1 (general registration statement under the Securities Act of 1933, used for new issuers) and Form F-6 (registration statement used by foreign issuers of American Depositary Receipts).

This listing of information provided by the SEC is not complete. Additional information can be found on the SEC web site (www.sec.gov) under "Researching Public Companies through EDGAR: A Guide for Investors." EDGAR is an acronym that stands for electronic data gathering, analysis, and retrieval.

Investor Relations The investor relations departments of many publicly held banks may provide the following information about their companies:

Annual reports
Quarterly reports
Proxy statements
Earnings releases
SEC filings
Other regulatory filings
Company information
Credit ratings
Investor presentations
Event calendars
Shareholder information
Press releases
Frequently asked questions

Bank investor relations departments can be accessed through the bank's web site. The information provided will vary from bank to bank.

Other Sources of Information Publicly traded stocks are closely followed by international credit rating agencies (e.g., Moody's, Fitch, and Standard & Poor's), securities research firms (e.g., Standard & Poor's, Value Line), investment banking/brokerage firms (e.g., Charles Schwab and Merrill Lynch), and online sources of financial information such as Morningstar, CNN-Money.com, and Yahoo! Finance. Some of these sources are free, and others charge fees for their services. By way of illustration: Yahoo! Finance provides free information about companies that are traded in the United States and abroad. For U.S. stocks, it provides the following:[6]

- Profile
  - Details
  - Business summary
  - Company websites
  - Corporate governance
  - Key executives
- Quotes
  - Summary
  - Real-time
  - Options
  - Historical prices

- Charts
  - Interactive (1 day to 5 years or more)
  - Basic chart
  - Basic technical analysis
- News and information
  - Headlines
  - Financial blogs
  - Company events
  - Message boards
- Company
  - Profile
  - Key statistics
  - SEC filings
  - Competitors
  - Industry
  - Components
- Analyst coverage
  - Analyst opinion
  - Analyst estimates
  - Research reports
  - Star analysts
- Ownership
  - Major holders
  - Insider transactions
  - Insider roster
- Financials
  - Income statement
  - Balance sheet
  - Cash flow

What Information Do You Need? The amount of information that is available about banks and bank stocks is overwhelming. Accordingly, the place to start is by asking why you want the information and your investment time horizon.[7] Are you are a short-term speculator, a long-term investor, or a bank customer wanting to know more about a particular bank? As shown in Table 9.1, if you are a day trader trying to profit from small changes in

TABLE 9.1 Information Required for Investment Decisions

Investment Time Horizon	Examples of Data Required
One day or less	Current information that affects the stock price Current stock price, bid-asked spreads, and trading volume Daily charts of stock prices
Short-term (1 year or less)	Current economic data and short-term projections for the markets served by the bank (regional, national, international) Changes in management, strategies, operations, mergers, etc. Bank's financial data Earnings projections Analysts' recommendations Credit ratings Technical indicators provided by charts
Long-term (1 year or more)	Bank's strategies for growth Projections of major factors affecting the bank, such as population growth in areas served, new technologies, and laws Bank's financial data Earnings projections Credit ratings Technical indicators provided by charts

stock prices, and your investment time horizon is one day or less, then you need current information about the stock price, bid-asked spreads, volume of trading, and charts to facilitate your trades.

Both short-term (one year or less holding period) and long-term investors require additional information before buying the stock. For example, a short-term investor might be interested in earnings projections for the next few quarters, analysts' recommendations, credit ratings, and technical indicators provided by charts. Long-term investors require additional information, such as the major factors affecting the bank like population growth in the markets they serve. After short-term and long-term investors acquire that stock, they still have to monitor that bank's performance by using the same type of information.

Suppose that you own a business, have bank deposits and borrowed funds, and make wire transfers to other firms. Deposits made in Federal Deposit Insurance Corporation- (FDIC-) insured institutions by a corporation, partnership, or unincorporated association are insured up to a maximum of $250,000.[8] But your deposits far exceed the maximum amount covered by deposit insurance. Therefore, you need to monitor the financial condition of that bank using the same type of information as short-term investors, such as the bank's financial data and credit ratings. Data about the banking system and individual banks are available on the FDIC Bank Data Guide web sites shown in Appendix 9A.

EVALUATING COMMERCIAL BANKS

An Overview of Commercial Bank Performance

The overview presents selected measures of financial performance for banks of different asset sizes. Then we will examine the financial performance of individual banks.

As shown in Table 9.2, there were 6,772 FDIC-insured commercial banks in early 2010. These banks include national banks, state chartered banks, and trust companies, except savings banks.[9]

Table 9.2 reveals that 83 large banks control 80.4 percent of the total assets. In other words, bank assets are highly concentrated in a few large banks. At the other end of the size spectrum, about 90 percent of the commercial banks have assets of $1 billion or less, and they hold 10.2 percent of total assets. Medium-size banks, with $1 billion to $10 billion in assets, hold the remaining 9.4 percent.

The *net interest margin* is the difference between interest and dividends earned on interest-bearing assets and interest paid to depositors and creditors, expressed as a percentage of average-earning assets. No adjustments are made for income that is tax exempt. The data show that banks of all sizes earned about the same amount—slightly less than 4 percent. However, there are significant differences in the *return on assets* (ROA), which is a comprehensive measure of profitability. The ROA was calculated by dividing net income (including gains or losses on securities and extraordinary items) by average total assets. The average ROA for all banks was 0.53, but for medium-size banks, it was substantially lower (0.11). The FDIC reported: "Implementation of FAS 166 *(*Accounting for Transfers and Servicing of Financial Assets and Extinguishments of Liabilities) and FAS 167 (Consolidation of Variable Interest Entities) caused a large amount of loans in securitized loan pools to be consolidated into the reported loan balances of a relatively small number of large insured institutions in the first quarter."[10] Fee income is another factor that can affect net income. The largest banks may have trust departments and other financial services that provide them with fee income that is not available to the smallest banks.

The *efficiency ratio* measures the proportion of net operating revenues that is absorbed by overhead expenses. Lower values indicate greater efficiency. A ratio of 55 is considered good. The data show that efficiency

TABLE 9.2 Selected Data for FDIC-Insured Commercial Banks, First Quarter 2010

	All Institutions	Assets Less Than $100 Million	Assets $100 Million to $1 Billion	Assets $1 Billion to $10 Billion	Assets Greater Than $10 Billion
Number of institutions	6,772	2,469	3,780	440	83
Total assets ($billions)	$12,086.5	$138.7	$1,098.1	$1,136.3	$9,713.4
Percentage of assets	100%	1.1%	9.1%	9.4%	80.4%
Net interest margin	3.89	3.92	3.80	3.75	3.92
Return on assets	0.53	0.45	0.43	0.11	0.59
Efficiency ratio	54.25	78.27	71.22	60.51	51.78
Core capital (leverage) ratio	8.44	11.19	9.36	9.34	8.19
Return on equity	4.82	3.84	4.38	1.01	5.32
Net loans and leases to deposits	78.03	70.66	78.84	84.86	77.13

Source: FDIC Quarterly Banking Profile, First Quarter 2010, Table III-A. FDIC-Insured Commercial Banks. www2.fdic.gov/qbp/2010mar/cb3.html.

is inversely related to the size of the banks. This, in part, explains why the smallest banks have lower ROAs than the largest ones.

Core capital (tier 1 capital) includes common equity capital plus noncumulative perpetual preferred stock plus minority interest in consolidated subsidiaries, less goodwill and other ineligible intangible assets. The core capital leverage ratio is a measure of financial leverage. It is the ratio of tier 1 capital to total assets.[11] The data show that the largest banks have the lowest capital-to-asset ratios, which results in the highest financial leverage. The implication of this is that, if all other things were equal, the largest bank's ROE will be more volatile than those of the smallest banks. The ROE is calculated by dividing net income (including gains or losses on securities and extraordinary items) by the average total equity capital.

Net loans and leases to deposits is an indicator of how effectively the bank is employing its deposits. The higher the number, the better. The data show that the smallest banks have the lowest numbers.

In summary, the asset size of a bank matters in evaluating its financial performance. Comparing the financial performance of small banks with those of large banks is like comparing apples and oranges. Don't do it!

Geography is another factor to consider. The financial crisis that began in 2007 had its greatest impact in California, Florida, and Nevada. Therefore, when selecting peer banks for purposes of comparison, geographic location should be taken into account.

Finally, the data shown in Table 9.2 is from the FDIC Quarterly Banking Profile that contains more financial information than is presented here. For those who want additional financial data about commercial banks, go to the FDIC web site referenced below the table.

Call Reports

The Reports of Condition and Income are commonly referred to as *call reports*. Every national bank, state member bank, and insured state nonmember bank is required to file a quarterly consolidated call report. Similarly, *thrift institutions* (e.g., credit unions, savings and loans, savings banks) file Thrift Financial Reports (TFR). The call reports and TFRs are publicly available sources of information and can be accessed through the FDIC web site listed in Appendix 9A. As will be explained later, start with the FDIC Institution Directory.

Call reports contain detailed financial information that exceeds what most readers of this book need to know. For example, the call report for Ally Bank is 70 pages long.[12] Ally Bank is owned by Ally Financial Inc., the 15th largest bank holding company in the United States, with total assets of $179.4 billion.[13] It was originally known as General Motors Acceptance Corporation, headquartered in Detroit, Michigan. In 2008, the name was changed to GMAC LLC, and the corporate organization changed from a finance company to a bank holding company. Its core business was automobile financing. In May 2010, GMAC LLC was renamed Ally Financial Inc. Ally Bank, a nonmember bank located in Midvale, Utah, is one of 20 entities in the holding company hierarchy. As a result of the financial crisis, the U.S. government became the major stockholder in Ally Bank.[14]

The easiest place to find individual bank data and start analyzing a bank's financial performance is the "FDIC Institution Directory" accessed via the advanced search box at the top of the FDIC web site (www.fdic.gov). Under "Find All," click on "Institutions" (www2.fdic.gov/idasp/index.asp). Type in the name of the bank and where it is located. It will give you

TABLE 9.3 FDIC Institution Directory

Key demographic information as of July 29, 2010

Ally Bank
6985 Union Park Center Suite 435
Midvale, UT 84047

FDIC Certificate #:	57803	Date Established:	8/2/2004
Bank Charter Class:	Federal Reserve Non-member	Date of Deposit Insurance:	8/2/2004
Primary Federal Regulator:	Federal Deposit Insurance Corporation	More Demographic Information →	
Primary Internet Web Address:	http://www.ally.com:80/	Generate History →	

Information Gateway

ID Report Selections: All Summary Information

Report Date: March 31, 2010

----------------**More Information**----------------

Current List of Offices	Bank Holding Company Ownership and Affiliates
Compare to Peer Group(s)	Regional Economic Conditions (FDIC RECON)
FFIEC Call/TFR Report ***6/30/2010 Latest Available***	Organization Hierarchy from the Federal Reserve System
FFIEC Uniform Bank Performance Report (UBPR)	FDIC CRA ratings
FDIC/OTS Summary of Deposits	Consumer Assistance from Primary Federal Regulator

Source: www2.fdic.gov/idasp/confirmation_outside.asp?inCert1=57803.

the FDIC certificate number. Click on the FDIC certificate number, and a report similar to the one shown in Table 9.3 will appear.[15] The "all summary information" (in the *ID Report Selection*) contains assets and liabilities, income and expenses, performance and condition ratios, and some demographic information.

The FDIC Institution Directory, under "More Information," lists additional reports, including the Federal Financial Institutions Examination

Council (FFIEC) Uniform Bank Performance Report (UBPR) that will be discussed shortly.

As shown in Table 9.4, Ally Bank had total assets (line 2) of $55.1 billion in March 2010, up from $36.3 billion in the previous year. Their total interest-bearing deposits (line 4) increased dramatically from $2.4 billion to $9.6 billion. Net loans and leases (line 7) increased by $7 billion. Most of their assets are "earning assets" (line 36), which is a good thing. On the liability side of the balance sheet, funds were raised from increases in deposits (line 17), other borrowed funds (line 23), and increases in equity capital (line 26).

In the income statement, net interest income (line 54) increased, but noninterest income (line 56) declined. Overall, their net income (line 70) showed a substantial gain.

Turning to the performance and condition ratios, we look at the same ratios we examined in Table 9.2. Notice that the performance ratios are expressed as a percent, and they are annualized. Ally Bank's net interest margin (NIM, line 81) increased to 2.64 percent. However, this is lower than the NIM for large banks (above $10 billion in assets) shown in Table 9.2 (3.92 percent).

Ally Bank's ROA (line 85) increased from a loss to a positive 1.63 percent. This is well above the 0.59 percent for the large banks in Table 9.2. Ally Bank's ROE is 11.15 percent compared with 5.32 percent for the large banks. One reason for their high returns is the low efficiency ratio (line 92) of 42.18 percent. Part of the explanation for this is that Ally has only 707 employees (line 1). Recall that the lower the number, the better. The efficiency ratio for the large banks is almost 52 percent. Ally's net loans and leases to deposits (line 99) is 113 percent compared with 77 percent for the large banks.

Finally, Ally Bank is well capitalized, with a core capital (leverage) ratio of 16.41 percent compared with 8.19 percent for the large banks.

In summary, the data shown in Table 9.4 reveals that between March 2009 and March 2010, Ally Bank recovered from its losses and became profitable, increased its capital, and improved its efficiency.

The demographic information in Table 9.4 provides some insights into Ally Bank's organization and regulation.

Uniform Bank Performance Report

The UBPR is a multi-page financial analysis of a commercial bank or savings bank that files the Consolidated Reports of Condition and Income (Call Report). The UBPR is organized by subject, e.g., earnings, balance sheet, asset quality, liquidity, and capital. Virtually all of the dollar values, ratios, peer group averages and percentile

TABLE 9.4 "All Summary Information"

	Ally Bank		
	6985 Union Park Ctr Suite 43 Midvale, UT 84047		
	FDIC Certificate #: 57803 Bank Charter Class: NM		
Definition	*Dollar figures in thousands*	Ally Bank Midvale, UT March 31, 2010	GMAC Bank Midvale, UT March 31, 2009
All Summary Information			
Assets and Liabilities			
1	Total employees (full-time equivalent)	707	531
2	**Total assets**	**55,172,742**	**36,366,230**
3	Cash and due from depository institutions	9,725,217	2,610,337
4	Interest-bearing balances	9,667,269	2,479,386
5	Securities	7,036,269	2,454,704
6	Federal funds sold & reverse repurchase agreements	0	0
7	Net loans & leases	34,599,709	27,545,651
8	Loan loss allowance	698,371	548,186
9	Trading account assets	0	0
10	Bank premises and fixed assets	68	177
11	Other real estate owned	7,800	73,707
12	Goodwill and other intangibles	1,129,404	428,190
13	All other assets	2,674,275	3,253,464
14	Life insurance assets	0	0
15	**Total liabilities and capital**	55,172,742	36,366,229
16	**Total liabilities**	**46,961,876**	**32,345,738**
17	Total deposits	30,559,056	22,527,450
18	Interest-bearing deposits	27,967,644	20,556,527
19	Deposits held in domestic offices	30,559,056	22,527,450
20	% insured	93.74%	89.15%
21	Federal funds purchased & repurchase agreements	1,001,500	0
22	Trading liabilities	0	0
23	Other borrowed funds	14,868,825	9,190,536
24	Subordinated debt	0	0
25	All other liabilities	532,495	627,752
26	**Total equity capital**	**8,210,866**	**4,020,491**

TABLE 9.4 *(Continued)*

Definition	*Dollar figures in thousands*	Ally Bank Midvale, UT March 31, 2010	GMAC Bank Midvale, UT March 31, 2009
27	Total bank equity capital	8,210,866	4,020,491
28	Perpetual preferred stock	0	0
29	Common stock	1,000	1,000
30	Surplus	9,596,142	3,878,700
31	Undivided profits	−1,386,276	140,791
32	Noncontrolling interests in consolidated subsidiaries	0	0
	Memoranda:		
33	Noncurrent loans and leases	350,150	721,471
34	Noncurrent loans that are wholly or partially guaranteed by the U.S. government	1,499	0
35	Income earned, not collected on loans	95,379	85,684
36	Earning assets	51,303,247	32,479,741
37	Long-term assets (5+ years)	13,436,482	10,669,936
38	Average Assets, year-to-date	55,237,822	34,624,402
39	Average Assets, quarterly	55,237,822	34,624,402
40	Volatile liabilities	14,996,025	4,383,337
41	Insider loans	0	2,525
42	FHLB advances	4,816,000	9,188,000
43	Loans and leases held for sale	4,984,973	4,903,787
44	Unused loan commitments	13,800,467	2,796,347
45	Tier 1 (core) risk-based capital	8,032,351	3,975,067
46	Tier 2 risk-based capital	421,135	318,886
47	Total risk weighted assets	33,409,565	25,280,063
48	Total unused commitments	13,800,467	2,796,347
49	Restructured Loans and leases	114,154	130,946
50	Derivatives	20,791,600	40,738,039
	Past due and nonaccrual assets	—	—
	Fiduciary and related services	—	—
Income and Expense		*(Year-to-date)*	*(Year-to-date)*
51	Number of institutions reporting	1	1
52	Total interest income	550,705	385,129
53	Total interest expense	211,304	286,359
54	Net interest income	339,401	98,770

(continued)

TABLE 9.4 *(Continued)*

Definition	*Dollar figures in thousands*	Ally Bank Midvale, UT March 31, 2010	GMAC Bank Midvale, UT March 31, 2009
55	Provision for loan and lease losses	40,626	280,207
56	Total noninterest income	118,545	131,151
57	Fiduciary activities	0	0
58	Service charges on deposit accounts	50	2
59	Trading account gains & fees	0	0
60	Additional noninterest income	118,495	131,149
61	Total noninterest expense	193,156	162,000
62	Salaries and employee benefits	18,324	12,528
63	Premises and equipment expense	241	228
64	Additional noninterest expense	174,591	149,244
65	Pre-tax net operating income	224,164	–212,286
66	Securities gains (losses)	7,148	–1,061
67	Applicable income taxes	6,640	–79,854
68	Income before extraordinary items	224,672	–133,493
69	Extraordinary gains - net	0	0
70	**Net income attributable to bank**	**224,672**	**–133,493**
71	Net income attributable to noncontrolling interests	0	0
72	Net income attributable to bank and noncontrolling interests	224,672	–133,493
73	Net charge-offs	25,442	136,684
74	Cash dividends	0	0
75	Sale, conversion, retirement of capital stock, net	0	0
76	Net operating income	217,738	–132,814
	Memo:		
	Gross fiduciary and related services income	—	—
Performance and Condition Ratios			
77	% of unprofitable institutions	N/A	N/A
78	% of institutions with earnings gains	N/A	N/A

Performance Ratios (%, annualized)		*(Year-to-date)*	*(Year-to-date)*
79	Yield on earning assets	4.29%	5.00%
80	Cost of funding earning assets	1.64%	3.72%
81	Net interest margin	2.64%	1.28%

TABLE 9.4 *(Continued)*

Definition	*Dollar figures in thousands*	Ally Bank Midvale, UT March 31, 2010	GMAC Bank Midvale, UT March 31, 2009
82	Noninterest income to earning assets	0.92%	1.70%
83	Noninterest expense to earning assets	1.50%	2.10%
84	Net operating income to assets	1.58%	−1.53%
85	Return on assets (ROA)	1.63%	−1.54%
86	Pretax return on assets	1.68%	−2.46%
87	Return on equity (ROE)	11.15%	−13.79%
88	Retained earnings to average equity (YTD only)	11.15%	−13.79%
89	Net charge-offs to loans	0.29%	2.11%
90	Credit loss provision to net charge-offs	159.68%	205.00%
91	Earnings coverage of net loan charge-offs (x)	10.41	0.50
92	Efficiency ratio	42.18%	70.46%
93	Assets per employee ($ millions)	78.04	68.49
94	Cash dividends to net income (YTD only)	0	0
	Condition Ratios (%)		
95	Loss allowance to loans	1.98%	1.95%
96	Loss allowance to noncurrent loans	199.45%	75.98%
97	Noncurrent assets plus other real estate owned to assets	0.65%	2.19%
98	Noncurrent loans to loans	0.99%	2.57%
99	Net loans and leases to deposits	113.22%	122.28%
100	Net loans and leases to core deposits	136.70%	144.57%
101	Equity capital to assets	14.88%	11.06%
102	Core capital (leverage) ratio	16.41%	11.38%
103	Tier 1 risk-based capital ratio	24.04%	15.72%
104	Total risk-based capital ratio	25.30%	16.99%
	Memoranda:		
105	Average assets	55,237,822	34,624,402
106	Average earning assets	51,390,815	30,793,663
107	Average equity	8,057,120	3,873,132
108	Average loans	35,183,122	25,944,453

(continued)

TABLE 9.4 (*Continued*)

Definition	*Demographic Information*	July 29, 2010	March 31, 2010	March 31, 2009
1	Status	Active	Active	Active
2	Bank Holding Company (Regulatory Top Holder)	See Note!	GMAC INC.	GMAC LLC
3	Certificate#	57803	57803	57803
4	Federal Reserve ID Number	3284070	3284070	3284070
5	Institution Name	Ally Bank	Ally Bank	GMAC Bank
6	City, State, Zip	Midvale, UT, 84047	Midvale, UT, 84047	Midvale, UT, 84047
7	Number of Domestic Offices	—	2	2
8	Number of Foreign Offices	—	N/A	N/A
9	Interstate Offices	—	Yes	Yes
10	Summary Of Deposits	—	June 30, 2009	June 30, 2008
11	Current List of Total Offices	Offices	—	—
12	Asset Concentration Hierarchy	All Other Specialization > 1 Billion	All other Over 1 Billion	Mortgage Lending Specialization
13	Subchapter S Corporation	—	No	No
14	County	Salt Lake	Salt Lake	Salt Lake
15	Metropolitan Statistical Area	Salt Lake City, UT	Salt Lake City, UT	Salt Lake City, UT
16	Established Date	August 2, 2004	August 2, 2004	August 2, 2004
17	Date of Deposit Insurance	August 2, 2004	August 2, 2004	August 2, 2004
18	Last Structure Change Process Date	October 28, 2009	—	—
19	Last Structure Change Effective Date	October 1, 2009	—	—
20	Ownership Type	—	Stock	Stock

TABLE 9.4 *(Continued)*

Definition	*Demographic Information*	July 29, 2010	March 31, 2010	March 31, 2009
21	Directly Owned by Another Bank?(CERT)	—	No	No
22	Trust Powers Granted	Yes	Yes	Yes
23	Bank Charter Class	Federal Reserve Non-member	Federal Reserve Non-member	Federal Reserve Non-member
24	Regulator	FDIC	FDIC	FDIC
25	Insurance fund membership	DIF	DIF	DIF
26	FDIC Quarterly Banking Profile Region	San Francisco	San Francisco	San Francisco
27	FDIC Geographic Region	San Francisco	San Francisco	San Francisco
28	FDIC Supervisory Region	New York	NEW YORK	NEW YORK
29	FDIC Field Office	Salt Lake City	Salt Lake City	Salt Lake City
30	Federal Reserve District	San Francisco	San Francisco	San Francisco
31	Office of the Comptroller of the Currency District	Western	Western	Western
32	Office of Thrift Supervision Region	West	West	West
33	Primary Web Address	http://www.ally.com:80/	N/A	N/A

Source: www2.fdic.gov/idasp/main2.asp.

> *rankings within the UBPR are computed from financial data reported by commercial banks and savings banks on the quarterly . . . . The UBPR compares the performance of a given bank both against itself over time and against the performance of a group of peer banks. Peer group average and percentile ranking data provide benchmarks to measure bank performance . . . . Most data found in the UBPR is derived directly from the Call Report filed by banks.*[16]

The UBPR is designed primarily for federal and state banking supervisors and the banks they supervise. Therefore, there is more detailed information in the reports than most nonregulators need to know.

TABLE 9.5 UPBR Summary Ratios for Ally Bank

FDIC Certificate # 57803 OCC Charter # 0 Public Report	FRB District/ID_RSSD 12 / 3284070 County: SALT LAKE						ALLY BANK; MIDVALE, UT Summary Ratios–Page 1						Summary Ratios 8/6/2010 3:45:29 PM		
	3/31/2010			3/31/2009			12/31/2009			12/31/2008			12/31/2007		
Earnings and Profitability	**BANK**	**PG 1**	**PCT**	**BANK**	**PG 1**	**PCT**	**BANK**	**PG 1**	**PCT**	**BANK**	**PG 1**	**PCT**	**BANK**	**PG 1**	**PCT**
Percent of Average Assets:															
Interest Income (TE)	4.49	4.16	62	4.40	4.43	45	4.38	4.37	49	5.13	5.25	38	5.71	6.17	26
– Interest Expense	1.72	0.99	87	3.27	1.48	96	2.52	1.29	95	3.66	2.06	95	3.97	2.96	93
Net Interest Income (TE)	2.77	3.12	29	1.13	2.90	4	1.86	3.02	9	1.47	3.12	5	1.74	3.19	5
+ Noninterest Income	0.97	1.21	47	1.50	1.22	68	1.25	1.38	56	2.23	1.16	85	2.58	1.25	87
– Noninterest Expense	1.57	2.67	9	1.85	2.65	15	1.67	2.83	11	2.58	2.94	43	2.02	2.66	21
– Provision: Loan & Lease Losses	0.33	1.34	17	3.20	1.57	82	6.59	1.72	96	1.71	1.18	72	0.46	0.30	76
Pretax Operating Income (TE)	1.83	0.39	83	–2.43	–0.05	16	–5.15	–0.08	7	–0.60	0.23	26	1.85	1.54	65
+ Realized Gains/Losses Sec	0.06	0.05	73	–0.01	0.03	17	0.15	0.02	87	0.00	–0.11	39	0.00	–0.02	53
Pretax Net Operating Income (TE)	1.89	0.45	84	–2.44	–0.04	16	–5.00	–0.12	7	–0.60	–0.06	29	1.85	1.51	68
Net Operating Income	1.83	0.25	92	–1.53	–0.01	18	–4.65	–0.21	9	–0.35	–0.16	30	1.18	0.98	64
Adjusted Net Operating Income	1.96	0.35	91	0.11	0.60	27	–3.96	0.21	8	0.60	0.37	41	1.39	1.09	76
Net Inc Attrib to Min Ints	0.00	0.00	82	0.00	0.00	80	0.00	0.00	77	N/A	0.00	N/A	N/A	0.00	N/A
Net Income Adjusted Sub S	1.83	0.25	92	–1.53	–0.02	18	–4.65	–0.24	9	–0.35	–0.16	30	1.18	0.97	63
Net Income	1.83	0.26	92	–1.53	–0.01	18	–4.65	–0.24	9	–0.35	–0.16	30	1.18	0.97	
Margin Analysis:															
Avg Earning Assets to Avg Assets	94.88	92.09	74	83.85	92.09	5	87.51	92.28	11	87.07	91.85	11	88.11	91.54	19
Avg Int-Bearing Funds to Avg Assets	82.99	80.99	57	87.48	81.73	84	84.54	81.24	65	83.94	81.95	60	84.01	81.54	64
Int Inc (TE) to Avg Earn Assets	4.73	4.54	54	5.25	4.84	70	5.00	4.75	60	5.89	5.73	57	6.48	6.75	32
Int Expense to Avg Earn Assets	1.82	1.08	88	3.90	1.61	97	2.88	1.40	96	4.20	2.25	99	4.51	3.25	96
Net Int Inc-TE to Avg Earn Assets	2.92	3.42	26	1.35	3.17	5	2.12	3.29	11	1.69	3.42	5	1.97	3.51	6

Loan & Lease Analysis:															
Net Loss to Average Total LN&LS	0.30	1.87	12	2.13	1.43	72	8.48	1.86	97	1.00	0.97	61	0.30	0.29	60
Earnings Coverage of Net Losses (X)	10.41	3.31	90	0.50	3.46	19	0.24	3.40	17	1.46	4.55	31	9.45	16.15	42
LN&SL Allowance to LN&LS Not HFS	2.30	2.62	46	2.36	2.08	67	2.68	2.53	62	1.77	1.84	54	0.48	1.25	5
LN&LS Allowance to Net Losses (X)	6.86	2.09	92	1.00	2.38	20	0.28	1.89	1	1.66	2.87	33	1.72	6.97	7
LN&LS Allowance to Total LN&LS	1.98	2.54	40	1.95	2.02	55	1.95	2.45	41	1.70	1.81	51	0.43	1.22	6
Total LN&LS-90+ Days Past Due	0.00	0.36	21	0.01	0.27	19	0.00	0.35	19	0.00	0.20	16	0.00	0.13	18
–Nonaccrual	0.99	3.99	15	2.56	2.67	56	0.90	3.76	13	2.18	2.02	62	0.64	0.77	48
–Total	0.99	4.54	10	2.57	3.10	46	0.91	4.33	9	2.18	2.36	55	0.64	0.96	39
Liquidity															
Net Non Core Fund Dependence	50.93	27.33	85	63.98	34.47	90	51.92	29.02	86	70.78	37.67	90	76.78	33.98	95
Net Loans & Leases to Assets	62.71	62.01	45	75.75	65.12	81	62.18	62.96	40	71.13	65.90	63	82.29	65.48	92
Capitalization															
Tier One Leverage Capital	16.41	8.82	94	11.38	8.26	88	15.42	8.69	95	11.06	8.21	86	11.48	8.05	92
Cash Dividends to Net Income	0.00	10.92	73	0.00	18.97	66	0.00	20.55	60	0.00	34.51	47	0.00	62.59	23
Retained Earnings to Avg Total Equity	11.15	–0.40	86	–13.79	–3.36	21	–33.74	–5.33	12	–3.18	–5.99	40	10.48	2.01	91
Rest+Nonac+RE Acq to Eqcap+ALLL	5.43	28.48	12	20.72	19.56	61	3.90	26.93	12	14.80	15.62	53	5.05	5.67	54
Growth Rates															
Total Assets	51.71	4.00	94	19.90	9.43	79	68.18	4.26	95	15.77	11.44	72	42.47	12.30	90
Tier One Capital	102.07	8.70	95	16.40	11.75	65	110.92	9.68	96	11.05	12.45	60	54.39	9.15	93
Net Loans & Leases	25.61	–2.04	89	12.26	5.80	75	47.00	–1.28	93	0.06	9.19	29	42.65	14.14	88
Short Term Investments	289.91	213.65	78	29.21	119.88	51	176.94	236.29	72	210.81	87.10	77	45.70	40.18	66
Short Term Non Core Funding	109.23	–16.35	98	11.58	7.82	62	134.89	–14.75	97	58.95	16.05	84	111.78	23.57	92
Average Total Assets		**49,070,578**			**34,984,778**			**41,876,220**			**32,034,066**			**24,067,407**	
Total Equity Capital		8,210,866			4,020,491			7,903,373			3,725,773			3,316,216	
Net Income		224,672			–133,493			–1,948,202			–112,399			282,820	
Number of banks in Peer Group		**177**			**189**			**180**			**187**			**187**	

The UPBRs can be accessed through the FDIC Institution Directory shown in Table 9.3 or through the FFIEC Central Data Repository's (CDR) web site.[17] The FFIEC is an interagency body empowered to prescribe uniform principles, standards, and report forms for the federal examination of financial institutions by federal regulators of financial institutions.[18]

The UPBRs were designed by bank regulators for bank regulators. They contain more detailed information than is needed by most bank directors, investors, and customers. Nevertheless, it is worthwhile looking at such reports.

Table 9.5 shows the summary ratios for Ally Bank. Note that it provides more detail than was provided in the previous table. For example, PG stands for peer group, and PCT stands for percentile ranking in the peer group. These data allow us to observe how Ally Bank is doing relative to its peers, rather than just comparing it with large banks with assets greater than $10 billion. There were 177 banks in its peer group. The table also shows data for prior years.

A caveat is in order. Notice that the earnings and profitability are expressed as a percentage of average assets. Recall from Table 9.4 that the performance ratios were expressed as a percentage and they were annualized. Therefore, the numbers are not strictly comparable. For example, the ROA in Table 9.4 (line 85) was 1.63. In Table 9.5, there is no label for ROA. However, ROA is defined as net income divided by average assets. So the last line in the first section of Table 9.5 that is labeled "net operating income" is Ally Bank's ROA of 1.83 percent. But this number has not been annualized.

The data also reveal that the ROA of 1.83% is substantially higher than the PG average of 0.26. Note that the ROA for this PG also differs from the ROA of large banks of 0.59 percent that was shown in Table 9.2.

Returning to Table 9.5, the ROA for Ally Bank is in the 92nd percentile, showing that they are doing much better than their peers in early 2010. However, Ally Bank did not do well in the previous years.

This section of Table 9.5 also shows each component of the income and expenses that went into the computation for the ROA. By looking at the PCT for very high and very low numbers, you can see how Ally Bank differs from its peers. For example, for noninterest expense, Ally Bank is in the 9th percentile. Noninterest expense is mainly employees, and Ally Bank had only 707 employees (Table 9.4, Line 1). Low noninterest expense means that it is operating efficiently.

The remainder of the UPBR summary ratios cover margin analysis, loans and leases, liquidity, capitalization, and growth rates. The data reveal that Ally Bank's performance has improved significantly over the time periods shown.[19]

APPENDIX 9A: FDIC BANK DATA GUIDE

Use this FDIC Bank Data Guide and the Internet links to find detailed information about specific banks.[20]

Bank Find www2.fdic.gov/idasp/main_bankfind.asp.

- ☐ Find out if your bank is FDIC-insured.
- ☐ Find the locations of your bank's branches.
- ☐ Find out if your bank has merged or been acquired.
- ☐ Review your bank's history.

Institution Directory (ID) www2.fdic.gov/idasp/index.asp.

- ☐ The latest comprehensive financial and demographic data for every FDIC-insured institution.
- ☐ Create reports and downloads to analyze prospective mergers and classes of competitors.
- ☐ Compare performance and condition data between individual institutions, peer groups, and time periods.

Call and Thrift Financial Reports www2.fdic.gov/Call_TFR_Rpts/.
FFIEC Central Data Repository (CDR): https://cdr.ffiec.gov/public/.

- ☐ Repository of the Report of Condition (call report) and Thrift Financial Report (TFR) filed since 1998 through FFIEC's Central Data Repository (CDR).

Summary of Deposits (SOD)/Market Share_www2.fdic.gov/sod/.

- ☐ Annual survey of branch office deposits as of June 30.
- ☐ Find a list of your institution's offices in Summary of Deposits (SOD).
- ☐ Create a Deposit Market Share Report that presents aggregates of each institution's deposits in any combined choice of states, metro areas, cities, counties, or zip codes.

Statistics on Depository Institutions (SDI) www2.fdic.gov/sdi/.

- ☐ Find individual and aggregate demographic and financial information (750+ items including balance sheets, income statements, and performance ratios) about banks and thrifts dated back to 1992.
- ☐ Compare financial information between institutions based on common characteristics including size, financial performance, location, established date, status (open versus inactive), charter type (state versus national, commercial bank versus savings institution), and business specialty.

- ☐ Create custom peer groups, reports, and downloads.
- ☐ SDI Tutorial: www2.fdic.gov/sdi/Internet_tutorial.pps.

Statistics at a Glance www.fdic.gov/bank/statistical/stats/.

- ☐ The latest quarterly statistics that define the banking industry and the most recent industry trends.

Regional Economic Conditions (RECON) www2.fdic.gov/recon/index.asp.

- ☐ Standard graphs, tables, and maps depicting economic conditions and how they changed over time for any state, metropolitan statistical area (MSA), or county.

Historical Statistics on Banking (HSOB) www2.fdic.gov/hsob/index.asp.

- ☐ Annual statistical information on the banking industry beginning in 1934.
- ☐ Commercial bank, savings institutions, and bank failure history.

FDIC Quarterly www.fdic.gov/bank/analytical/quarterly/index.html.

- ☐ Timely analyses of economic and banking trends at the national and regional level.
- ☐ Combines data from two retired publications: the *FDIC Outlook* and the *FDIC Banking Review*.

Quarterly Banking Profile (QBP) www2.fdic.gov/qbp/index.asp.

- ☐ Quarterly report card for the banking industry.
- ☐ Summarized financial results in the form of analyses, graphs, and statistical tables for all FDIC-insured institutions.
- ☐ Results are published approximately 55 days after the end of each quarter, beginning with December 31, 1994.

FDIC State Profiles www.fdic.gov/bank/analytical/stateprofile/index.html.

- ☐ Quarterly data sheets of banking and economic conditions in each state.

Center for Financial Research (CFR) www.fdic.gov/bank/analytical/cfr/index.html.

- ☐ Innovative research on topics that are important to the FDIC's role as a deposit insurer and bank supervisor.
- ☐ CFR programs explore developments affecting the banking industry, risk measurement and management methods, regulatory policy, and related topics of interest to the FDIC.

CHAPTER 10

Payments Systems

MONEY

Think of banks as the heart of the financial system and payments as the blood supply that is delivered through the arteries—the payments systems. *Payments* can be referred to as *money,* which can be described by its functions. The primary function of money is that it is a generally accepted means of exchange in terms of a defined unit of account. Another function of money is that it serves as a store of value. A wide range of things are used as money. For example, money includes cash, checks, credit cards, gold and silver, wire transfers, and other means of exchange.

Payments systems are defined as the mechanisms, rules, institutions, people, markets, and agreements that make the exchange of payments possible. They are essential in supporting economic growth. Like many other aspects of banking, payments systems evolve over time.

LEGAL TENDER

Congress and the courts grant some forms of money the special status of being *legal tender* that creditors must accept as payments for debts.[1] The history of legal tender involves various laws. For example, the U.S. Constitution (Article 1, Section 8) granted "The Congress shall have Power . . . To coin Money, regulate the Value thereof, and of foreign Coin, and fix the Standard of Weights and Measures." The Emergency Farm Mortgage Act of 1933 (Title III, Section 43) directed the secretary of the Treasury to authorize U.S. notes and coins and Federal Reserve notes to be legal tender for all debts public and private. The Coinage Act of 1965, Section 31 U.S.C. 5103, titled "Legal Tender," states that "United States coins and currency (including Federal Reserve notes and circulating notes of Federal Reserve banks and national banks) are legal tender for all debts, public charges, taxes, and dues." However, "private businesses are free to develop their own policies on whether or not to accept cash unless there is a State law which says otherwise. For example, a bus line may prohibit payment of fares in pennies or dollar bills. In addition, movie theaters, convenience stores, and gas stations may refuse to accept large denomination currency (usually notes above $20) as a matter of policy."[2] In other words, the sale of gas or movie tickets is one form of a "conditional sales contract" that sets a limit on the denomination of the currency used to purchase goods or services.

Currency

Table 10.1 shows the annual production figures for U.S. notes, by denomination, for fiscal years 2000–2009. The data reveal that fewer small dollar value notes and more large value dollar notes are being produced. There are various explanations for these trends. Individuals may want to hold some minimum amount of small-denomination currency for liquidity reasons and to buy goods and services. The large-denomination notes can be used as a store of value, for transactions, and as an international currency. "The Federal Reserve estimates that as much as two-thirds of currency in circulation is held abroad. . . . In addition to being used as a store of value, U.S. currency is also broadly used for transaction purposes in officially dollarized countries, such as Panama, Ecuador, El Salvador, and East Timor, and other countries where the U.S. dollar co-circulates with local currencies."[3]

Alternatively, the trends may reflect the increased use of other forms of payments, such as credit and debit cards, stored-value cards, and electronic payments. Some merchants have started to accept only card payments for safety and convenience reasons.[4] While cash protects the anonymity of the user, from the merchant's perspective, it is costly to handle and less secure than electronic payments.[5] On the other hand, it is extremely difficult to counterfeit currency, whereas credit cards and some other means of payments can be stolen or fraudulent.[6] Thus, there are strengths and weaknesses to using both currency and other means of payment.

Seigniorage refers to the interest saved by the U.S. Treasury from having currency, which is non-interest-bearing debt, circulate as a medium of exchange. It is also the profit for the Treasury, where profit is the difference between the interest earned on assets financed by issuing currency and the cost of issuing and redeeming it. Seigniorage is influenced by the costs of metals, production costs, and other factors. The weakened demand associated with the recession that began in 2007 and the shift in payment systems resulted in the seigniorage per dollar falling to $0.58 in fiscal year (FY) 2007 to $0.55 in FY 2008.[7] In addition, the cost of producing coins

TABLE 10.1 Annual Production Figures of U.S. Notes, Fiscal Years 2000–2009

Denomination	FY 2000	FY 2001	FY 2002	FY 2003	FY 2004
$ 1	5,190,400,000	5,145,600,000	2,880,000,000	3,699,200,000	4,147,200,000
$ 2	N/A	N/A	N/A	N/A	121,600,000
$ 5	640,000,000	979,200,000	1,350,400,000	550,400,000	627,200,000
$ 10	492,800,000	652,800,000	1,100,800,000	249,600,000	403,200,000
$ 20	2,707,200,000	1,017,600,000	1,068,800,000	2,700,800,000	2,707,200,000
$ 50	N/A	N/A	N/A	102,400,000	211,200,000
$100	N/A	201,600,000	604,800,000	854,400,000	515,200,000
Denomination	**FY 2005**	**FY 2006**	**FY 2007**	**FY 2008**	**FY 2009**
$ 1	3,475,200,000	4,512,000,000	4,147,200,000	3,577,600,000	2,636,800,000
$ 2	N/A	230,400,000	N/A	N/A	N/A
$ 5	576,000,000	800,000,000	1,401,600,000	1,203,200,000	384,000,000
$10	512,000,000	851,200,000	83,200,000	1,094,400,000	345,600,000
$20	3,059,200,000	889,600,000	1,971,200,000	633,600,000	716,800,000
$50	345,600,000	N/A	428,800,000	N/A	371,200,000

Source: U.S. Bureau of Engraving and Printing, annual production figures, www.moneyfactory.gov/uscurrency/annualproductionfigures.html.

increased because of higher metal prices—again reducing seigniorage. Pennies and nickels were actually produced at a loss of $47 million in 2008, down from a loss of $98.6 million in the previous year. Seigniorage for all currency produced was $706.2 million in FY 2008, down 29.7 percent from the previous period.[8]

RETAIL PAYMENTS

Good-Bye, Checks

Over time, retail payments to buy goods and services have evolved from using cash to using checks and other means of payment such as credit cards, debit cards, and banking by cell phone. A *check* is a written order from one party (payer) to another (payee) requiring the payer's financial institution to pay a specified sum on demand to the payee or to a third party specified by the payee.[9] The Check Clearing for the 21st Century Act (the Check 21 Act) enacted in 2003 encouraged the use of electronic check clearing. This included printed images of checks (*substitute checks*) that can be used for processing instead of the original paper check. In addition, the automated clearing house (ACH) system developed to truncate checks and make the payments electronically (i.e., electronic check presentment, ECP).[10] In *truncation,* the information on a check is captured and processed electronically. The truncated check is not returned to the writer. Large dollar value business-to-business payment transactions between domestic or foreign institutions that have offices located in the United States are settled in real time through the Clearing House Interbank Payment Systems (CHIPS). Thus, because of the growth of ECP, the number of checks being written declined.[11] Equally important, more people are using various forms of electronic banking, including direct deposits, preauthorized payment, and online banking.[12] In 2007, about 70 percent of the checks cleared were paper, and 30 percent were cleared electronically.[13] Simply stated, the number of checks, written, paid, and converted to ACH payments have declined.[14] The expectation is that they will continue to do so, both in the United States and in the United Kingdom. Another factor contributing to the decline of checks is that some banks are offering online checking accounts because many routine transactions, such as deposits, withdrawals, and funds transfers, can be handled online or at an automated teller machine (ATM). For example, Bank of America, with $2.364 trillion in assets (June 2010), offers online checking accounts to its customers. In the United States, Bank of America serves more than 57 million consumers, and more than 29 million of them use its online services.[15] Similarly, Ally Bank, an online bank with about $179 billion in assets (March 2010), describes itself as a direct bank, which means customers manage their checking account online, by phone, or by ATM.[16]

In the United Kingdom, "at its meeting on 16 December 2009, the Board of the Payments Council agreed to set a target end date of 31 October 2018 for the cheques clearings in Great Britain and Northern Ireland."[17] The Payments Council said:

> *The number of cheques is falling at 12 percent per annum and most major retailers and other merchants no longer accept them. Alongside growth in existing electronic payment methods, there is continuing innovation in new alternatives to cheques. . . . Given the steady fall in cheque use, the choice is between managing the decline and leaving developments to market forces. . . . The Payments Council Board has agreed to set a target date of 31st October 2018 to close the central cheque clearing. Over the next nine years the Payments Council will work to ensure that where alternatives already exist they are promoted and explained; and where innovation and new options are required, they are put in place.*[18]

The Payments Council is the nongovernmental organization that represents banks and clearing companies and sets strategy for U.K. payments.

The conversion from our current paper-based system of payments to electronic systems faces some obstacles in the United States. Unlike the United Kingdom, where a few large institutions dominate the country, there are more than 7,000 financial service providers and hundreds of thousands of billers in the United States, many of whom may not have the technology to provide a seamless network for billing and collections.

Hello, Plastic Cards

Plastic cards and electronic means of payment are replacing paper as a means of exchange. For example, a *credit card* indicates the holder has been granted a line of credit. It enables the holder to make purchases or withdraw cash up to a prearranged limit. The credit granted can be settled in full by the end of a specified period or can be settled in part, with the balance taken as extended credit. Interest is based on the terms of the credit card agreement, and the holder is sometimes charged an annual fee.[19] A *bankcard* is a general-purpose credit card, issued by a financial institution under agreement with the bankcard companies (e.g., Visa, MasterCard, Discover), that customers can use to purchase goods and services and to obtain cash against a line of credit established by the bankcard issuer. A *debit card* is a payment card issued as either a *personal identification number* (PIN)-based debit

ATM card or as a signature-based debit card from one of the bankcard associations. A payment card is issued to a person for purchasing goods and services through an electronic transfer of funds from a demand deposit account rather than using cash, checks, or drafts at the point-of-sale.[20] And a *stored-value card* is a card-based payment system that assigns a value to the card. The card's value can be stored on the card itself (on the magnetic strip or in a computer chip) or in a network database. As the card is used for transactions, the transaction amounts are subtracted from the card's balance. As the balance approaches zero, some cards can be reloaded through various methods, and others are designed to be discarded. These cards are often used in closed systems for specific types of purchases.[21] Finally, payments can be made and funds transferred by phone or online from anywhere in the world where there is an Internet connection.

A Federal Reserve Study, "U.S. Households' Access to and Use of Electronic Banking, 1989–2007," revealed: "Consumers are increasingly embracing electronic technology as a means of making payments and managing their personal finances. Data from the 2007 Federal Reserve Payments Study show a continuing shift away from paper-based transactions, such as payments by cash and check, and toward electronic transactions, in particular, automated deposits and payments and payments by debit card."[22] For example, 80 percent of households reported that they used direct deposit for income or benefits payments in 2007, indicating that electronic banking (*e-banking*) is becoming an increasingly important part of the payments system. E-banking includes the use of ATMs, debit cards, direct deposit, preauthorized payments, phone banking, smart cards, prepaid cards, and online banking. The number of ATMs increased from a few hundred in the early 1980s to more than 400,000 in 2007. Most consumers with Internet access at home use online banking. Thus, households are making greater use of ATMs and online banking and less use of brick-and- mortar banks and their branches. Consumers are also increasing their use of mobile banking and payments via such devices as cell phones and personal digital assistants (PDAs) like BlackBerrys. "In Zagreb, Croatia, consumers can board the local streetcar and pay their fare via their mobile phone. In Kuala Lumpur, Malaysia, consumers can use their mobile phone to pay for parking and restaurant meals. In Stockholm, Sweden, consumers can buy a cup of coffee using their mobile phone."[23]

Another study estimated that debit card holders would purchase \$1.616 trillion in 2010, up from \$311 billion in 2000.[24]

With these new ways of making payments come new sources of fee income. For example, under new rules (Regulation E, Electronic Fund Transfers, and Regulation DD, Truth in Savings pertaining to overdraft services), banking institutions must give customers an opportunity to opt in to programs that charge a fee to cover ATM use, one-time debit card transactions when there are insufficient funds to cover the transaction, and point-of-sale overdrafts. "Overdraft fees can exceed the amount of the overdraft benefit and can occur multiple times in a single day, depending on the type of transaction and clearing practices of the institution."[25] It should also be noted that banks can earn interest on *float funds*—funds held by an institution during the check-clearing process before they are made available to a depositor.

Finally, a 2009 Federal Deposit Insurance Corporation (FDIC) national survey revealed that about 17 million adults reside in households that are *unbanked;* that is, they did not have access to a checking or savings account.[26] In addition, about 21 million adults are *underbanked;* that is, they have a checking account or savings account, but they rely instead on alternative financial services (AFS), including nonbank money orders, nonbank check cashing, payday lending, pawnshops, rent-to-own stores, and refund anticipation loans. The unbanked and underbanked were concentrated in certain racial and ethnic minorities (e.g., black, American Indian, Hispanic), low-income people, unmarried heads of households, those with no college degree, and younger age groups.[27]

The most commonly cited reasons for using these AFS transactions instead of banks were convenience and costs. Some respondents stated that it was easier to get a payday loan or money at pawnshops than to qualify for a bank loan and that it was more convenient to do so.

Informal Value Transfer Systems

Informal value transfer systems (IVTS) refer to any nonbank system where someone receives money for the purpose of making those funds, or an equivalent value, available to someone else in a different geographic location. Such systems date back to 5,800 B.C., and they are called by a variety of names: *hawala* (Middle East, Pakistan, Afghanistan), *hundi* (India), *fei-ch'ien* (China), *phoe kuan* (Thailand), and underground banking.

Originally, IVTS were used for trade finance because of the dangers of traveling with gold and other forms of payment. The majority of transactions using IVTS are legitimate. But IVTS also are used to facilitate both criminal activities and the funding of terrorism.[28] They may legally operate in the United States, so long as they abide by applicable state and federal laws, including registering with the Financial Crimes Enforcement Network (FinCEN) and complying with anti-money-laundering and counterterrorist-financing provisions of the Bank Secrecy Act (BSA), which are applicable to all money transmitters and to certain other money service businesses (MSBs).[29]

These IVTS serve as an alternative for traditional financial institutions for a variety of reasons, including political instability, lack of easy access to financial institutions, efficiency, security, and anonymity. Equally important, many emerging economies do not have modern financial systems that can handle international funds transfers for individuals living in rural areas or other areas that are not serviced by financial institutions. Finally, IVTS are low cost and reliable. Some argue that they are lower cost and more reliable than banks. A key feature of the IVTS is that they are informal. They depend on *trust* based on family or other ties. They are not based on contractual agreements.

Hawala By way of illustration, a hawala requires four participants: the sender of funds in one country, the receiver in another, and IVTS operators in both countries to facilitate the transfer or remittance.[30] The IVTS operators are also called *hawaladars*. The hawaladars in different countries are connected by family ties, ethnicity, or gang alliances where trust is established. *Hawala* can be defined as "transfer" or "wire" in Arabic, or "money transfer without money movement." Moreover, there is no paper trail. In the following example, Amar in the United States wants to send $50,000 to Rahman in Pakistan. If he goes to a bank to transfer the funds, the bank would want him to open an account, charge fees for the international transfer, and charge for differences in the exchange rates. Equally important, dealing with a bank would leave a paper trail. Instead, as shown in Table 10.2, (1) Amar gives $50,000 to Yasmeen, a local hawaladar. (2) Yasmeen gives

TABLE 10.2 Hawala

	United States	Pakistan
1	Amar gives $50,000 to local IVTS operator (hawaladar)	
2	U.S. hawaladar gives code to Amar	
3	U.S. hawaladar contacts IVTS operator in Pakistan, with payment instructions and code	Pakistani hawaladar receives payment instructions and code
4	Amar contacts Rahman and provides code	Rahman receives code from Amar
5		Rahman contacts the Pakistani hawaladar, gives him the code, and receives the Pakistani equivalent of $50,000, less fees
	Direct Transfer	
1	Amar gives funds to Yasmeen Yasmeen contacts Ghulam	Ghulam receives instructions Ghulam pays Rahman

Amar a code, or a means of communication. (3) Yasmeen contacts Ghulam, his counterpart in Pakistan, with payment instructions and the code. The international contacts are made by phone, fax, or e-mail. (4) Amar contacts Rahman and gives him the code. Finally, Rahman contacts Ghulam and gives him the code for the settlement. Rahman then receives the local equivalent of $50,000, less fees charged by the operators and differences in exchange rates, and the settlement process is complete. The payments usually take place within a day. The methods used depend on the degree of trust between the two hawaladars and the need to obscure the transactions.

Contemporary IVTS The basic process is similar to the one just described. However, in this case, funds are transferred. The owners of cash-intensive businesses may accept money from clients to transfer overseas. Examples of cash-intensive businesses include grocery stores, import-export businesses, restaurants, phone-card stores, and used car dealers. The funds are included with funds from the business and deposited in a local bank. When sufficient funds are accumulated, they are wire-transferred to accounts in the United Arab Emirates (UAE), London, New York, or Hong Kong. These are considered IVTS hub regions. Dubai in the UAE is widely used because it has a large population of expatriate workers from India and Pakistan who use hawalas to send money home. In addition, Dubai has a large gold market.

From these hubs, funds are wire-transferred again to IVTS operators overseas, where the funds can be withdrawn.

The process can be made obscure to outside observers by using multiple accounts, nominee accounts, false names, and couriers to carry out some of the steps. "So long as there remains a divergence between the US and other countries in financial development, banking efficiency, taxation levels, and laws pertaining to foreign exchange transfers, there will exist a demand for the *Hawala* and other means of moving money across the globe. More importantly, difference in regulation and supervision standards across countries will create loopholes to be exploited by *Hawala* operators."[31]

While many IVTS transactions are legal, some involve money laundering and are illegal. By way of illustration, Abad's Carnival French Ice Cream in Brooklyn, New York, was convicted of operating as a money transmitter without an appropriate state license. According to court records, $22.2 million was deposited by cash, checks, and wire transfers into 12 accounts held at multiple U.S. banks from 1996 through 2003, including from a separate company under the same ownership. The deposits typically were structured to avoid reporting requirements. These funds were then consolidated into a central account in the United States using checks and wire transfers from the 12 separate accounts. From that central account, $21.9 million was wired to accounts held in 25 other countries on behalf of U.S. customers. The recipient IVTS operators who controlled the accounts in those countries then exchanged the funds into local currency and distributed the payments to the intended beneficiaries.[32]

In 2009, Mauricio Alfanso Mazza-Alaluf was convicted of providing IVTS services without a license. Mazza-Alaluf used his U.S. bank accounts to assist with thousands of transactions totaling hundreds of millions of dollars after physically carrying millions of U.S. dollars through Los Angeles International Airport. Mazza-Alaluf then deposited the funds in bank accounts in the United States to relay payments from Chilean businesses and individuals to U.S. customers, clearing informal transfers between entities through accounts in his own name.[33]

Money Laundering

Laws *Money laundering* is the conversion of the monetary proceeds of criminal activity into funds with an apparently legal source and without revealing the true nature, source, or ownership of those proceeds.[34] Stated otherwise, it is disguising illegal proceeds by introducing them into legitimate commerce and finance.[35] Money laundering also includes using legitimate funds for illegal purposes, such as financing terrorism. Thus, money laundering occurs in connection with bribery and kickbacks, drug trafficking, fraud, tax evasion, terrorism, and other illegal activities. Congress enacted the following laws concerning money laundering:

- *Bank Secrecy Act of 1970*. The Bank Records and Foreign Transaction Reporting Act is commonly referred to as the BSA of 1970. It was the first federal legislation targeting money laundering and other white-collar crimes, including tax evasion. It is called the BSA because it helps provide information to law enforcement agencies about the secret use of foreign accounts by U.S. customers by creating a paper trail. While the BSA aided in tracking money launderers, it did not make money laundering illegal per se. Nevertheless, some money launderers were prosecuted for violating the BSA and under the Racketeer-Influenced and Corrupt Organizations (RICO) statutes.
- *Money Laundering Control Act of 1986*. Money laundering became a federal crime when the BSA was amended by the Money Laundering Control Act of 1986 and again with the Money Laundering Prosecution Act of 1988 (part of the Omnibus Anti-Drug Abuse Act).
- *Annuzio-Wylie-Anti-Money Laundering Act of 1992*. The Housing Community Development Act of 1992, commonly referred to as the

Annuzio-Wylie-Anti-Money Laundering Act, permits the secretary of the Treasury to require any financial institution (including employees, officers, and directors) to file suspicious transaction reports (STRs). The banks are prohibited from notifying the person who is the subject of the report. In addition, all businesses must keep customer identification records for currency transactions between $3,000 and $10,000 and report suspicious transactions regardless of their size.

- *Money Laundering Suppression Act of 1994.* Beginning April 1, 1996, all banks, thrifts, and credit unions were required to file suspicious activity reports (SARs) with the FinCEN.[36] FinCen is the U.S. Department of Treasury's lead agency in the fight against money laundering.
- *Antiterrorism and Effective Death Penalty Act (AEDPA) of 1996.* The Antiterrorism and Effective Death Penalty Act of 1996 makes it a crime to engage in financial transactions with governments or countries designated as supporting international terrorism or to provide material support or resources to a designated foreign terrorist organization (FTO).
- *USA PATRIOT Act of 2001.* Following the September 11, 2001, terrorist attacks on the United States, Congress passed the USA PATRIOT Act (formally known as the Uniting and Strengthening America by Providing Appropriate Tools Required to Intercept and Obstruct Terrorism Act of 2001).[37] The intent of the law is to deter terrorists and others from using the U.S. financial system anonymously to launder money.

All financial institutions must develop, administer, and maintain anti-money-laundering (AML) programs that ensure compliance with the BSA. This includes the record keeping, reporting, and compliance with each federal financial institution's rules. The definition of *financial institutions*, in the context of BSA and AML, includes commercial banks, all subsidiaries of bank holding companies, Edge and Agreement corporations, U.S. branches and agencies of foreign banks, savings and loan associations, and credit unions; federally regulated securities brokers, dealers, and investment companies; MSBs, currency dealers, or exchangers; check cashers and issuers of traveler's checks, money orders, or stored valuc; sellers or redeemers of traveler's checks, money orders, or stored value; and funds transmitters; persons subject to supervision by state or federal bank supervisory authority; casinos and card clubs; futures commission merchants, introducing brokers, commodity pool operators, and commodity trading advisors; and individuals and/or groups engaging in IVTS. Finally, insurance companies and mutual funds were added to the list.

The BSA and AML programs apply to all operational areas of the financial institutions. They must be written and approved by the board of directors (or its equivalent) and noted in the minutes of the board. These programs must include:

- Internal controls to assure compliance with the BSA.
- Independent testing of the financial institution's compliance with BSA.
- The designation of one individual who is responsible for coordinating and monitoring compliance on a daily basis.
- Training personnel.
- Customer identification programs (CID) including account opening procedures and verifying the customer's identity. The customer due diligence (CDD) must include risk assessment procedures in connection with the customer and/or transactions and have sufficient information to determine if the filing of a SAR is warranted.

In April 2010, The Federal Financial Institutions Examination Council (FFIEC) revised the BSA/AML Examination Manual.[38] The significant updates include:

Bulk currency shipments BSA/AML.

Compliance program structures.

Core examination procedures for assessing the BSA/AML compliance program.

Currency transaction reporting exemptions.

Funds transfers.

Suspicious activity reporting.

Automated clearing house transactions.

Electronic cash.

Trade finance activities.

Electronic banking.

Third-party payment processors.

Fines Failure to comply with BSA/AML laws and regulations can result in large fines. For example, consider the fine imposed on Wachovia Bank. On March 17, 2010, FinCEN announced the assessment of a civil money penalty, in the amount of $110 million, against Wachovia Bank, the fourth largest commercial bank in the United States. The action represents the largest penalty action to date in 2010 against a financial institution by FinCEN for violations of the Bank Secrecy Act, including failures to:

- Institute and maintain an effective anti-money-laundering program to prevent, detect, and report suspicious activity within the bank.

- Timely file suspicious activity and currency transaction reports, thereby greatly diminishing the value of the reports to both law enforcement and regulatory agencies.
- Comply with the due diligence requirements of Section 312 of the USA PATRIOT Act to enable the detection and reporting of any known or suspected money-laundering activity involving foreign correspondent banking.
- Apply systems and controls to manage the risk of money laundering within the bank's business lines, such as remote deposit capture, pouch and cash letter activity, and the repatriation of bulk cash from Mexico to the United States.[39]

The charges were in connection with Latin American drug trafficking. "Wachovia admitted it didn't do enough to spot illicit funds in handling $378.4 billion for Mexican-currency-exchange houses from 2004–2007. That's the largest violation of the Bank Secrecy Act, an anti-money-laundering law, in U.S. history—a sum equal to one-third of Mexico's current gross domestic product."[40] Wachovia is now a unit of Wells Fargo.

LARGE-INTERBANK PAYMENTS

In the United States, large-interbank payments, or wholesale payments as they are commonly called, are used by banks, businesses, and governments for both domestic and international transactions. The large-interbank payments are made over the Fedwire® or by using CHIPS. International payments also may involve the Society for Worldwide Interbank Financial Telecommunications (SWIFT).[41]

Fedwire

Interbank payments can be transferred over the Fedwire, an electronic funds transfer system that is operated by the Federal Reserve.[42] "Fedwire Services are designed to offer a secure, reliable method of handling large value, time-critical payments and maintaining and transferring U.S. government and certain government agency, government-sponsored enterprises, and international organization book-entry securities."[43] It is used by depository institutions, agencies, and branches of foreign banks, the U.S. Department of Treasury, entities designated by the secretary of the Treasury, foreign central banks, and foreign monetary authorities, and others.

The Fedwire is a *real-time gross settlements (RTGS) system* that settles each transaction individually as it occurs, rather than processing transactions in a batch. It operates from 9:00 P.M. eastern time (ET) on the preceding calendar day and ends at 6:30 P.M. ET, Monday through Friday, excluding designated holidays. The Fedwire provides cash concentration payments, settling positions with other financial institutions and/or clearing arrangements, submitting federal tax payments, and buying and selling Federal Reserve funds. About 7,300 depository institutions and certain other financial institutions utilize Fedwire funds transfers. In 2009, there were 127.4 million transfers, and the average daily value of a transfer was $2.5 million.[44]

Because the Federal Reserve grants payment finality, the payments are final and irrevocable. Stated otherwise, the Federal Reserve assumes the credit risk associated with the transfer of funds. Therefore, the Federal Reserve places net debt caps on banks based on their creditworthiness, which is determined by their capital and supervisory rating. It also requires institutions to have sufficient funds, either in the form of account balances or overdraft capacity, or a payment order may be rejected. Intraday central bank credit in the form of daylight overdrafts is generally available to Fedwire participants. The aggregate average daylight overdrafts averaged $62 billion per day in 2008.[45]

CHIPS

Foreign exchange transactions arise from international trade and investments, as well as from hedging and speculation in foreign currencies. The settlement transactions result in U.S. dollars being exchanged for another currency such as the French franc. There are two settlements in such transactions: dollars being settled in the United States and the foreign currency being settled in the other country's payment system.

Both domestic and international funds transfers use CHIPS. It was established in 1853 and owned by 20 of the largest banks in the United States.[46] It began operating in 1970 as an electronic replacement for paper checks for international dollar payments. Today, CHIPS is responsible for more than 95 percent of U.S. dollar cross-border and nearly half of all domestic wire transactions, totaling $1.5 trillion daily to banks, businesses, and individuals. In 2009, CHIPS processed payments with a value of $179.3 billion.[47]

Suppose that a German firm bought $5 million in parts from a U.S. manufacturing firm. The German firm instructed its bank in Frankfurt to debit its account in euros for the dollar equivalent of $5 million and then to pay the U.S. supplier's bank in New York. The German bank has a branch in New York, and it makes the $5 million payment to the U.S. bank.

As the funds are transferred throughout the day, CHIPS calculates each participant's single net position vis-à-vis all of the other participants. In other words, CHIPS nets or offsets mutual obligations to reduce the number of obligations that the participants must deal with. This system of settlement is called *multilateral netting*. Each of the CHIPS participants has a bilateral agreement and credit limit with the other CHIPS participants. When all of the positions are settled at the end of the day (*same-day settlement*), those banks with a net credit position receive a Fedwire funds transfer, and the CHIPS account at the Federal Reserve Bank of New York has a zero position. Now the transaction between the German and U.S. banks is final.

SWIFT

SWIFT incorporated in Belgium, is a cooperative owned by member banks throughout the world to facilitate payments and financial messages among its members and standardize financial transactions, thereby lowering their costs.[48] The SWIFT system is used primarily for communications, while the actual transfers of funds are done by CHIPS and the Fedwire. It also engages in custody and asset servicing, supporting the automation of investment funds distribution, regulation, and compliance, such as meeting the transaction reporting requirements, Islamic finance and Murabaha (which includes a money transfer and a commodity trade, typically involving two banks and two brokers), and foreign exchange.

Additional Settlement Institutions

CLS Bank The CLS Bank specializes in the settlement of foreign exchange (FX) transactions.[49] It is owned by the foreign exchange community and operates the largest multicurrency cash settlement system. It settles 17 major currencies: U.S. dollar, Euro, U.K. pound, Japanese yen, Swiss franc, Canadian dollar, Australian dollar, Swedish krona, Danish krone, Norwegian krone, the Singapore dollar, the Hong Kong dollar, the New Zealand dollar, the Korean won, the South African rand, the Israeli shekel, and the Mexican peso.

DTC The Depository Trust Company (DTC) is owned by the Depository Trust and Clearing Corporation (DTCC).[50] It provides clearing and settlement of corporate securities and commercial paper. In 2009, DTC settled transactions worth more than $299 trillion. It is a member of the U.S. Federal Reserve System.

CHAPTER 11

Other Financial Services

Banks provide a variety of services, such as cash management services, wealth management, and other services covered in this chapter, in order to earn fee income, to cross-sell their products, and to enhance relationships with their customers.[1] Service charges on deposit accounts, trading gains and losses, and fiduciary and servicing fees are the largest sources of noninterest income for banks.[2]

CASH MANAGEMENT SERVICES

Cash management is the process of combining banking services, data collection, and communications systems to enhance the collection, control, and utilization of cash for domestic and international business concerns. Cash management services help businesses collect their receivables faster and make their payments more efficiently. Faster collections reduce the firm's float. *Float* is the dollar amount of checks that have been received by the firm and are in the process of collection but have not yet been converted into cash. Firms typically want to reduce the float when collecting funds owed to them. Conversely, they want to take advantage of float when making payments to others. As explained in the previous chapter, the *Check 21 Act* has helped reduce the float—funds held by an institution during the check-clearing process before they are made available to a depositor. The act permits institutions to make digital images of checks, truncate the original paper check, and process the payment information electronically. Thus, customers send their checks to, say, American Express, which makes digital images of them and then digitally processes the payments. The original checks are not returned to customers.

Cash Concentration for Collection of Funds

Many business concerns, such as a grocery store chain, receive retail payments and make relatively small daily deposits in the various cities where the stores are located. Cash concentration brings all of the deposits together in one account so that the firm's corporate headquarters can use those funds efficiently.

Controlled Disbursement

Banks can help business concerns make better use of their cash resources by controlling disbursements (e.g., payments). A zero balance account is one technique. This is a bank account that most of the time has a zero dollar balance. When a check drawn against a business is presented to its bank for collection, the bank notifies the business, which then deposits the appropriate amount to cover the check. By using a zero balance account, businesses minimize the amount of funds deposited in non-interest-earning bank accounts.

Lock Boxes for Collections

A *lock box* is a post office box of a business concern that is used to receive payments for goods and services that it sold to customers. For example, for those still using paper checks, bill payments made to retail stores and utilities are sent to a post office box in a city that minimizes the mail time in transit. Instead of retail customers sending payments to the company headquarters in Seattle, for instance, payments from customers in the Southeastern United States are sent to a post office box in Atlanta that reduces mailing time from three days to one day. A bank in Atlanta empties the post office box several times each day, deposits the checks, and notifies the receiving company of its collections. The company can then invest those funds or reduce its debts. Companies may have lock boxes located in various cities, depending on the size and scope of their operations.

Letters of Credit

The growth of international trade gives rise to domestic firms making and receiving payments from foreign firms for goods and services bought and sold. Banks play an important role here by providing letters of credit, foreign exchange, and other financial services that facilitate the flow of funds.

A basic *letter of credit* is a bank's written guaranty to make a payment to an exporter on behalf of an importer, under specified conditions. There are numerous types of letters of credit. For example, a *revolving letter of credit* is for a stated amount that can be drawn on multiple times. It is used when a seller is going to make multiple shipments to a buyer. The revolving letter of credit allows the seller to receive payment for each shipment without the need for a separate letter of credit for each shipment. A *standby letter of credit* guarantees payment in the case of the buyer's default on the purchase. With a *confirmed letter of credit,* a second bank adds its guaranty of payment in the event of payment default by the issuing bank.

Bankers' acceptances are used to finance the shipment or temporary storage of goods, usually in connection with international trade. A *bankers' acceptance* is a time draft drawn on a bank that has been stamped "accepted" by the bank. By accepting the draft, the bank makes an unconditional promise to pay the holder of the draft a stated amount at a specified date.[3]

Syndication/Shared National Credits

Commercial banks have learned from investment banks that syndication can be profitable. When underwriting new securities issues, a group of investment banking firms, called the *syndicate,* buy stocks and bonds from the corporation or government issuing the new securities and then sell them to the public. The originating investment bank is the syndicate manager. Each firm in the syndicate agrees to buy a stipulated amount of the new issue, and their profit is the difference between the price paid to the issuer of the security and the price at which it is sold to investors.

Commercial banks have applied that same strategy to underwrite large commercial loans and loan commitments that they either hold or sell to other financial institutions, such as small banks that buy parts of syndicated loans to diversify their portfolios. "A shared national credit (SNC) is any large syndicated loan and/or formal loan commitment, and any asset such as real estate, stocks, notes, bonds, and debentures taken as debts previously contracted, extended to borrowers by a federally supervised institution, its subsidiaries, and affiliates that aggregates to $20 million or more and is shared by three or more unaffiliated federally supervised institutions or a portion of which is sold to two or more unaffiliated federally supervised institutions."[4]

In 1977, the Board of Governors of the Federal Reserve System, the Federal Deposit Insurance Corporation (FDIC), and the Office of the Comptroller of the Currency (OCC) established a program to review and classify SNCs made by U.S. banks, foreign banking organizations (FBOs), and nonbank institutions. Nonbanks include independent investment brokerages, investment vehicles, hedge funds, and other institutional investors.

> *The interagency Shared National Credit (SNC) Review for 2009 found credit quality deteriorated to record levels with respect to large loans and loan commitments held by U.S. bank organizations, foreign bank organizations (FBO), and nonbanks such as securitization pools, hedge funds, insurance companies, and pension funds. Total loss of $53 billion identified in the 2009 review exceeded the*

combined loss of the previous eight SNC reviews and nearly tripled the previous high in 2002. The declining credit quality is attributed to weak economic conditions affecting most industries and weak credit underwriting standards leading up to 2008.

Credit quality deteriorated across all entities, but nonbanks held 47 percent of classified assets in the SNC portfolio, despite making up only 21.2 percent of the SNC portfolio. U.S. bank organizations, which make up 40.8 percent of the SNC portfolio, held 30.2 percent of the classified assets. FBOs, which make up 38.0 percent of the SNC portfolio, held 22.8 percent of the classified assets.[5]

TRUST SERVICES, PRIVATE WEALTH, AND ASSET MANAGEMENT

Wealth and asset management refers to custom-tailored services provided to high-net-worth individuals to help manage their assets and estates. Because it is available only to high-net-worth individuals, it is also called *private banking* or some similar term. For example, in Atlanta, SunTrust's personal financial services include high-net-worth banking, asset management, estate planning, trust services, family office services, investment services, credit advisory services, and insurance.[6] Regions Bank (Birmingham, Alabama) offers "Trust and Asset Management: Preserving, Protecting, and Managing Your Wealth."[7] In addition to working with high-net-worth individuals, they also offer trust and agency services for both municipal and corporate clients by administering bond issues, escrow accounts, and other related services.

In contrast, State Street Corporation's "State Street Global Advisors (SSGA)" is a global leader in asset management that sophisticated financial institutions worldwide rely on for their investment needs. It had $1.8 trillion under management in June 2010.[8] It also has 24-hour global trading capability with trading desks in Boston, London, and Hong Kong.

Deutsche Bank (Germany) and others use the term *private wealth management*.[9] Deutsche Bank stresses the "personal relationship" between the bank managers and their clients. It manages roughly € 2,000 billion in assets and provides financial services in more than 70 countries.

These and other trust services provide fee income to banks, and there is no capital requirement for trust departments.

Trust Services

Trusts were created during the Crusades. When English knights went in search of the Holy Grail, someone had to manage their land and property.

Women had no legal standing at that time, so the knights' property was put in trust for someone else to manage. Over the years, common law recognized trusts. Today a *trust* is a legal entity that can hold and manage assets for one or more beneficiaries for as long as the trust exists. All trusts have the same general structure. A *trust* is established by a grantor (the creator of the trust), who transfers assets to a trust that is managed by the trustee for the benefit of the beneficiaries in accordance with the terms of the trust agreement. The trustee may be an individual or a trust institution such as a trust company or trust department, or both could be cotrustees. The trustee receives fee income for managing the trust. The amount of fee income depends on the market value of the trust and the services provided. Most of the fee income comes from investment management, administration and custody services, and benefits consulting.

Today, trust institutions

> *are banks and trust companies that exercise powers granted by a state or national regulatory authority to administer accounts in a fiduciary capacity. Typical fiduciary accounts include trusts; estates; guardianships; conservatorships; various corporate agencies, such as a paying agent, registrar of bonds, or transfer agent; and investment management/advisory services, as well as accounts for which the institution exercises investment discretion on behalf of another. Although custody and safekeeping accounts are not considered fiduciary accounts, trust institutions are important providers of custody and safekeeping services to both retail and institutional clients.*[10]

Trust institutions act as agents for trustees. For example, the trustee for a corporate employee benefit program hires a trust institution as the agent to invest and manage the funds. The trustee tells the agent how the funds are to be managed, and the agent carries out the orders for a fee. However, the agent does not have the same fiduciary responsibility as a trustee when managing the funds. For example, if the trustee tells the agent to invest all of the funds in one volatile stock, the agent will do so. If the trust institution was the trustee for those funds, it would have to invest the funds prudently, taking into account risk, diversification, and other factors.

Trust institutions usually are organized into two or three lines of business. One line of business deals with employee benefit programs, another with personal trusts and estates, and the third with corporate trusts. Personal trusts manage assets for individuals and their beneficiaries. Corporate or fiduciary trusts, for example, act as trustees for bond issues, and they are responsible for dispensing interest payments to bondholders, maintaining escrow accounts, and other related tasks.

The corporate trust business in the United States is dominated by large banks such as State Street Corporation, with US$22.6 trillion in assets under custody and administration and US$2.1 trillion under management as of March 31, 2011. It provides a wide range of financial services, including investment management, research and trading, and investment servicing.[11] Similarly, Northern Trust Corporation is a leading provider of investment management, asset and fund administration, and fiduciary and banking solutions for corporations, institutions, and affluent individuals worldwide.[12] The Bank of New York Mellon Corporation (BNY Mellon) provides asset management, securities servicing and treasury services, wealth management, and other services.[13] Other large banking organizations also offer a variety of trust and investment services.

The employee benefit line of business deals with deferred compensation plans. The three principal types of deferred compensation are profit-sharing plans, defined-benefit plans, and defined-contribution plans, such as the popular 401(k) plans. The funds from defined-contribution plans can be invested in mutual funds and other investments.

Trusts are not limited to financial institutions. The federal government is the trustee for funds that have been established by law. The federal old-age, survivors, and disability insurance fund, Medicare, and federal supplemental insurance are the largest funds they manage.

Types of Trusts

Business Trusts can be created for any purpose that is not illegal. Trusts are used for business, investment, and estate management. In terms of historical development, trusts were a widely used form of corporate organization by which several corporations engaged in the same line of business formed a trust to conduct their business without having to merge. In the 1870s and 1880s, the trusts were business monopolies in oil, coal, tobacco, and other industries. These monopolies, and their anticompetitive behavior, gave rise to the passage of the Sherman Antitrust Act of 1890. This was the first of a series of acts that dealt with antitrust activities. Others acts include the Clayton Act and the Federal Trade Commission Act of 1914, the Robinson-Patman Act of 1936, and the Celler Antimerger Act of 1950. Section 7 of the Clayton Act prohibited one firm from acquiring the stock of a competitor when the effect was to lessen competition. The Celler Act strengthened Section 7 of the Clayton Act by prohibiting one firm from acquiring the assets of competitors when the effect is to reduce competition. Bank and other types of mergers involve both stock and/or asset acquisitions, and bank mergers are subject to antitrust scrutiny before they are approved.

Today, holding companies and consortiums have replaced trusts as a common form of business organization. For example, bank and financial holding companies control most of the bank assets in the United States. A *consortium* is any association or partnership. *Consortium* also is defined as an association of financial institutions for effecting a venture requiring extensive financial resources, especially in international finance. A consortium of some of the largest banks in the world and a technology vendor established Global Trust Enterprise in 1999 for the purpose of providing businesses with a single electronic authentication of identity that they can use in electronic commerce. Global Trust then formed a legal entity called IdenTrust that will vouch for the identity of trading parties—business customers of banks—doing business on the Internet.[14] Their motto is "We Put the Trust in IDENTITY." The banks initially involved in IdenTrust include ABN Amro, Bank of America, Bankers Trust, Barclays Bank, CIBC, Chase Manhattan, Citigroup, Deutsche Bank, Hypo Vereinsbank, and Sanwa Bank. In 2002 and 2003, it acquired Digital Signature Trust Company and eFinance Corporation.

Real Estate Investment Trusts The real estate investment trust (REIT) is a financial device used by investors to buy shares in a trust that owns and may operate income-producing real estate.[15] It must invest at least 75 percent of total assets in real estate and derive at least 75 percent of gross income from real estate rents or interest on mortgage loans. In addition, it must distribute 90 percent of its income to its shareholders annually in the form of a cash dividend.

There are three different types of REITs. Equity REITs own and operate income-producing real estate. Mortgage REITs lend funds to the owners and/or operators of income-producing real estate, such as apartments, hotels, office buildings, shopping centers, and warehouses. Hybrid REITs both own income-producing real estate and lend money to real estate owners and operators. Some REITs specialize in particular types of properties, such as shopping centers, office buildings, or multifamily residential properties (apartments). A number of REITs are actively traded on major stock exchanges. There are about 1,100 public and privately held REITs in the United States.

Trust Company A *trust company* is a corporation formed for the purpose of taking, accepting, and executing all lawful trusts committed to it and acting as trustee, executor, guardian, fiscal agent, or transfer agent for stocks and bonds, wealth management, and so forth. The U.S. Trust Company of New York was the nation's first trust company, established in 1853.[16] In 2007, U.S. Trust and Bank of America combined to form U.S. Trust, Bank of America Private Wealth Management.

Many banks have established trust departments within their banks to provide additional services to their customers, such as estate planning. Trusts are used by individuals for estate planning, to distribute their assets, and to reduce their taxes. There are several types of widely used trusts.

Revocable Living Trust A revocable living trust (also known as *living trust* or *inter vivos trust*) allows the grantor to retain control over the assets during his or her lifetime. All trust assets are included in the estate for tax purposes.

Credit Shelter Trust A credit shelter trust is designed to take full advantage of estate tax credits for individuals. The maximum estate tax exclusion amount was $3.5 million in 2009.[17]

Marital Trust A marital trust shelters from the estate tax any amount that is transferred to the surviving spouse in trust for their benefit if the trust qualifies for the marital deduction.

Irrevocable Trust Trust assets in an irrevocable trust may be excluded from estate tax by the estate tax exclusion amount. In addition, irrevocable trusts are used to own life insurance policies to avoid estate taxes and to protect trust assets from creditors.

Other Types of Trusts Several other types of trusts are listed here to illustrate other uses. This listing of trusts is not complete.

Charitable Trust Charitable trusts are designed to benefit particular charities, educational institutions, or religions.

Trust Deposit Money or property is deposited with a bank but not commingled with other property or deposits of the bank. The money or property is to be returned in kind to the depositor or for some special purpose such as payment of a particular debt obligation of the depositor.

Unit Investment Trusts Unit investment trusts (UITs) are used for investment purposes. A UIT is a registered investment company (i.e., mutual fund) that buys and holds a relatively fixed portfolio of stocks, bonds, and other securities until the trust's termination date. When the trust is dissolved, the proceeds are paid to the shareholders. The fact that UITs have relatively fixed portfolios makes it different from other mutual funds that have portfolios that are actively traded.

The reason for the relatively fixed portfolio is that stock UITs are structured to replicate the performance of a particular stock index, and they hold only the stocks in that index. From time to time, stocks in the index may change, and then the portfolio is changed accordingly. For example, SPDR

S&P 500 ETF (pronounced "Spiders"), which stands for Standard & Poor's Depository Receipts, is an exchange traded fund (ETF) linked to the S&P 500 stock index. The SPDRs are traded on the New York Stock Exchange under the ticker symbol SPY.[18] They are designed to provide investment results that, before expenses, correspond to the price and yield performance of the S&P 500 Stock Index.

Similarly, SPDR Dow Jones Industrial Average ETF (DIA) is an index-based product that mirrors the Dow Jones Industrial Average, and there are UITs that mirror other market sectors and industries.[19]

Correspondent Banking

The vast majority of banks do not engage in international banking on a regular basis. But some banks do have regular customers who buy and sell foreign goods and services. On those occasions when a customer requires international banking services, banks use a correspondent bank that provides such services. "Correspondent Banking is the provision of a current or other liability account and related services to another institution used to meet its cash clearing, liquidity management and short-term borrowing or investment needs."[20] *Correspondent banks* are large banks that provide the gamut of banking products and services to other banks in exchange for fees and/or deposits. Typically, correspondent banks providing international banking services are money center banks (large banks located in New York and other money centers), large regional banks, and foreign banks located in the United States. Some correspondent banks maintain deposits in foreign banks that can be used to facilitate trade by making or receiving payments; this is commonly referred to as *trade finance*. Other services may include foreign exchange of currencies, letters of credit and introduction, and credit information on overseas firms. In addition to the services mentioned, correspondent banks make international loans and sell participation in those loans to other banks. They also deal in swaps and provide investment and other services.

Banks that deal in international trade depend on correspondent banks. Wells Fargo, for example, offers more than 50 products and services for correspondent banks, including:[21]

- Treasury management
- Credit services
- Foreign exchange
- International trade and finance
- Investment management
- Insurance services

Similarly, ABN AMRO Bank N.V., a large European bank, provides payment services, euro and multicurrency clearing, cash letter and collection services, trade services, and letters of credit including documentary collections and bank guarantees that are crucial instruments in global trade.[22]

Anti-Money-Laundering Principles for Correspondent Banking

> *The Wolfsburg Group consists of the following leading international financial institutions: ABN AMRO Bank N.V., Banco Santander Central Hispano S.A., Bank of Tokyo-Mitsubishi Ltd., Barclays Bank, Citigroup, Credit Suisse Group, Deutsche Bank AG, Goldman Sachs, HSBC, J. P. Morgan Chase, Société Générale, UBS AG. Their anti-money laundering principles support the aim of Wolfsberg Group members to prevent the use of their worldwide operations for criminal purposes. Accordingly, the Wolfsberg Group established Due Diligence Standards for their correspondent banking clients. For example, the correspondent bank must know where its customer's ultimate parent is headquartered because certain jurisdictions have inadequate anti-money laundering standards, insufficient regulatory supervision, or presenting greater risk for crime, corruption or terrorist financing. They must know if Politically Exposed Persons (PEP) are involved in the management or ownership of the company. Also, certain types of businesses are internationally recognized as creating particular vulnerability to money laundering, corruption or terrorist financing. Therefore, all Correspondent Banking Clients shall be subjected to appropriate due diligence to assure that an institution is comfortable conducting business with that client.*[23]

CHAPTER 12

A Guide to Islamic Banking

Mohamed Ariff

This chapter is a guide to the essential operating principles and practices of Islamic banking in some 80 countries in the world. This simplified introduction focuses on how such banks make profits following two fundamental methods of pricing their services: (1) Bank deposits and investments are priced using profit-loss-risk-sharing (PLS) contracts in place of interest in conventional banks, and (2) mortgages, leases, and banking services are based on fee and markup instead of interest/fees. The central theme is that this new form of banking that began in 1963 has grown to the present size of about US$500 billion in equity, with total assets of US$4,000 billion, making profits successfully in many legal jurisdictions as a new form of pricing banking products. The organization, the working principles, and selected key terms used in this form of banking are explained here. Included also is the philosophical bases on which this different form of pricing banking services is justified.

ISLAMIC BANKING, AN ALTERNATIVE INTERMEDIATION

This chapter provides an introduction—a beginner's guide—to the current practices of *Islamic banking* as found in 2010 in about one-third of the world.[1] Islamic financial institutions are legal entities that are licensed as financial corporations under banking laws of a given legal jurisdiction in a country to operate in one or more of the following areas: banking, insurance, treasury and money market trades, bonds, equity, mutual funds, and bills markets. For directors of banks, it is essential to remember that such financial transactions as are carried out by Islamic financial institutions are controlled by the same modern laws as those applied to conventional banks with one additional set of laws. That additional set of laws requires that banks use PLS as the basis (*not* interest rate) for financial contracting, that fees and markups to recover costs of financial services are used (*instead* of interest rates), and that credits/equity financing are not given to firms producing intoxicants (except for medical use), gambling, prostitution, and activities considered to be antisociety.

One further requirement is that the bank officers reveal the full extent of information relevant to contracts ahead of contracting, witnessed by a competent person: This arises from a doctrine of avoidance of excessive risk bearable by a contracting person or firm. Islamic financial institutions, therefore, originate and transact in similar banking/financial products but with special contract provisions to avoid receipt or payment of interest and to earn profits under PLS terms and/or *fee-based, marked-up* (FMU) terms in the contracts (*not* interest and fees as is done by conventional banks). In a broader context, these institutions use an alternative mechanism to price financial products: It is an alternative intermediation.

Islamic banks form one class of licensed financial institutions, and they engage in any typical banking transactions using PLS and FMU to make profits. Those engaging in PLS and FMU in insurance are classed as *Takaful* insurance, those engaging in funds management are Islamic mutual funds, and so on. Non-interest-based bonds are traded by authorized firms doing transactions in *sukuk* bonds, which are traditional bonds based on PLS issuers with asset-backed borrowing contracts. Credit cards have been issued based on predesignated cash accounts earning a PLS income, and card payments are made without the use of interest. Islamic banking and finance normally refers to the more restricted practices of profit seeking by a bank using PLS and FMU in place of interest while carrying out just about the same transactions as a typical conventional bank. Thus, an Islamic bank takes deposits, creates savings accounts, lends money to customers, finances the mortgage purchase of a property, invests a customer's funds, issues a bill of lading, and so on—but always without the use of interest in the contractual agreements.[2]

The rest of the chapter is organized into six sections to explain Islamic banking practices (and not other Islamic financial institutions). The typical organizational structure of an Islamic bank is provided in the second section. It should be noted that the key difference of this new form of banking is the presence of a surveillance body, the Board of Scholars (*Shari'ah* Board), which ensures that the products offered by a bank are in line with the avoidance of interest-based financial services. The popular press has either ridiculed this idea as a religious surveillance board or called it a good thing! The latter view is supported because there is a layer of control beyond the money-hungry or corrupt influences of bad banking practices[3] and inadequate central bank oversight[4] that are the reality in current banking environments in many countries. In the third section, we discuss the general principles of financial transactions that are permitted in an Islamic bank under the strict doctrine of avoiding receipt or payment of interest in financial transactions and promoting full disclosures. The reader will find in the fourth section a quick introduction to what the balance sheet and income statement of an Islamic bank look like. In that section, we explain the underlying operating principles of the items in the accounting statements. In the fifth section, the reader will find an explanation of some special terms and how they are used. The chapter ends with some suggestions as to the likely direction this new niche banking may take in the near future.

Organization of an Islamic Bank

The organization chart of an Islamic bank operating under PLS and FMU resembles that of a typical conventional bank. As is the case in a conventional bank, there is a board of directors with legislated fiduciary duties imposed on them by the laws of the country in which a bank license is issued. These laws are corporation laws, trust laws, banking laws and prudential regulations, income tax laws, laws relating to legal transfer of ownership, disclosure laws, and accounting and financial reporting regulations. This aspect of the Islamic bank is exactly the same as is the case for a conventional bank. All these laws apply fully to an Islamic bank as they apply to a conventional bank.

Below the board of directors is the president and Chief Executive Officer (CEO), who may also be a member of the board. He is required to be qualified to manage the banking operations and is responsible to the board to carry out its policies. Increasingly, in almost all countries, there is an audit board that reports to the board to ensure that the activities of a bank are compliant with the laws and regulations. This is also found in an Islamic bank. Banks, being special because of their fractional-reserve money-creating ability, are supervised by a central bank or a separate prudential authority, whose visiting examiners constitute a supervisory board of commissioners reporting to the board of directors and bypassing the president. This is also the case in Islamic banks. The only exception is the case of an Islamic bank that is not by law required to be supervised by a central bank. Of course, this is an exception in Islamic banking, as it is also in conventional banking. That situation is not desirable because unsupervised banks, be they Islamic or conventional, have greater frequency of failing.[5]

Unlike the case of a conventional bank, the Islamic bank has a board of scholars—the *Shari'ah* Board—whose members are trained to ensure that the banking products offered are designed and sold in compliance with Islamic laws (as well as applicable conventional banking laws). In the current shortage of such diversely trained people, more broadly trained religious scholars are filling this board, with the unintended consequence that their advice appears to be much more focused on broader ethical standards than would be the case with strict adherence to Islamic financial transaction laws. The duty of this board, which gives independent advice to a board of directors, thus bypassing the CEO, is to ensure that the banking transactions do not include receipt or payment of interest-based activities and that the products offered to the customers pass the test of reasonableness in risk as required under the Islamic law of risk (*gharar*), which is that the risk is not excessive or bordering on gambling. This board also ensures that new banking products that are offered also pass the test of not being excessively risky for a given class of customers and that products provide full disclosure—nothing in fine print.

Surveillance activities of this board thus introduce a degree of conservatism—in current circumstances since the global financial crisis, a much needed conservatism—in the business practices of banks. Some say the presence of this intervener *within each bank* introduces a moral compass that possibly reduces the high-risk activities that are often reported in adventurous banks that actually create serious systemic risks through high-risk financing leading to financial crises.[6] Two examples are the Barings Bank closure in the United Kingdom due to excessive speculation on Japanese yen futures contracts and the mortgage-backed and collateralized debt obligations as innovations, in the case of the global financial crisis in 2007, brought on by inadequate disclosures to subprime borrowers of the consequence to their housing ownership if (a) interest rates went up and (b) real estate prices begin to fall.

The board of scholars would not have approved a financial practice that is based on excessive speculation, even though the CEO and board of directors of Barings Bank would have wanted the excessive speculation on Japanese yen futures that produced huge profits for Baring Bank and bonuses for its directors. The scholars would have deemed that trade as too risky, closer to gambling, for the safety of shareholder equity. So, having this special surveillance is a good thing. Inducing people to take loans they would not be able to pay back—the subprime loan—would be considered a risky contract for that class of borrowers and would not be approved by such a board. It borders on gambling, and it also fails to pass the requirement that the customer must be told up front all information relating to a product; that is, if the property market collapses, the borrowers will lose heavily.

Recent commentaries on the activities of this board reflect two views. Some have criticized this as an inroad of religious doctrine into banking practices. Most good practices in financial transactions arise from some preexisting ethical considerations that may be found in religious literature. Another concern is that these specialists charge exorbitant fees, sitting on many boards, a rich source of money, for them, given the current shortage of such trained men. Many of them are religious scholars, but many are also secular individuals trained in laws: Few of them are non-Muslims who are known to be experts in this regard. It should also be noted that Islamic banking customers need not belong to the Islamic faith. A member of the board of scholars could be any person, as long as the person has the required training.

Another view about this board is that it is necessary to ensure that a bank does not earn income from interest as receipts or pay interest, since that is an essential part of being Islamic banking. In the absence of a central bank providing inspection on this aspect, there is a need for this board within the bank. Customers who wish to have certainty that there is ongoing oversight of practices and the imposition of rules are assured by the board's presence. It is a sanitizing exercise. Hence, the second view is that this board is a good thing. A consequence of this board is that Islamic banks in general are more conservatively managed, not just to avoid interest-based activities but also to avoid activities based on excessive risk taking bordering on gambling (which arises from religious advice to avoid anything bordering on gambling) to limit the damage to community that may arise from excessive risk taking in financial activities. An example of this is the design of structured banking products such as the collateralized debt obligations (CDOs) that have been shown to have been partly responsible for the global financial crisis in 2007–2008.[7] Personnel working in such a bank have to be trained in the special requirements of Islamic banking products and to fully disclose information before the customer signs a financial contract.

As shown in Figure 12.1, other than this special board, the divisions reporting to the CEO are identical to those found in any conventional bank. The CEO as an incumbent board member is responsible for the effective management of specialized divisions: secretariat, internal audit, operations, treasury, loans (which may be more than one division, depending on the size of the bank), international banking, branch offices, and business development. All these divisions bring to bear different expertise and professional skills to the successful operation and management of a bank. These divisions need to be directed to ensure that they operate as required under conventional banking laws and Islamic banking principles. The larger the bank, the greater the number of divisions under the CEO. These divisions are very similar in Islamic banks, and these banks compete in the same market for personnel and look for the same qualities in personnel as is the case in conventional banking.

With facilities for training at professional levels within large banks, there are also now new institutions that certify Islamic banking training, and senior personnel are being trained in Islamic banking. Such trained manpower is increasingly coming to the job market with knowledge of the product design and operations of a PLS, FMU, and risk-revelation skills in banking

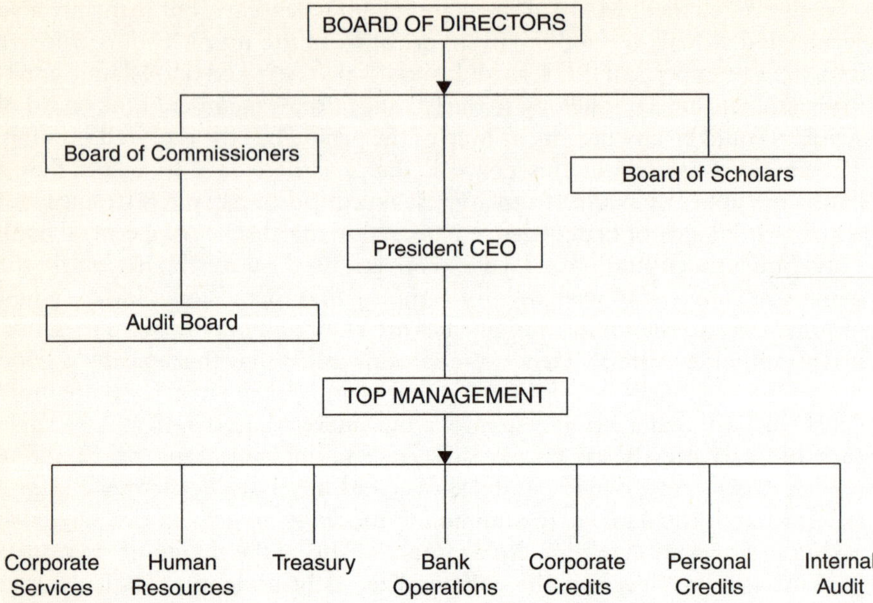

FIGURE 12.1 Typical Organization Chart of an Islamic Bank

operations.[8] It may take few years before there are sufficient numbers of people trained in the intricacies of these new niche banking practices.

The upshot of this discussion is that the Bank *Mualamat* (using a more descriptive name than the overly extended "Islamic" banking term) is a form of banking specializing in a new niche to implement financial practices based on PLS and FMU to price contracts. The organization chart of such a bank has to have an additional committee of trained legal persons to ensure that the financial practices and the products on offer to customers are in line with the three injunctions on avoidance of interest, avoidance of excessive risk in financial contracts, and full disclosures. These, it is claimed, make such a bank more conservative and thus safer for communities doing business with such banks. However, the safety can be compromised by poor operational controls. In many developing countries, such banks have room for improving operational processes to ensure that risk is managed well.

Fundamental Principles of Islamic Banking

This section is intended to introduce the important principles of operating Islamic banks that differ from those of conventional banks for pricing banking products.

Avoidance of interest-based financial transactions is the first principle. Profits are made by applying PLS and FMU principles to normal savings and investment transactions by customers (in addition to fee-based markup products). In all time deposits, negotiable certificates of deposit (NCD), and investment deposits, an Islamic bank earns profits using PLS contracts. In the case of investment products such as a mutual fund, the bank is required to ensure that the incomes of the mutual funds are from economic activities not prohibited in Islamic laws: examples are gambling, prostitution, and production of prohibited food and drinks. The profit share is declared a period *after* the deposit is made, and the current popular period is one month later for a savings account. The third principle is the widespread use of FMU in what are termed trade-in-*non*-financial assets by a bank. These are lease contracts for machinery purchase, for example, a barge by a shipping company or the purchase of a house by a household, both of which are nonfinancial assets. The final principle is the requirement that the customer is informed of the level of risk of a financial contract if there is undue risk of loss in investing in a product. In all these, risk cannot be excessive to the contracting parties. Furthermore, the risks that are assumed cannot resemble the odds of a gamble.

A Digression to History Should humanity avoid interest in financial transactions has been a fascinating topic of great thinkers for some 4,000 years and in canon law. Our first record of prohibition of excessive interest rates in financial transactions—the first usury law—is a stone tablet by Hammurabi of Mesopotamia (modern-day Syria-Iraq). His prescribed punishment for this malpractice was execution! He specified a charge of a third of money lent as interest as usurious interest. Hindu scriptures such as the Upanishad had injunctions against such interest. The Torah has references to the people of Jewish faith to avoid interest in financial transactions. Christianity has the largest number of scripture-based commandments in both New and Old Testaments prohibiting all forms of interest in general, not just usurious interest.

The Muslim scripture has six key commandments prohibiting financial transactions based on interest. Some scholars interpret this prohibition as meaning only excessive interest, *riba,* meaning usurious interest, rather than small interest amounts. For more than 1,400 years from the advent of Islam, there have been scholars who interpreted these commandments as permitting dealing in interest, but all were agreed that excessive interest or usury is not permitted. Since the mid-1950s, the pendulum has swung the other way, with the consensus among scholars that no form of interest is good for society. Contemporary scholars' interpretation is now closer to that of Christianity's prohibition of interest right up to 1752, when the

Catholic Church lifted the strict biblical verses on interest. Since the middle of the twentieth century, a majority consensus has emerged among Muslim scholars that no interest is permitted in financial transactions, and usurious interest is certainly banned.[9]

The key provision under Islamic canon law states: "Thou . . . shall not take usury, compounded over and over." This means that the use of capital by a rich person (or entity) to gain excessive profits is an advantage secured by indebting another person (or another entity) needing funds, which is considered an uncharitable act forbidden in God's law. Hence, by making a morally justified financial gain by lending the capital to a person, the lender must *share in the risk of the venture* of the person putting the money to work. Then afterward, the lender should obtain the *pre*-agreed share of the profit coming from the venture *subsequently* and not impose an interest *ex ante*. This is the origin of the legal requirement in Islamic banking canon law that, up front, the borrower reveals the risk of the venture, the lender agrees to partake of the risk ex ante, and both parties agree to a ratio of profit deemed as fair for the inherent risk in the financial transaction. A silent partner may require a small share, and a very risky investment such as financing a satellite may involve high risk, such that the contract term for PLS reflects the higher risk level. It is also required that the contract is witnessed in writing by a third person of legal standing.

Hence, a financier providing funds to an entrepreneur building a roadway as a turnkey project may agree to share 25 percent of the profits from toll charges collected rather than lend funds at a fixed interest rate without waiting to ensure that the financier has in fact participated in the risk of building the road. If an entrepreneurial activity is a single economic act for both entrepreneur and financier, the act of financing the project cannot be separated from the economic act of building the road. Why should the financing be considered a matter unrelated to the completion of the project by imposing repayment of the loan ahead without regard to sharing in the risk of completion of the project? This is the fundamental principle of the risk-share and profit-share argument as a feature of fairness in contracts in Islamic law. Prefixing the reward in the form of interest payments unrelated to the risk of completion of a project does not lead to risk-sharing-reward-sharing, and thus an interest-based contract places the borrower at an unequal position of exploitation. If one is to practice this risk-sharing, then reward-sharing principle strictly, an alternative mode of financial contracting is needed. That is what Islamic banks do. How they do this is a matter of evolving practices that have emerged after half a century of trial and error, leading to possible future refinements in this practice. It must be admitted, current practice is a crude form of this!

The core banking activities include a safekeeping function, savings, and extending credit. Safekeeping is an age-old practice that existed when money as a store of value evolved millennia back. For example, this was done by pious Catholics going to Jerusalem as pilgrims in the eleventh century when they left their money (and valuables) in the custody of the church. Later the Knights Templar took over this business. King Louis XIV disposed of the Knights Templar in 1307 with a false charge of devil worship in order to acquire the wealth of this banking group to pay off his war debt. This brought an end to the Knights Templar acting as a bank, and the church continued receiving pilgrims' deposits in financial transactions. Modern banking evolved after 1752 A.D., when the church gave a watered-down interpretation of the 13-century ban on interest. This mellowing of the attitude toward interest was largely fostered by the more egalitarian attitude in Germany after Luther's epoch-making break with the Roman Catholic Church. In fact, some German rulers gave implicit permission to wealthy German financiers long before the ban was lifted to take over the lending businesses based on interest from other non-German ethnic groups.

This practice of safekeeping deposits at banks and then lending those funds at interest led to the modern-day banking in the Netherlands in the sixteenth century as fully backed lending (not fractional-reserve lending). The second core activity of a bank is savings deposited over a time period in a savings account, and the third is the extension of credit or a loan to buy nonfinancial assets, such as a house, a car, a boat, or a factory.

From about the mid-eighteenth century, banks actually created credit by using the fractional-reserve banking principle, which multiplies money by the reciprocal of the liquidity ratio of money in deposits. Although there is discussion in 2010 of increasing the regulatory capital base of about 8 percent under current laws, fractional banking is well entrenched and likely to survive in both Islamic and conventional banking.

What reward should be paid to customers for safekeeping? This case is simple. As was the practice in banking for centuries, money placed in checking accounts does not get any returns since the service of safekeeping provided by the bank is sufficient reward if the principal is returned. So Islamic banks do not pay a return in all cash-safekeeping accounts. For nonmoney items kept in bank safe deposit boxes, customers are charged a fee for safekeeping. Since the 1970s, with a change in a bank regulation in some countries, conventional banks started to pay interest to checking account holders. But the interest paid is a paltry amount. In countries with about 6 percent interest rates for savings accounts (in 2010), this payment for checking deposits is less than 1 percent, and banks recover this payment by imposing a minimum sum in checking deposits and a fee on the check-clearing process. The net effect is that the checking account in conventional banks gets almost zero returns, as is also the case in Islamic banking.

Savings accounts are different because savings depositors should earn a return for letting the bank use the money for money creation under the fractional-reserve ratio and also for the risk that a bank may lose the money, even if it is covered by deposit insurance. There may also be a loss of value of money over time due to inflation. The permitted practice in Islamic banking as regards reward for savings is for the bank to accept the deposit without promising *prefixed interest,* as is the case by a conventional bank promising a *preagreed* interest. At the end of each month, an increase (it is called a *dividend distribution*) is announced by Islamic banks. In theory, this increase is based as a share of the actual profits of the bank for that month. By this practice, the savers get to earn a return commensurate with the profitability of the bank—at least that is the principle—and the use of interest is avoided. Studies have shown that the so-called distribution of profits as is termed a dividend payment is slightly higher than the market rates of interest in the prior month. Some commentators have called this a formality of making the same old interest payment instead of really agreeing to a certain ratio of sharing the bank's actual profits. After about half a century of practice, there is no consensus on how to share the bank's profits with savings deposit holders under profit-risk-sharing principles.

Why the return declared at the end of a month has no bearing on the profitability of the bank is an issue that requires additional research. Orthodox Muslim scholars have used this as a major weapon to call Islamic banking a scam by modern-day Muslim countries. Hence, this issue is important in that these critiques point out that the practice of Islamic banking has to be consistent with the Islamic law of profit-share rather than merely *compliant.* Indeed, repackaging the profit-share as equal to interest in the market is not consistent with the injunction of the profit-sharing principle.

This writer believes that the return to savings account holders will be greater than the interest rates if profit-sharing in its true sense is actually practiced. The average return on equity in modern banks is 11 percent to 33 percent, according to the Bank for International Settlements, (BIS) reports over some 20 years. The equity of banks forms at most about 15 percent of the total assets, meaning that most of the total assets is from money created on the fractional-reserve to savings-deposit principle *applied to deposits.* The average rate of return depositors have been getting in conventional banks is about half a percent higher than the Treasury yields, which translates to about 5 percent to 6 percent in the United States during the last 90 years. Obviously, a move to pin the return on the profitability of the bank will yield a higher return to savers as anywhere between 3.7 percent and 11 percent if a profit share is agreed, say, as one-third of bank shareholders' profits. As Islamic banking evolves in the future, this issue has to move in this direction.

Bankers point out that the real profits will be known only at the end of the year (accounting standards require this), and so the return cannot be based on such a simple way. With modern accounting and technology, it is possible for banks to know how much profit they are making in a month and thus base the return to the savings accounts as an interim ratio of profits. At the end of the year, an adjustment amount should be given to equate the returns to date to equal some defined preagreed share of the profits of the bank on a yearly basis. This aspect requires additional research to provide policy guidelines. If the banks share their profits in a predetermined ratio, it is highly likely that the return would be larger than the market interest rates. This will spur incentives to save in any country. The jury is out on this issue. Any banks offering, say, a third of the profits to savings depositors at each six-month period will steal the market overnight, and that will be consistent with the profit-share idea!

A perverse way of reasoning to justify low returns is to argue that the savers are sure of avoiding perdition by participating in an Islamic savings deposit, so why worry about the economic profit-share ratio? Surveys indicate that about 3 of 10 persons in majority-Muslim countries wish to participate in this form of savings deposits. Add to this the rich individuals who could tailor-make the profit-share via syndicated loans for large funding projects and earn higher returns than is possible in bank-based deposits today. Firms directly tapping the rich loan-money providers under profit shares can also cut out the bank as middlemen by using financial agents and thus access cheaper loans in this niche marketplace. This is the incentive for big banks coming to dinner as Islamic bankers in this new century in locations such as London, Singapore, and Zurich to lend to high-net-worth individuals on a truly profit-sharing basis.

Laws can vary from country to country. For example, Iranian law permits "minimum return is to be given to the depositors" as provided in one section of banking laws. Giving an increase to the amount of deposit is encouraged in Islamic jurisprudence, though the borrower (a bank) is not required to give a return, since borrowing is contingent on risk sharing and profit sharing. But a borrower going the extra mile to give some return above the principal is considered to act in a benevolent manner. Such a behavior—another is donating the interest earned to charity—is considered exemplary in the canon law of Islam. Hence, in practice, savers do expect to get back principal and a minimum additional payment by the bank in Iran. Though documented findings are not available as yet, oral evidence suggests that this return has been around the inflation rate in that country.

This ensures that the savers preserve the purchasing power of their wealth in savings accounts.

Under the interpretation of forbearance of interest on strictly religious grounds (there are customers who want to observe this for fear of hellfire if they received or paid interest), the PLS contracts ensure first that both parties share in the risk of the venture and that there is a preagreed share of the profits from the venture. This is how the profit-share agreements are made. Prominent banks and institutions that are creating custom-made contracts using PLS contracts—for example, UBS and HSBC—negotiate the profit-share ratios and then tailor a debenture agreement for investing large sums in infrastructural and industrial projects. Thus, it is possible to have profit-sharing contracts, especially in long-term development funding and projects. This leads to sharing in the risk and higher returns, to savers, should the project become successful.

This form of loan agreement under profit sharing is called the *mudaraba* or *murabaha,* depending on some differences between the two, but these are PLS contracts for a term of time (both are debt contracts). Since Islamic banks are new and not too large, operating mostly in developing countries, most of the lending activities are based on lending bank funds in savings deposits to traders of goods and services as loans for one year or less. It is attractive in a small community whereby entrepreneurship can be rekindled by the bank that is lending on this basis. The agency problem in a small community of closely linked people of defaulting on sharing profits or engaging in false contracting is rather small. However, this form of lending in more developed economies with anonymous borrowers and lenders requires a more formal mechanism that has yet to be invented to overcome the agency problem. As the Islamic banks become larger, new structures are needed to prevent the agency problem of false projects being financed by PLS lenders, leading to huge fraudulent losses.

Mortgage Lending The core banking activity of financing purchases of real assets requires FMU techniques to price this contract. A buyer of a property approaches the bank for credit. The bank adds a markup as the cost over the period of lending a given principal amount to immediately purchase the real asset and then resell the real asset to a borrower. The problem here is to predict the price of an apartment in Fifth Avenue or Hoboken, say, 20 years from now. The usual shortcut taken by an Islamic bank—a very unsatisfactory method of determining the cost of funding—is to consider a markup based on the current cost of money in the loan market in conventional banks. This leads to a markup based on ruling interest rates. However, once the markup is added, and the amortization of loan-plus-markup is computed, the Islamic principle requires that the amortization is based on equal treatment of principal and markup payment, according to the concept in Islamic law that the asset is now owned by the borrower. Conventional banks recover all the interest payments in the first periods of repayments, leaving the purchaser to build equity at a later date, after most of the interest is recovered. Typically, a 20-year loan begins to build significant equity in the property after about 10 years of repayments.

This should not be the case in amortization under Islamic principles. Under an Islamic mortgage amortization, the owner of the property builds equity, according to strict interpretation, from the first payment on an equal basis. Islamic banks have adopted conventional banking practices on amortization, which, in the opinion of scholars in this area, would not be a fair practice, requiring different modes yet devised to compute amortization. Also in mortgage financing by conventional banks, stamp duty (a tax) is charged only once at the time the borrower buys a real estate asset. Under Islamic law, the banks buy the real estate asset, and then the customer buys it from the banks. Hence, under current stamp duty requirements in conventional laws, an Islamic mortgage would incur double stamp duty. To avoid this unequal treatment of the same economic activity, countries under civil law jurisdictions normally pass amendments to such laws as needed to place both banks on equal footing. Directors need to bear this in mind.

Full Disclosure of Risk Finally, under the board of scholars guidelines, it is a requirement that the parties to a contract must reveal the full extent of risk in a financial transaction ex ante. Such laws have been passed in many developed countries since 2002, after the Enron-Worldcom-Maxwell frauds. If the purchase of a ship is financed by a bank, then the ship owner-operator requiring the finance must reveal the actuarial facts about the ship, such as accident rates on the route taken (apart from the seaworthiness of the ship), and the banker must reveal the risk of money being invested in the project. Thus, all contracts must provide up-front material facts to a transaction that is witnessed by a third party. Further, there is the requirement that the bank—a public institution—does not offer a financial transaction that has excessive risk bordering on gambling because gambling is not permitted under canon law in many religions.

This injunction fosters conservatism and avoids adventurous financing by banks. In Islamic insurance, financing is permitted, since there is a way of quantifying the risk and compensating it. In commodity futures contracts, for example, wheat futures, a futures contract is permitted only after there is evidence that wheat seeds have formed, and not before the formation of the asset being contracted for, as a requirement to have assets backing a financial contract. Some consider this a function of the board of scholars, thus making community banking safer than it has been under conventional banking. That may be a good thing, especially if the bank operates in communities with low-income customers.

Other Banking Services Banks engage in investment services in addition to core banking transactions. The requirement is that the securities in which a customer's money is invested are from businesses that do not engage in interest-based activities,[10] gambling, production or distribution of intoxicants, or prostitution. The Islamic Dow-Jones Index, for example, has identified that about 40 percent of the firms listed on the New York Stock Exchange fulfill these criteria. The principle is that capital should be made available only to foster socially responsible economic activities and not activities that place the community (and family) at risk. As long as the returns to the investors are from activities congenial to community welfare, then that investment instrument becomes a permitted (*halal*) Islamic investment. Many ethical funds have operated in the United States on somewhat similar criteria since the 1970s, although they do not trace their origin to Islamic laws.

There are an increasing number of Islamic investment firms around the world, of which about 120 are mutual funds. These funds could include in their holdings the *sukuk* bonds, which are not based on interest but on income from vested firms. For example, a firm that owns property and collects rent may set aside a portion of the rent as belonging to a special purpose company (SPC)—the vested firm. The vested firm will pay the promised profit sharing and the principal on due dates. Thus, borrowing requires asset-backed lending. Some say this will make free-for-all sovereign borrowing less attractive since governments need to specify an earning asset as the SPC to service the loan, so the problems of sovereign debt that have plagued humanity over millennia could be brought under control.

It is sufficient in this brief introduction not to extend and limit this discussion to bank-relevant factors. We summarize the main principles of the Islamic banking operations here. Participation in risk sharing with full disclosure of the risk of a financial contract is a must in financial transactions; a witness is also required to attest to the revelation of information. This means no asymmetric information exists at the time of contracting. It relies on a number of ways of promoting this idea. There is no guarantee that one participant in a contract may not bluff his way into the contract (thus perpetrating asymmetric information and agency costs) despite all these controls, thus leading to possible loss. This is a fact of life in mass-based societies, and new control procedures and monitoring devices are needed to ensure that after the contract, the parties live up to the revelations made beforehand. This problem associated with risk sharing and profit sharing is not highlighted in the literature, though it is a major problem. This is a position entirely consistent with modern finance that the return-risk paradigm is an increasing function of the amount of risk taken, but as of yet, there is no way to ensure how this is specified *ex ante* in a profit-sharing contract.

Add to that the avoidance of interest in transactions, which is based on the principle of PLS with the sharing ratio depending on the risk of the project and also on the extent to which the lender is committing time to the project (absentee owner or participating lender may be as an independent director in the project). Convenience deposits, which are checking accounts, are merely deposits, and no return is given for them. Strictly financial transactions, such as saving accounts, investments, and loans, are based on PLS but with risk-sharing agreements. Finally, FMU as a principle is applied in financing purchases of *non*-financial assets, such as a home, commercial office, or equipment. Like a lease agreement, which is for a shorter period, mortgage lending is over a longer period, and it requires ownership to be preserved from the first payment by borrowers on split of markup repayments.

Financial Statements of an Islamic Bank

The financial statements of an Islamic bank are interpreted in this section. Currently, an independent institute based in Bahrain has developed several accounting standards for the preparation of the financial accounts of an Islamic financial institution: Accounting and Auditing Organization for Islamic Financial Institutions (AAOIFI). They have fostered comparisons across banks that adopt these standards, in addition to the usual applicable conventional accounting standards. International Islamic banking practices are apt to converge in the near future to these standards already being adopted by banks. On the banking regulatory side, there is the Islamic Financial Services Board (IFSB, founded in 2004), which works closely with the BIS, International Monetary Fund (IMF), and World Bank to develop standards on capital requirements, nonperforming loans, and risk-weighting assets as applied to Islamic banks. Thus, over time, Islamic banks will converge to best practices in this regard, although at present it is difficult to compare financial statements of banks operating in faraway places such as the Philippines and Switzerland. Islamic banks are not comparable unless they adopt uniform reporting standards. Studies show that only a minority of them have done so.

The first thing to note is that the traditional accounting framework is similar to conventional banks. That is, there is a balance sheet, the income statement, and the cash flow statement. There is the asset side to the balance sheet equaling the liability plus owners' equity. The income report reports income; deducts costs, depreciation, and so on to tax; and then computes the net income. The cash flow statement records the sources and uses of capital. Banks also report the statement of retained earnings after paying dividends to the shareholders. The differences in all these reports are the *absence* of interest income and interest payments. Thus, for example, in a profit-and-loss statement, profit share payments take the place of interest receipts and payments.

On the structural side, the financial statements are similar. However, the items recorded in the statements come from the management of the bank using only PLS and FMU activities. In addition, Islamic banks often set aside a small part of the year's profits as a contribution to the welfare of the poor in the community the bank serves. Conventional banks do not have this item but rather an expense item before tax for promotion of football or art activities, not as part of the profits set aside to promote sports and arts. The second and final different item in an Islamic bank is a religious contribution—a wealth tax called *zakat*—paid by rich people into the bank to be mixed with the bank's set-aside profits for the poor. In Iranian jurisdictions, this small account is about 1 percent to 4 percent of the total profits of banks. These two items are strictly after taxes and after profits in the case of the Islamic bank. It should be emphasized that the last item is a very tiny portion of the income statements and may be missing in some Islamic banks, as it is voluntary contribution by the bank. Furthermore, people often contribute charity money directly to charities. Therefore, a bank may not receive any charity money into its account. As shown in Table 12.1, the charity activities are not recorded. This sum, if any, is contributed to institutions that take care of the poor and the orphans. All other items are equivalent to items found in conventional bank reports.

Revenues in income statements refer to the income received through PLS and FMU activities of lending by the bank (not interest-based activities). The costs incurred are material costs, wage costs, overhead costs, depreciation costs, and cost of PLS given to the savings depositors *as dividends*. The earnings before tax is the amount on which a tax is paid. (In most cases, there is a corporate tax, although in some jurisdictions, there is no tax on corporate income.) The resulting number is the net income. Thus, the income statement appears to use the same structure, but the items entered on the statement are not involved in interest-based activities.

The balance sheet can be interpreted in a similar manner. The asset side has current assets that are cash or cash owed to the bank, including deposits with the central bank, payments due to the bank from PLS and FMU activities, and an adjustment for nonperforming loans. The current liabilities are the accounts payable, tax payable, and cash payable to other parties. Thus, what is missing are the marketable securities based on interest (if marketable securities based on profit share are available, there will be an entry for this item) and loans by banks to be repaid based with interest (if PLS is incurred, this item will be there). In some locations of Islamic banking—Bahrain and Malaysia—short-term bills fulfilling the norms of

TABLE 12.1 A Stylized Representation of Balance Sheet and Income Statements

A: Balance Sheet	
Cash	Accounts payable
Cash due	Deposits
Securities in	Deferrals
Receivables	Short-term borrowing
Gross Assets	Long-term borrowing
Depreciation	Shareholder equity
Net Assets	Retained earnings
	Reserves
Total Assets	Liabilities + Equity

B: Income Statement	
	Revenue (PLS or FMU)
	Cost
	Materials
	Wages
	Depreciation
	Overhead
	Deposit dividends
	Dividend distribution to depositors
	Income before taxes
	Taxes
	Net Income

Islamic financial products are available. In such cases, there will be entry of marketable securities.

On the asset side is plant and equipment with accumulated depreciation and current depreciation. There is the book value of the loans and investments. On the other side of the balance sheet, long-term liabilities are items of capital borrowing (tier 2 capital) using profit sharing. Then at the end is the equity account of shareholders, which would pay dividends to shareholders as in conventional banks.

Thus, the financial statements are as easily interpretable as conventional bank reports. However, in some cases, the same items have different meanings, as the item is generated by applying profit-sharing or fee-and-markup financial activities. As previously mentioned, the accounting standards applied to the preparation of these accounts are increasingly in compliance with the standards issued by the Bahrain-based institute. The same is the case on banking standards as complying with the IFSB schedules. That would mean that, in the near future, Islamic bank reports from very diverse economies can reasonably be compared and their relative performance evaluated.

SPECIAL QUESTION ON INTERMEDIATION BY BANKS

This section explains some of the terminology already used in this chapter, as well as additional terms that are needed to understand the operation of Islamic banks. Some reference has to be made to nonbank activities, such as investments and insurance. These traditional nonbank activities are becoming more widespread by universal banks after the 1999 Graham-Leach-Bliley Act in the United States and similar changes to bank regulations in the United Kingdom and other countries. In such places, we also observe Islamic banking activities are on the increase.

Three Approaches to Banking

The debate about the merit of banking as we see in conventional banking practices has led to three distinct views. Banking is viewed as a necessary licensed activity that fosters less risk taking by the masses because of delegated monitoring by banks on behalf of the savers, mobilization of savings at low cost, promoting delegated monitoring of users of funds on behalf of the depositors, ensuring efficient payments to factors of production, and today, helping economic agents transfer risk either for the agents or for the bank itself when the bank repackages risky holdings and sells them off to those who want to undertake that risk for higher returns. That these objectives are consistent with the promotion of community welfare is not at all debatable. Thus, these five objectives are accepted as worthwhile for a modern society, and resources are spent to ensure that these objectives are achieved.

Is there an alternative mode to this conventional intermediation? Whether these objectives must be achieved only by conventional banks is at the heart of this debate. Proponents of free banking advocate that the regulated nature of banking makes it costly to deliver these objectives. They claim that under free banking, there will be more monitoring of banks by depositors, savers, borrowers, and others, using the market to get information. It follows that the market will punish the bad banks and promote the good ones, so that in the end, the banks will be able to deliver these functions more efficiently than at present with politician-devised institutions. There will be less chance of the central banks, purporting to do good, actually not doing the right thing for society. They advocate free trade in banking instead of license-based banking, where the suprainstitutions of central banks and world institutions have failed to create safe banking. Rather, this nonfree but regulated banking practice over two and a half centuries has promoted concentrating the wealth of countries in a few elites of the society. Equally important, the world has become indebted with the interest-on-interest-based lending practices.

Another point of view that can be traced back to Benjamin Franklin is the idea that fractional banking has led to the creation of a wealthy class of banks and their owners and hangers-on. These bank owners have permeated the world with so much debt that the citizens are paying a huge price in the form of the interest (from paying higher tax to service government debt) that is being paid to the bank from the taxes collected by the politicians, who have no qualms about borrowing to ensure their reelection. This line of reasoning takes the view that a bank with $1,000 can lend $6,670 for a 15 percent PLS under fractional bank lending and that this is the source of indebtedness in the world. There are very scary amounts of indebtedness of developed and developing countries quoted in the literature, which is mostly studies by respectable scholars and commentators who bolster this argument.

The final point of view is that interest-based banking is the source of the problem. When society replaces interest with risk-shared and profit-shared lending in financial activities, the society will be much better off than under one-sided, interest-based lending because depositors become profit-sharing owners of banks, and bank runs will not happen that badly except in very bad banks. Islamic banking appears to come from this angle, although the first argument for the avoidance of interest is based on God-revealed doctrine in all world religions.

So, there is on ongoing debate as to which form of banking is prosociety and which have not provided adequate banking services to the community at large. Taken in this context, Islamic banking (with finance included) appears to argue that the ethical dimension of risk-share-reward-share is at the center of the argument that favors this new niche banking (and finance) that has been growing since its first formation in 1963.[11] Islamic banking practices were ubiquitous for almost 1,400 years, as well as earlier in the forms practiced in the Eastern Mediterranean area. But over the last 50 years, these practices have now become formalized into this new niche banking and finance. This idea has gained acceptance because of customers' willingness to do business under PLS and FMU banking as being favorable to them. Thus, banks have begun to provide such new services. Examples of new entrants to this service include HSBC, Citigroup, Barclays, and some Swiss, Australian, and German banks. The largest numbers of Islamic banks are found in countries with significant Muslim populations, in Sudan, Malaysia, Bahrain, Iran, and Turkey (where it is not called Islamic because of constitutional restrictions on the use of the word *Islamic*).

Thus, Islamic banking fills a niche for special clients. It fulfills the need of some customers who do not wish to participate in harmful activities; in their minds, interest-based financial transactions are harmful because of unequal contracting, and funds should be cut off for intoxicant production, gambling, and prostitution, just as ethical U.S. investment firms avoid firms producing weapons. Therefore, this is simply a niche market that is there to harness another source of funds into the broader banking system so the conventional banks will continue to dominate. After all, the assets of all the Islamic banks in the world after almost 50 years of growth add up to the total assets of the fourth largest single bank in the world! This indicates that Islamic banking should be approached as niche banking, just as 70 years ago investment banking was so considered and developed. Under this scenario, then, it is a different functional structure for this niche market and no more. Therefore, one needs to understand how best to operate these new entities.

Selected Islamic Product Terms

It has come to be accepted over the years that convenience deposits are simply what they are. They do not earn a return. The deposited money is safeguarded for either use by the depositor for issuance of checks or withdrawal by the depositor. In the conventional banking in some countries, such deposits attract a very tiny interest rate, and the user of this service is required to place a sizable amount; otherwise, a service fee is charged. In a sense, even conventional banks appear to treat checking deposits as something not close to savings, and the return given is paltry. These are thus no-compensation deposits. The savings deposits are considered funds meant to obtain a reward for placement in savings. These are thus considered *mudaraba* (profit-share) deposits attracting a return at the end of each month *after* the depositor had shared in the risk of the bank's investing activity. There are variations of this that are referred to by other terms. The bank is considered an agent (*mudarib*) for investment.

On the part of the bank lending on the *mudaraba* basis, the borrower agrees to pay a ratio of the profits from the projects or venture to which the borrowed money is put to use. The bank then receives the reward on a regular basis, usually after a period but not in arrears, the sum of money returned at the ratio of preagreed profits generated by the project. In such an agreement, the *mudaraba* borrower only parts with that portion of profits commensurate with the services provided by a bank (or the direct investor if the contract is with a direct lender). If the banker (or the direct lender) actually sits in the project team (as a director of the board of a turnkey project for a road construction), then there is both a financial service and a management service of participating in the project management. Thus, the reward to the bank (or the direct lender) will be larger than would be the case if money is the only thing that was lent.

How to vary the profit ratio is a matter that has still not been well developed because most of the Islamic banks' funds are used for short-term projects in developing countries that are more trade-related than industrial ventures. However, the bigger banks are now directly negotiating larger loans. For example, a German state body borrowed 400 million euros in 2006 on a profit-share basis. As the Islamic banks gather more experience in large-scale lending, there may be some form of categorizing loans based on their quality and then varying the profit shares accordingly. Thus *mudaraba* financing may take a larger role in facilitating financing than is at present possible under preagreed interest rate arrangements.

The other form of financial transaction is an equity share in the firm, be it as silent owners or as active owners of the firm. The reward in this case will be the residual income after the debt holders have been paid their profit share. This reward is the dividend and the retained earnings in the firm. Such contracts are called *musharaka* (share) contracts, and they are exactly equal to the dividend share certificates in conventional practice. There is one variation, though, in Islamic *musharaka* funding: the finite-period equity funding, which can be repaid with dividends either as diminishing *musharaka* payments on a periodic basis or as a balloon payment *musharaka,* when the sum given is paid off with the dividends cumulated. The latter is akin to the ship financing by European nobility in the fifteenth and seventeenth centuries. As the reward for such financing is decided after the financier participated in the risk of the firm before getting a claim to the residual earnings (part being distributed as dividends), this has never been a bone of contention in the anti-interest-rate literature. Thus, common stock is a non-interest-based permitted instrument, except when the issuer engages in prohibited activities (interest earnings, production of intoxicants for sale to persons, gambling, and prostitution).

Another item to be discussed in this chapter is the *ijaara* contract, which is a buy-and-lease-back agreement that involves buying property, adding a markup, and then requiring regular payments to recover the up-front payment by a bank. Importantly, this is a bank financing the asset and then selling that asset to a borrower, who takes ownership. It has been claimed that this is akin to the conventional mortgage, except that the equity created in the agreement starts from the first payment in equal proportion to the money paid out. There are views expressed that the Islamic bank's practice of pricing the markup on interest rates is contrary to this principle. *Mudahraba* is the name given to a real estate (mortgage) contract compared with lease (*ijara*) contracts.

In addition to these forms of contracts (deposits for safekeeping, savings deposits, shares, leasing-mortgage), Islamic banks are beginning to hold Treasury bonds that are based on PLS contracts named *sukuk*. The outstanding value of the *sukuk* bond market in 2010 was estimated as $100 billion in six locations. It is a loan contract with two innovations developed four centuries ago in the Turkish empire. First, a *sukuk* issuer creates a special firm, SPC, into which the issuer vests a stream of its income to serve as the assets from which the loan agreement will be serviced. In this manner, *sukuk* is asset-backed lending based on profit sharing. This instrument can also be held by an Islamic mutual fund that may wish to add no-risk Treasury bonds to its portfolio of risky securities. In addition, *sukuk* bonds can be designed and issued by private lenders. Such issues are relatively new, as in the case of an issue in 2010 by Commerce Bank in Malaysia. This will be a boon to *Takaful* insurance firms since such instruments are Islamic investable debt instruments, which are in short supply now. Note that a bank can use this form of lending to risky customers to make lending and borrowing safer on the principle of profit sharing with a SPC to provide asset backing.

Islamic banks do many other things. They provide advisory services for fees, as does an investment bank issuing securities in the primary market. Letters of credit may be given by a bank for a fee, as can the accounts receivable factored at a discounted price by a factoring company. Thus, there are many types of financial transactions that are the same as those in conventional banks, except that the instrument is not one that is issued by a firm that engages in production of intoxicants, gambling, or prostitution, or receives income in the form of interest.

FUTURE DIRECTION

It is debatable whether the world will take notice of the challenges fractional-reserve-based banking has produced via non-risk-sharing lending practices, such as debt-laden economies and individuals because of interest-on-interest lending and also institutions such as central banks and world banks that are mostly not delivering what they are supposed to for the greater welfare of human society. It appears that the niche banking called Islamic banks, though based on fractional-reserve banking but not interest-on-interest, discourages loans without participation in the risk of loss or funding without asset backing. It does not extend credit to socially harmful production activities. Its profit-and-risk-share foundation lends itself very well for rural and infrastructural development in all countries without the current debt burden created by interest-based lending: This makes depositors a junior owner of the banks with fewer shares than common shareholders.

Despite its ideals, Islamic banks have to date borrowed most of the ideas (except in the areas of forward and futures instruments, which are not permitted as yet by the board of scholars) from conventional banks and adapted the contracts to become compliant with the principle of avoiding interest. Some commentators have called this a sheepish practice of making essentially interest-based decisions in Islamic banks but making the contract compliant with the letter of the law rather than the spirit of true profit sharing or fair markup. An extreme view expressed by one scholar is that this practice has made Islamic banking a $300 billion scam! What is needed is thinking out of the box to design instruments and products that are *consistent* with Islamic principles rather than compliant, wherein lie challenges for boards of directors, presidents and CEOs, and Islamic scholars to go deeper into the principles explained in this chapter. The well-trained new entrants to the market have enough credibility to move in this way—this writer firmly believes so—and that is the new direction for changes to come.

A practical issue is how to use derivatives to overcome the riskiness of the Islamic banking operations: gap risk, exchange risk, price risk, balance sheet risk. Here, given the risk-averse nature of the board of scholars, the prohibition on the use of derivatives is a stumbling block to making Islamic banks safer from price change (basis) risk. The *Shari'ah* Board members, who are to be both secular and religious scholars, should be educated in the intricacies of these new financial instruments. They are then likely to find ways and means of structuring such new instruments (not bordering on gambling risk) to be added to Islamic banking products. New thinking is needed here to interpret what exactly the case laws on risk (*gharar* in Islam) have to say about the difference between the derivatives and gambling. Believers are required not to take too much risk in life and to avoid risky financial ventures, essentially because the full disclosure is not possible when risk is very high. But then risk pricing is permitted in *Takaful* insurance, provided the profits of the insurance firm are returned to the policyholders after all management expenses. Why, then, is the risk of derivatives considered excessive risk in banking?

Finally, there is a huge shortage of skilled management personnel in Islamic banks. Only since the 2000s have efforts been made to address this. As more trained personnel come onstream, the design of new products, no doubt at a slow pace now, will increasingly be in the true spirit of the profit-loss-share principle and the markup principle. That may herald innovations that are not simply complying with the letter of the law but are in fact at the core of the design of these instruments. The large players entering the market place—HSBC, Citibank, Barclays, NAB—have the resources and trained personnel to achieve these things. With a better-trained workforce and competition in banking, truly profit-sharing lending practices and fair markups in lease-mortgage contracts may emerge to replace the compliance culture that pervades current practices in Islamic banking and finance. Perhaps the one message to the directors of banks is to keep this strategic thought in mind in managing their banks.

■ ■ ■

Mohamed Ariff held a chair in finance and headed the finance faculty at Monash University in Melbourne, Australia, before moving to Bond University, where he is currently a professor of finance. He earned his postgraduate degrees from the University of Wisconsin–Madison and the University of Queensland. He holds an upper II honors degree from the National University of Singapore, where he worked for 14 years.

In recent years, Mohamed has added the consolidation of Islamic banking and finance principles within the broader framework of modern banking and finance concepts to his finance research interests. He and two others won a large Australian Research Council Linkage grant to research Islamic banking. His other continuing research interest is capital market studies, particularly of markets in the Asia-Pacific region, which has resulted in cited publications in the leading literature of finance and financial economics.

Mohamed served during 2004–2006 as the elected president of the 23-year-old Asian Finance Association and has consulted for international institutions and private banks and firms. He has worked and lectured in several major universities in the United States, Europe, Asia, and Australia.

CHAPTER 13

The View from the Top

Recommendations from a Superintendent of Banks

John D. Harrison*

TIPS FOR BANK DIRECTORS

1. The first tip concerns director education. Directors must understand their responsibilities—what is expected from them. They have legal duties that include selecting and maintaining competent management. They have to establish the policies, procedures, and business objectives for the bank. They have to oversee the performance of the bank to ensure that it is following their policies, procedures, and objectives. The objectives must include meeting the credit needs of the communities they serve and complying with all federal and state laws and procedures. However, always remember, board members do not run the bank; they just hire the management that does.
2. The directors must have access in advance of board meetings to all of the information that is needed to make decisions requiring their input. Along this line, board members should ask hard questions before voting on the issues.
3. Always maintain complete independence from management, with the interest of the bank coming first. This is especially true for audits, credit decisions, and risk management.

*This chapter summarizes an interview in November 2010 with John D. Harrison, Superintendent of Banks, Alabama State Department of Banking. Based on his vast experience as a bank regulator and as a banker, John was asked to give some tips for bank directors, borrowers, and investors in banks.

4. Know the current and expected capital requirements of the bank. Have a plan to raise new capital in a timely manner as needed.
5. Liquidity management in today's economic environment is a critical issue for banks. This includes both on-balance-sheet and off-balance-sheet sources that can be available when needed. Have a plan to meet these needs.
6. Have policies and procedures in place that allow the bank to grow and have reasonable returns.
7. Avoid any and all conflicts of interest that could cause possible preferential treatment of insiders. It is important to understand that every decision made by you, as a director, has both civil and possibly criminal liabilities.
8. Continuing education is essential for bank directors about new banking laws and regulations, accounting issues, and other developments affecting banks. This includes the Federal Deposit Insurance Corporation's (FDIC's) Regional Directors' and Officers' College, in-house training programs, and other sources.

TIPS FOR BORROWERS

1. Each bank is different. Some banks specialize in particular types of loans, while others offer a wide array of products and services. Prospective borrowers should seek banks with the expertise and knowledge that meet their needs.
2. Banking relationships are important. Does the loan officer understand your financial needs?
3. What are the terms of the loan (fees, interest rates, covenants, assignment of deeds, collateral, insurance)?
4. What about contingency plans if problems occur?
5. What happens if the bank has regulatory problems?

TIPS FOR INVESTORS

1. As previously noted, each bank is different. What type of assets does the bank hold? What geographic area does the bank serve?
2. Who are the major stockholders? Although it is hard to determine as an outside investor, what is the management style of the bank?
3. Who is on the board of directors? Do they have knowledge and expertise in banking?
4. What is the bank's financial performance (earnings, capital, liquidity, dividends) compared with its peers? And how has it done in previous recessions?

5. What relationships does the bank have with its customers, community, employees, and regulators?

WHAT LIES AHEAD

The current economic crisis, which has hit the financial industry particularly hard, has been a real education for not only bankers and bank directors but also borrowers and stockholders. The banks that have not fared well during the difficult times all exhibit similar characteristics. They are characterized by boards of directors that have not exercised the prudence and sound judgment discussed here. They have deferred to the decisions of a few to the detriment of many and the safety and soundness of the institution they pledged to protect. Bankers lost sight of what risk means, and borrowers were caught up in the euphoria of cheap credit by overextending themselves far beyond their ability to recover. Unfortunately, the stockholders of these institutions were the big losers. They watched their investment evaporate as the financial condition of the bank they were encouraged to buy stock in crumbled. The good banks, on the other hand, have weathered the storm well. Their board members are staunchly independent; they question everything, especially why the bank should take exorbitant risks to chase unrealistic yields; and they recognize the value of a strong capital position and the role it plays in shaping the institution's strategic plans as well as its future. These banks have proven they are grounded in their service to the communities they represent. They will remain strong and will be the leaders in the exciting and challenging financial times we face.

■ ■ ■

John D. Harrison has been Superintendent of Banks, Alabama State Department of Banking, since 2005. The State Banking Department regulates state-chartered banks and trust companies, nondepository lenders, and mortgage loan originators, among other duties. Alabama's State Banking Department is fifth in the nation based on the number of assets under supervision.

John also serves as co-chairman of the Alabama Rural Action Commission. From 2003 to 2005, he was the director for the Alabama Department of Economic and Community Affairs. Prior to working for the State of Alabama, John was president and chief executive officer of First Citizens Bank of Luverne, Alabama. In addition, he is the owner and president of Crenshaw Land and Timber Company, and he served as mayor of Luverne (1988–2003). John is a graduate of Troy University and Louisiana State University's Graduate School of Banking.

Notes

The URLs and web sites listed in the Notes were correct at the time the book was written. However, some URLs and web sites changed over time and may no longer be valid.

Preface

1. For example, Barclays Group US Inc, a bank holding company in the United States, is owned by Barclays PLC in the United Kingdom. Barclays operates in more than 50 countries. Similarly, Taunus Corporation is the North American subsidiary bank holding company owned by Germany's Deutsche Bank AG. It has a presence in more than 70 countries.

CHAPTER 1 Lessons Learned from Banking Crises

1. Liaquat Ahamed, *Lords of Finance* (New York: Penguin, 2009), 4.
2. Ibid.
3. Bank of America. 2009. "About Bank of America Corporation," *Bank of America Corporation 2008 Annual Report*, Bank of America Corporation did not provide an exact number of foreign countries in which it has offices.
4. Top 50 BHCs (as of 3/31/09), National Information Center, www.ffiec.gov/nicpubweb/nicweb/Top50Form.aspx.
5. U.S. Census Bureau, *Statistical Abstract of the United States 2009,* Table 2, Population: 1960–2007, 2008.
6. Data are from the U.S. Census Bureau, *Statistical Abstract of the United States 2009* and *Statistical Abstract of the United States 1995.*
7. Code of Federal Regulations: Title 12: Banks and Banking: PART 204—Reserve Requirements of Depository Institutions (Regulation D).
   (1) *Depository institution* means:
      (i) Any insured bank as defined in section 3 of the Federal Deposit Insurance Act (12 U.S.C. 1813(h)) or any bank that is eligible to apply to become an insured bank under section 5 of such Act (12 U.S.C. 1815)
      (ii) Any savings bank or mutual savings bank as defined in section 3 of the Federal Deposit Insurance Act (12 U.S.C. 1813(f), (g))
      (iii) Any insured credit union as defined in section 101 of the Federal Credit Union Act (12 U.S.C. 1752(7)) or any credit union that is eligible to

apply to become an insured credit union under section 201 of such Act (12 U.S.C. 1781)

(iv) Any member as defined in section 2 of the Federal Home Loan Bank Act (12 U.S.C. 1422(4))

(v) Any insured institution as defined in section 401 of the National Housing Act (12 U.S.C. 1724(a)) or any institution which is eligible to apply to become an insured institution under section 403 of such Act (12 U.S.C. 1726)

8. Federal National Mortgage Association, SEC Form 10-Q, March 31, 2009, 1.
9. Financial Crisis Inquiry Commission, "Securitization and the Mortgage Crisis," Preliminary Staff Report, April 7, 2010.
10. They acquired a large amount of subprime and Alt-A mortgages. These terms are defined later in the article.
11. Text from Ginnie Mae, "Who We Are...," www.ginniemae.gov/about/about.asp?section=about.
12. For additional information about the FHLBs, see their web page: www.fhlbanks.com.
13. Morton L. Bech and Tara Rice, "Profits and Balance Sheet Developments at U.S. Commercial Banks in 2008," *Federal Reserve Bulletin,* June 2009, A63, A71.
14. www.fdic.gov/news/news/speeches/chairman/spjan1410.html#_ftn1.
15. Board of Governors of the Federal Reserve System, "Selected Interest Rates," Release H.15.
16. For a listing of Sovereign Wealth Funds, see the Sovereign Wealth Fund Institute: www.swfinstitute.org/fund-rankings/.
17. The term *shadow banking* was first used by Paul McCulley in a speech at the Kansas City Federal Reserve Bank's annual conference in Jackson Hole, Wyoming, 2007.
18. Zoltran Pozsar, Tobias Adrian, Adam Ashcraft, and Haely Boesky, "Shadow Banking," Federal Reserve Bank of New York Staff Report No. 458, July 2010.
19. Financial Crisis Inquiry Commission, "Shadow Banking and the Financial Crisis," Preliminary Staff Report, May 4, 2010, 4, http://fcic-static.law.stanford.edu/cdn_media/fcic-reports/2010-0505-Shadow-Banking.pdf.
20. Darryl E. Getter, Mark Jickling, Marc Labonte, and Edward V. Murphy, "Financial Crisis? The Liquidity Crunch of 2007," CRS Report for Congress, September 21, 2007.
21. For additional information about FICO credit scores, see: www.myfico.com/CreditEducation/. FICO is a product of the Fair Isaac Corporation. FICO scores range from 300 to 850. The higher the score, the lower the credit risk.
22. Fannie Mae News Release, "Fannie Mae Announces 2005 Conforming Loan Limit of $359,650," February 1, 2005, www.fanniemae.com/newsreleases/2005/3445.jhtml?p=Media&s=News+Releases.
23. For data on housing prices, see the S&P/Case-Shiller Home Price Indices, www.standardandpoors.com/indices/sp-case-shiller-home-price-indices/en/us/?indexId=spusa-cashpidff–p-us—.

24. Federal Reserve Bank of Richmond, "Markets, Trends, and Statistics, First Quarter 2009. US Residential Mortgage Delinquency Rates Data Seasonally Adjusted, 1998:Q1–2009:Q1," www.richmondfed.org/banking/markets_trends_and_statistics/trends/pdf/delinquency_and_foreclosure_rates.pdf.
25. Financial Crisis Regulatory Commission, op. cit. (footnote #9).
26. Additional discussion of CDS can be found in Chapter 5.
27. "Table 19: Amounts Outstanding of Over-the-Counter (OTC) Derivatives," *BIS Quarterly Review,* June 2009, A103; "Table 19: Amounts Outstanding of Over-the-Counter (OTC) Derivatives, *BIS Quarterly Review,* June 2007, A103.
28. Board of Governors of the Federal Reserve System, Federal Reserve Press Release, September 16, 2008 (re AIG), www.federalreserve.gov/newsevents/press/other/20080916a.htm.
29. Robert C. Merton, "Observations on the Financial Crisis: Systemic Risk, Financial Innovation, Models, and Regulatory Recommendations," presentation at the Allied Social Science Associations meeting, Atlanta, GA, January 3, 2010.
30. Harry M. Markowitz, "Modern Portfolio Theory: Financial Engineering, and Their Role in Financial Crises," *Conference Proceedings Quarterly* (CFA Institute), December 2009, 1–6.
31. Ray Ball, "The Global Financial Crises and the Efficient Market Hypothesis: What Have We Learned?" *Journal of Applied Corporate Finance* 21, no. 4 (Fall 2009): 8–16.
32. Richard W Fisher, President, Federal Reserve Bank of Dallas, "The Egocentricity of the Present," remarks before a Federal Reserve Bank of Dallas community forum, San Antonio, Texas, April 9, 2008.
33. 12 U.S.C. 1831f(g)(1)(A); 12 C.F.R. 337.6(a)(2); FDIC Advisory Opinion, "Brokered Deposits: Are Funds Deposited in a Special Reserve Bank Account for the Exclusive Benefit of Customers Brokered Deposits under Sections 29 and 29A of the FDI Act," Valerie J. Best, Counsel. FDIC—94—39, August 17, 1994.
34. Claudio Borio, "Ten Propositions about Liquidity Crisis," (BIS working papers no. 293, November 2009), 1.
35. Office of the Comptroller of the Currency, "Request for Comment on Proposed Interagency Liquidity Guidance," *OCC Bulletin* 2009-21. The guidance can be found in the *Federal Register* 74, no. 127 (Monday, July 6, 2009): 32035.
36. Board of Governors of the Federal Reserve System, "Report Pursuant to Section 129 of the Emergency Economic Stabilization Act of 2008: Bridge Loan to the Bear Stearns Companies Inc. Through JPMorgan Chase Bank, N.A.," March 14, 2008, www.federalreserve.gov/monetarypolicy/files/129bearstearnsbridgeloan.pdf.
37. President's Working Group on Financial Markets. "Hedge Funds, Leverage, and the Lessons of Long-Term Capital Management," Report of the President's Working Group on Financial Markets, April 1999, 23.
38. "Strengthening the Resilience of the Banking Sector—Consultative Document," Bank for International Settlements, December 2009, www.bis.org/publ/bcbs164.htm.
39. FDIC Quarterly Banking Profile, Commercial Bank Performance, Table III-A, FDIC Insured Commercial Banks, Third Quarter, 2009.

40. U.S. Census Bureau, *Statistical Abstract of the United States 2009,* Table 729.
41. FDIC Quarterly Banking Profile (2009), Table III-A, All FDIC Insured Institutions, First Quarter 2009.
42. Amir E. Khandani, Andrew W. Lo., and Robert C. Merton, "Systemic Risk and the Refinancing Ratchet Effect," MIT Sloan Research Paper No. 4750-09; Harvard Business School Finance Working Paper No. 1472892, September 15, 2009. Available at SSRN: http://ssrn.com/abstract=1472892.
43. Net Noncore Funding Dependence Ratio ("NNCFD Ratio") and Short-Term Net Noncore Funding Dependence Ratio ("STNNCFD Ratio") are reported in the Uniform Bank Performance Report; for additional analysis on this topic, see Thomas B. King, Daniel A. Nuxoll, and Timothy J. Yeager, "Are the Causes of Bank Distress Changing? Can Researchers Keep Up?" (FDIC CFR Working Paper No. 2005-03, 2005), www.fdic.gov/bank/analytical/cfr/2005/wp2005/CFRWP_2005-03_nuxoll1.pdf.
44. FDIC Quarterly Banking Profile, Third Quarter 2009, Table 1-A.
45. Central Intelligence Agency, *The World Fact Book/Iceland* (2009), www.cia.gov/library/publications/the-world-factbook/geos/ic.html.
46. Peter Gumble, "Iceland: The Country That Became a Hedge Fund," CNNMoney.com., December 1, 2008. http://money.cnn.com/2008/12/01/magazines/fortune/iceland_gumbel.fortune/.
47. Brian O'Keefe, "The Man behind 2009's Biggest Bank Bust," CNNMoney.com, October 12, 2009.
48. Colonial BancGroup, *2008 Annual Report,* 2009.
49. Ibid., 51.
50. Federal Reserve, "Charge-Off and Delinquency Rates on Loans and Leases at Commercial Banks," Federal Reserve Statistical Release, Third Quarter 2009.
51. *Delinquency rate* refers to loans that are at least one payment past due, but it does not include loans in the process of foreclosure.
52. Federal Reserve Bank of Richmond, "U.S. Residential Mortgage Delinquency Rates," 2009, www.richmondfed.org/banking/markets_trends_and_statistics/trends/pdf/delinquency_and_foreclosure_rates.pdf.
53. Board of Governors of the Federal Reserve System, "Federal Reserve Statistical Release H 15. Selected Interest Rates, Historical Data, 2009," www.federalreserve.gov/releases/h15/data.htm.
54. FDIC, "Quarterly Banking Profile, All Institutions Performance, Third Quarter 2009," www2.fdic.gov/qbp/2009sep/qbpall.html.
55. Comptroller of the Currency, "OCC's Quarterly Report on Bank Trading and Derivatives Activities, Second Quarter 2009," www.occ.gov/topics/capital-markets/financial-markets/trading/derivatives/dq209.pdf.
56. Lorenzo Bini Smaghi, Member of the Executive Board of the European Central Bank, "What Has the Financial Crisis Taught Us? The Global Dimension and International Policy Cooperation," Speech at the 21st Century Forum 2010, Beijing, September 7, 2010. *BIS Review,* 114/2010.
57. Benton E. Gup, "International Banking Crises: The Real Estate Connection," in *International Banking Crises: Large-Scale Failures, Massive Government Intervention* (Westport, CT: Quorum, 1999).

58. Chip Cummins, Dana Cimilluca, and Sara Schaefer Muñoz, "Dubai's Woes Shake U.A. E., Region," *Wall Street Journal,* November 27, 2009, C1, C3; Nikhil Lorade and Summer Said, "Dubai Discusses Debt Revamp," *Wall Street Journal,* December 1, 2009, C1, C3.
59. Edward Fennell, "Dubai's Golden Sands Lose Their Lustre," TimesOnLine, December 10, 2009, business.timesonline.co.uk/tol/business/law/article6950725.ece.
60. Abu Dhabi is part of the UAE.
61. "Dubai's Debt Reckoning," *Wall Street Journal,* November 28–29, 2009, A14.
62. U.S. Census Bureau, "U.S. & World Population Clocks," www.census.gov/main/www/popclock.html.
63. U.S. Census Bureau, "National Population Projections Released 2008, Table 1, Projections of the Population and Components of Change for the United States: 2010 to 2050," www.census.gov/population/www/projections/summarytables.html.
64. William C. Hunter, George G. Kaufman, and Michael Pomerleano, *Asset Price Bubble: The Implications for Monetary, Regulatory and International Policies* (Cambridge, MA: MIT Press, 2003), xxv.

CHAPTER 2 The Economic Role of Financial Intermediaries

1. On July 21, 2010, President Barack Obama signed the Dodd-Frank Wall Street Reform and Consumer Protection Act into law, which, in part, permanently raises the current standard maximum deposit insurance amount (SMDIA) to $250,000.
2. United States General Accounting Office, "Risk-Focused Bank Examinations: Regulators of Large Banking Organizations Face Challenges," GAO/GGD-00-48, January 2000, p. 18; www.gao.gov/archive/2000/gg00048.pdf.
3. For additional information about FDIC insurance coverage, see www.fdic.gov/deposit/deposits/insured/basics.html.
4. "Alternative Financial Services, a Primer," *FDIC Quarterly* 3, no. 1 (2009).
5. Board of Governors of the Federal Reserve System, "Assets and Liabilities of Commercial Banks in the US-H8," Release, February 5, 2010.
6. The example and Figure 2.3 are based on Hyun Song Shin, "Financial Intermediation and the Post-Crisis Financial System" (BIS Working Papers No. 304, March 2001, p. 2).
7. Data for 1921 are from Board of Governors of the Federal Reserve System, *All-Bank Statistics, United States 1896–1959,* 33. Data for 2009 are from FDIC, *The FDIC Quarterly Banking Profile,* Fourth Quarter, 2009, Table IV-A.
8. FDIC, *History of the Eighties, Lessons for the Future,* vol. 1, 199.
9. Lisa M. DeFerrari and David E. Palmer, "Supervision of Large Complex Banking Organizations," *Federal Reserve Bulletin,* February 2001, 47.
10. Ibid., 50.

11. U.S. GAO, "Risk-Focused Bank Examinations," 11.
12. SIVs are a type of investment fund. For example, they can borrow short-term and lend long-term in asset-backed securities or other investments. The ABSs include, but are not limited to, mortgages and credit cards. Their investments can be segregated into various tranches of risk and maturities. SIVs are discussed in Chapter 5.
13. For additional information, see the National Information Center, www.ffiec.gov/nicpubweb/nicweb/Top50Form.aspx.
14. Bank of America, *Investor Fact Book,* Full Year 2009, p. 2; http://investor.bankofamerica.com.
15. For additional information, see JPMorgan Chase, www.jpmorganchase.com/corporate/About-JPMC/about-us.htm.
16. FDIC, "FDIC Quarterly Banking Profile, Second Quarter 2010, All FDIC Institutions," www2.fdic.gov/qbp/2010mar/grbook/QBPGR.pdf.
17. Eugene N. White, "Were Banks Special Intermediaries in Late Nineteenth Century America?" Review, Federal Reserve Bank of St. Louis, May–June 1998, 13–32.
18. Sheila Bair, "Remarks by FDIC Chairman Sheila Bair at the 45th Annual Bank Structure and Competition Conference," Chicago Federal Reserve Bank, Chicago, May 7, 2009.
19. Gary Gorton and Andrew Metrick, "Regulating the Shadow Banking System" (working paper, September 15, 2010), http://ssrn.com/abstract =1676947.
20. Ibid., 6.
21. Timothy J. Geithner, "Reducing Systemic Risk in a Dynamic Financial System," Remarks at the Economic Club of New York, Federal Reserve Bank of New York, June 9, 2008.
22. Ron J. Feldman and Mark Lueck, "Are Banks Really Dying This Time?" *The Region,* Federal Reserve Bank of Minneapolis, September 2007.
23. Nout Wellink, Chairman of the Bank for International Settlement, "Risk Management & Financial Stability—Basel II & Beyond," remarks at the GARP 2007 8th Annual Risk Management Convention, New York, February 27, 2007; Malcolm D. Knight, General Manager of the Bank of International Settlements, "Some Reflections on the Future of Originate-to-Distribute Model in the Context of the Current Financial Turmoil," Euro 50 Group Roundtable, London, April 21, 2008.
24. This section is based on the following articles: FDIC, "FDIC National Survey of Unbanked and Underbanked Households," December 2009; Christine Bradley, Susan Burhouse, Heather Gratton, and Rae Ann Miller, "Alternative Financial Services: A Primer," *FDIC Quarterly* 3, no. 1 (2009).

CHAPTER 3 The Evolving Legal Environment

1. This chapter is based, in part, on Benton E. Gup and James W. Kolari, *Commercial Banking, The Management of Risk, 3rd ed.* (Hoboken, NJ: John Wiley & Sons, 2004). Reprinted with permission of John Wiley & Sons, Inc.

2. National Information Center, "All Institution Types Defined," www.ffiec.gov/nicpubweb/Content/HELP/Institution%20Type%20Description.htm.
3. FDIC, "Historical Statistics on Banking, Index to Notes on Insured Commercial Banks," www2.fdic.gov/hsob/hsobnotes.asp.
4. Zoltran Pozsar, Tobias Adrian, Adam Ashcraft, and Haely Boesky, "Shadow Banking," Federal Reserve Bank of New York Staff Report No. 458, July 2010.
5. Ibid.
6. Ross M. Robertson, Comptroller of Bank Supervision, *A Historical Perspective* (Washington, DC: Office of the Comptroller of the Currency, 1995), 16.
7. Bills of exchange are a written order issued by the drawer instructing a second party, the drawee, to pay a stated amount of money on some date in the future.
8. An insured bank as defined in section 3(h) of the Federal Deposit Insurance Act [12 U.S.C. 1813 (h)].
9. Dodd-Frank Wall Street Reform and Consumer Protection Act (formerly referred to as H.R. 4173). The bill is named after Connecticut Senator Christopher Dodd and Massachusetts Rep. Barney Frank. The enrolled version of the bill is www.gpo.gov/fdsys/pkg/BILLS-111hr4173ENR/pdf/BILLS-111hr4173ENR.pdf. An enrolled bill is the final copy of a bill that has been passed in identical form by both houses. It must be certified by an officer of the house of origin (the Clerk of the House or the Secretary of the Senate) and then sent on for the signatures of the Speaker of the House, the President of the Senate, and the U.S. President. The text of the enrolled bill is identical to the public law.
10. Sheila Bair, Chairman, FDIC, "Implementing the Dodd-Frank Wall Street Reform and Consumer Protection Act," before the Committee on Banking, Housing, and Urban Affairs, U.S. Senate, September 30, 2010.
11. This has been referred to as the "Volcker Rule" because the concept of restricting banks from making certain kinds of proprietary trades, if they are not on behalf of their customers, was introduced by former Federal Reserve Chairman Paul Volcker.
12. Marc Steckel, Associate Director, Division of Insurance and Research, FDIC, "Statement on Executive Compensation Oversight after the Dodd-Frank Wall Street Reform and Consumer Protection Act of 2010" before the Committee on Financial Services, U.S. House of Representatives, September 24, 2010; www.fdic.gov/news/news/speeches/chairman/spsep2410.html.
13. This section is based, in part, on Benton E. Gup and James W. Kolari, *Commercial Banking: The Management of Risk,* 3rd ed. (Hoboken, NJ: John Wiley & Sons, 2005), Chapter 1.
14. For additional details, see FDIC, "Deposit Insurance Frequently Asked Questions," www.fdic.gov/edie/fdic_info.html.
15. SBV Financial Group, "About SBV Financial Group," http://ir.svb.com/; Emily Maltby, "Entrepreneurs Find Success with Specialty Lenders," *Wall Street Journal,* April 26, 2010, B8.
16. Bank of America, "Corporate Profile," http://investor.bankofamerica.com/phoenix.zhtml?c=71595&p=irol-irhome.
17. FDIC, "Quarterly Banking Profile Graph Book, Number of Institutions by Asset Concentration Group," December 31, 2009, www2.fdic.gov/QBP/grgraph.asp.

18. For additional information, see Benton E. Gup and Robert Brooks, *Interest Rate Risk Management: The Banker's Guide to Using Futures, Options, Swaps and Other Derivatives* (New York: McGraw-Hill, 1993); *Interest Rate Risk: Comptroller's Handbook* (Washington, DC: OCC, 1997).
19. This section is based, in part, on Benton E. Gup and James W. Kolari, *Commercial Banking: The Management of Risk,* 3rd ed. (Hoboken, NJ: John Wiley & Sons, 2005), Chapter 2.
20. For an overview of the Federal Reserve System, see *The Federal Reserve System: Purposes and Functions,* 9th ed. (Washington, DC: Board of Governors of the Federal Reserve System, 2005). Their powers have been expanded under the Dodd-Frank Act that is explained in Chapter 3.
21. Ibid., 59–60.
22. Ibid.
23. J. Seiberg, "Scrapped: Uniform 150-Day Rule for Writing Off Past-Due Loans," *American Banker*, February 11, 1999, 3.
24. BIS Mission Statement, www.bis.org/about/mission.htm.
25. C. J. Lindgren, G. Garcia, and M. I. Saal, *Bank Soundness and Macroeconomic Policy* (Washington, DC: International Monetary Fund, 1996).
26. G. Hanc, "The Banking Crises of the 1980s and Early 1990s: Summary and Implications," *FDIC Banking Review* 11, no. 1 (1998): 1–55.
27. Basel Committee on Banking Supervision's Core Principles, *Core Principles for Effective Banking Supervision* (Basel, Switzerland: Bank for International Settlement, Basel Committee on Banking Supervision, 1997).
28. Rieker Matthias, "Dimon: New Rules Will Cost Customers," *Wall Street Journal,* September 15, 2010, C17.
29. FDIC, "Historical Statistics on Banking: Index to Notes on Insured Commercial Banks," www2.fdic.gov/hsob/hsobnotes.asp.

CHAPTER 4 Asset/Liability Management

1. This chapter is based, in part, on Benton E. Gup and James W. Kolari, *Commercial Banking: The Management of Risk,* 3rd ed. (Hoboken, NJ: John Wiley & Co., 2004). Reprinted with permission of John Wiley & Sons, Inc.
2. No adjustments are made for income that is tax exempt. FDIC, "Fourth Quarter 2009," *FDIC Quarterly Banking Profile* 4, no. 1 (2010): 20.
3. Ibid., Table 1-A.
4. Historical data on market rates of interest rates can be found in Board of Governors of the Federal Reserve System, "Federal Reserve Statistical Release H.15—Selected Interest Rates," www.federalreserve.gov/releases/h15/data.htm.
5. Suzanne L. Clair, Alison T. Touhey, and Lemoine J. Tuberville, "Nowhere to Go but Up: Managing Interest Rate Risk in a Low-Rate Environment," *Supervisory Insights, FDIC* (Winter 2009): 3–15.
6. FDIC, "FDIC Issues Interest Rate Risk Advisory," Press Release, January 7, 2010, www.fdic.gov/news/news/press/2010/pr1002.pdf.

7. FDIC, "Certificates of Deposit: Tips for Savers," www.fdic.gov/deposit/deposits/certificate/index.html.
8. For additional information, see www.fdic.gov/regulations/resources/rates/. Or go to the FDIC web site and type "Weekly Rate Caps" in the advanced search box.
9. For additional information, see Federal Financial Institutions Examination Council (FFIEC), "UBPR User's Guide," www.ffiec.gov/ubprguide.htm.
10. Christine M. Bradley and Lynn Shibut, "The Liability Structure of FDIC-Insured Institutions: Changes and Implications," *FDIC Banking Review*, 2006, www.fdic.gov/bank/analytical/banking/2006sep/article1/.
11. *Federal funds* refers to the purchase or sale of excess reserves of banks that are members of the Federal Reserve System.
12. The Federal Home Loan Bank System provides liquidity to member institutions that hold mortgages in their portfolios and facilitates the financing of home mortgages by making low-cost loans, called *advances*, to those members.
13. *Primary credit* refers to loans made by the Federal Reserve to generally sound depository institutions on a very short-term basis, typically overnight, at a rate above the Federal Open Market Committee (FOMC) target rate for federal funds. For additional information, see "The Federal Reserve Discount Window," www.frbdiscountwindow.org/discountwindowbook.cfm?hdrID=14&dtlID=43#primary.
14. UBPRs are publicly available for all banks at the FFIEC web site: www.ffiec.gov/. They contain detailed information concerning bank performance and other information. See the "UBPR Users Guide" for definitions of terms, www.ffiec.gov/ubprguide.htm. UPBRs are discussed further in Chapter 9.
15. Ally Bank, Midvale, Utah, RSSD 3284070.
16. Top 50 Bank Holding Companies, March 31, 2010, www.ffiec.gov/nicpubweb/nicweb/Top50Form.aspx.
17. Suzanne L. Clair, Alison T. Touhey, and Lemoine J. Tuberville, "Nowhere to Go but Up:Managing Interest Rate Risk in a Low-Rate Environment," *Supervisory Insights, FDIC* (Winter 2009): 6.
18. "Interagency Statement on Funding and Liquidity Risk Management," Office of the Comptroller of the Currency, Board of Governors of the Federal Reserve System, FDIC, Office of Thrift Supervision, National Credit Union Administration, *Federal Register* 75, no. 54 (March 22, 2010), Notices, 13656–13666. For a discussion of the liquidity crisis, see Claudio Borio, "Ten Propositions about Liquidity Crisis" (BIS Working Papers No. 293, November 2009), 1.
19. Ben S. Bernanke, "Reflections on a Year of Crisis," at the Federal Reserve Bank of Kansas City's Annual Economic Symposium, Jackson Hole, Wyoming, August 21, 2009. www.federalreserve.gov/newsevents/speech/bernanke20090821a.htm.
20. Ben S. Bernanke, "Causes of the Recent Financial and Economic Crisis," before the Financial Crisis Inquiry Commission, Washington, DC, September 2, 2010. federalreserve.gov/newsevents/testimony/bernanke20100902a.htm.
21. Ibid.

22. Ibid. Also see Gary B. Gorton, "The Panic of 2007," paper presented at "Maintaining Stability in a Changing Financial System," a symposium sponsored by the Federal Reserve Bank of Kansas City, held in Jackson Hole, Wyoming, August 21–23, 2008; the paper is available at www.kansascityfed.org/publications/research/escp/escp-2008.cfm.
23. Kathy M. Kristof and Andrea Chang, "Federal Regulators Seize Crippled IndyMac Bank," *Los Angeles Times,* July 12, 2008, http://articles.latimes.com/2008/jul/12/business/fi-indymac12.
24. Sheila C. Bair, "Systemically Important Institutions, and the Issue of 'Too Big to Fail,'" before the Financial Crisis Inquiry Commission, Washington, DC, September 2, 2010. www.fcic.gov/hearings/pdfs/2010-0902-Bair.pdf.
25. Statement of John Corston, Acting Deputy Director, Complex Financial Institution Branch, Division of Supervision and Consumer Protection, FDIC on "Systemically Important Institutions and the Issue of 'Too Big To Fail," before the Financial Crisis Inquiry Commission, Washington, DC, September 1, 2010. www.fdic.gov/news/news/speeches/chairman/spsep0110.html.
26. There are some accounting issues involving whether repos should have been counted as "sales" or "borrowing" and balance sheet leverage. For additional information, see Susanne Craig and Mike Spector, "Repos Played a Key Role in Lehman's Demise," *Wall Street Journal,* March 13, 2010; Michael Rapoport, "Bank of America, Citigroup Incorrectly Hid Billions in Repo Debt," *Wall Street Journal,* May 26, 2010.
27. Basel III is discussed in Chapter 8. The LCR is discussed in John Walsh, Acting Comptroller of the Currency, Testimony before the Committee on Banking, Housing, and Urban Affairs, United States Senate, September 30, 2010.
28. Based on an article by Eugene A. Bonte and Gregg A. Dieguez, "Spread Management: How to Maintain Profitability," *Savings and Loan News,* November 1979, 54–59.
29. Frederick R. Macaulay, *The Movements of Interest Rate, Bond Yields and Stock Prices in the United States since 1856* (New York: National Bureau of Economic Research, 1938). For bank's use of duration, see George G. Kaufman, "Measuring and Managing Interest Rate Risk: A Primer," *Economic Perspectives, Federal Reserve Bank of Chicago* (August–September 1984): 16–29.
30. Board of Governors of the Federal Reserve System "Advisory on Interest Rate Risk Management," Board of Governors of the Federal Reserve System, January 6, 2010.
31. *Principles for Sound Stress Testing Practices and Supervision* (Basel: Switzerland: Bank for International Settlements, 2009), www.bis.org/publ/bcbs155.pdf.
32. Ibid., 4.

CHAPTER 5 Hedging and Risk Management

1. The definition of *derivative* and many of the other terms used in this chapter are taken from the "Glossary of Terms," used in the "OCC's Quarterly

Report on Bank Trading and Derivatives Activities," Fourth Quarter 2009, www.occ.treas.gov/ftp/release/2010-33a.pdf.

2. FDIC, "Quarterly Banking Profile," Full Year 2009, Table III-A.
3. OCC, "OCC's Quarterly Report on Bank Trading and Derivatives Activities," Fourth Quarter 2009.
4. United States General Accounting Office, "Financial Derivatives: Actions Needed to Protect the Financial System," GAO/GGD-94-133, May 1994; "Overview on Derivatives," Preliminary Staff Report, Financial Crisis Inquiry Commission, June 29, 2010.
5. Ibid. "Overview on Derivatives."
6. FDIC, "Advisory on Interest Rate Risk Management," January 6, 2010.
7. "OCC's Quarterly Report on Bank Trading and Derivatives Activities," 4.
8. See Miguel A. Segoviano and Manmohan Singh, "Counterparty Risk in the Over-the-Counter Derivatives Market" (IMF Working Paper WP/08/258, November 2008).
9. Benton E. Gup, *Too Big to Fail: Policies and Practices in Government Bailouts* (Westport, CT: Praeger, 2004), Chapter 2.
10. Greg Robb, Minutes of the Board of Governors of the Federal Reserve System, March 14, 2008, quoted "Bear Stearns Too Interconnected to Fail, Fed Says," *MarketWatch,* June 27, 2008, www.marketwatch.com/story/fed-believed-bear-stearns-was-too-interconnected-to-fail.
11. Ibid.
12. Commodity Futures Trading Commission, "CFTC Glossary," www.cftc.gov/ConsumerProtection/EducationCenter/CFTCGlossary/glossary_b.html.
13. The basic definitions presented here are from the CMEGroup, "Glossary," www.cmegroup.com/education/glossary.html; and the Bank for International Settlements, Julian S. Alworth, "The Valuation of US Dollar Interest Rate Swaps," (BIS Economic Paper No. 35, January 1993), www.bis.org/publ/econ35.pdf.
14. The legal definition of a *swap agreement* in the Gramm-Leach-Bliley Act, Sec. 206, is: "For purposes of subsection (a)(6), the term "swap agreement" means any individually negotiated contract, agreement, warrant, note, or option that is based, in whole or in part, on the value of, any interest in, or any quantitative measure or the occurrence of any event relating to, one or more commodities, securities, currencies, interest or other rates, indices, or other assets, but does not include any other identified banking product, as defined in paragraphs (1) through (5) of subsection (a)." www.sec.gov/about/laws/glba.pdf.
15. For additional information, see Benton E. Gup and Robert Brooks, *Interest Rate Risk Management: A Banker's Guide to Using Futures, Options, Swaps and Other Financial Instruments* (Chicago: Probus, 1993).
16. Susanne Walker, "Ten-Year Swap Spread Turns Negative on Renewed Demand for Risk," *Bloomberg BusinessWeek,* March 23, 2010, com/news/2010-03-23/ten-year-swap-spread-drops-to-low-on-renewed.
17. The example is from the United Kingdom's HM Revenue & Customs, "CTM72890—Financial instruments: overview: currency swap: example," www.hmrc.gov.uk/manuals/ctmanual/ctm72890.htm.

18. William K. Sjostrom, "The AIG Bailout," *Washington and Lee Law Review* 66 (2009): 943–991, http://ssrn.com/abstract=1346552.
19. Ibid.
20. Alan Greenspan, Testimony before the Senate Banking Committee, Financial Crisis Inquiry Commission, Wednesday, April 7, 2010.
21. For additional information, see the Federal Housing Finance Agency (FHFA), which regulates Fannie Mae, Freddie Mac, and the 12 Federal Home Loan Banks: www.fhfa.gov/; www.fanniemae.com/kb/index?page=home; and www.freddiemac.com/.
22. For additional information, see Ginnie Mae, www.ginniemae.gov/.
23. John Krainer, "Recent Developments in Mortgage Finance," *FRSBSF Economic Letter,* 2009-33, October 26, 2009.
24. The *spot yield* is the annualized discount rate and the yield to maturity on the most recently issued Treasury securities with a designated maturity. For additional information, see Interest Rate Options, CBOE, www.cboe.com/LearnCenter/pdf/IRO.pdf.
25. See the Commodities Futures Trading Commission's monthly reports on "Bank Participation Reports in Futures and Options Markets," www.cftc.gov/MarketReports/BankParticipationReports/index.htm.
26. For additional information about the CMEGroup, see www.cmegroup.com/company/index.html.
27. For additional information about the CFTC, see www.cftc.gov/About/MissionResponsibilities/index.htm.
28. For additional information about Treasury futures and options, see CBOT Treasury Futures and Options—Reference Guide, 2006, www.insigniafutures.com/docs/CBOT_Treasuries.pdf.
29. CMEGroup, "The U.S. Treasury Futures Delivery Process," www.cmegroup.com/trading/interest-rates/files/CL-100_TFDPBrochureFINAL.pdf.
30. Julie L. Williams, Chief Counsel and First Senior Deputy Comptroller, Office of the Comptroller of the Currency, Testimony before the Committee on Banking, Housing, and Urban Affairs, United States Senate, September 15, 2010. She notes that covered bonds do not appear to fall within the definition of ABSs under federal securities law.
31. Michael H. Krimminger, Deputy to the Chairman, FDIC, "Covered Bonds: Potential Uses and Regulatory Issues," Statement to the Committee on Banking, Housing, and Urban Affairs, United States Senate, September 15, 2010.
32. FDIC Press Releases—PR-85-2008: "JPMorgan Chase Acquires Banking Operations of Washington Mutual," September 25, 2008, www.fdic.gov/news/news/press/2008/pr08085.html.
33. Steven L. Schwarcz, "The Conundrum of Covered Bonds," Working Paper, August 31, 2010.
34. Chairman Ben S. Bernanke, "The Future of Mortgage Finance in the United States," Speech at the UC Berkeley/UCLA Symposium: The Mortgage Meltdown, the Economy, and Public Policy, Berkeley, California, October 31, 2008,

www.federalreserve.gov/newsevents/speech/bernanke20081031a.htm. For additional information, see Diana Hancock and Wayne Passmore, "Three Mortgage Innovations for Enhancing the American Mortgage Market and Promoting Financial Stability," preliminary draft presented at the UC Berkeley/UCLA symposium: The Mortgage Meltdown, the Economy, and Public Policy, Berkeley, California, October 31, 2008.

35. This section is based on Basel Committee on Banking Supervision, "Report of Special Purpose Entities," September 2009. Executive Summary and Overview.
36. Ibid., 79–84. For additional details, see FDIC Press Release, "FDIC Board Finalizes Regulatory Capital Rule for Statements of Financial Accounting Standards," December 16, 2009. Also see OCC, Department of the Treasury; Board of Governors of the Federal Reserve System; FDIC; and OTS, Department of the Treasury, ACTION: Final rule. Risk-Based Capital Guidelines; Capital Adequacy Guidelines; Capital Maintenance: Regulatory Capital; Impact of Modifications to Generally Accepted Accounting Principles; Consolidation of Asset-Backed Commercial Paper Programs; and Other Related Issues, Final Rule," December 16, 2009, www.fdic.gov/news/board/DEC152009no2.pdf.
37. Governor Susan Schmidt Bies, "Enterprise Risk Management and Mortgage Lending," Speech at the National Credit Union Administration 2007 Risk Mitigation Summit, January 11, 2007.
38. Most of the risks listed in the table are from U.S. General Accounting Office, "Risk-Focused Bank Examinations: Regulators of Large Banks Face Challenges," GAO/GGD-00-48, January 2000, p. 18, www.gao.gov/archive/2000/gg00048.pdf.
39. COSO, "Enterprise Risk Management: Integrated Framework," Executive Summary, September 2004. For additional information about ERM, see John Fraser and Betty J. Simkins, Eds., *Enterprise Risk Management: Today's Leading Research and Best Practices for Tomorrow's Executives* (New York: John Wiley & Sons, 2010).
40. Ibid.
41. Ibid.
42. Senior Supervisors Group, "Observations on Risk Management Practices during Recent Market Turbulence," Federal Reserve Bank of New York, March 6, 2008, www.newyorkfed.org/newsevents/news/banking/2008/SSG_Risk_Mgt_doc_final.pdf.

CHAPTER 6 Commercial and Industrial Loans

1. This chapter is based, in part, on Benton E. Gup and James W. Kolari, *Commercial Banking: The Management of Risk,* 3rd ed. (Hoboken, NJ: John Wiley & Sons, 2004). Reprinted with permission of John Wiley & Sons, Inc.
2. See the Board of Governors of the Federal Reserve System, "Survey of Terms of Business Lending," Federal Reserve Statistical Release E.2, March 24, 2010, www.federalreserve.gov/releases/e2/current/default.htm.

3. Interest rate data are from the Board of Governors of the Federal Reserve System, Federal Reserve Statistical Release H.15, "Selected Interest Rates, May 24, 2010," www.federalreserve.gov/releases/h15/current/.
4. Timothy F. Geithner, Treasury Secretary, Remarks before the American Enterprise Institute on Financial Reform, March 22, 2010, www.treas.gov/press/release/tg600.htm.
5. Board of Governors of the Federal Reserve System, "Survey of Terms of Business Lending."
6. Board of Governors of the Federal Reserve System, "Shared National Credits Program 2010 Review," September 2010.
7. FICO: Fair Isaac Corp. is traded on the NYSE under the symbol FICO.
8. For additional information about FICO scores, see Chapter 7 and the Fair Isaac web site, www.fico.com/en/Pages/default.aspx.
9. www.onlinecheck.com/business_funding/business_loans.html.
10. The limits apply to a bank's total unimpaired capital and surplus, which equals their tier 1 and tier 2 capital. For additional details, see 12 USC 84.
11. SNCs are discussed in Chapter 11.
12. "FDIC's Participation in the Shared National Credit Program," Report No. AUD-07-012, September 2007. This definition applies to banks supervised by a federal banking agency (e.g., OCC, FDIC); www.fdicoig.gov/reports07/07-012-508.shtml.
13. Kenneth Temkin and Roger C. Kormendi, "An Exploration of a Secondary Market for Small Business Loans," SBA Office of Advocacy (SBAHQ-01-C-0150), April 2003, www.sba.gov/advo/research/rs227_tot.pdf.
14. U.S. Small Business Administration, "2009 Recovery Act: Frequently Asked Questions," www.sba.gov/sites/default/files/Virginia_Newsletter_Special_FY_2009.pdf.
15. For additional information about the SBA resources for small business lending, see www.sba.gov/localresources/index.html.
16. See Board of Governors, "Survey of Terms of Business Lending."
17. The *Wall Street Journal* section on "Bonds, Rates & Yields," gives the current prime rate, LIBOR, and other interest rates.
18. For information about SBA loan guarantee programs, see www.sba.gov/financialassistance/borrowers/guaranteed/.
19. For additional details, see Internal Revenue Code Ruling 55-540.
20. The continuous yield is determined by calculating $e^{in} = (2.718)^{0.12 \times 1} = 12.7483\%$, where e = Euler's constant and where e^{in} is the limit of $(1 + i/m)^{nm}$.
21. Risk-based capital weights are not considered here because commercial loans have a 100 percent risk weighting.
22. If the increased equity results in the bank being perceived by investors as less risky, the cost of borrowing may be reduced, which may lower the WACC.
23. For additional discussion of the use of the Z (zeta) score in loan pricing, see Edward I. Altman, "Valuation, Loss Reserves, and Pricing of Commercial Loans," *Journal of Commercial Lending* (August 1993): 8–25.

CHAPTER 7 Real Estate and Consumer Lending

1. This chapter is based, in part, on Benton E. Gup and James W. Kolari, *Commercial Banking: The Management of Risk,* 3rd ed. (Hoboken, NJ: John Wiley & Sons, 2004). Reprinted with permission of John Wiley & Sons, Inc.
2. Remarks by FDIC Chairman Sheila C. Bair to the Wharton School, University of Pennsylvania, International Housing Finance Program, Philadelphia, June 18, 2010.
3. For additional data and information on housing, see U.S. Census Bureau, Housing Topics, www.census.gov/hhes/www/housing.html.
4. Fannie Mae and Freddie Mac were placed into conservatorship on September 6, 2008. The Federal Housing Finance Agency (FHFA), their former regulator, was appointed the conservator.
5. See the FHL Bank systems web site for additional details: www.fhlbanks.com/.
6. "Guidelines for Real Estate Lending Policies," Office of the Comptroller of the Currency (OCC) *Advisory Letter*, AL2003-7, August 8, 2003; "Credit Risk Management for Home Equity Lending," OCC 2005-22; www.occ.treas.gov/ftp/bulletin/2005-22a.pdf. Also see 12 CFR 34, Subpart D, Appendix A.
7. FDIC Quarterly Banking Profile, First Quarter 2010, "Loan Portfolio Composition," www2.fdic.gov/qbp/2010mar/grbookbw/QBPGRBW.pdf.
8. For additional information about private mortgage insurance, see the Federal Reserve Bank of San Francisco, "Consumer Information: Private Mortgage Insurance," www.frbsf.org/publications/consumer/pmi.html.
9. For information about current mortgage rates and terms, see www.bankrate.com/ and www.lendingtree.com/.
10. For additional information about COFI, see the Federal Reserve Bank of San Francisco, "COFI: Frequently Asked Questions," www.fhlbsf.com/cofi/faq.asp#0.
11. The mortgage rates are from www.bankrate.com. Data are the average overnight rates for June 18, 2010.
12. Fannie Mae Loan Limits, www.fanniemae.com/aboutfm/loanlimits.jhtml.
13. For additional information about FICO credit scores, see www.myfico.com/CreditEducation/. FICO is a product of the Fair Isaac Corporation. FICO scores range from 300 to 850. The higher the score, the lower the credit risk.
14. For additional information, see the National Reverse Mortgage Lenders Association (NRMLA), www.reversemortgage.org/.
15. Texas Constitution, Article XIV, Section 50(a)(6)(B), commonly known as the home equity section.
16. Federal Reserve Statistical Release, "Consumer Credit," G19, June 7, 2010, www.federalreserve.gov/releases/g19/20100607/.
17. Ibid.
18. Also see Benton E. Gup, *Bank Failures in the Major Trading Countries of the World: Causes and Remedies* (Westport, CT: Quorum, 1998).
19. For current data on auto financing, see Federal Reserve Statistical Release G.20, "Finance Companies," www.federalreserve.gov/releases/g20/current/g20.htm.

20. Jane J. Kim, "A Car Loan That Outlasts Your Car," *Wall Street Journal,* September 30, 2003, D1, D4.
21. Credit cards are defined by Regulation Z and in 12 CFR 226.2 (a)(15).
22. Ben Woolsey and Matt Schulz, "Credit Card Statistics, Industry Facts, Debt Statistics," *Credit Cards.com,* www.creditcards.com/credit-card-news/credit-card-industry-facts-personal-debt-statistics-1276.php.
23. For additional information about Visa, see www.visa.com; for MasterCard, see www.mastercard.com; for American Express, see www.americanexpress.com; for Discover, see www.discovercard.com.
24. U.S. Government Accountability Office, "CREDIT CARDS: Rising Interchange Fees Have Increased Costs for Merchants, but Options for Reducing Fees Pose Challenges," GAO 10-45, November 2009, p. 7.
25. FDIC, "From the Examiner's Desk: Amendments to Regulation Z: Compliance Challenges for Bankers and Examiners," *Supervisory Insights* (Summer 2010): 12.
26. Ibid., 19.
27. U.S. Department of Commerce, *Statistical Abstract of the United States 2009,* Table 1149. The latest data are for 2004.
28. U.S. Government Accountability Office, "CREDIT CARDS," 6.
29. For additional details, see HUD, "What Is a Manufactured Home?" www.hud.gov/offices/hsg/ramh/mhs/faq.cfm.
30. When a customer leases a car, he or she pays a monthly rental use tax. This is in lieu of a sales tax if the car were purchased.
31. The CARD Act of 2009 outlawed the "double billing cycle" or "two cycle average daily balance" method of computing finance charges.
32. For detailed information about interest rate calculations, see: David Thorndike, *Thorndike Encyclopedia of Banking and Financial Tables, Revised Edition* (Boston: Warren, Gorham & Lamont, 1980).
33. An alternative method for computing APR is presented in Chapter 7 Real Estate and Consumer Lending
34. Gregory Elliehausen, "The Cost of Bank Regulation: A Review of the Evidence," *Federal Reserve Bulletin* (April 1998): 252–253.
35. Clive Briault, Director, Prudential Standards, Financial Services Authority, ZEW/AEI Conference on Regulation and Supervision of Financial Markets and Institutions in the EU, Mannheim, Germany, July 10, 2003.
36. R. Russell Bailey, "Fair Lending Implications of Credit Scoring Systems," *FDIC Supervisory Insights,* June 23, 2005.
37. OCC, "Truth in Lending Act," OCC Bulletin 2010-14, March 25, 2010.
38. Board of Governors of the Federal Reserve System, "What Your Credit Card Company Has To Tell You," www.federalreserve.gov/consumerinfo/wyntk_creditcardrules.htm.

CHAPTER 8 Bank Capital: Capital Adequacy

1. Basel Committee on Banking Supervision, "Strengthening the Resilience of the Banking Sector—Consultative Document," December 2009.

2. Dodd-Frank Wall Street Reform and Consumer Protection Act, Section 616, www.gpo.gov/fdsys/pkg/BILLS-111hr4173ENR/pdf/BILLS-111hr4173ENR.pdf.
3. Basel Committee on Banking Supervision, "Strengthening the Resilience of the Banking Sector—Consultative Document," December 2009, p. 4.
4. Federal Deposit Insurance Corporation (FDIC) *Quarterly* 4, no. 1 (2010): 25.
5. *FDIC Annual Report,* 2001, 86.
6. FDIC, "Introduction—Capital," www.fdic.gov/regulations/resources/directors_college/sfcb/capital.pdf.
7. Ben S. Bernanke, Chairman, Federal Reserve, at the Federal Reserve Bank of Chicago 46th Annual Conference on Bank Structure and Competition, Chicago, May 6, 2010.
8. Bank Holding Company Act of 1956, Gramm-Leach Bliley Act of 1999.
9. Richard J. Rosen, "The Role of Securitization in Mortgage Lending," *Chicago Fed Letter,* Number 244, November 2007.
10. For additional information, see the Bank for International Settlements, www.bis.org.
11. Tier 2 is limited to no more than 100 percent of tier 1 capital.
12. D. Wessel, "Revised Bank Rules Help Spread Woes," *Wall Street Journal,* September 20, 2007, A7.
13. A. Estrella, "A Prolegomenon to Future Capital Requirements," *Economic Policy Review,* Federal Reserve Bank of New York, July 1995, 1–12.
14. FDIC, *History of the Eighties: Lessons for the Future*, vol. 1 (Washington, DC: FDIC, 1998), 57.
15. In 1997, regulators added an *S* to CAMEL to stand for sensitivity. For additional information about CAMEL, Board of Governors of the Federal Reserve System, Division of Banking Supervision and Regulation, SR-97-4 (SUP), "Interagency Guidance on Common Questions About the Application of the Revised CAMELS Rating System," March 5, 1997.
16. Ibid, *History of the Eighties,* 80.
17. N. Wellink, "Basel II and Financial Institution Resiliency," remarks by Dr. Nout Wellink, President of the Netherlands Bank and Chairman of the Basel Committee on Banking Supervision, at the Risk Capital 2007 conference, Paris, June 27, 2007.
18. For more information about Basel I, see B. Gup, *The New Basel Capital Accord* (New York: Thomson/Texere, 2004).
19. David Jones and John Mingo, "Industry Practices in Credit Risk Modeling and Internal Capital Allocations: Implications for a Models-Based Regulatory Capital Standard: Summary of Presentation," *FRBNY Economic Policy Review* (October 1998): 53.
20. FDIC, "FDIC Board Approves Basel II-Based Standardized Approach Capital Proposal as an Alternative to the Current Rules," Press Release, June 26, 2008.
21. For additional discussion of the failure of market discipline, see Sheila C. Bair, Chairman, FDIC, on the causes and current state of the financial crisis before the Financial Crisis Inquiry Commission, January 14, 2010; Benton E. Gup, "Market Discipline: Is it Fact or Fiction?" (working paper, 2005), 67–94, http://papers.ssrn.com/sol3/papers.cfm?abstract_id=449841.

22. Adjustments to the Basel II market risk framework announced by the Basel Committee, Bank for International Settlements, June 18, 2010; the details are listed in the "Annex" attached to the announcement: www.bis.org/press/p100618.htm.
23. Ibid.
24. Bank for International Settlements (BIS), "The Group of Governors and Heads of Supervision Reach Broad Agreement on Basel Committee Capital and Liquidity Reform Package," July 26, 2010, Annex at www.bis.org/press/p100726/annex.pdf.
25. Ibid.
26. BIS, "Comprehensive Response to the Global Banking Crisis," Press Release, September 7, 2009.
27. BIS, "Group of Governors and Heads of Supervision Announces Higher Global Minimum Capital Standards," Press Release, September 12, 2010, www.bis.org/press/p100912.htm.
28. "U.S. Banking Agencies Express Support for Basel Agreement," Joint Press Release, Board of Governors of the Federal Reserve System, OCC, FDIC, September 12, 2010; www.federalreserve.gov/newsevents/press/bcreg/20100912a.htm.
29. Basel Committee, "Strengthening the Resilience of the Banking Sector," 60–61.
30. COSO, "Enterprise Risk Management–Integrated Framework, Executive Summary," 2004.
31. Susan Schmidt Bies, "Enterprise Risk Management and Mortgage Lending," at the National Credit Union Administration 2007 Risk Mitigation Summit, January 11, 2007.
32. COSO, "Enterprise Risk Management."
33. For further discussion, see Robert L. Burns, "Economic Capital and the Assessment of Capital Adequacy," *FDIC Supervisory Insights*, Winter 2004; Basel Committee on Banking Supervision, "Range of Practices and Issues in Economic Capital Frameworks," March 2009, www.bis.org/publ/bcbs152.pdf.
34. Basel Committee, "Range of Practices and Issues."
35. U.S. GAO, "Risk Based Capital," GAO-070253, February, 2007.
36. Donald L, Kohn, Vice Chairman, Federal Reserve, "Risk Management and Its Implications for Systemic Risk," before the Subcommittee on Securities, Insurance, and Investment, Committee on Banking, Housing, and Urban Affairs, U.S. Senate, June 19, 2008.
37. Basel Committee, "Range of Practices and Issues," 5.
38. In June 2009, the FASB issued Statement No. 166, "Accounting for Transfers of Financial Assets" (FAS 166), and Statement No. 167, "Amendments to FASB Interpretation No. 46(R)" (FAS 167), which change the way entities account for securitizations and special purpose entities. Both FAS 166 and FAS 167 take effect as of the beginning of each bank's first annual reporting period that begins after November 15, 2009.
39. *FDIC Quarterly* 4, no. 2 (2010): 24, 25.
40. FASB, "Summary of Statement No. 159, the Fair Value Option for Financial Assets and Financial Liabilities—Including an Amendment of FASB Statement No. 115" (2009), www.fasb.org/st/summary/stsum159.shtml.

41. Kevin J. Bailey, Deputy Comptroller, OCC, testimony before the U.S. House of Representatives Subcommittee on Capital Markets, Insurance, and Government Sponsored Enterprises, March 12, 2009.
42. For a detailed discussion of this issue, see Benton E. Gup and Thomas Lutton, "Potential Effects of Fair Value Accounting on U.S. Bank Regulatory Capital," *Journal of Applied Finance* 18, nos. 1–2 (2009): 38–48.
43. FASB, "FASB Issues Statements 166 and 167 Pertaining to Securitizations and Special Purpose Entities," News Release, June 12, 2009.
44. Alan Greenspan, "Technology and Financial Services," speech before the Journal of Financial Services Research and American Enterprise Institute Conference, Washington, DC, April 14, 2009.
45. Stefan Walter, Secretary General, Basel Committee on Banking Supervision, "Basel II and Revisions to the Capital Requirements Directive," before the European Parliament Committee on Economic and Monetary Affairs on the Basel Committee on Banking Supervision reform program, May 3, 2010.
46. Nout Wellink, "The Basel Committee and Regulatory Reform" before the Institute of International Finance 2010 Spring Meeting, Vienna, Austria, June 11, 2010.
47. Basel Committee on Banking Supervision, "Countercyclical Capital Buffer Proposal," Consultative Document, BIS, July 2010.
48. Ibid. pp. 2–3.
49. Basel Committee, "Strengthening the Resilience of the Banking Sector," p. 6.
50. Sheila C. Bair, Financial Crisis Inquiry Commission.
51. Basel Committee on Banking Supervision, BIS, "Adjustments to the Basel II Market Risk Framework," June 18, 2010.
52. Susan Burhouse, John Field, George French, and Keith Ligon, - "Baseland the Evolution of Capital Regulation: Moving Forward and Looking Back," An Update on Emerging Issues in Banking, FDIC, February 13, 2003.

CHAPTER 9 Evaluating Bank Performance

1. NASDAQ Market Indices, Bank Index (symbol IXBK). http://dynamic.nasdaq.com/dynamic/bank_0.stm. For additional information about the FTSE Global Classification System, see www.ftse.com/index.jsp.
2. ABA NASDAQ Community Bank Index Methodology, https://indexes.nasdaqomx.com/docs/methodology_ABAQ.pdf.
3. Yahoo! Finance, Citigroup, Inc. (C), http://finance.yahoo.com/q/pr?s=C+Profile.
4. Federal Financial Institutions Examination Counci (FFIEC), National Information Center, http://www.ffiec.gov/nicpubweb/nicweb/InstitutionProfile.aspx?parID_Rssd=1951350&parDT_END=99991231.
5. For additional information, see SEC, "The Laws That Govern the Securities Industry," www.sec.gov/about/laws.shtml.
6. For additional information, see Yahoo! Finance, http://finance.yahoo.com/.
7. For additional information about stocks, see Benton E. Gup, *Investing Online* (Hoboken, NJ: Wiley-Blackwell, 2003).

8. For additional information about deposit insurance coverage, see FDIC, "Deposit Insurance FAQ," https://www.fdic.gov/edie/fdic_info.html#11g.
9. For additional information about the definition of an FDIC-insured commercial bank, see Chapter 3 or FDIC, "Historical Statistics on Banking," Index to Notes on Insured Commercial Banks, www2.fdic.gov/hsob/hsobnotes.asp.
10. FDIC, "New Accounting Rules Affect Reported Cash Flows," *FDIC Quarterly Banking Profile,* First Quarter 2010, volume 4, no. 2, www2.fdic.gov/qbp/2010mar/qbp.pdf.
11. The Core Capital leverage ratio should not be confused with the tier 1 risk-based capital ratio that only considers risk-based assets.
12. FDIC Certificate Number 57803. RSSD-ID 3284070.
13. National Information Center, Top 50 Bank Holding Companies (as of March 21, 2010). www.ffiec.gov/nicpubweb/nicweb/Top50Form.aspx.
14. For information on the government investment, see U.S. Department of Treasury, Press Room, TG563, Written Testimony of Ron Bloom, Senior Advisor to the Secretary of the Treasury, and Jim Millstein, Chief Restructuring Officer, U.S. Department of the Treasury, before the Congressional Oversight Panel, February 25, 2010. www.treas.gov/press/releases/tg563.htm.
15. To find the Institution Directory on the internet, go to the FDIC web page (www.fdic.gov/). On the left side of the web page are "Quick Links by User." Under that heading, click on "Bankers, Resources for banking professionals." Or just type "Institution Directory" into the search window.
16. FFIEC, "About the Federal Financial Institutions Examination Council (FFIEC) Central Data Repository (CDR) Public Data Distribution (PDD) website and its data," https://cdr.ffiec.gov/Public/HelpFileContainers/WelcomeAdditionalInfo.aspx.
17. FFEIC CDR's Public Data Distribution web site: https://cdr.ffiec.gov/public/.
18. For additional information, see www.ffiec.gov/.
19. https://cdr.ffiec.gov/public/Reports/UbprReport.aspx?rptCycleIds=61%2c56%2c58%2c52%2c47&rptid=283&idrssd=3284070.
20. FDIC "Bank Data Guide," www.fdic.gov/bank/statistical/guide/bankdataguide.pdf.

CHAPTER 10 Payments Systems

1. For the history of legal tender in the United States, see Benton E. Gup, "The Changing Role of Legal Tender: An Historical Perspective," in *Marketing Exchange Relationships, Transactions, and Their Media,* ed. Franklin S. Houston, 239–246 (Westport, CT: Quorum, 1994).
2. U.S. Department of Treasury, "FAQs, Currency, Legal Tender Status." The Treasury Department stopped issuing U.S. notes in January 21, 1971, www.treasury.gov/resource-center/faqs/Currency/Pages/legal-tender.aspx.
3. Louise Roseman, Director, Division of Reserve Bank Operations and Payment Systems, Board of Governors of the Federal Reserve System, statement before the

Subcommittee on Domestic Monetary Policy and Technology of the Committee on Financial Services, U.S. House of Representatives, July 20, 2010.

4. Wilco Bolt and Sujit Chakrovorti, "Economic of Payment Cards: A Status Report," *Economic Perspectives,* Federal Reserve Bank of Chicago, Fourth Quarter 2008, 15–27.
5. Federal Reserve Bank of Chicago, "Competitive Forces Shaping the Payments Environment: What's Next?—A Conference Summary," *Chicago Fed Letter,* No. 241b, August 2007.
6. Marcela M. Williams and Richard G. Anderson, "Currency Design in the United States and Abroad: Counterfeit Deterrence and Visual Accessibility," *Review,* Federal Reserve Bank of St. Louis, September–October 2007, 371–414, For discussions of payments fraud, see conference papers on that topic in *Economic Perspectives,* Federal Reserve Bank of Chicago, First Quarter 2009; Louise L. Roseman, testimony.
7. Audit Report of the U.S. Mint's Fiscal Years 2008 and 2007 Financial Statements, Office of the Inspector General, OIG-09-015, December 8, 2008, p. 26, www.treasury.gov/about/organizational-structure/ig/Documents/oig09015.pdf.
8. Ibid., 27.
9. FFIEC IT Retail Payment Systems Examination Handbook, February 2010, http://ithandbook.ffiec.gov/it-booklets/retail-payment-systems.aspx.
10. For additional information on the clearing process, see National Automated Clearing House Association (NACHA): The Electronic Payments Association, www.nacha.org/.
11. Paul W. Bauer and Geoffrey R. Gerdes, "The Check Is Dead! Long Live the Check! A Check 21 Update," *Economic Commentary,* Federal Reserve Bank of Cleveland, June 2009; Geoffrey R. Gerdes and Kathy C. Wang, "Recent Payment Trends in the United States," *Federal Reserve Bulletin* 94 (2008).
12. Catherine J. Bell, Jeanne Hogarth, and Eric Robins, "U.S. Households' Access to and Use of Electronic Banking, 1989–2007," *Federal Reserve Bulletin,* July 2009, A99–A121.
13. Gerdes and Wang, "Recent Payment Trends."
14. Board of Governors of the Federal Reserve System, "The 2007 Federal Reserve Payments Study: Noncash Payment Trends in the United States: 2003–2006," December 10, 2007, http://frbservices.org/files/communications/pdf/research/2007_payments_study.pdf.
15. Bank of America, *Investor Factbook,* Mid-Year 2010, p. 2, http://investor.bankofamerica.com/phoenix.zhtml?c=71595&p=irol-reportsother.
16. Ally's web site: www.ally.com/bank/interest-checking-account/#tabs=default.
17. Payments Council, United Kingdom, www.paymentscouncil.org.uk/.
18. Payments Council, "Cheque Replacement," www.paymentscouncil.org.uk/payments_plan/-/page/856/.
19. FFIEC IT Retail Payment Systems Examination Handbook, February 2010, http://ithandbook.ffiec.gov/it-booklets/retail-payment-systems.aspx.
20. Ibid.

21. Ibid. Also see U.S. Census Bureau, Table 1148, "Percent of Households Using Selected Electronic Banking Technologies: 1995–2007," 2010 Statistical Abstract.
22. Bell, Hogarth, and Robbins, "U.S. Households' Access."
23. Ibid.
24. U.S. Census Bureau, Table 1150, "Debit Cards-Holders, Number, Transactions, and Volume, 2000 and 2007, and Projections, 2010," 2010 Statistical Abstract.
25. Federal Deposit Insurance Corporation (FDIC) "FDIC Sets Out Overdraft Payment Program Guidance," FDIC Press Release, August 11, 2010, https://mail.google.com/a/cba.ua.edu/#inbox/12a62572619feb3e; Also see Office of the Comptroller of the Currency (OCC) "Overdraft Protection," *OCC Bulletin,* OCC 2010-15, April 12, 2010.
26. FDIC, "FDIC National Survey of Unbanked and Underbanked Households," December 2009, 12. Also see FDIC, "Addendum to the 2009 FDIC National Survey of Unbanked and Underbanked Households: Use of Alternative Financial Services," September 2010.
27. FDIC, "Addendum," 11.
28. For further details about ARSs, see Financial Action Task Force, "Money Laundering & Terrorist Financing Typologies, 2004–2005," June 10, 2005. Also see Benton E. Gup, *Money Laundering and Financing Terrorism, and Suspicious Activities* (New York: Nova Science, 2007).
29. U.S. Department of Treasury, FinCEN, Advisory FIN-2010-A011, "Informal Value Transfer Systems," September 1, 2010, www.fincen.gov/statutes_regs/guidance/pdf/FIN-2010-A011.pdf.
30. The example is based on one that appears in FinCEN, "Informal Value Transfer Systems," *FinCEN Advisory* 33 (March 2003): 4.
31. Tarik M. Yousef, Testimony before the U.S. Senate Committee on Banking, Housing, and Urban Affairs, Subcommittee on International Trade and Finance, Hearing on "Hawala and Underground Terrorist Financing Mechanisms," November 14, 2001.
32. U.S. Department of Treasury, "Informal Value Transfer Systems." Also see *United States v. Banki*, 2010 U.S. Dist. LEXIS 51330, 2010 WL 2076770 (S.D.N.Y. 2010).
33. Ibid. Also see *United States v. Mazza-Alaluf*, 607 F.Supp.2d 484 (S.D.N.Y. 2009).
34. U. S. Senate, "Current Trends in Money Laundering," Report prepared for the Permanent Subcommittee on Investigations of the Committee on Government Affairs, 102nd Cong., 2nd Sess. S. Hrg. 102–123, December 1992, p. 1.
35. U.S. Department of the Treasury, "Program Performance Report," Fiscal Year 2000, 2001, p. 145.
36. For more information about FinCen, see www.fincen.gov.
37. Public Law 107-56. A short title for the USA PATRIOT Act is the "International Money Laundering Abatement and Financial Anti-Terrorism Act of 2001."
38. FinCEN, "The 2010 Version of the Bank Secrecy Act/Anti-Money Laundering Examination Manual," News Release, April 29, 2010, www.fincen.gov/news_

room/nr/html/20100429.html. The 2010 version of the manual is located on the FFIEC BSA/AML InfoBase at: www.ffiec.gov/bsa_aml_infobase/default.htm.

39. FinCEN, "Civil Money Penalty Assessed against Wachovia Bank," March 17, 2010, www.fincen.gov/bsaviolations.html.
40. Michael Smith, "Wachovia's Drug Habit," Bloomberg News, July 2, 2010, www.bloomberg.com/news/print/2010-07-07/wachovia-s-drug-habit.html.
41. For a discussion of global trends in payments, see Morton L. Bech, Christine Preisig, and Kimmo Soramäki, "Global Trends in Large-Value Payments," *Economic Policy Review,* Federal Reserve Bank of New York (September 2008): 59–81.
42. Board of Governors of the Federal Reserve System, Fedwire, www.federalreserve.gov/paymentsystems/fedfunds_about.htm.
43. Board of Governors of the Federal Reserve System, "Fedwire Services," www.frbservices.org/fedwire/index.html.
44. Board of Governors of the Federal Reserve System, "Fedwire Funds Services," www.federalreserve.gov/paymentsystems/fedfunds_ann.htm.
45. Board of Governors of the Federal Reserve System, www.federalreserve.gov/paymentsystems/fedfunds_coreprinciples.htm#executive.
46. CHIPS, "CHIPS Celebrates 40th Anniversary Milestone," Press Release, April 6, 2010, www.chips.org/press_releases/pressReleaseDocs/070431.php. Also see The Clearing House, "About Us," www.theclearinghouse.org/about/000211f.php.
47. The Clearing House, "Chips Annual Statistics From 1970 to 2010," www.chips.org/docs/000652.pdf.
48. For additional information about SWIFT, see the web site: www.swift.com/home/index.page?lang=en.
49. CLS Group, "About CLS," www.cls-group.com/About/Pages/default.aspx.
50. DTCC, "About DTCC: Our Business," www.dtcc.com/about/business/.

CHAPTER 11 Other Financial Services

1. This chapter is based, in part, on Benton E. Gup and James W. Kolari, *Commercial Banking: The Management of Risk*, 3rd ed. (Hoboken, NJ: John Wiley & Sons, 2004). Reprinted with permission of John Wiley & Sons, Inc.
2. Federal Deposit Insurance Corporation (FDIC), "Composition of Commercial Banks' Noninterest Income," *FDIC Quarterly Banking Profile,* Graph Book, First Half 2010, www2.fdic.gov/QBP/grgraph.asp.
3. "Bankers' Acceptances," in *Comptroller's Handbook* (Washington, DC: Office of the Comptroller of the Currency (OCC), 1999).
4. Board of Governors of the Federal Reserve System, FDIC, OCC, Office of Thrift Supervision (OTS), "Shared National Credits Program, 2009 Review," September 24, 2009, p. 4, www.federalreserve.gov/newsevents/press/bcreg/bcreg20090924a1.pdf.
5. Ibid.

6. SunTrust: https://www.suntrust.com/portal/server.pt/community/managing_wealth/254.
7. Regions Bank: www.regions.com/personal_banking/trust_asset.rf.
8. SSGA. www.ssga.com/about_ssga/about_ssga_hm.html.
9. For details, see www.db-privatebanking.com.sg/index_home.html.
10. FDIC, "2005 FDIC Trust Report." No Trust Reports were published after 2005. www.fdic.gov/bank/individual/trust/report2005.html.
11. State Street Corporate Fact Sheet: www.statestreet.com/wps/portal/internet/corporate/home/aboutstatestreet/corporateoverview/factsheet/!ut/p/c4/04_SB8K8xLLM9MSSzPy8xBz9CP0os3i_0CADCydDRwN3d0tzA89gNxczHydnIwNjI_3g1Lz40GD9gmxHRQB9i1Ox/.
12. Northern Trust, "About Northern Trust," www.northerntrust.com/pws/jsp/display2.jsp?TYPE=irLanding&XML=pages/ntirlanding/0802/1203536410667_429.xml.
13. For additional information, see www.bnymellon.com/assetmanagement/.
14. For additional information, see www.identrust.com.
15. For additional information, see the National Association of Real Estate Investment Trusts, NAREIT, at www.nareit.org/home.cfm.
16. For additional information, see U.S. Trust, www.ustrust.com.
17. For additional information, see IRS, "Estate Tax," www.irs.gov/businesses/small/article/0,,id=164871,00.html.
18. SPDR® is a registered trademark of Standard & Poor's Financial Services LLC and has been licensed for use by State Street Corporation. For additional information, see https://www.spdrs.com/.
19. See https://www.spdrs.com/product/.
20. The Wolfsberg Group, www.wolfsberg-principles.com/corresp-banking.html.
21. Wells Fargo, "Correspondent Banking," www.wellsfargo.com/com/cobank/index.jhtml.
22. ABN AMRO Group, Correspondent Banking. www.abnamro.com/en/clients/commercial-merchant-banking/correspondent-banking.html.
23. "Wolfsberg AML Principles for Correspondent Banking," 2008, www.wolfsberg-principles.com/corresp-banking.html.

CHAPTER 12 A Guide to Islamic Banking

1. As at 2010, published reports indicate 76 countries in which Islamic institutions are operating under some form of official licensing arrangements. After the Bank of London amended the U.K. laws to permit the licensing of this form of niche banking, many more countries, including countries with no Muslim population, are rushing to amend their laws to get into this niche banking. The attraction is the large pool of money that is likely to be attracted to this form of banking from customers who would like to lend on the basis of profit-share deposits. Middle Eastern and Muslim states are promoting this: for a summary of the current status of this new industry, see M. Ariff, "Introduction to Islamic

Financial Institutions," in *Fundamentals of Islamic Banking: Theory, Practice & Education,* ed. M. Ariff and M. Iqbal (Northampton, MA: Edward Elgar, 2010).

2. The term *Islamic bank* has come to be accepted widely. However, a more appropriate name is one that is descriptive of its proper practices is bank *Mualamat.* This latter term avoids the connotation that the bank has something to do with Islam. Apart from the injunction in that religion to avoid interest in financial activities, almost all the instruments are based on pre-Islamic contract terms as these evolved over time to the present day. The only thing that such a bank has with Islam is the practice of a doctrine (as was also the case in Catholicism till 1752 A.D.) that all forms of interest are forbidden by God. There is a wide body of respectable literature ranging from Aristotle to Benjamin Franklin to some modern-day thinkers that the interest-based debt-pricing banking system is not conducive to human welfare and that fractional reserve banking and the attendant interest earned by the organizers encourages more debt.
3. There are contemporary examples of how banks have colluded with firms to perpetrate wrong practices. For example, Citibank accepted wrongdoing in helping Enron commit fraud and paid a fine of $120 million in 2003, as did also JPMorgan Bank, which paid a fine of $135 million.
4. The governor of Bank Indonesia, a central bank, was removed for requiring an officer to be removed from Bank Duta for losing US$300 million in 1996. There was political pressure in this removal during the period of Suharto's presidency.
5. Across the world, there are many episodes of failures of banking when a bank or a class of deposit-taking firms are exempted from central bank oversight. In Australia, there were two such banks in Adelaide and Brisbane, which failed, causing huge losses. The Malaysian government spent some US$900 billion in the early 1980s to rescue credit unions outside the supervision of its central bank. The Asian financial crisis of July 1997 actually came after Thailand's 52 credit unions outside central bank supervision were bailed out in the first half of 1997, prompting investor interest on corruption. The special purpose vehicles created after the easing of banking regulations in the United States led to unsupervised banklike firms providing US$5.2 trillion outside the Federal Reserve's supervision that led to credit explosion prior to the great financial crisis.
6. Despite this, it is always possible some errant bankers may engage in practices that are contrary to this oversight function. There was a case in 2009 of such malfeasance in Bank Islam Malaysia, the largest Islamic bank, founded in 1982. An errant officer used funds of the bank, to the tune of US$300 million, in derivative positions in an offshore operation, and that led to a one-time loss of this amount of money. This happened because of lack of operational controls rather than sanctioned practice.
7. See Gillian Tett, *Fools Gold* (London: Financial Times, 2009). It has been shown that the ballooning of CDOs to US$12 trillion, when the clients returned this new product to the New York and London banks, actually depleted the bank capital that led to the liquidity trap in September 2008 and then the global financial crisis. The damage done by subprime lending was in early 2006–2007, while the damage by CDOs was severe and felt in 2008; see M. Ariff, John Farrar

(2011). "Global Financial Crisis: Antipodean Perspective," Edward Elgar Ltd., UK and USA. (forthcoming in mid-2011).

8. For a while a Bahrain-based institute was training personnel in Islamic banking for the regional markets. A number of universities have started to offer programs to train graduates in banking with specialization in Islamic banking product design and operations. However, the number of university students graduating in this regard is very small. In 2003, an international body was founded, International Center for Education in Islamic Finance (INCEIF) that began a certifying program in Islamic banking. The Islamic Financial Services Board (IFSB) was founded in 2005 to establish prudential standards in association with the world institutions such as the Bank for International Settlements (BIS) on banking norms. In addition, the Islamic Development Bank's training institute conducts intensive training programs around the world, usually in central banks, to train regulators and private bankers in Islamic banking. There is no requirement that a student has to be a Muslim to enter any of these.
9. One of the six commandments on interest rates states that lending resulting in twofold and threefold in interest payments is harmful and thus must not be practiced, while other commandments specify that giving to charity the money from interest rather than devouring it is commendable. Except in the Jewish scripture, the ban on interest appears to be applicable to all humans: Jewish scripture forbids interest only among the Jewish people. See also R. Zaman, "Usury (*Riba*) and the Place of Bank Interest in Islamic Banking and Finance," *International Journal of Banking and Finance* 6, no. 1 (2009): 1–15, which is a historical review of usury as being different from interest for more than 1,400 years and positing that equating the two is a recent consensus promoted in the last century.
10. This requirement is put into practice in a less restrictive manner since all firms are not unlikely to have dealings purely on profit-sharing basis, given the ubiquitous nature of interest in commerce. So this rule is interpreted to mean that about 10 percent of the firm's operation may include engaging in interest-based contracts to qualify as an investable firm for mutual fund investments.
11. In April 2010, the popular press across the world reported that a new fund has been established as a Christian investment fund, meaning that it follows strict Christian guidelines. Thus, there are wider interest groups, not just from Islamic jurisprudence, and simple ethics-based lending firms are being formed.

Glossary

1. The Library of Congress, Thomas, "Over-the-Counter Derivatives Markets Act of 2009" (H.R. 3795 Introduced in House, SEC. 111. DEFINITIONS). http://thomas.loc.gov/cgi-bin/query/F?c111:1:./temp/~c1116BhH0D:e1213.

Glossary

This glossary is intended to provide a general understanding of selected terms used in the book and in connection with banking and finance. Therefore, some definitions are not complete. By way of illustration, a *swap* is defined in the Glossary as "the simultaneous purchase and sale of currencies or interest rate products in spot and forward market transactions. Swap contracts are traded over-the-counter." However, in legislation to enact the "Over-the-Counter Derivatives Markets Act of 2009"[1] the term *swap* means any agreement, contract, or transaction that

> *(i) is a put, call, cap, floor, collar, or similar option of any kind for the purchase or sale of, or based on the value of, one or more interest or other rates, currencies, commodities, securities, instruments of indebtedness, indices, quantitative measures, or other financial or economic interests or property of any kind;*
>
> *(ii) provides for any purchase, sale, payment, or delivery (other than a dividend on an equity security) that is dependent on the occurrence, non-occurrence, or the extent of the occurrence of an event or contingency associated with a potential financial, economic, or commercial consequence;*
>
> *(iii) provides on an executory basis for the exchange, on a fixed or contingent basis, of one or more payments based on the value or level of one or more interest or other rates, currencies, commodities, securities, instruments of indebtedness, indices, quantitative measures, or other financial or economic interests or property of any kind, or any interest therein or based on the value thereof, and that transfers, as between the parties to the transaction, in whole or in part, the financial risk associated with a future change in any such value or level without also conveying a current or future direct or indirect ownership interest in an asset (including any enterprise or investment pool) or liability that incorporates the financial risk so transferred, including any agreement, contract, or transaction commonly known as an interest rate swap, a rate floor, rate cap, rate collar, cross-currency rate swap, basis swap, currency swap, total return swap, equity index swap, equity swap, debt index swap,*

debt swap, credit spread, credit default swap, credit swap, weather swap, energy swap, metal swap, agricultural swap, emissions swap, or commodity swap;

(iv) is an agreement, contract, or transaction that is, or in the future becomes, commonly known to the trade as a swap; or

(v) is any combination or permutation of, or option on, any agreement, contract, or transaction described in any of clauses (i) through (iv).

(B) EXCLUSIONS—The term "swap" does not include:

(i) any contract of sale of a commodity for future delivery or security futures product traded on or subject to the rules of any board of trade designated as a contract market under section 5 or 5f;

(ii) any sale of a nonfinancial commodity for deferred shipment or delivery, so long as such transaction is physically settled;

(iii) any put, call, straddle, option, or privilege on any security, certificate of deposit, or group or index of securities, including any interest therein or based on the value thereof, that is subject to the Securities Act of 1933 (15 U.S.C. 77a et seq.) and the Securities Exchange Act of 1934 (15 U.S.C. 78a et seq.);

(iv) any put, call, straddle, option, or privilege relating to foreign currency entered into on a national securities exchange registered pursuant to section 6(a) of the Securities Exchange Act of 1934 (15 U.S.C. 78f(a));

(v) any agreement, contract, or transaction providing for the purchase or sale of one or more securities on a fixed basis that is subject to the Securities Act of 1933 (15 U.S.C. 77a et seq.) and the Securities Exchange Act of 1934 (15 U.S.C. 78a et seq.);

(vi) any agreement, contract, or transaction providing for the purchase or sale of one or more securities on a contingent basis that is subject to the Securities Act of 1933 (15 U.S.C. 77a et seq.) and the Securities Exchange Act of 1934 (15 U.S.C. 78a et seq.), unless such agreement, contract, or transaction predicates such purchase or sale on the occurrence of a bona fide contingency that might reasonably be expected to affect or be affected by the creditworthiness of a party other than a party to the agreement, contract, or transaction;

(vii) any note, bond, or evidence of indebtedness that is a security as defined in section 2(a)(1) of the Securities Act of 1933 (15 U.S.C. 77b(a)(1));

(viii) any agreement, contract, or transaction that is—

(I) based on a security; and

(II) entered into directly or through an underwriter (as defined in section 2(a)(11) of the Securities Act of 1933) (15 U.S.C.

77b(a)(11)) by the issuer of such security for the purposes of raising capital, unless such agreement, contract, or transaction is entered into to manage a risk associated with capital raising;

(ix) any foreign exchange swap;

(x) any foreign exchange forward;

(xi) any agreement, contract, or transaction a counterparty of which is a Federal Reserve bank or the United States Government, or an agency of the United States Government that is expressly backed by the full faith and credit of the United States; and

(xii) any security-based swap, other than a security-based swap as described in paragraph (38)(C).

DEFINITIONS

2/28 Adjustable rate mortgages (ARMs). The interest rate is fixed for the first 2 years, and then it can be adjusted for the next 28 years. This is also called a *hybrid mortgage.*

Accrual basis means that revenues are recognized in the accounting period when they are earned, regardless of when the cash is received.

Acid test ratio is a narrow measure of liquidity derived by dividing cash, marketable securities, and accounts receivable by current liabilities.

Adjustable rate mortgages are mortgage loans that have interest rates and payments that are subject to change over time.

Affinity credit card plans offer bank credit cards to members of a particular organization (e.g., universities, clubs, and unions).

Agency problems, as used here, refer to the ability of the lender (the principal) to influence the behavior of the borrower (the agent).

Agreement corporation is a corporation chartered by a state to engage in international banking, so named because the corporation enters into an agreement with the Federal Reserve's Board of Governors that it will limit its activities to those permitted.

Alt-A mortgages may lack full documentation, have higher loan-to-value ratios and debt-to-income ratios, or have other features that do not conform to Government Sponsored Enterprises' lending guidelines. They are riskier than mortgages that are prime rated but less risky than subprime mortgages.

Alternative financial services are financial services offered outside the Federal Deposit Insurance Corporation-insured institutions.

Alternative mortgage instruments is a generic term that covers a smorgasbord of mortgage instruments where the terms of the contract can change or where they differ from the traditional mortgage loan.

Annual percentage rate (APR) is the percentage cost of credit on an annual basis.

Assets represent resources that the company owns or controls. Assets include financial assets (cash, investments, receivables) and real assets (property, plant, and equipment); some firms also have intangible assets (patents, trademarks).

Asset-backed securities (ABS) are financial securities backed by loans, leases, accounts receivable, credit card debt, or real estate loans (e.g., *securitization*).

Asset-based lending is a form of commercial and industrial lending where the assets of a company are used to secure the company's obligation to the lender. Much greater weight is given to the market value of the collateral in asset-based lending than in regular commercial and industrial loans.

Asset/liability management (ALM) refers to the simultaneous management of both assets and liabilities for the purpose of maximizing profits, mitigating interest rate risk, providing liquidity, and enhancing the market value of banks.

Assumable mortgage. Some mortgage loans, such as home loans backed by the Veterans Administration (VA), are assumable, which means that they can be passed on to a new owner if the property is sold.

Asymmetric information, or private information, is information used by one party that is not available to others.

ATM. Automatic teller machine.

At-the-Money. When the strike price of a put or call option is equal to price of the underlying security or commodity.

Audit is an evaluation process that assures you that the financial statements followed generally accepted accounting principles (GAAP).

Average collection period indicates the average number of days that a firm waits before receiving cash from sales made on credit.

Balloon mortgage loans are relatively short-term loans, such as five years. At the end of that period, the entire amount of the loan comes due, and a new loan is negotiated.

Bank refers to Federal Deposit Insurance Corporation-insured banks chartered in the United States that accept deposits (other than trust funds) and make loans [12 U.S.C. 1813 (h)].

Bankcard is a general-purpose credit card, issued by a financial institution under agreement with the bankcard companies (e.g., Visa, MasterCard),

Bankers' acceptance is a time draft drawn on a bank that has been stamped "accepted" by the bank. By accepting the draft, the bank makes an unconditional promise to pay the holder of the draft a stated amount at a specified date.

Bank holding company (BHC) is a company that owns and/or controls one or more U.S. banks or one that owns, or has controlling interest in, one or more banks. A bank holding company may also own another bank holding company, which in turn owns or controls a bank; the company at the top of the ownership chain is called the *top holder*.

Basel I and II refer to the Basel Committee on Banking Supervision's risk-based bank capital standards.

Basis is the difference between the spot or cash price of a commodity and the price of the nearest futures contract for the same or a related commodity (typically calculated as cash minus futures).

Basis risk is the risk associated with an unexpected widening or narrowing of the basis between the time a hedge position is established and the time that it is lifted.

Basket swap. A credit default swap (CDS) covering multiple credit default events.

Bilateral netting. A legally enforceable arrangement between a bank and a counterparty that creates a single legal obligation covering all included individual contracts. This means that a bank's receivable or payable, in the event of the default or insolvency of one of the parties, would be the net sum of all positive and negative fair values of contracts included in the bilateral netting arrangement.

Bills of exchange are written orders issued by the drawer instructing a second party—the drawee—to pay a stated amount of money on some date in the future.

Brokered deposits are deposits issued by a financial institution and purchased by an investor through a third-party intermediary (i.e., .a deposit broker).

BSA/AML. Bank secrecy act/anti-money laundering laws.

Buydown. A high mortgage interest rate is offset by paying points at the time of closing.

Call Option. The option buyer pays a fee (*premium*) to the seller for the right to buy the underlying asset at an agreed price (*strike* or *exercise price*) until the contract expires (*expiry*).

Call reports refer to the reports of condition and income every national bank, state member bank, and insured state nonmember bank is required to file quarterly with bank regulators.

CAMEL rating stands for **C**apital, **A**sset quality, **M**anagement, **E**arnings, and **L**iquidity. CAMEL ratings are used by bank regulators to evaluate bank performance on a scale of 1 (good) to 5 (failing).

Capital arbitrage. See *regulatory arbitrage.*

Capital market instruments are long-term securities such as stocks and bonds.

Cash basis means that revenues and expenses are recognized when they are received or paid.

Clearing House Interbank Payment System (**CHIPS**) is used for the real-time settlement of large dollar value business-to-business payment transactions between domestic or foreign institutions that have offices in the United States.

Closed-end loans. See *nonrevolving loans.*

Collateral is an asset pledged against the performance of an obligation.

Collateralized debt obligation (**CDO**) is an asset-backed security (ABS) that can be based on residential real estate, commercial real estate, corporate bonds, or other assets. The CDOs are divided into tranches that have different maturities and priorities for repaying the loans.

Commercial bank is a financial institution that is owned by stockholders, operates for a profit, and engages in various lending activities.

Commercial mortgage loans consist of nonresidential and nonfarm commercial buildings and other business real estate.

Compilation is data presented, in the form of financial statements, that is the representation of management without undertaking to express assurance on the statements.

Compliance risk. The current and prospective risk to earnings or capital arising from violations of, or nonconformance with, laws, rules, regulations, prescribed practices, internal policies and procedures, or ethical standards.

Confirmed letter of credit. A second bank adds its guaranty of payment in the event of payment default by the issuing bank.

Consortium. Any association or partnership.

Construction and land development loans are secured by real estate. They are made to finance the construction of new structures, additions, alterations, or demolitions to make way for new structures.

Cooperative bank. State-chartered savings associations located in Massachusetts, New Hampshire, Rhode Island, and Vermont.

Core banks are large banks with $250 billion or more in assets.

Core capital includes common equity capital plus noncumulative perpetual preferred stock plus minority interest in consolidated subsidiaries, less goodwill and other ineligible intangible assets.

Core deposits are defined in the Uniform Bank Performance Report (UBPR) User Guide as the sum of demand deposits, all negotiable orders of withdrawal (NOW) and automatic transfer accounts (ATS), money market deposit accounts (MMDA), savings, other savings deposits, and time deposits under $100,000.

Corporate culture can be defined as the way we do things in this organization.

Corporation. An artificial person or legal entity with rights, privileges, and liabilities separate from those of the owners.

Counterparty risk refers to the failure of a counterparty, such as financial institutions (e.g., banks, broker dealers, and other nonbanking institutions), in a derivatives contract. It is the loss due a counterparty that fails to deliver on its over-the-counter (OTC) derivative obligation.

Covered bonds are debt obligations issued by financial institutions. They are backed by the institution's promise to pay and by a dynamic pool of assets (i.e., cover pool) pledged as collateral. The underlying assets are typically high-quality assets that are subject to the eligibility requirements.

Credit bureau. A credit reporting agency that is a clearinghouse for information on the credit ratings of individuals or firms. The three largest U.S. credit bureaus are Equifax, Experian, and TransUnion.

Credit card is any card, plate, or device that may be used from time to time and over and over again to borrow money or buy goods and services *on credit* (i.e., a loan).

Credit CARD Act. The full title of the law is the Credit Card Accountability, Responsibility and Disclosure Act of 2009.

Credit default swap (CDS) is a bilateral financial contract in which a buyer seeking protection on loans makes periodic payments to a seller who is offering financial protection if a predefined credit event occurs.

Credit derivative. A financial contract that allows a party to take, or reduce, credit exposure (generally on a bond, loan, or index). Credit default swaps, total return swaps, and credit spread options are examples of credit derivatives.

Credit event in swap contracts usually refers to default on a loan, bankruptcy, and debt restructuring.

Credit facilities. Some commercial and industrial loans are referred to as credit facilities. The term also applies to agreements that may or may not result in loans.

Credit risk is the risk to earnings and capital that a borrower or counterparty may not meet the terms of the loan contract, resulting in losses to the lender.

Credit unions are financial cooperative institutions with a common federal, state, or corporate affiliation.

Current ratio is a broad measure of liquidity derived by dividing current assets by current liabilities.

Data processing servicers. Entities primarily engaged in providing infrastructure for hosting or data processing services. These establishments may provide specialized hosting activities, such as web hosting, streaming services, or application hosting; application service provisioning; or general time-share mainframe facilities to clients. Data processing establishments provide complete processing and specialized reports from data supplied by clients or provide automated data processing and data entry services.

Daylight overdrafts. See *overdrafts*.

Debit card. It looks like a plastic credit card and may be used to make purchases, but no credit is extended. The funds are withdrawn or transferred from the cardholder's account to pay for the purchases.

Debt coverage is measured by *times interest earned,* which is computed by dividing earnings before interest and taxes (EBIT) by interest expense.

Debt ratio indicates the proportion of a firm's total assets financed with borrowed funds.

Default risk is the risk that the borrower will not repay the loan or may violate other terms of the loan agreement.

Delinquency rate refers to loans that are at least one payment past due, but it does not include loans in the process of foreclosure.

Deposit broker is any person engaged in the business of placing deposits, or facilitating the placement of deposits, of third parties with insured depository institutions.

Depository institutions include Federal Deposit Insurance Corporation-insured banks (commercial banks, savings banks, mutual savings banks), insured credit unions, and other institutions defined by law in Code of Federal Regulations: Title 12: Banks and Banking: Part 204—Reserve Requirements of Depository Institutions (Regulation D).

Derivative. A contract of sale of a commodity for future delivery. A financial contract whose value is derived from the performance of underlying market factors, such as interest rates, currency exchange rates, commodity, credit, and equity prices. Derivative transactions include a wide assortment of financial contracts, including structured debt obligations and deposits, swaps, futures, options, caps, floors, collars, forwards, and various combinations thereof.

Diversification means investing in assets whose returns are not perfectly positively correlated.

Dividend payout ratio is the percentage of earnings paid to common stockholders in the form of cash dividends.

Documentation refers to all of the documents needed to legally enforce a loan contract and protect a bank's interest.

Dodd-Frank Act. Dodd-Frank Wall Street Reform and Consumer Protection Act of 2010.

Dollar gap is the difference between the dollar amount rate-sensitive assets and rate-sensitive liabilities.

Domestic branch of a domestic bank. A branch that resides in the United States and whose parent is also located in the United States.

Domestic entity other. Domestic institutions that engage in banking activities, usually in connection with the business of banking in the United States.

Due-on-sale clause. Some mortgage loans contain a *due-on-sale clause*, which means that the mortgage loan is not transferable to the new buyer and the balance of the loan must be paid to the lender when the house is sold.

Duration is defined as the weighted average *time to maturity* to receive all cash flows from a financial instrument. Time is measured in terms of years and months.

Duration drift. Every day bonds come closer to maturity. Similarly, the duration of debt instruments changes over time.

Duration gap compares the effects of changes in interest rates on the duration of a bank's assets and liabilities to determine the *economic value* of stockholders' equity.

Earnings per share (EPS) is derived by dividing income available for common stock by the number of shares outstanding. Basic EPS represents the income from continuing operations and net income. Diluted EPS takes into account the effect of conversion of convertible securities, warrants, and stock options.

E-banking, or electronic banking, includes the use of automated teller machines (ATMs), debit cards, direct deposit, preauthorized payments, phone banking, online banking, smart cards, and prepaid cards.

Economic capital is the difference between a given percentile of a loss distribution and the expected loss. It is a statistical concept measuring risk and the bank's estimate of the amount of capital needed to support its risk-taking activities. Economic capital is not the amount of *regulatory capital* held.

Economic value is the theoretical value of a bank's equity, taking into account the duration of both the assets and liabilities. It is not the market value of the equity.

ECP, or electronic check presentment, is used for clearing checks.

EDGAR is an acronym that stands for Electronic Data Gathering, Analysis, and Retrieval.

Edge Act/Agreement Corporation. An organization chartered by the Federal Reserve to engage in international banking and financial operations. Edge corporations can be broken into domestic branches, banking institutions, or investment institutions.

Effective yield of a loan takes the payment accrual basis and the payment frequency into account.

Efficiency ratio measures the proportion of net operating revenues that are absorbed by overhead expenses. Lower value indicates greater efficiency.

Enterprise risk management (ERM) is a process affected by an enterprise's board of directors, management, and other personnel that is applied across an enterprise to identify, assess, and manage risks within its risk appetite and provide reasonable assurance of achieving its objectives.

Equity capital is the book value of assets less the book value of liabilities.

Equity capital ratio is the bank's equity capital, exclusive of the allowance for loan and lease losses, divided by the bank's total assets.

Euro. The official currency of most members of the European Union.

Eurocurrency. Certificates of deposit (CDs), bonds, deposits, or any capital market instrument issued outside the national boundaries of the currency in which the instrument is denominated (for example, eurodollars or Swiss francs).

Eurodollars. U.S. dollar-denominated deposits placed in banks outside the United States. Holders may include individuals, companies, banks, and central banks. London Interbank Offered Rate (LIBOR) is the interest rate paid on Eurodollars.

European-style put and call options. The holder can exercise the option only on the last business day before the expiration date.

Exchange rate. The price of one currency stated in terms of another currency.

Exchange-traded fund (ETF). An investment vehicle holding a commodity or other asset that issues shares that are traded like a stock on a securities exchange.

Exercise Price. See *strike price.*

Expiry is the expiration date of a put or call option or a futures contract.

Fair Isaac Corporation (FICO) credit scores. FICO consumer credit scores are widely used by banks and other lenders to determine a borrower's credit risk. They are also used by Equifax and TransUnion for their credit reports. For additional details, see www.myfico.com/Default.aspx.

Fair value. The valuation of various assets and liabilities on the balance sheet—including trading assets and liabilities, available-for-sale securities, loans held for sale, assets and liabilities accounted for under the fair value option, and foreclosed assets—involves the use of fair values (Federal Deposit Insurance Corporation definition).

Federal Deposit Insurance Corporation (FDIC). An independent agency of the U.S. government that insures selected deposits at FDIC-insured banks and savings associations.

Federal Deposit Insurance Corporation Improvement Act of 1991 (FDICIA). Increased bank capital requirements. FDICIA included prompt corrective action (PCA) rules of how to deal with undercapitalized banks.

Federal funds refers to the purchase or sale of excess reserves of banks that are members of the Federal Reserve System.

Federal Home Loan Bank advances. The Federal Home Loan Bank System provides liquidity to member institutions that hold mortgages in their portfolios and facilitates the financing of home mortgages by making low-cost loans, called *advances,* to those members.

FIFO. See *LIFO*.

Finance company. Financial intermediary that makes loans to individuals or businesses.

Financial holding company. A financial entity engaged in a broad range of banking-related activities, created by the Gramm-Leach-Bliley Act of 1999. These activities include insurance underwriting, securities dealing and underwriting, financial and investment advisory services, merchant banking, issuing or selling securitized interests in bank-eligible assets, and generally engaging in any nonbanking activity authorized by the Bank Holding Company Act.

Financial institutions, in the context of the bank secrecy act/anti-money laundering (BSA/AML) laws, include commercial banks; all subsidiaries of bank holding companies; Edge and Agreement corporations; U.S. branches and agencies of foreign banks; savings and loan associations; credit unions; federally regulated securities brokers, dealers, and investment companies; money service businesses (MSBs, currency dealers or exchangers; check cashers; issuers of traveler's checks, money orders, or stored value; sellers or redeemers of traveler's checks, money orders, or stored value; and funds transmitters); persons subject to supervision by state or federal bank supervisory authority; casinos; card clubs; futures commission merchants; introducing brokers; commodity pool operators; and commodity trading advisors. Individuals and/or groups engaging in informal value transfer systems (IVTS), insurance companies, and mutual funds were added to the list.

Financial intermediaries are economic entities whose principal function is to manage the financial assets of other economic entities, such as business concerns and individuals. They bring savers, investors, and borrowers together by selling securities to savers and investors for money and then investing or lending the money to other entities.

Financial leverage is the relationship between debt and equity. The higher the debt/equity ratio, the higher the degree of financial leverage.

Financial Stability Oversight Council identifies risks to financial stability that could arise from financial distress or from the ongoing activities of large bank and nonbank financial companies and payment systems or that could arise outside the financial services marketplace.

Float funds. Funds held by an institution during the check-clearing process before they are made available to a depositor.

Foreign bank generally refers to any U.S. operation of a banking organization headquartered outside the United States.

Foreign banking organization (FBO). Foreign banking organizations can acquire or establish freestanding banks or bank holding companies in the United States. These entities are regulated and supervised as domestic institutions.

Foreign banking organization as a BHC. A foreign banking organization that also acts as a bank holding company and is thus supervised by the Board of Governors of the Federal Reserve.

Foreign banking organization of a BHC. A foreign banking organization that is owned or controlled by a bank holding company.

Foreign branch of a U.S. bank. A branch that resides outside the United States but has a parent located in the United States.

Foreign entity other. Foreign institutions that engage in banking activities usually in connection with the business of banking in the countries where such foreign institutions are organized or operating.

Foreign exchange transaction risk is the risk to capital and earnings arising from the conversion of a bank's financial statements from one currency to another.

Forward markets refer to future delivery.

Forward price is the ratio of the currency amounts to be paid at the expiration of the currency swap.

Forwards are private, cash-market agreements between a buyer and seller for the future delivery of a commodity at an agreed price. In contrast to futures contracts, forward contracts are not standardized and not transferable.

Funding liquidity. See *liquidity.*

Futures are standardized contracts for the purchase and sale of financial instruments or physical commodities for future delivery on a regulated commodity futures exchange.

Gharar is the Islamic law of risk.

Government-sponsored entities (GSEs) include Fannie Mae, Freddie Mac, and Ginnie Mae.

Grace period is the time within which any credit extended can be repaid without incurring a finance change due to a periodic interest rate.

Graduated payment mortgages (GPMs) are fixed-rate mortgage loans where monthly payments are low at first and then rise over a period of years. Because the monthly payments on GPMs are so low in the early years, there is *negative amortization*—the monthly payments are insufficient to pay the interest on the loan.

Growing equity mortgages (GEMs) are 15-year fully amortized home mortgage loans that provide for successively higher debt service payments over the life of the loan.

Harmonization is having uniform international bank regulations to avoid divergent standards.

Hedging refers to trades used to reduce risk.

Home equity line of credit (HELOC) can be a traditional second mortgage or a revolving line of credit, in which case the line of credit has a second mortgage status but would be the first lien if the borrower has no mortgage debt outstanding when the credit line was established.

Hybrid mortgage. See *2/28 adjustable rate mortgages.*

Ijaara in Islamic banking refers to a buy-and-lease-back agreement that involves buying property.

Immunization occurs when the duration of a bank's assets and liabilities are equal to zero. Immunization protects the value of equity from changes in market rates of interest.

In-the-money option. When the strike price of a call (put) option is below (higher than) the price of the underlying asset.

Income risk refers to the risk of losing income when movements in bank borrowing and lending rates are not perfectly synchronized.

Industrial bank A limited-service financial institution that raises funds by selling certificates called *investment shares* and by accepting deposits. Often called Morris Plan banks or industrial loan companies. Industrial banks are distinguished from commercial loan companies because industrial banks accept deposits in addition to making consumer loans. Industrial banks differ from commercial banks because they do not offer demand deposit (checking) accounts. Industrial banks are not regulated by the Federal Reserve.

Informal value transfer systems (IVTS) refer to any nonbank system where someone receives money for the purpose of making those funds, or an equivalent value, available to someone else in a different geographic location.

Insurance company provides compensation based on the happening of one or more contingencies.

Insured branch of an FBO (federal and state). An insured branch accepts retail deposits and must apply for federal deposit insurance.

Interchange fees in credit card transactions are the amount paid by the merchant's bank to the card user's bank and the card network that processes the transaction.

Interest-only mortgages. The interest-only mortgage lets the borrower pay only the interest portion of the loan for some predetermined period, and then the loan payments are adjusted to fully amortize over the remaining life of the loan.

Interest rate repricing refers to the time when the interest rate on an instrument is adjusted.

Interest rate risk is the risk to earnings and capital that interest rates may change unfavorably.

Interest rates are the price paid for the use of money.

Intermediate-term interest rates. Interest rates on debt securities with maturities ranging from three to five years.

Inventory turnover ratio is calculated by dividing the cost of goods sold by inventory. As a general rule, the higher the turnover, the faster the company can realize profits.

Investment bank/company. Acts as underwriter or agent that serves as intermediary between an issuer of securities and the investing public.

Jumbo mortgage is one that is larger than the limits set by Fannie Mae and Freddie Mac. In 2010, the single-family loan limit was $417,000 in the 48 contiguous states and $625,500 in Alaska, Hawaii, and the Virgin Islands. Mortgage loans exceeding these loan limits are called *nonconforming loans*.

Large cap. See *market capitalization*.

Large complex banking organizations (LCBOs) are very large bank holding companies and financial holding companies that engage in a wide variety of permissible activities. They are determined by their asset size, the extent of international operations, participation in large-value payment and settlement systems, and other factors.

Late charges. Borrowers are required to make their monthly payments by a certain date or pay a late charge. Late charges cover the costs of handling delinquent accounts and add to the lender's fee income.

LEAPS. Long-Term Equity AnticiPation Securities are long-term options that expire at dates up to two years and eight months in the future.

Lease. A contract that enables a user—the lessee—to secure the use of a tangible asset over a specified period of time by making payments to the owner—the lessor.

Legal risks arise from unenforceable contracts, lawsuits, or adverse judgments that may negatively affect the operations or the financial condition of the bank.

Legal tender includes U.S. coins and currency (including Federal Reserve notes and circulating notes of Federal Reserve banks and national banks).

Lender liability means that the lender may be sued by borrowers or others for losses and damages.

Letter of credit. A written commitment by a bank to make a payment to an exporter on behalf of an importer, under specified conditions.

Leverage ratio can be defined as debt obligations divided by equity. One example of leverage is the tier 1 leverage capital ratio (tier 1 capital/average assets).

Liabilities represent what the company owes to others. Liabilities due to be paid within one year, or within an operating cycle, are called *current liabilities.* The remainder of the liabilities includes long-term debts and leases and deferred liabilities.

LIBOR (the London Inter-Bank Offered Rate) is the interest rate that high-credit-quality banks (AA-rated or above) charge one another for short-term financing in international markets. It is the rate paid on eurodollar deposits.

LIFO (last in, first out) method of inventory valuation. Alternatively, there is **FIFO** (first in, first out).

Liquidity. *Market liquidity* refers to assets that can be converted into cash quickly with little or no loss in value. *Funding liquidity* is the ability to raise cash or its equivalents by selling assets or borrowing funds.

Liquidity coverage ratio (LCR) is part of Basel III. It requires banks to have high-quality liquid assets that should be equal to or greater than their net cash outflows over 30 days. Net cash outflows are the expected cash inflows less cash outflows adjusted for stress conditions.

Liquidity crisis is a sudden and prolonged evaporation of both market and funding liquidity with potentially serious consequences for the stability of the financial system and the real economy.

Liquidity risk is the risk to earnings and capital related to a financial intermediary's ability to meet its financial obligations to depositors or borrowers.

Loan agreement. When the bank decides to grant a loan, all of the terms of the loan are put into a contract called a *loan agreement.*

Loan brokers are individuals or firms who act as agents or brokers between the borrower and the lender.

Loan covenants are conditions in the loan contract that the borrower must meet.

Lock boxes are mailboxes where retail customers send their payments for goods and services purchased.

Long. One who has bought a security or commodity is said to be long. The opposite of being short.

Long net futures positions or short net positions occur when all open long futures positions and open short positions in an account are offset against each other; the difference is either a surplus of long or of short positions.

Long-term interest rates. Interest rates on debt securities with maturities of five years or longer.

Manufactured home is a structure that is transportable in one or more sections. In traveling mode, the home is 8 feet or more in width and 40 feet or more in length. A manufactured home is designed and constructed to the federal manufactured construction and safety standards and is labeled as such.

Margin. The minimum investment needed to maintain a stock/securities trading position. It is usually expressed as a percentage of the contract's value.

Market capitalization. There is no generally accepted meaning of this term. However, a working definition is that a stock market capitalization of $10 billion or more is large-cap, $2 billion to $9.99 million is mid-cap, and less than $2 billion is small-cap.

Market liquidity. See *liquidity.*

Market risk is the risk that price changes can affect both on- and off-balance-sheet values of assets and liabilities.

Medium cap. See *market capitalization.*

Member bank is a member of the Federal Reserve System, including all nationally chartered banks and any state-chartered or mutual savings banks that apply for membership and are accepted.

Money is a generally accepted means of exchange and store of value in terms of a defined unit of account.

Money market deposit account (MMDA) is a bank account designed to compete with money market funds. It offers a relatively low rate of interest and the ability to withdraw funds. There can be no more than six withdrawals per calendar month or statement cycle, of which no more than three can be by check, draft, or debit card.

Money market instruments are short-term debt securities such as commercial paper.

Money market mutual fund (MMF) is an open ended *mutual fund* that invests in short-term debt securities.

Moral hazard is the risk that the borrower, who now has the loan, might use the funds to engage in high-risk activities in expectation of earning higher returns.

Mortgage is a written conveyance of title to real property.

Mortgage-backed securities (MBS) are securitized mortgage loans. A type of collateralized debt obligation (CDO). An MBS is a CDO that represents a claim on the cash flows from mortgage loans.

Mortgage insurance. Private mortgage insurance for conventional mortgage loans is required by some lenders to reduce the default risk by insuring against loss on a specified percentage of the loan, usually the top 20 percent to 25 percent.

Mudaraba or murabaha are forms of profit-sharing loan contracts used in Islamic banking.

Mutual savings bank is a financial institution that accepts deposits primarily from individuals and places a large portion of its funds into mortgage loans.

Naked credit default swaps are swaps in which the holder has no risk of financial loss if the underlying security fails.

National banks are commercial banks chartered by the Office of the Comptroller of the Currency (OCC). They have the word *National* or *NA* for National Association in their names. They are required to be members of the Federal Reserve System and the Federal Deposit Insurance Corporation.

National Information Center (NIC) is a central repository of data about banks and other institutions for which the Federal Reserve has a supervisory, regulatory, or research interest, including both domestic and foreign banking organizations operating in the United States.

National rates and rate caps are the maximum interest rates determined by the Federal Deposit Insurance Corporation that can be paid on deposit products that apply to less than well-capitalized institutions.

Negative amortization. See *graduated payment mortgage.*

Net interest income (NII) is interest income less interest expense.

Net interest margin (NIM) is the difference between interest and dividends earned on interest-bearing assets and interest paid to depositors and creditors, expressed as a percentage of average-earning assets. No adjustments are made for income that is tax exempt.

Net profit margin on sales is computed by dividing net income by net sales. It is the percent of profit earned for each dollar of sales.

Net stable funding ratio (NSFR) is part of Basel III. It requires that a bank's available stable funding should at least equal its required stable funding.

Net working capital is the arithmetic difference between current assets and current liabilities. It represents a cushion for creditors' short-term loans.

Nominal interest rate is the interest rate stated in a loan agreement.

Nonconforming loans. See *jumbo mortgages*.

Noncore funding sources of funds include time deposits over $100,000, brokered deposits, foreign office deposits, and borrowed funds from Federal Home Loan Banks.

Nondepository trust company accepts and executes trusts but does not issue currency. Nondepository trust companies can be either Federal Reserve members or nonmembers.

Nonmember banks. This subset includes all commercial banks that are state-chartered and *not* members of the Federal Reserve System. Commercial banks include all Bank Insurance Fund (BIF), Savings Association Insurance Fund (SAIF), and BIF/SAIF-insured commercial banks and industrial banks. Effective March 31, 2006, the FDIC merged the BIF and the SAIF into a new fund, the Deposit Insurance Fund (DIF). All institutions carrying BIF, SAIF, and BIF/SAIF insurance were transitioned to DIF accordingly.

Nonrevolving loans or closed-end loans must be repaid within a set period, such as 48 months. Automobile loans that must be repaid within 48 months are an example of closed-end loans.

Notional amount. The nominal or face amount that is used to calculate payments made on swaps and other risk management products. This amount generally does not change hands and is thus referred to as notional.

Office of the Comptroller of the Currency (OCC) charters, regulates, and supervises national banks.

Open-end loans. See *revolving loans*.

Operational risk refers to failed processes, people, systems, and events that can have adverse effects on banks and other organizations.

Options are contracts that give the bearer the right, but not the obligation, to be long or short a futures contract on a security or commodity at a specified price within a specified time period. The specified price is called the *strike price*. The futures contract that the long may establish by exercising the option is referred to as the *underlying futures contract*.

Out-of-the-money option. When the strike price of a call (put) option is higher (lower) than the price of the underlying asset.

Overdraft. An overdraft occurs when a customer writes a check on uncollected funds or when there are insufficient funds in the account to cover the withdrawal. Overdrafts for less than one day are called *daylight overdrafts*.

Par value is the face value of a debt security. For example, a bond can have a face or par value of $1,000.00.

Participations. Banks buy and sell parts of loans to other banks. The parts of the loans are participations.

Partnership. A voluntary contract between two or more individuals who agree to carry on a business together in specified terms of participation, profits, and losses.

Payment accrual basis refers to the number of days used in the interest rate calculation on a loan.

Payments systems are the means by which financial transactions are settled. The payments system involves the clearing of checks, electronic deposits and transfers, settlement of credit card transactions, wire transfers, and other aspects of the movement of funds.

PDAs. Personal digital assistants (e.g., BlackBerry, HP, Palm).

Peer groups in uniform bank performance reports (UBPRs) are based on asset size, number full service branches, location, and other factors.

PIN number (PIN) is a personal identification number.

Points. In addition to charging interest on borrowed funds, lenders charge both fixed-rate and adjustable-rate mortgage borrowers additional fees or points to increase their income and to cover the costs of originating and closing mortgage loans. A *point* is 1 percent of the principal amount of a mortgage loan, and points are prepaid interest.

Preemption. The National Bank Act of 1864 preempted state laws that tried to direct or control the activities of the banks granted under federal law.

Premium. The purchase price of an option.

Prepayment (stored-value) cards. A certain dollar amount is prepaid into an account, and deductions are made for each transaction.

Price risk. The price of an asset, such as bonds, can decline in value.

Primary credit refers to loans made by the Federal Reserve to generally sound depository institutions on a very short-term basis, typically overnight, at a rate above the Federal Open Market Committee's (FOMC) target rate for federal funds. Secondary credit is available to depository institutions that are not eligible for primary credit.

Primary securities are all debt and equity securities issued by business concerns and individuals. Bonds, notes, loans, mortgages, and stocks are examples of primary securities issued by business concerns.

Prime rate is the base rate of interest on corporate loans made by banks.

Prompt corrective action (PCA). See *Federal Deposit Insurance Corporation Improvement Act.*

Prudential regulation of banks deals with their safety and soundness in order to protect depositors' funds and the economic stability of the economy.

Put option. The option buyer pays a fee (*premium*) to the seller for the right to sell the underlying asset at an agreed price (*strike* or *exercise price*) until the contract expires (*expiry*).

Rate caps. See *national rate caps.*

Real bills doctrine held that banks borrowed short-term funds and made short-term self-liquidating loans.

Real-time gross settlements (RTGS). The system settles each transaction individually as it occurs, rather than processing transactions in batches.

Regulatory arbitrage. Finding legal ways to get around restrictions imposed by laws or regulations.

Reports of condition and income are commonly referred to as *call reports.*

Repurchase agreements, or repos, are short-term contracts to sell and repurchase financial assets, such as Treasury securities, at a future date. From the point of view of the institution buying the security, it is a **reverse repo.**

Reputational risk. The potential that negative publicity regarding an institution's business practices, whether true or not, will cause a decline in the customer base, costly litigation, or revenue reductions.

Retail banking. Banking services provided to individuals and to small business concerns.

Return on assets (ROA). A comprehensive measure of profitability, measuring the productivity for shareholders, bondholders, and other creditors. It is calculated by dividing net income by total assets.

Return on equity (ROE) measures the rate of return on the stockholders' investment in the corporation, which includes their paid-in capital, as well as retained earnings. It is calculated by dividing net income by total stockholders' equity.

Reverse mortgages are designed for senior citizens, 62 and older, who own their houses free and clear and want to increase their incomes by borrowing against the equity in their houses.

Review of accounting data refers to performing inquiry and analytical procedures that provide an accountant with a reasonable basis for expressing limited assurance that there are no material modifications that should be made to the statements for them to be in conformity with generally accepted accounting principles.

Revolving letter of credit is a *letter of credit* for a stated amount that can be drawn upon multiple times.

Revolving loans are used to finance borrowers' temporary and seasonal working capital needs for business concerns. The bank is obligated to make the loans up to the maximum amount of the loan, if the borrower is in compliance with the terms of the agreement. They usually have a maturity of two years or more. Revolving loans also refer to open-ended consumer loans, such as credit card loans.

Risk refers to the probability of loss and the variability of returns. Low risk is usually associated with low returns, and high risk with high returns.

Risk-weighted assets of banks are assigned four risk weights: 0 percent, 20 percent, 50 percent, and 100 percent, depending on their relative risk. Zero percent reflects the lowest risk, and 50 percent is the highest risk category.

Savings and loan association. A financial institution that accepts deposits primarily from individuals and channels its funds primarily into residential mortgage loans.

Savings bank. Banking institution organized to encourage thrift by paying interest dividends on savings. Savings banks can have state and federal affiliations, for example, state savings banks and federal savings banks.

Scotoma is a term used by psychologists to mean a culturally induced blind spot.

Second mortgage. See *home equity line of credit (HELOC).*

Secondary credit. See *primary credit.*

Secondary securities are claims against financial intermediaries that may take the form of demand deposits (checking accounts), money market deposit accounts (MMDAs), savings deposits, life insurance policies, mutual fund shares, and other types of claims.

Securities broker/dealer. Entities primarily engaged in acting as agents (i.e., brokers) between buyers and sellers in buying or selling securities on a commission or transaction fee basis.

Securitization is the packaging and selling of loans, such as mortgage and credit card loans. These are asset-backed securities (ABS).

Seigniorage refers to the interest saved by the U.S. Treasury from having currency, which is non-interest-bearing debt, circulate as a medium of exchange. It is also the profit for the Treasury, where profit is the difference between the interest earned on assets financed by issuing currency and the cost of issuing and redeeming it.

Settlement is the formal process by which ownership of real property, evidenced by the title, is transferred from the seller to the buyer.

Shadow banking system refers to the whole alphabet soup of levered-up nonbank investment conduits, vehicles, and structures.

Shared appreciation mortgage (SAM) is a mortgage loan arrangement whereby the borrower agrees to share in the increased value of the property (usually 30 percent to 50 percent) with the lender in return for a reduction in the fixed-interest rate at the time the loan is made.

Shared national credits (SNCs). Participation by three or more unaffiliated banks (supervised by a federal credit agency) in a syndicated loan or formal loan commitments in excess of $20 million are called shared national credits.

Shari'ah board is an Islamic bank's board of scholars.

Short. The promise to sell a certain quantity of a commodity or security at a specified price in the future. The opposite of being long.

Short-term interest rates. Interest rates on debt securities with maturities of less than three years.

Small-cap. See *market cap.*

Smart cards are credit and debit cards containing silicon chips capable of storing data and making simple computations that are being introduced into the payments system in China, Europe, and the United States.

Sole proprietor has the legal right or exclusive title to a business.

Special purpose vehicle (SPV), also referred to as a *special purpose entity (SPE),* are off-balance-sheet legal entities used to isolate risky assets from the parent organization or company and transfer the risks to others. They are also referred to as *bankruptcy remote entities.*

Speculators are traders who attempt to profit by anticipating the prices of financial instruments and commodities.

Spot market is the market in which cash transactions for the physical commodity occur, and the item is bought and sold for cash and delivered immediately.

Spot yield is the annualized discount rate and the yield to maturity on the most recently issued Treasury securities with a designated maturity.

Standby letter of credit is a contingent claim that involves a bank's agreement to pay an agreed-upon amount on presentation of evidence of default or nonperformance of the party whose obligation is guaranteed.

State member banks. This subset includes all commercial banks that are state-chartered and members of the Federal Reserve System. Commercial banks include all Bank Insurance Fund (BIF), Savings Association Insurance Fund (SAIF), and BIF/SAIF-insured commercial banks and industrial banks. (Effective March 31, 2006, the FDIC merged the BIF and the SAIF into a new fund, the Deposit Insurance Fund (DIF). All institutions carrying BIF, SAIF, and BIF/SAIF insurance were transitioned to DIF accordingly.)

Stockholders' equity represents the owners' investment in the business.

Stored-value card. See *prepayment card.*

Strategic risk. The current and prospective impact on earnings or capital arising from adverse business decisions, improper implementation of decisions, or lack of responsiveness to industry changes.

Strike price. The option buyer pays a fee (*premium*) to the seller, for the right to buy (a *call option*) or sell (a *put option*) the underlying asset at an agreed price (*strike* or *exercise price*) until the contract expires (*expiry*).

Structured investment vehicles (SIVs) are a type of off-balance-sheet investment fund. They can borrow short-term and lend long-term in asset-backed securities or other investments. The asset-backed securities include, but are not limited to, mortgages and credit cards. Their investments can be segregated into various tranches of risk and maturities.

Subchapter S corporations have 100 or fewer shareholders, and they are taxed as a partnership.

Subprime real estate loans. Simply stated, subprime means high risk. There is no uniform definition of subprime real estate loans. They refer to high-risk mortgage loans made to borrowers with low credit scores (e.g., Fair Isaac Corporation (FICO) Credit scores below 660), high loan-to-value ratios, and/or high debt-to-income ratios. Subprime loans also include loans originated by lenders specializing high-risk mortgage loans, such as 2/28 adjustable rate mortgage loans, and nonconforming loans, which are real estate loans that do not conform to the Government Sponsored Entity's loan standards.

Substitute checks are printed images of checks used for check processing.

Sukuk bonds are traditional Islamic non-interest-bearing bonds based on profit-loss-risk-sharing issuers with asset-backed borrowing contracts.

Swap refers to the simultaneous purchase and sale of currencies or interest rate products in spot and forward market transactions. Swap contracts are traded over-the-counter.

Swap rate. In a swap, it is the fixed interest rate that the receiver gets in exchange for the uncertainty of paying a floating rate (LIBOR) over time.

Swap spread. In a swap, it is the difference between the swap rate and the government bond yields for the same maturity.

Swaption is an option on a swap. Purchasing a swaption would allow a party to set up, but not enter into, a potentially offsetting swap at the time they execute the original swap.

Systemic risk occurs when bank failures are potentially contagious and only then if the losses in one bank cascade into other banks or other economies throughout the world.

Takaful is a form of insurance in Islamic banking.

TED spread is the difference between the three-month T-bill interest rate and three-month LIBOR. It is a measure of credit risk in the economy.

Term loan. A single loan for a stated period of time (e.g., five years) or a series of loans on specified dates. Term loans are used for a specific purpose, such as acquiring machinery, renovating a building, or refinancing debt.

Thrifts primarily accept savings account deposits and invest most of the proceeds in mortgages. Savings banks, savings and loan associations, and credit unions are examples of thrift institutions.

Tier 1 leverage ratio is tier 1 capital divided by average quarterly consolidated assets (from the most recent call report) less goodwill and other intangibles.

Tier 1 risk-based capital ratio is tier 1 capital divided by risk-weighted assets. Tier 1 capital is the core capital. See *core capital.*

Tier 2 risk-based capital ratio is tier 2 capital divided by risk-weighted assets. Tier 2 capital is the sum of allowance for loan and lease losses (limited to 1.25 percent of risk-weighted assets), perpetual preferred stock that is not part of tier 1 capital, intermediate-term preferred stock, and subordinated debt.

Total risk-based capital ratio is the sum of tier 1 risk-based capital and tier 2 risk-based capital. The minimum total risk-based capital ratio is 8 percent.

Time draft. A means of payment that is similar to a predated check.

Times interest earned. See *debt coverage.*

Top holder is the company at the top of the ownership chain in a bank holding company (i.e., it controls all of the companies). See *bank holding company.*

Total risk-based capital. The sum of tier 1 plus tier 2 capital. Tier 1 capital consists of common shareholders' equity, perpetual preferred shareholders' equity with noncumulative dividends, retained earnings, and minority interests in the equity accounts of consolidated subsidiaries. Tier 2 capital consists of subordinated debt, intermediate-term preferred stock, cumulative and long-term preferred stock, and a portion of a bank's allowance for loan and lease losses.

True lease. See Internal Revenue Code Ruling 55-540 for the details. It deals with lease payments and tax deductions.

Truncation. The payment information on a check is captured and processed electronically. The truncated check is not returned to the writer.

Trust. A legal entity that can hold and manage assets for one or more beneficiaries for as long as the trust exists.

Unbanked. Households that do not have a checking or savings account.

Underbanked. Households that have a checking account or savings account, but they rely instead on alternative financial services.

Underwater. The market value of real estate that is being used as collateral is worth less than the amount of the loan that was used to acquire the property.

Uniform bank performance report (UBPR) is an analytical tool created by bank regulators for supervisory, examination, and bank management purposes.

Uninsured agency of an Foreign Banking Organization (federal and state) does not accept retail deposits and need not apply for Federal Deposit insurance.

Uninsured branch of an Foreign Banking Organization (federal and state) does not accept retail deposits and need not apply for federal deposit insurance.

U.S. branches and agencies of Foreign Banking Organizations are entities contained within and controlled by a foreign banking organization.

Value at risk (VaR) is a statistical measure that banks use to quantify the maximum expected loss, over a specified horizon and at a certain confidence level, in normal markets.

Volcker Rule, introduced by former Federal Reserve Chairman Paul Volcker, a part of the Dodd-Frank Act. It restricts banks from proprietary trading and sets limits on certain relationships and investments in hedge funds and private equity funds.

Wholesale banking. Services provided to medium-size and large business concerns and governments.

Zero coupon bonds pay the principal amount at maturity and have no periodic interest payments.

References

The URLs and web sites listed in the References were correct at the time the book was written. However, some URLs and web sites changed over time and may no longer be valid.

CHAPTER 1 Lessons Learned from Banking Crises

Ahamed, Liaquat. *Lords of Finance*. New York: Penguin, 2009.

Bailey, Kevin J., Deputy Comptroller, Office of the Comptroller of the Currency. Testimony before the U.S. House of Representatives Subcommittee on Capital Markets, Insurance, and Government Sponsored Enterprises, March 12, 2009.

Bair, Sheila C., Chairman, Federal Deposit Insurance Corporation. Statement on the Causes and Current State of the Financial Crisis before the Financial Crisis Inquiry Commission, January 14, 2010.

Ball, Ray. "The Global Financial Crises and the Efficient Market Hypothesis: What Have We Learned?" *Journal of Applied Corporate Finance* 21, no. 4 (Fall 2009): 8–16.

Bank of America Corporation 2008 Annual Report. "About Bank of America Corporation," 2009.

Bank for International Settlements. "Table 19: Amounts Outstanding of Over-the-Counter (OTC) Derivatives." *BIS Quarterly Review* (June 2007): A103.

Bech, Morton L., and Tara Rice. "Profits and Balance Sheet Developments at U.S. Commercial Banks in 2008," *Federal Reserve Bulletin* (June 2009): A63, A71.

Board of Governors of the Federal Reserve System. Federal Reserve Press Release, September 16, 2008. (Re AIG). www.federalreserve.gov/newsevents/press/other/20080916a.htm.

Board of Governors of the Federal Reserve System. "Report Pursuant to Section 129 of the Emergency Economic Stabilization Act of 2008: Bridge Loan to the Bear Stearns Companies Inc. through JPMorgan Chase Bank, N.A., March 14, 2008. www.federalreserve.gov/monetarypolicy/files/129bearstearnsbridgeloan.pdf.

Board of Governors of the Federal Reserve System. Federal Reserve Statistical Release H.15. "Selected Interest Rates, Historical Data, 2009." www.federalreserve.gov/releases/h15/data.htm.

Code of Federal Regulations. Title 12: Banks and Banking: Part 204—Reserve Requirements of Depository Institutions (Regulation D).

Colonial BancGroup. 2008 Annual Report, 2009.

Cummins, Chip, Dana Cimilluca, and Sara Schaefer Muñoz. "Dubai's Woes Shake U.A.E., Region." *Wall Street Journal.* November 27, 2009, C1, C3.

"Dubai's Debt Reckoning." *Wall Street Journal.* November 28–29, 2009, A14.

FannieMae News Release. "Fannie Mae Announces 2005 Conforming Loan Limit of $359,650." February 1, 2005. www.fanniemae.com/newsreleases/2005/3445.jhtml?p=Media&s=News+Releases.

FDIC. Statistics on Banking, *Historical 1934–1994,* vol. 1. 1995.

FDIC. *History of the Eighties, Lessons for the Future,* vol. 1. 1999.

FDIC. "Statistics at a Glance, Historical Trends as of March 31, 2009."

FDIC. "Quarterly Banking Profile, Commercial Bank Performance. Table III-A, FDIC Insured Commercial Banks, Third Quarter, 2009."

FDIC. "Quarterly Banking Profile, All Institutions Performance, Third Quarter 2009." www2.fdic.gov/qbp/2009sep/qbpall.html.

Federal Deposit Insurance Corporation Failed Bank List.

Federal Reserve Bank of Richmond. "Markets, Trends and Statistics, First Quarter 2009. US Residential Mortgage Delinquency Rates Data Seasonally Adjusted, 1998:Q1–2009:Q1." www.richmondfed.org/banking/markets_trends_and_statistics/trends/pdf/delinquency_and_foreclosure_rates.pdf.

Fennell, Edward. "Dubai's Golden Sands Lose Their Lustre." *TimesOnLine*, December 10, 2009. http://business.timesonline.co.uk/tol/business/law/article6950725.ece.

Fisher, Richard W., President, Federal Reserve Bank of Dallas. "The Egocentricity of the Present." Remarks before a Federal Reserve Bank of Dallas Community Forum, San Antonio, Texas, April 9, 2008.

Getter, Darryl E., Mark Jickling, Marc Labonte, and Edward V. Murphy. "Financial Crisis? The Liquidity Crunch of 2007." CRS Report for Congress, September 21, 2007.

Ginnie Mae. "Who We Are. . . ." www.ginniemae.gov/about/about.asp?section=about.

Gumble, Peter. "Iceland: The Country That Became a Hedge Fund." *CNNMoney.com,* December 1, 2008. http://money.cnn.com/2008/12/01/magazines/fortune/iceland_gumbel.fortune/.

Gup, Benton E. "International Banking Crises: The Real Estate Connection," in *International Banking Crises: Large-Scale Failures, Massive Government Intervention.* Westport, CT: Quorum, 1999.

Gup, Benton E., and Thomas Lutton. "Potential Effects of Fair Value Accounting on US Bank Regulatory Capital." *Journal of Applied Finance* 18, nos. 1–2 (2009): 38–48.

Hunter, William C., George G. Kaufman, and Michael Pomerleano. *Asset Price Bubble: The Implications for Monetary, Regulatory and International Policies.* Cambridge, MA: MIT Press, 2003.

Khandani, Amir E., Andrew W. Lo, and Robert C. Merton. "Systemic Risk and the Refinancing Ratchet Effect" (MIT Sloan Research Paper No. 4750-09; Harvard Business School Finance Working Paper No. 1472892, September 15, 2009): http://ssrn.com/abstract=1472892.

King, Thomas B., Daniel A. Nuxoll, and Timothy J. Yeager. "Are the Causes of Bank Distress Changing? Can Researchers Keep Up?" (FDIC Center for Financial Research Working Paper No. 2005–03, 2005). www.fdic.gov/bank/analytical/cfr/2005/wp2005/CFRWP_2005-03_nuxoll1.pdf.

"Liquidity Analysis: Decades of Change." *FDIC Supervisory Insights* 4, no. 2 (Winter 2007). (Freely adapted from a presentation by Leonard Matz, International Director, BancWare Academy for SunGard BancWare, at Federal Financial Institutions Examination Council (FFIEC) Capital Markets Specialist Conference in June 2007).

Lorade, Nikhil, and Summer Said. "Dubai Discusses Debt Revamp." *Wall Street Journal*, December 1, 2009, C1, C3.

Markowitz, Harry M. "Modern Portfolio Theory: Financial Engineering, and Their Role in Financial Crises." *CFA Institute, Conference Proceedings Quarterly* (December 2009): 1–6.

Merton, Robert C. "Observations on the Financial Crisis: Systemic Risk, Financial Innovation, Models, and Regulatory Recommendations." Presentation at the ASSA Meeting, Atlanta January 3, 2010.

National Information Center, "Top 50 BHCs, National Information Center." www.ffiec.gov/nicpubweb/nicweb/Top50Form.aspx.

Office of the Comptroller of the Currency. "OCC's Quarterly Report on Bank Trading and Derivatives Activities, Second Quarter 2009." www.occ.gov/topics/capital-markets/financial-markets/trading/derivatives/dq209.pdf.

Office of the Comptroller of the Currency. "Request for Comment on Proposed Interagency Liquidity Guidance." *OCC Bulletin* 2009-21. The guidance can be found in the *Federal Register* 74, no. 127 (Monday, July 6, 2009): 32035.

O'Keefe, Brian. "The Man behind 2009's Biggest Bank Bust." *CNNMoney.com*, October 12, 2009.

President's Working Group on Financial Markets. "Hedge Funds, Leverage, and the Lessons of Long-Term Capital Management." April 1999.

Smaghi, Lorenzo Bini, Member of the Executive Board of the European Central Bank. "What Has the Financial Crisis Taught Us? The Global Dimension and International Policy Cooperation." Speech at the 21st Century Forum 2010, Beijing, September 7, 2010. *BIS Review* 114/2010.

"Summary of Statement No. 159, The Fair Value Option for Financial Assets and Financial Liabilities—Including an Amendment of FASB Statement No. 115": www.fasb.org/st/summary/stsum159.shtml.

"The World's Biggest Banks." *Global Finance*, October 2008, 111.

U.S. Census Bureau. "National Population Projections, Released 2008, Table 1, Projections of the Population and Components of Change for the United States: 2010 to 2050." www.census.gov/population/www/projections/summarytables.html.

U.S. Census Bureau. *Statistical Abstract of the United States 2009*.

U.S. Census Bureau. *Statistical Abstract of the United States 1995*.

U.S. Census Bureau. "U.S. & World Population Clocks." www.census.gov/main/www/popclock.html.

12 U.S.C. 1831f(g)(1)(A); 12 C.F.R. 337.6(a)(2). FDIC Advisory Opinion. "Brokered Deposits: Are Funds Deposited in a Special Reserve Bank Account for the Exclusive Benefit of Customers Brokered Deposits Under Sections 29 and 29A of the FDI Act." Valerie J. Best, Counsel. FDIC-94-39, August 17, 1994.

CHAPTER 2 The Economic Role of Financial Intermediaries

Bair, Sheila. Remarks by FDIC Chairman Sheila Bair at the 45th Annual Bank Structure and Competition Conference, Chicago Federal Reserve Bank; Chicago, May 7, 2009.

Bank of America. *Investor Fact Book*. Full Year 2009, p. 2.

Board of Governors of the Federal Reserve System. "All-Bank Statistics, United States 1896–1959," 33.

Board of Governors of the Federal Reserve System. "Assets and Liabilities of Commercial Banks in the US–H8." Release, February 5, 2010.

Bradley, Christine, Susan Burhouse, Heather Gratton, and Rae Ann Miller. "Alternative Financial Services: A Primer." *FDIC Quarterly* 3, no. 1 (2009).

DeFerrari, Lisa M., and David E. Palmer. "Supervision of Large Complex Banking Organizations." *Federal Reserve Bulletin* (February 2001): 47.

FDIC. "National Survey of Unbanked and Underbanked Households," December 2009.

FDIC. *Quarterly Banking Profile*, 4th Quarter, 2009.

FDIC. *Quarterly Banking Profile*, Second Quarter 2010.

Federal Deposit Insurance Corporation. *History of the Eighties, Lessons for the Future*, vol. 1, 199.

Feldman, Ron J., and Mark Lueck. "Are Banks Really Dying This Time?" *The Region*, Federal Reserve Bank of Minneapolis, September, 2007.

Geithner, Timothy J. "Reducing Systemic Risk in a Dynamic Financial System." Remarks at the Economic Club of New York, June 9, 2008.

Gorton, Gary, and Andrew Metrick. "Regulating the Shadow Banking System" (Working paper, September 10, 2010). http://ssrn.com/abstract=1676947.

Knight, Malcolm D., General Manager of the Bank of International Settlements. "Some Reflections on the Future of Originate-to-Distribute model in the Context of the Current Financial Turmoil" at the Euro 50 Group Roundtable, London, April 21, 2008.

Shin, Hyun Song. "Financial Intermediation and the Post-Crisis Financial System" (Bank of International Settlements Working Paper 304, March 2101).

United States General Accounting Office. "Risk-Focused Bank Examinations: Regulators of Large Banks Face Challenges." GAO/GGD-00-48, January 2000.

Wellink, Nout, Chairman of the Bank for International Settlement. "Risk Management & Financial Stability—Basel II & Beyond." Remarks at the GARP 2007 8th Annual Risk Management Convention, New York, February 27, 2007.

White, Eugene N. "Were Banks Special Intermediaries in Late Nineteenth Century America?" *Review*, Federal Reserve Bank of St. Louis (May–June 1998): 13–32.

CHAPTER 3 The Evolving Legal Environment

Bair, Sheila, Chairman, Federal Deposit Insurance Corporation. "Implementing the Dodd-Frank Wall Street Reform and Consumer Protection Act." Before the Committee on Banking, Housing, and Urban Affairs, U.S. Senate, September 30, 2010.

Bank of America. "Corporate Profile." http://investor.bankofamerica.com/phoenix.zhtml?c=71595&p=irol-irhome.

Bank of International Settlements. Mission Statement. www.bis.org/about/mission.htm.

Board of Governors of the Federal Reserve System. "All Regulations." www.federalreserve.gov/bankinforeg/reglisting.htm#R.

Bank for International Settlement, Basel Committee on Banking Supervision. "Core Principles for Effective Banking Supervision." April 1997.

FDIC. "Historical Statistics on Banking, Index to Notes on Insured Commercial Banks." www2.fdic.gov/hsob/hsobnotes.asp.

FDIC. "Quarterly Banking Profile Graph Book, Number of Institutions by Asset Concentration Group." December 31, 2009.

Federal Reserve Bank of New York. "Banking Institutions and Their Regulators." 2003. www.newyorkfed.org/banking/regrept/BIATR.pdf.

Gup, Benton E., and Robert Brooks. *Interest Rate Risk Management: The Banker's Guide to Using Futures, Options, Swaps and Other Derivatives*. New York: McGraw-Hill, 1993.

Gup, Benton E., and James W. Kolari. *Commercial Banking: The Management of Risk*, 3rd ed. Hoboken, NJ: John Wiley & Sons, 2005.

Hanc, G. "The Banking Crises of the 1980s and Early 1990s: Summary and Implications." *FDIC Banking Review* 11, no. 1 (1998): 1–55.

Lindgren, C. J., G. Garcia, and M. I. Saal. *Bank Soundness and Macroeconomic Policy*. Washington, DC: International Monetary Fund, 1996.

Maltby, Emily. "Entrepreneurs Find Success with Specialty Lenders." *Wall Street Journal*, April 26, 2010, B8.

Matthias, Rieker. "Dimon: New Rules Will Cost Customers." *Wall Street Journal*, September 15, 2010, C17.

National Information Center. "All Institution Types Defined." http://www.ffiec.gov/nicpubweb/nicweb/nichome.aspx.

Office of the Comptroller of the Currency. *Interest Rate Risk: Comptroller's Handbook*. Washington, DC: Office of the Comptroller of the Currency, 1997.

Pozsar, Zoltran, Tobias Adrian, Adam Ashcraft, and Haely Boesky. "Shadow Banking." Federal Reserve Bank of New York Staff Report No. 458, July 2010.

Robertson, Ross M., Comptroller of Bank Supervision. *A Historical Perspective*. Washington, DC: Office of the Comptroller of the Currency, 1995.

SBV Financial Group "About SBV Financial Group": http://ir.svb.com/.

Seiberg, J. "Scrapped: Uniform 150-Day Rule for Writing Off Past-Due Loans." *American Banker*, February 11, 1999, 3.

Steckel, Marc, Associate Director, Division of Insurance and Research, FDIC. "Statement on Executive Compensation Oversight after the Dodd-Frank Wall

Street Reform and Consumer Protection Act of 2010." Before the Committee on Financial Services, U.S. House of Representatives, September 24, 2010.

Treacy, William F. "Credit Risk Ratings at Large U.S. Banks." *Federal Reserve Bulletin*, November 1998, 901.

CHAPTER 4 Asset/Liability Management (ALM)

Bair, Sheila, C. "Systemically Important Institutions, and the Issue of 'Too Big to Fail.'" Before the Financial Crisis Inquiry Commission, Washington, DC, September 2, 2010. www.fcic.gov/hearings/pdfs/2010-0902-Bair.pdf.

Bernanke, Ben S. "Reflections on a Year of Crisis." At the Federal Reserve Bank of Kansas City's Annual Economic Symposium, Jackson Hole, Wyoming, August 21, 2009. www.federalreserve.gov/newsevents/speech/bernanke2009 0821a.htm.

Bernanke, Ben S. "Causes of the Recent Financial and Economic Crisis." Before the Financial Crisis Inquiry Commission, Washington, DC, September 2, 2010. http://federalreserve.gov/newsevents/testimony/bernanke20100902a.htm.

Board of Governors of the Federal Reserve System. "Advisory on Interest Rate Risk Management." January 6, 2010.

Bonte, Eugene A., and Gregg A. Dieguez. "Spread Management: How to Maintain Profitability." *Savings and Loan News* (November 1979): 54–59.

Bradley, Christine M., and Lynn Shibut. "The Liability Structure of FDIC-Insured Institutions: Changes and Implications." *FDIC Banking Review*, 2006.

Clair, Suzanne L., Alison T. Touhey, and Lemoine J. Tuberville. "Nowhere to Go but Up: Managing Interest Rate Risk in a Low-Rate Environment." *Supervisory Insights*, FDIC (Winter 2009): 3–15.

Corston, John, Acting Deputy Director, Complex Financial Institution Branch, Division of Supervision and Consumer Protection, Federal Deposit Insurance Corporation. "Systemically Important Institutions and the Issue of 'Too Big to Fail.'" Before the Financial Crisis Inquiry Commission, Washington, DC, September 1, 2010. www.fdic.gov/news/news/speeches/chairman/spsep0110.html.

Craig, Susanne, and Mike Spector. "Repos Played a Key Role in Lehman's Demise." *Wall Street Journal*, March 13, 2010.

FDIC. "FDIC Issues Interest Rate Risk Advisory." Press Release, January 7, 2010.

FDIC. "Certificates of Deposit: Tips for Savers." www.fdic.gov/deposit/deposits/certificate/index.html.

Federal Reserve Bank of St. Louis. "National Economic Trends." May 2010.

Gorton, Gary B. "The Panic of 2007." Paper presented at "Maintaining Stability in a Changing Financial System," a symposium sponsored by the Federal Reserve Bank of Kansas City, held in Jackson Hole, Wyoming, August 21–23, 2008.

Gup, Benton E., and James W. Kolari. *Commercial Banking: The Management of Risk*, 3rd ed. New York: John Wiley & Co., 2004.

Kaufman, George G. "Measuring and Managing Interest Rate Risk: A Primer." *Economic Perspectives*, Federal Reserve Bank of Chicago (August–September 1984): 16–29.

Kristof, Kathy M., and Andrea Chang. "Federal Regulators Seize Crippled IndyMac Bank." *Los Angeles Times,* July 12, 2008. http://articles.latimes.com/2008/jul/12/business/fi-indymac12.

Macaulay, Frederick R. *The Movements of Interest Rate, Bond Yields and Stock Prices in the United States since 1856*. New York: National Bureau of Economic Research, 1938.

National Information Center, Top 50 Bank Holding Companies: www.ffiec.gov/nicpubweb/nicweb/Top50Form.aspx.

Office of the Comptroller of the Currency, Board of Governors of the Federal Reserve System, Federal Deposit Insurance Corporation, Office of Thrift Supervision, National Credit Union Administration. "Interagency Statement on Funding and Liquidity Risk Management." *Federal Register* 75, no. 54 (March 22, 2010): Notices, 13656–13666.

Rapoport, Michael: "Bank of America, Citigroup Incorrectly Hid Billions in Repo Debt." *Wall Street Journal*, May 26, 2010.

Uniform Bank Performance Report. Ally Bank, March 31, 2010. https://cdr.ffiec.gov/public/Reports/UbprReport.aspx?rptCycleIds=60%2c54%2c58%2c52%2c47&rptid=283&idrssd=3284070.

Walsh, John, Acting Comptroller of the Currency. Testimony before the Committee on Banking, Housing, and Urban Affairs, United States Senate, September 30, 2010.

CHAPTER 5 Hedging and Risk Management

Alworth, Julian S. "The Valuation of US Dollar Interest Rate Swaps" (Bank of International Settlements Economic Paper No. 35, January 1993). www.bis.org/publ/econ35.pdf?noframes=1.

Basel Committee on Banking Supervision. "Report of Special Purpose Entities." September 2009.

Bernanke, Ben S. "The Future of Mortgage Finance in the United States." Speech at the UC Berkeley/UCLA Symposium: The Mortgage Meltdown, the Economy, and Public Policy, Berkeley, California, October 31, 2008. www.federalreserve.gov/newsevents/speech/bernanke20081031a.htm.

Bies, Susan Schmidt. "Enterprise Risk Management and Mortgage Lending." Speech at the National Credit Union Administration 2007 Risk Mitigation Summit, January 11, 2007.

Chicago Board of Trade. "Treasury Futures and Options: Reference Guide, 2006." www.insigniafutures.com/docs/CBOT_Treasuries.pdf.

Chicago Board Options Exchange. "Interest Rate Options." www.cboe.com/LearnCenter/pdf/IRO.pdf.

CMEGroup. "Interest Rate Products." www.cmegroup.com/trading/interest-rates/us-treasury/5-year-us-treasury-note_contract_specifications.html.

Committee of Sponsoring Organizations of the Treadway Commission (COSO). "Enterprise Risk Management: Integrated Framework, Executive Summary." September 2004.

Commodity Futures Trading Commission. "Glossary." www.cftc.gov/ConsumerProtection/EducationCenter/CFTCGlossary/glossary_b.html.

Commodity Futures Trading Commission. "Mission and Responsibilities." www.cftc.gov/About/MissionResponsibilities/index.htm.

Commodities Futures Trading Commission. "Bank Participation Reports." www.cftc.gov/MarketReports/BankParticipationReports/index.htm.

FDIC. "Advisory on Interest Rate Risk Management." January 6, 2010.

FDIC. "Quarterly Banking Profile." Full Year 2009, Table III-A.

FDIC, Office of the Comptroller of the Currency, Department of the Treasury; Board of Governors of the Federal Reserve System; and Office of Thrift Supervision, Department of Treasury. "Risk-Based Capital Guidelines; Capital Adequacy Guidelines; Capital Maintenance: Regulatory Capital; Impact of Modifications to Generally Accepted Accounting Principles; Consolidation of Asset-Backed Commercial Paper Programs; and Other Related Issues, Final Rule." December 16, 2009. www.fdic.gov/news/board/DEC152009no2.pdf.

FDIC Press Release. "FDIC Board Finalizes Regulatory Capital Rule for Statements of Financial Accounting Standards." Press Release. December 16, 2009.

FDIC Press Release PR-85-2008. "JPMorgan Chase Acquires Banking Operations of Washington Mutual." Press release PR 85 2008 September 25, 2008. www.fdic.gov/news/news/press/2008/pr08085.html.

Federal Reserve. Statistical Release H.15 Selected Interest Rates (Daily), May 18, 2010.

Fraser, John, and Betty J. Simkins, eds. *Enterprise Risk Management: Today's Leading Research and Best Practices for Tomorrow's Executives*. New York: John Wiley & Sons, 2010.

Greenspan, Alan. Testimony before the Senate Banking Committee, Financial Crisis Inquiry Commission, Wednesday, April 7, 2010.

Gup, Benton E. *Too Big to Fail: Policies and Practices in Government Bailouts*. Westport, CT: Praeger, 2004.

Gup, Benton E., and Robert Brooks. *Interest Rate Risk Management, A Banker's Guide to Using Futures, Options, Swaps and Other Financial Instruments*. Chicago: Probus, 1993.

Hancock, Diana, and Wayne Passmore. "Three Mortgage Innovations for Enhancing the American Mortgage Market and Promoting Financial Stability." Preliminary draft presented at the UC Berkeley–UCLA symposium "The Mortgage Meltdown, the Economy, and Public Policy," Berkeley, CA, October 31, 2008.

Krainer, John. "Recent Developments in Mortgage Finance." *FRSBSF Economic Letter*, 2009-33, October 26, 2009.

Krimminger, Michael H., Deputy to the Chairman, Federal Deposit Insurance Corporation. "Covered Bonds: Potential Uses and Regulatory Issues." Statement to the Committee on Banking, Housing, and Urban Affairs, United States Senate, September 15, 2010.

Office of the Comptroller of the Currency, Department of the Treasury; Board of Governors of the Federal Reserve System; Federal Deposit Senior Supervisors Group. "Observations on Risk Management Practices during Recent

Market Turbulence." Federal Reserve Bank of New York, March 6, 2008. www.newyorkfed.org/newsevents/news/banking/2008/SSG_Risk_Mgt_doc_final.pdf.

"Overview on Derivatives." Preliminary Staff Report, Financial Crisis Inquiry Commission, June 29, 2010.

Robb, Greg. Minutes of the Board of Governors of the Federal Reserve System, March 14, 2008, quoted "Bear Stearns Too Interconnected to Fail, Fed Says." *MarketWatch*, June 27, 2008. www.marketwatch.com/story/fed-believed-bear-stearns-was-too-interconnected-to-fail.

Segoviano, Miguel A., and Manmohan Singh. "Counterparty Risk in the Over-the-Counter Derivatives Market." (IMF Working Paper WP/08/258, November 2008).

Sjostrom, William K. "The AIG Bailout." *Washington and Lee Law Review* 66 (2009): 943–991. http://ssrn.com/abstract=1346552.

United Kingdom's HM Revenue & Customs. "CTM72890—Financial Instruments: Overview: Currency Swap: Example." www.hmrc.gov.uk/manuals/ctmanual/ctm72890.htm.

United States General Accounting Office. "Financial Derivatives: Actions Needed to Protect the Financial System." GAO/GGD-94-133, May 1994.

United States General Accounting Office. "Risk-Focused Bank Examinations: Regulators of Large Banks Face Challenges." GAO/GGD-00-48, January 2000. www.gao.gov/archive/2000/gg00048.pdf.

Walker, Susanne. "Ten-Year Swap Spread Turns Negative on Renewed Demand for Risk." *Bloomberg Businessweek,* March 23, 2010. www.businessweek.com/news/2010-03-23/ten-year-swap-spread-drops-to-low-on-renewed-demand-for-risk.html.

Williams, Julie L., Chief Counsel and First Senior Deputy Comptroller, Office of the Comptroller of the Currency. Testimony before the Committee on Banking, Housing, and Urban Affairs, United States Senate, September 15, 2010.

CHAPTER 6 Commercial and Industrial Loans

Altman, Edward I. "Valuation, Loss Reserves, and Pricing of Commercial Loans." *Journal of Commercial Lending* (August 1993): 8–25.

Board of Governors of the Federal Reserve System. "Federal Reserve Statistical Release H.15: Selected Interest Rates." www.federalreserve.gov/releases/h15/current/.

Board of Governors of the Federal Reserve System. "Shared National Credits Program 2010 Review." September 2010.

Board of Governors of the Federal Reserve System. "Federal Reserve Statistical Release E.2: Survey of Terms of Business Lending." www.federalreserve.gov/releases/e2/current/default.htm.

Geithner, Timothy F., Treasury Secretary. Remarks before the American Enterprise Institute on Financial Reform, March 22, 2010. www.treas.gov/press/release/tg600.htm.

Gup, Benton E., and James W. Kolari. *Commercial Banking: The Management of Risk*, 3rd ed. New York: John Wiley & Sons, 2004.

Temkin, Kenneth, and Roger C. Kormendi. "An Exploration of a Secondary Market for Small Business Loans." Small Business Association Office of Advocacy (SBAHQ-01-C-0150), April 2003. www.sba.gov/advo/research/rs227_tot.pdf.

U.S. Small Business Administration. "2009 Recovery Act: Frequently Asked Questions." www.sba.gov/idc/groups/public/documents/sba_homepage/recovery_act_faqs.pdf.

CHAPTER 7 Real Estate and Consumer Lending

Bailey, R. Russell. "Fair Lending Implications of Credit Scoring Systems." *FDIC Supervisory Insights*, June 23, 2005.

Bair, Shelia, FDIC Chairman. Speaking at the Wharton School, University of Pennsylvania, International Housing Finance Program, Philadelphia, June 18, 2010.

Board of Governors of the Federal Reserve System. "Mortgage Debt Outstanding." March 2010.

Briault, Clive, Director, Prudential Standards, Financial Services Authority. Speaking at the ZEW/AEI Conference on Regulation and Supervision of Financial Markets and Institutions in the EU, Mannheim, Germany, July 10, 2003.

Elliehausen, Gregory. "The Cost of Bank Regulation: A Review of the Evidence." *Federal Reserve Bulletin* (April 1998): 252–253.

"Examiner's Desk: Amendments to Regulation Z: Compliance Challenges for Bankers and Examiners." *Supervisory Insights,* FDIC, Summer 2010.

FDIC. "Loan Portfolio Composition." Quarterly Banking Profile, First Quarter, 2010. www2.fdic.gov/qbp/2010mar/grbookbw/QBPGRBW.pdf.

Federal Reserve Bank of San Francisco. "COFI: Frequently Asked Questions." www.fhlbsf.com/cofi/faq.asp#0.

Federal Reserve Statistical Release. "Consumer Credit, G19." June 7, 2010. www.federalreserve.gov/releases/g19/Current/.

Gup, Benton E. *Bank Failures in the Major Trading Countries of the World: Causes and Remedies*. Westport, CT: Quorum Books, 1998.

Gup, Benton E., and James W. Kolari. *Commercial Banking: The Management of Risk*, 3rd ed. Hoboken, NJ: John Wiley & Sons, 2004.

Kim, Jane J. "A Car Loan That Outlasts Your Car." *Wall Street Journal*, September 30, 2003, D1, D4.

Office of the Comptroller of the Currency. "Guidelines for Real Estate Lending Policies." *OCC Advisory Letter*, AL2003-7, August 8, 2003; "Credit Risk Management for Home Equity Lending." *OCC Bulletin* 2005-22. www.occ.gov/news-issuances/bulletins/2005/bulletin-2005-22.html.

Office of the Comptroller of the Currency. "Truth in Lending Act." *OCC Bulletin* 2010-14, March 25, 2010.

Texas Constitution. Article XIV, Section 50(a)(6)(B).

Thorndike, David. *Thorndike Encyclopedia of Banking and Financial Tables*, rev. ed. Boston: Warren, Gorham & Lamont, 1980.

U.S. Department of Commerce. *Statistical Abstract of the United States 2009.*

U.S. Federal Housing Finance Board. "Rates & Terms on Conventional Home Mortgages, Annual Summary." www.census.gov/compendia/statab/2010/tables/10s1156.xls.

U.S. Government General Accountability Office. "CREDIT CARDS: Rising Interchange Fees Have Increased Costs for Merchants, but Options for Reducing Fees Pose Challenges." GAO 10-45, November 2009.

Woolsey, Ben, and Matt Schulz. "Credit Card Statistics, Industry Facts, Debt Statistics." www.creditcards.com/credit-card-news/credit-card-industry-facts-personal-debt-statistics-1276.php.

CHAPTER 8 Bank Capital: Capital Adequacy

"All-Bank Statistics, United States, 1896–1955." *Statistical Abstract of the United States* 1989, 1993, 2010.

Bailey, Kevin J., Deputy Comptroller, Office of the Comptroller of the Currency. Testimony before the U.S. House of Representatives Subcommittee on Capital Markets, Insurance, and Government Sponsored Enterprises, March 12, 2009.

Bair, Sheila C., Chairman, Federal Deposit Insurance Corporation. Testimony on the causes and current state of the financial crisis before the Financial Crisis Inquiry Commission, January 14, 2010.

Bank for International Settlements. "Comprehensive Response to the Global Banking Crisis." Press Release, September 7, 2009.

Bank for International Settlements. "Group of Governors and Heads of Supervision Announces Higher Global Minimum Capital Standards." Press Release, September 12, 2010. www.bis.org/press/p100912.htm.

Basel Committee on Banking Supervision, Bank for International Settlements. "Adjustments to the Basel II Market Risk Framework." June 18, 2010.

Basel Committee on Banking Supervision, Bank for International Settlements. "Countercyclical Capital Buffer Proposal." Consultative Document, July 2010.

Basel Committee on Banking Supervision. "Range of Practices and Issues in Economic Capital Frameworks." March 2009. www.bis.org/publ/bcbs152.pdf.

Basel Committee on Banking Supervision, Bank for International Settlements. "The Group of Governors and Heads of Supervision Reach Broad Agreement on Basel Committee Capital and Liquidity Reform Package." Annex July 26, 2010. www.bis.org/press/p100726/annex.pdf.

Basel Committee on Banking Supervision. "Strengthening the Resilience of the Banking Sector—Consultative Document." December 2009.

Bernanke, Ben S., Chairman, Federal Reserve. At the Federal Reserve Bank of Chicago 46th Annual Conference on Bank Structure and Competition, Chicago, May 6, 2010.

Board of Governors of the Federal Reserve System, Office of the Comptroller of the Currency, and Federal Deposit Insurance Corporation, "U.S. Banking Agencies Express Support for Basel Agreement." Joint Press Release, September 12, 2010. www.federalreserve.gov/newsevents/press/bcreg/20100912a.htm.

Bies, Susan Schmidt. "Enterprise Risk Management and Mortgage Lending." At the National Credit Union Administration 2007 Risk Mitigation Summit, January 11, 2007.

Burhouse, Susan, John Field, George French, and Keith Ligon, "Basel and the Evolution of Capital Regulation: Moving Forward and Looking Back." An Update on Emerging Issues In Banking, FDIC, January 14, 2003.

Burns, Robert L. "Economic Capital and the Assessment of Capital Adequacy." *Supervisory Insights,* FDIC, Winter 2004.

Committee of Sponsoring Organizations of the Treadway Commission (COSO). "Enterprise Risk Management: Integrated Framework," Executive Summary, September 2004.

Dodd-Frank Wall Street Reform and Consumer Protection Act, Section 616. www.gpo.gov/fdsys/pkg/BILLS-111hr4173ENR/pdf/BILLS-111hr4173ENR.pdf.

Estrella, A. "A Prolegomenon to Future Capital Requirements." *Economic Policy Review,* Federal Reserve Bank of New York (July 1995): 1–12.

FDIC. Annual Report, 2001.

FDIC. "Introduction: Capital." www.fdic.gov/regulations/resources/directors_college/sfcb/capital.pdf.

FDIC. "FDIC Board Approves Basel II-Based Standardized Approach Capital Proposal as an Alternative to the Current Rules." Press Release, June 26, 2008.

FDIC Quarterly 4, no. 1 (2010).

FDIC Quarterly 4, no. 2 (2010).

Financial Accounting Standards Board. "FASB Issues Statements 166 and 167 Pertaining to Securitizations and Special Purpose Entities." News Release, June 12, 2009.

Financial Accounting Standards Board. "Summary of Statement No. 159, the Fair Value Option for Financial Assets and Financial Liabilities—Including an Amendment of FASB Statement No. 115." 2009. www.fasb.org/st/summary/stsum159.shtml.

Greenspan, Alan. "Technology and Financial Services." Speech before the Journal of Financial Services Research and American Enterprise Institute Conference, Washington, DC, April 14, 2009.

Gup, B. The New Basel Capital Accord. New York: Thomson/Texere, 2004.

Gup, Benton E., and Thomas Lutton. "Potential Effects of Fair Value Accounting on US Bank Regulatory Capital." *Journal of Applied Finance* 18, nos. 1–2 (2009): 38–48.

Jones, David, and John Mingo. "Industry Practices in Credit Risk Modeling and Internal Capital Allocations: Implications for a Models-Based Regulatory Capital Standard: Summary of Presentation." *FRBNY Economic Policy Review,* October 1998.

Kohn, Donald L., Vice Chairman, Federal Reserve. "Risk management and Its Implications for Systemic Risk." Before the Subcommittee on Securities, Insurance, and Investment, Committee on Banking, Housing, and Urban Affairs, U.S. Senate, June 19, 2008.

Rosen, Richard J. "The Role of Securitization in Mortgage Lending." *Chicago Fed Letter* 244, November. 2007.

United States Government Accountability Office. "Risk Based Capital." GAO-070253, February 2007.

Walter, Stefan, Secretary General, Basel Committee on Banking Supervision. "Basel II and Revisions to the Capital Requirements Directive." Before the European Parliament Committee on Economic and Monetary Affairs on the BCBS's reform program, May 3, 2010.

Wessel, D. "Revised Bank Rules Help Spread Woes." *Wall Street Journal,* September 20, 2007, A7.

Wellink, N. "Basel II and Financial Institution Resiliency." Remarks by Dr Nout Wellink, President of the Netherlands Bank and Chairman of the Basel Committee on Banking Supervision, at the Risk Capital 2007 conference, Paris, June 27, 2007.

Wellink, Nout. "The Basel Committee and Regulatory Reform." Before the Institute of International Finance 2010 Spring Meeting Vienna, Austria, June 11, 2010.

CHAPTER 9 Evaluating Bank Performance

"ABA NASDAQ Community Bank Index Methodology." https:indexes.nasdaqomx.com/docs/methodology_ABAQ.pdf.

Ally Bank. "All Summary Information." FDIC. www2.fdic.gov/idasp/main2.asp.

Ally Bank. UBPR Summary Ratios. https://cdr.ffiec.gov/public/Reports/UbprReport.aspx?rptCycleIds=61%2c56%2c58%2c52%2c47&rptid=283&idrssd=3284070.

FDIC. "Bank Data Guide." www.fdic.gov/bank/statistical/guide/bankdataguide.pdf.

FDIC. "Deposit Insurance FAQ." www.fdic.gov/edie/fdic_info.html#11g.

FDIC. "Historical Statistics on Banking, Index to Notes on Insured Commercial Banks." www2.fdic.gov/hsob/hsobnotes.asp.

FDIC. Quarterly Banking Profile, First Quarter 2010, Table III-A. Federal Deposit Insurance Corporation-Insured Commercial Banks.

FDIC. "New Accounting Rules Affect Reported Cash Flows." FDIC Quarterly Banking Profile, First Quarter 2010. www2.fdic.gov/qbp/2010mar/qbp.pdf.

Federal Financial Institutions Examination Council. "National Information Center: Citigroup." www.ffiec.gov/nicpubweb/nicweb/InstitutionProfile.aspx?parID_Rssd=1951350&parDT_END=99991231.

FFEIC. "Central Data Repository's Public Data Distribution Web Site." https://cdr.ffiec.gov/public/.

Gup, Benton E. *Investing Online* (Hoboken, NJ: Wiley-Blackwell, 2003).

National Information Center. "Top 50 Bank Holding Companies." www.ffiec.gov/nicpubweb/nicweb/Top50Form.aspx.

Securities and Exchange Commission. "The Laws That Govern the Securities Industry." www.sec.gov/about/laws.shtml.

U.S. Department of Treasury. Written Testimony of Ron Bloom, Senior Advisor to the Secretary of the Treasury, and Jim Millstein, Chief Restructuring Officer, U.S. Department of the Treasury. Before the Congressional Oversight Panel, February 25, 2010. www.treas.gov/press/releases/tg563.htm.

Yahoo! Finance. "Citigroup, Inc. (C)." http://finance.yahoo.com/q/pr?s=C+Profile.

CHAPTER 10 Payments Systems

Ally Bank. www.ally.com/bank/interest-checking-account/#tabs=default.

"Audit Report of the U.S. Mint's Fiscal Years 2008 and 2007 Financial Statements." Office of the Inspector General, OIG-09-015, December 8, 2008, p. 26. www.treas.gov/inspector-general/audit-reports/2009/oig09015.pdf.

Bank of America. *Investor Factbook, Mid Year 2010*. http://investor.bankofamerica.com/phoenix.zhtml?c=71595&p=irol-reportsother.

Bauer, Paul W., and Geoffrey R. Gerdes. "The Check Is Dead! Long Live the Check! A Check 21 Update." Economic Commentary, Federal Reserve Bank of Cleveland, June 2009.

Bech, Morton L., Christine Preisig, and Kimmo Soramäki. "Global Trends in Large-Value Payments." *Economic Policy Review*, Federal Reserve Bank of New York (September 2008): 59–81.

Bell,Catherine J., Jeanne M. Hogarth, and Eric Robbins. "U.S. Households' Access to and Use of Electronic Banking, 1989–2007." *Federal Reserve Bulletin* 95 (2009). www.federalreserve.gov/Pubs/Bulletin/2009/articles/onlinebanking/default.htm.

Board of Governors of the Federal Reserve System. "Fedwire Funds Services." www.federalreserve.gov/paymentsystems/fedfunds_about.htm.

Board of Governors of the Federal Reserve System. "Fedwire Funds Service: Annual." www.federalreserve.gov/paymentsystems/fedfunds_ann.htm.

Board of Governors of the Federal Reserve System. "The 2007 Federal Reserve Payments Study, Noncash Payment Trends in the United States: 2003–2006." http://frbservices.org/files/communications/pdf/research/2007_payments_study.pdf.

Bolt, Wilco, and Sujit Chakrovorti. "Economic of Payment Cards: A Status Report." *Economic Perspectives*, Federal Reserve Bank of Chicago, Fourth Quarter (2008): 15–27.

"Chips Annual Statistics from 1970 to 2011." www.chips.org/docs/000652.pdf.

"CHIPS Celebrates 40th Anniversary Milestone." CHIPS Press Release, April 6, 2010. www.chips.org/press_releases/pressReleaseDocs/070431.php.

CLS Group. "About CLS." www.cls-group.com/About/Pages/default.aspx.

"Competitive Forces Shaping the Payments Environment: What's Next?—A Conference Summary." *Chicago Fed Letter*, Federal Reserve Bank of Chicago, Number 241b, August 2007.

"FDIC Sets Out Overdraft Payment Program Guidance." FDIC Press Release, August 11, 2010. https://mail.google.com/a/cba.ua.edu/#inbox/12a62572619feb3e.

"FDIC National Survey of Unbanked and Underbanked Household." FDIC, December 2009.

"FDIC National Survey of Unbanked and Underbanked Household: Use of Alternative Financial Services." FDIC, September 2010.

FFIEC IT Retail Payment Systems Examination Handbook. February 2010. www.ffiec.gov/ffiecinfobase/booklets/Retail/retail.pdf.

Financial Action Task Force. "Money Laundering & Terrorist Financing Typologies, 2004–2005." June 10, 2005.

Financial Crimes Enforcement Network (FinCEN). "Civil Money Penalty Assessed against Wachovia Bank." March 17, 2010. www.fincen.gov/bsaviolations.html.

FinCEN. "The 2010 Version of the Bank Secrecy Act/Anti-Money Laundering Examination Manual." News Release, April 29, 2010. www.fincen.gov/news_room/nr/html/20100429.html.

Gerdes, Geoffrey R., and Kathy C. Wang. "Recent Payment Trends in the United States." *Federal Reserve Bulletin* 94 (2008).

Gup, Benton E. "The Changing Role of Legal Tender: An Historical Perspective." In *Marketing Exchange Relationships, Transactions, and Their Media*, ed. Franklin S. Houston, 239–246. Westport, CT: Quorum, 1994.

Gup, Benton E. *Money Laundering and Financing Terrorism, and Suspicious Activities*. New York: Nova Science, 2007.

Office of the Comptroller of the Currency "Overdraft Protection." *OCC Bulletin*, OCC 2010-15, April 12, 2010.

Payments Council. www.paymentscouncil.org.uk/.

Payments Council. "The Future of Cheques." www.paymentscouncil.org.uk/payments_plan/.

Roseman, Louise L., Director, Division of Reserve Bank Operations and Payment Systems, Board of Governors of the Federal Reserve System. Statement before the Subcommittee on Domestic Monetary Policy and Technology of the Committee on Financial Services, U.S. House of Representatives, July 20, 2010.

Smith, Michael. "Wachovia's Drug Habit." *Bloomberg*, July 7, 2010, www.bloomberg.com/news/print/2010-07-07/wachovia-s-drug-habit.html.

United States v. Mazza-Alaluf, 607 F.Supp.2d 484 (S.D.N.Y. 2009).

U.S. Bureau of Engraving and Printing, Department of Treasury. "Annual Production Figures." www.moneyfactory.gov/uscurrency/annualproductionfigures.html.

U.S. Census Bureau. *2010 Statistical Abstract*, Table 1148.

U.S. Department of Treasury. "FAQs: Currency, Legal Tender Status." www.ustreas.gov/education/faq/currency/legal-tender.shtml.

U.S. Department of the Treasury. Program Performance Report, Fiscal Year 2000, 2001.

Department of Treasury, Financial Crimes Enforcement Network. "Informal Value Transfer Systems." Advisory FIN-2010-A011, September 1, 2010. www.fincen.gov/statutes_regs/guidance/pdf/FIN-2010-A011.pdf.

U. S. Senate. "Current Trends in Money Laundering." Report prepared for the Permanent Subcommittee on Investigations of the Committee on Government Affairs, 102nd Cong., 2nd Sess. S. Hrg. 102-123, December 1992.

Williams, Marcela M., and Richard G. Anderson. "Currency Design in the United States and Abroad: Counterfeit Deterrence and Visual Accessibility." *Review*, Federal Reserve Bank of St. Louis, September–October 2007, 371–414.

Yousef, Tarik M. Testimony before the U.S. Senate Committee on Banking, Housing, and Urban Affairs, Subcommittee on International Trade and Finance, Hearing on "Hawala and Underground Terrorist Financing Mechanisms." November 14, 2001.

CHAPTER 12 A Guide to Islamic Banking

Ariff, M. "Introduction to Islamic Financial Institutions." In *Fundamentals of Islamic Banking: Theory, Practice & Education*, ed. M. Ariff and M. Iqbal. Northampton, MA: Edward Elgar, 2010.

Divanna, J. *Understanding Islamic Banking: The Value Proposition That Transcends Culture*. Oxford: Oxford University Press, 2003.

Dowd, K. "The case for financial laissez-faire." *Economics Journal* 106 (1996): 679–687.

Dowd, K. "Free Banking." In *Handbook of International Banking*, ed. A. Mullineux and V. Murinde, 173–191. Cheltenham, UK: Edward Elgar, 2003.

El-Gamal, M. A. *Islamic Finance: Law, Economics, and Practice*. NY: Cambridge University Press, 2006.

Hayek, F. A. *Denationalisation of Money*. Hobart Paper Special Paper No. 70, London: Institute of Economic Affairs, 1976.

Iqbal, M. *A Mini Guide to Islamic Banking and Finance*. Northampton, MA: Edward Elgar, 2006.

Kane, E. J. *The Gathering of Crisis in Federal Deposit Insurance*. Cambridge, MA: MIT Press, 1985.

Khan, M. S., and A. Mirakhor. *Theoretical Studies in Islamic Banking and Finance*. Oxford: Oxford University Press, 2005.

Miller, M., R. Ippolito, and L. Zhang (1998). "Shareholders and Stakeholders: Human Capital and Industry." *Economic Journal* 108 (1998): 490–508.

Mirakhor, A. (1987). "Analysis of Short-Term Asset Concentration in Islamic Banking" (IMF Working Paper No. 67, Washington, DC, 1987).

Morris, V. B. *Guide to Understanding Islamic Investing*. New York: Lightbulb Press, 2005.

Mullineux, A., and V. Murinde, eds. *Handbook of International Banking*. Cheltenham, UK: Edward Elgar, 2003.

Saleem, M. Islamic Banking: A $300 Billion Deception.

Tett, Gillian. Fools Gold. London: Financial Times, 2009.

White, L. H. *Free Banking in Britain: Theory, Experience and Debate 1800–1845*. New York: Cambridge University Press, 1984.

Zaman, R. "Usury (*Riba*) and the Place of Bank Interest in Islamic Banking and Finance. *International Journal of Banking and Finance* 6, no. 1 (2009): 1–15.

Index

A

B

C

D

U

V

W